A Russian Prince in the Soviet State

A Russian Prince in the Soviet State

HUNTING STORIES, LETTERS FROM EXILE,
AND MILITARY MEMOIRS

Vladimir Sergeevich Trubetskoi

Translated from the Russian and edited by Susanne Fusso

NORTHWESTERN UNIVERSITY PRESS / EVANSTON, ILLINOIS

Northwestern University Press
Evanston, Illinois 60208-4210

Copyright © 2006 by Northwestern University Press.
Published 2006. All rights reserved.

Printed in the United States of America

10 9 8 7 6 5 4 3 2 1

ISBN 0-8101-1655-3

Library of Congress Cataloging-in-Publication Data

Trubetskoĭ, Vladimir, kniaz', 1892–1937.
    [Selections. English]
    A Russian prince in the Soviet state : stories, letters from exile, and Notes of a
cuirassier / Vladimir Sergeevich Trubetskoi ; translated from the Russian and
edited by Susanne Fusso.
        p. cm. — (Studies in Russian literature and theory)
    Includes bibliographical references.
    ISBN 0-8101-1655-3 (cloth : alk. paper)
    1. Trubetskoĭ, Vladimir, kniaz', 1892–1937. 2. Trubetskoĭ, Vladimir, kniaz',
1892–1937—Correspondence. 3. Russia. Armiia. Leĭb-gvardii kirasirskiĭ Eia
Velichestva polk—History. I. Fusso, Susanne. II. Title. III. Series.
PG3470.T764A28 2005
891.78'4209—dc22

                                                                        2005000329

⊗ The paper used in this publication meets the minimum requirements of the
American National Standard for Information Sciences—Permanence of Paper for
Printed Library Materials, ANSI Z39.48-1992.

Contents

Illustrations

Gallery follows page 110.

Acknowledgments

This translation owes its existence to my long and close friendship with Mikhail Andreevich (Misha) Trubetskoi, the grandson of Vladimir Sergeevich Trubetskoi. Misha embodies the resilience, humor, and linguistic brilliance that are the hallmark of the Moscow Trubetskois and that shine through every page of Vladimir Trubetskoi's writings. I am very grateful to him and to his late father Andrei Vladimirovich Trubetskoi for granting me permission to translate Vladimir Trubetskoi's surviving works. Misha was also of enormous help in the actual process of translation and annotation, and provided the photographs for this edition.

Many other people have assisted me in bringing this project to fruition. Olga Monina and Sergei Semionov offered encouragement and hospitality during my stays in Moscow. At a crucial early stage of the work, part of the translation was read by Susan Harris, Priscilla Meyer, Robert D. Richardson Jr., and William Trousdale, and their enthusiastic response was a valuable source of support. The reader for Northwestern University Press, distinguished Slavist and seasoned hunter Marvin Kantor, steered me in the direction of seeking expert help with the specialized terminology of hunting and the military. This help was generously provided by two of my Wesleyan colleagues. David Boule, director of scientific support services, read the hunting stories and provided many excellent suggestions. William J. Barber, Andrews Professor of Economics, Emeritus, former technical sergeant in the U.S. Army, and veteran of World War II, kindly read the "Notes of a Cuirassier" and helped me to find idiomatic translations of military terms. Translation and annotation queries were also answered by Sergei Bunaev, Darcy Dickinson, Noah Isenberg, Alexander Lehrman, Joyce O. Lowrie, Bruce Masters, H. Stern, Phillip B. Wagoner, and Jolee West. Gary Saul Morson provided invaluable assistance in the final stages of the project. Paul Mendelson did a brilliant job of copyediting the manuscript, offering numerous valuable suggestions. Thanks are also due to Susan Betz and Rachel Delaney of the Northwestern University Press for their work on bringing the project to completion.

Acknowledgments

Wesleyan University provided generous sabbatical time, a project grant for travel to Moscow, and a subvention to assist in the publication of the photographs.

My deepest gratitude is owed to my husband, Professor Joseph M. Siry, whose patient and steadfast support made the completion of this work a joyful moment in my life.

Introduction

Vladimir Sergeevich Trubetskoi (1892–1937) belonged to a generation of
Russians that suffered more than its share. He was born into an environment
of the highest privilege—economic, social, cultural, and intellectual—and
died (in all probability) in an Uzbekistan prison cell at the age of forty-five
with a single shot to the back of the neck. His surviving writings reflect his experiences of prewar comfort and postrevolutionary poverty, uncertainty, and
disenfranchisement, all described with humor and ironic detachment.

Trubetskoi was a member of one of Russia's most ancient and distinguished noble families, which produced some of the nation's finest warriors,
artists, and scholars.[1] His own father, Prince Sergei Nikolaevich Trubetskoi
(1862–1905), was an important philosopher and historian of ancient philosophy, and the first elected rector of Moscow University.[2] Sergei Nikolaevich
was a towering figure, intellectually, spiritually, and physically. (The poet
Boris Pasternak famously described him and his brother Evgenii Nikolaevich,
both professors at Moscow University, as "two elephants in frock coats without waists, clambering up onto the rostrum.") Sergei Nikolaevich Trubetskoi
was a shining example of liberal humanism at its best, beloved and respected
by even the most radical of his students. During the unrest leading up to the
1905 Revolution, much of which was centered in the student population,
Sergei Nikolaevich fearlessly defended the autonomy of the university from
both government interference and outside political agitators. His application
in June 1905 to Tsar Nicholas II for university autonomy is a tough defense of
the right of the professoriate to elect its own administrators rather than having them appointed by the government like civil servants. Trubetskoi argued
that only "the honor of being elected by the faculty" can give administrators
the necessary authority in "the eyes of students, society, and their own colleagues."[3] After winning university autonomy from the tsar in August 1905,
and being elected rector on September 2, Trubetskoi was forced to close the
university on September 22 because it had become the site of mass demon-
strations in which only a minority of the participants were students. Trubetskoi's statement to the students is worth quoting, for it shows him upholding

the same principle of university autonomy that he had defended against the government:

> I have always and everywhere defended the unconditional freedom of civic po-
> litical meetings . . . , but nevertheless I say to you now, not only as rector and
> professor, but as a social activist, that the university is not the place for politi-
> cal meetings, that the university cannot and must not be a public square, just
> as the public square cannot be a university, and any attempt to turn the uni-
> versity into such a square or to turn it into a place for public meetings will in-
> evitably destroy the university as such.[4]

Exhausted by the stress of the summer and fall of 1905, Trubetskoi collapsed and died on September 29 while on university business in St. Petersburg. The transportation of his body and his funeral were the occasion for huge demon-strations in Moscow and St. Petersburg.[5]

Sergei Nikolaevich's two sons, Nikolai Sergeevich (1890–1938) and Vladimir, had very different personalities and interests. As Vladimir indicates in chapter 1 of "Notes of a Cuirassier," Nikolai emulated his father in display-ing a precocious talent for scholarship. He published his first scholarly article at the age of fifteen and went on to become a member of the Prague Lin-guistic Circle and one of the outstanding linguists of the twentieth century.[6] Vladimir was more drawn to athletic and artistic pursuits, especially music and theater. He spent a very short time studying physics and mathematics at Moscow University before becoming a cadet in the navy, serving on the de-stroyer *Horseman,* part of the escort of the tsar's private yacht *Standard.*[7] As he describes at the beginning of "Notes of a Cuirassier," his desire to marry his fiancée, Elizaveta Vladimirovna Golitsyna, as soon as possible led him to for-sake the navy and enter the Blue Cuirassier Life Guards Cavalry Regiment in 1911. The surviving portion of his memoirs describes this period of his life in detail.

Trubetskoi served with distinction in World War I, receiving the St. George's Cross (Russia's highest military honor) for bravery in the 1914 Bat-tle of Gumbinnen (now Gusev) in East Prussia. After recovering from his wounds, he was placed on the staff of General Aleksei Alekseevich Brusilov on the Southwestern front. Impressed by Trubetskoi's intelligence and culture, Brusilov named him commander of the first separate automobile subunit in the Russian Army.

The October (Bolshevik) Revolution of 1917 destroyed the world of the Trubetskois. At the beginning of 1918, Trubetskoi joined a conspiratorial group of former Guards officers that tried to rescue the tsar from captivity. Their efforts failed, and the tsar, his wife, their four daughters and hemophil-iac son were shot and bayoneted to death in the cellar of a house in Ekaterinburg later in 1918. Trubetskoi did not engage in any other forms of resistance to the Bolshevik government and did not attempt to emigrate, unlike the majority of his extended family.

In 1920, during the Civil War, Trubetskoi responded to an appeal by his old commander Brusilov to "All Former Officers, Wherever They May Be," to join the Red Army. As V. P. Polykovskaia writes:

> Trubetskoi's relatives remember his story of how Brusilov singled him out in a waiting room full of officers and, after inviting him into his study, began the conversation with the words, "Prince, the cart has gotten stuck, and there is no one but us to pull it out. Without the army, Russia cannot be saved."[8]

On his way to Oriol to serve in the Red Army on the southern front, Trubetskoi stopped in Bogoroditsk (in the Tula region, south of Moscow and north of Oriol) to visit his family and share his rations with them, and was arrested because of his "aristocratic" appearance. While in prison he developed tubercular symptoms, and after his release he was demobilized and went home to his family.

Bogoroditsk, the estate owned by the Bobrinskiis (relatives of the Trubetskois), was built for Empress Catherine II by the architect Ivan Starov in the 1760s. It was famous for its park, designed by A. I. Bolotov in the 1780s, which combined elements of the formal French seventeenth-century garden and the picturesque garden of English Romanticism. In his story, "How We Fished for Grandmother," Trubetskoi gives a precise description of the topography of Bogoroditsk: the war-ravaged palace and still-romantic grounds on one side of the river and pond Uperta, faced by the town on the other side, with all its streets fanning out from the central square so that their visual focus is the palace facade.[9] The witty illustrations to Trubetskoi's stories by his nephew Vladimir Mikhailovich Golitsyn (the addressee of the "Letters from Exile") often include in the background the looming specter of Catherine's palace, like a vision of the old world commenting on the new one.

The Trubetskois, Golitsyns, and Bobrinskiis lived in a wing of the Bogoroditsk palace, going out by day to earn their keep giving music and language lessons. Trubetskoi served the Red Army as a remount officer. It was during this period that he gathered the material for the stories that were later published in the popular periodical *Vsemirnyi sledopyt* (*World Pathfinder*) in 1927–28, marking the beginning of his career as a writer.

With the easing of the atmosphere as the Civil War ended and the New Economic Policy began, the Trubetskois moved briefly back to Moscow, where neither work nor living space was available, before settling in nearby Sergiev Posad in 1923. Polykovskaia writes, "The Russian nobility settled around the St. Sergius Monastery in search of a saving refuge, and living every day as if it were their last, they found consolation in the nearness of the sacred place."[10] Trubetskoi worked by day as a pianist for silent movies and by night played in a band at a restaurant. His son Andrei remembered that Vladimir took a very professional approach to his work, viewing each movie in advance and making a list of the appropriate musical numbers to accompany each scene.[11] Both in Bogoroditsk and in Sergiev Posad, the Trubetskoi family maintained high spirits, and their household was the site of charades and amateur theatricals. It was in Sergiev Posad, in 1926, that Trubetskoi became friendly with the writer Mikhail Prishvin, who encouraged Trubetskoi's own literary efforts. The two men shared a passionate love for hunting; as Andrei Trubetskoi recalled, "Hunting in all its varieties was an important spiritual safety valve for him in those difficult times." He also remembered that one of his father's hunting hounds would pull the children away from each other when they were fighting: "Who taught her to do this, I don't know, but I well remember the delicate nip of her teeth on my trousers, and not only on them."[12] Trubetskoi's stories, published under the name "V. Vetov," enjoyed modest popularity in the 1920s.

The atmosphere changed for the worse in the 1930s. *World Pathfinder* was shut down because of its "harmful adventure tendency." Prishvin wrote in his diary in 1930: "The Prince [Vladimir Trubetskoi] said, 'Sometimes I feel so sorry for my homeland that it becomes a physical pain.' "[13] Waves of arrests began, targeting various sectors of the scholarly intelligentsia. In Moscow, scholars of language and literature were accused of creating a pro-monarchy organization supposedly directed from "headquarters" in Vienna by Prince Nikolai Sergeevich Trubetskoi, Vladimir's brother. In January 1934, Trubetskoi and his eldest daughter Varvara (Varia) were arrested and exiled to central Asia for ten years. They settled in Andijon (Andizhan), Uzbekistan, and were joined by the rest of the family, Elizaveta Vladimirovna and six other children (another son was born in Andijon in 1935). Here Trubetskoi worked as a pianist in the ballet studio and in cafés, began his memoirs ("Notes of a Cuirassier" is the only surviving section), and wrote more stories, the kernels of which survive in the "Letters from Exile" to Vladimir Golitsyn.

On July 29, 1937, Trubetskoi and Varia were rearrested, along with the two other eldest children. The family legend has it that during the search of their home, one of the boys succeeded in hiding several of his father's notebooks in his younger brother's wide trousers, thus saving the "Notes of a Cuirassier," without beginning or end, for posterity. The rest of the family made their way back to Moscow. The family learned that Trubetskoi and Varia had been sentenced to "Ten years of prison camp without right of correspondence," a formula that is now understood to have meant summary execution. It was only in 1991 that the family received the official information that Trubetskoi and his daughter had been shot on October 30, 1937. Of the other children, Aleksandra died in prison camp, Grigorii spent ten years there, Vladimir Vladimirovich lost a leg in World War II, and Andrei served his country in the army and the partisans, only to be sent to the Gulag for six years at war's end.[14] But perhaps the most heart-wrenching story is that of Trubet-skoi's wife, Elizaveta, of whom he speaks with such knightly devotion in the "Notes of a Cuirassier" and who appears in a photograph of 1912 as a fairy-tale princess with silken hair flowing down over a brocade cape. When Andrei Trubetskoi returned to Moscow at the end of World War II, he learned of the hunger and terror in which his mother and siblings had lived. Soldiers confis-cated the typewriter that had been their sole source of income. One brother worked carting bread to stores, and would bring home the crumbs that re-mained in the cart. After he was drafted, Elizaveta was forced to go begging in neighboring villages. Everything of any value (the sewing machine, the Bible) was sold. At a certain point a refugee from the occupied western re-gions of the Soviet Union, a vulgar, greedy woman, was lodged with the fam-ily. When Elizaveta asked her not to curse in front of the children, she became incensed, threatened Elizaveta, and moved out. Andrei Trubetskoi writes in his memoir:

> One day my mother and sister Irina met [the refugee woman] on the street. She was wearing new felt boots and a new quilted jacket, and instead of a greet-ing she yelled, "Ah, you're still walking around? Well, you won't be walking around for long!" And a little while later, at the beginning of January 1943, two men in sheepskin coats arrested our mother.[15]

Elizaveta Vladimirovna Trubetskaia died in Butyrki Prison one month later, probably of typhus.

In a 1935 letter, Vladimir Trubetskoi spoke disparagingly of his own talents as a writer:

> You keep suggesting that I continue to occupy myself with literature—for some reason I don't feel like it: my characters are either ideologically inconsis-tent, or exaggerated to the point of caricature and parody, my style is old-fashioned, and today people find it insipid and "lacking in vivid imagery." Ap-parently I haven't kept pace with literature.

Indeed, Trubetskoi fits the mold neither of the "ideologically consistent" so-cialist realist writer nor of the experimental modernist in the style of some of his great contemporaries. His hunting stories, narrated by his alter ego Vladimir Sergeevich Khvoshch, are, at least at first glance, humorous tales of two indefatigable and inventive hunters. Trubetskoi's comic and narrative gifts should not be underestimated, but there is also a more serious under-current to the stories: Khvoshch is clearly a déclassé nobleman, now forced to scrounge for food and supplies in close collaboration with the lower-class townsman Bochonkin. In the ruined palace that looms over the Bogoroditsk landscape, the two hunters, looking for leftover supplies of small-shot, find instead the green tub imported from England in which the counts who owned the estate used to have their children bathed. Bochonkin and Khvoshch quickly put the tub to use in their goose hunting, but it also symbolizes the idle life of luxury of the prewar nobility, to which Khvoshch offers a remarkable, ironic elegy in "The Death of the Dirigible." Perhaps the most important theme of the stories, though, is a different kind of nobility—an inborn nobility of intelligence, skill, and passion that is shared by the disenfranchised aristocrat, the townsman who accepts him as a friend, and the unforgettable hunting dog Gobbler, who dies after a heroic fox hunt. Bochonkin's epitaph for the dog commemorates her death with an allusion to the prerevolutionary calendar: she died, he writes, "na Kazanskuiu"—"on the feast of the Kazan icon of the Mother of God."

When speaking of his attempts to write his memoirs, Trubetskoi seems just as despairing as when discussing his own fiction: "After all, memoirs have above all to be truthful, and in order for my memoirs to be published—I would have either to lie, or to keep silent about a whole series of interesting things that played a major role in my life." Nevertheless, by 1937 Trubetskoi was well along in writing his memoirs, which he conceived in four parts: (1) "Memoirs of Youth," ending with his service in the navy; (2) "Memoirs of a Cuirassier," part of which has survived and is translated here; (3) "Memoirs of a Man in the Trenches," ending with the Revolution; and (4) "Notes of a Musician." Polykovskaia argues that he began with the "Notes of a Cuirassier" because it was the part of his memoirs with the greatest chance of being published.[16] He wished to memorialize the Guards officers who had been among the early casualties in World War I (and, although he doesn't mention it, in the Civil War, since many of the officers he mentions were executed by the Bolsheviks).

I have placed the "Letters from Exile" before the "Notes of a Cuirassier" in this edition, because Trubetskoi's recollections of the glittering prewar world of an elite Russian Guards regiment are enriched by an understanding of the situation of central Asian exile in which he wrote them down. Snatching a few hours between mornings playing piano in the ballet studio and late nights in the restaurant band, struggling with the heat, the insect-borne illnesses, and the problems of a large, uprooted family, Trubetskoi had to have performed a heroic act of the imagination in order to conjure up his life in 1911–12 with the precise, vivid detail—as he says, "photographic accuracy"—of the "Notes of a Cuirassier."

Trubetskoi's stories and memoirs offer a glimpse of what life was like for a man who had been thoroughly invested in imperial Russia but who also tried to make a life for himself in the new Soviet state. The "Letters from Exile," in particular, are a self-portrait of a person who met every development in his life as an opportunity to learn something—about the face veil, about irrigation ditches, about the courage and resourcefulness of his own daughters when attacked by rapists. Trubetskoi was writing to his nephew Vladimir Mikhailovich Golitsyn, who was also in exile and who died of hunger and pellagra in prison in 1943. Trubetskoi used his verbal gifts to turn what must have been difficult, painful events into an occasion for lightness and humor, an opportunity to amuse Golitsyn, who was in a similar situation and was under no illusions about what lay behind Trubetskoi's brave wit. Vladimir Trubetskoi's stories and memoirs will offer amusement for the contemporary reader as well, but they may also offer an inspiring example of how a person can live through large-scale social and political upheaval with grace and true nobility.

NOTE ON THE TEXT

The original texts of "The Extraordinary Adventures of Bochonkin and Khvoshch" were published in the journal *Vsemirnyi sledopyt* (*World Pathfinder*) in 1927–28. The "Letters from Exile" were first published with some omissions in the journal *Zolotoi vek* (*The Golden Age*), no. 4 (1993): 27–36, but I worked from a typescript provided by the Trubetskoi family. The "Notes of a Cuirassier" were published in the journal *Nashe nasledie* (*Our Heritage*), 1991, nos. 2, 3, and 4; and as a separate book: *Zapiski kirasira* (Moscow: Rossiia, 1991). My explanatory notes to "Notes of a Cuirassier" are heavily indebted to the notes compiled by G. V. Vilinbakhov for the *Nashe nasledie* edition (no. 4), and by Vera Pavlovna Polykovskaia for the book edition. In the "Notes of a Cuirassier," I have added chapter titles to help orient the reader.

In my translations I have used a modified Library of Congress transliteration. The hard sign is omitted, and the soft sign is either omitted or replaced by *i* when necessary; the letter *ë* is represented as *o* or *io*.

A Russian Prince in the Soviet State

The Extraordinary Adventures of
Bochonkin and Khvoshch

How We Fished for Grandmother

WHEN I FOUND myself in the town of B., at first I didn't suspect that fate would settle me here for a whole seven years.[1] Before this I had never even known that such a town existed, but in fact, as it later turned out, remarkable people lived here.

At first the place seemed boring to me. It took me about an hour to see all the sights. They consisted of the enormous town pond, on one side of which the entire town was situated in a fanlike layout. On the other side of the pond stood a palace built in the time of the Empress Catherine, and next to the palace an old park. The water in the pond was green, and the palace was white and dilapidated. One side of the pond was called the "town side," and the other the "Count's side." One end of the town abutted on the village of Upertovka, the other on the village of Viazovka. All around, for dozens of miles—fields . . .

This exhausted the touristic sights, unless you count several huge, red, absolutely empty tanks that stood at the intersections in case of fire, and the railroad station named "Waitville." What these round tanks were supposed to do in case of fire, I was never able to determine in my whole seven years of residence in B. There were fires, but the tanks didn't play any role in them. And as for the railroad station "Waitville," its very name clearly defined its purpose—to wait . . . to wait endlessly—sometimes for days on end—for the arrival or departure of the passenger train, which circulates here along a remote branch line, ruled not at all by the schedule but simply by the wise old proverb, "make haste slowly."

But please don't think that it was sarcastic passengers who gave the station the name of "Waitville." Nothing of the sort! The name is completely official. It was devised by the prescient tsarist authorities . . .

For the rest the town was like any other town: a drugstore, police station, town baths, movie house, cathedral, and market square. In a word, it didn't differ at all from a thousand of our godforsaken little towns, in which old-timers live who can't remember anything.

So—this all seemed quite boring to me, when one beautiful spring, capricious fate drove me here.

I didn't know anyone here; I had no one to socialize with, and when I had free time I would go over to the "Count's side," where I would ramble along a shady path on the bank of the pond. There was never anyone on this path during the day. Only in the evenings would there be mass strolling by the local cavaliers and ladies, engaged in mutual conquering of hearts.

It was the beginning of summer. According to my custom, I was taking a postprandial walk along the lower path on the bank of the pond, observing two suns, one of which mercilessly shone from the heavens, and the other no less insolently looked out from the mirrorlike surface of the pond. My ennui was just as stagnant as the pond water at my feet.

As I came around a bend, I stopped, amazed by an unaccustomed sight: fifteen or twenty dressed and undressed men were standing and sitting on the path. A couple of them were sitting in the trees, right over the water. They had lariats in their hands; others had guns; still others had fishing poles. Still others had nothing in their hands, but stood to the side chewing sunflower seeds in deep thought. I went up to these last and humbly asked why these people had gathered.

"They want to pull Grandmother out," answered a respectable citizen with galoshes on his bare feet, spitting out a shell.

"How on earth did she get into the pond?" I asked in amazement.

"How on earth she got there, I really don't know, but it's been many a year that they've been unable to pull her out."

My amazement continued to grow.

"But why on earth does she throw herself into the pond every year? Is she insane?"

It was the citizen's turn to look at me in bewilderment and ask, "And just where might you be from?"

"Moscow . . ."

"Moscow? So that's why you don't know! It's fish that we call Grandmother."

"What kind of fish are they? Pike?"

"Not fish, but one big fish . . . one might say it's a carp sort of fish . . . That's what they're trying to catch."

"Is there really only one fish in the whole pond?"

"No, what are you talking about? There are lots of carp, and big ones, but—there's only one Grandmother. She's extremely enormous . . . literally!. So everyone is interested in catching her. The old men say she's more than a hundred years old."

I approached the water. There were people standing here, silently and intensely looking into an alder bush that was sticking out of the water. I also started inspecting the bush, but I didn't see anything suspicious in the turbid, overgrown water.

"Under the tree root, she went under the root," someone's whisper could be heard in the crowd.

I looked at the huge rotten root, the end of which was sticking out about twenty paces from the shore. For one instant a strange object appeared out of the water. It was the dorsal fin of a carp, of monstrous proportions.

"Bang!" a deafening shot resounded at that moment from the top of a tree. The water around the tree root began to seethe, and at the same second two naked men plunged into the water.

"She got away!" the shooter cried. "Swim to the right . . . chase her back . . . Hey, you with the lariats, where are you going? Not there . . . more to the right . . . Ugh, you stupid devils, come on out!"

"No, Grandmother is clever, all right," they were saying in the crowd. "You can't do anything with her, it'll never work."

"Why don't you try catching her with a net?" I asked the fishermen.

"What can you do with a net here? Bushes, roots, ruts . . . you'll just tear the mesh."

"But she can't always be next to the shore!"

"You, Citizen, don't know what you're talking about, and yet you're giving advice. This isn't the first year that these people have been trying to catch that old lady. That means they must have tried every method already. The old lady only comes to this shore once a year, to spawn. She'll hang around here for about a week, then she'll go away, and then just try finding her in the whole pond, and you can see for yourself that it's not a small pond."

I didn't want to argue and I fell silent, since the people gathered here didn't impress me as being serious; these lariats and gunshots smacked of the frivolousness of amateurs.

"These aren't real fishermen and hunters," I thought. "How can they fail to hit a huge fish spawning right by the shore? They're so inexperienced! They probably don't know that when we look at a fish in the water, we experience a kind of optical illusion because of the refraction of light. A specialist once taught me how to aim not at the fish itself but lower, and in my day I succeeded in killing some rather large pike that way. I'm going to come here with my gun tomorrow and I'll take care of Grandmother in no time!"

The hundred-year-old carp had really piqued my interest. When I got home I thought about her for a long time, planning how best to deal with this denizen of the pond.

My imagination ran wild: the town pond seemed to be an ocean, and the old Grandmother a whale. Then I got the idea of getting a harpoon involved in the action. I spent a long time whittling my strong oak cane with a sharp knife, and finally I made it into a kind of harpoon, sharpening its iron tip with a file and making sharp notches in it like a real harpoon. I decided to load my gun with a cartridge holding only a small amount of powder, and to insert my homemade harpoon into the barrel after attaching a length of strong twine to it. That way, after I shot Grandmother with the harpoon, I could easily pull her out onto the shore.

In the evening I made some practice runs, shooting light sticks out of the gun at a target. The practice runs were quite satisfactory, and I lay down to sleep delighted by my invention. I was enraptured by my own ingenuity; it seemed to me that I had thought up something very original and witty, and I was sure that tomorrow I would put all the local hunters to shame.

My alarm clock roused me from bed at exactly four o'clock in the morning. After a hasty snack, I set off for the "Count's side," taking along my invention. I skirted the pond and quickly walked along the lower path. The hunters had not yet arrived, and I was apparently the first one there. I was already approaching the familiar tree root when I suddenly noticed a man I didn't know, who was coming to meet me from the opposite side. The stranger didn't look like a fisherman, since he had neither lariat nor gun nor even a fishing pole. In one hand he was carrying an old cast-iron kettle, the kind that is used for cooking food; in the other he had a large basket that apparently held something heavy. A long pole, the end of which he held pressed under his arm, dragged after him along the ground.

I came alongside him right opposite that same tree root where Grandmother had been spawning the day before. I stepped aside to let the bizarre stranger go by; but he unexpectedly stopped short at that very moment. Looking at me with a suspicious sidelong glance, he lowered his burden to the ground. For a time we observed each other silently; the stranger looked at me with a far from sympathetic air.

"After all, what do I have to do with him?" I thought, and after going close to the shore I began to stow the long rope of my harpoon in even zigzags on the ground. On the decks of whaling ships, this is exactly the way they stow the cable from the harpoon which is inserted into the whaling gun. I tied the free end of the rope to a long branch on the shore. Having finished dealing with the rope, I looked at the water: Grandmother was not there yet. I turned my glance to the stranger.

Sitting on his haunches several paces from me, he was pulling some rather strange objects from the basket. First of all there appeared an old rusted electric bell with green spools, then an insulated wire, a large electric battery, an ordinary thick wire, putty, and finally a large round tin box. All this the stranger laid out carefully and in an extremely businesslike way on the grass.

"What in the world is this character doing here?" I asked myself in irritation, looking at my neighbor.

8

He possessed the kind of appearance that impresses itself firmly in the memory: he was short and slightly bowlegged, wearing a dark-blue peasant shirt, with a red unshaven face, light-brown hair, and a long red nose, on which sat spectacles that lent his whole figure a particular seriousness and concentration. The unshakable confidence that was reflected on the stranger's face, the professorial manner with which he manipulated his portable power station, spoke of the fact that he did not like to fool around with trifles.

The stranger put the electric bell on the bottom of the kettle, opened the tin box, and started to pour its contents into the kettle. A dark powder poured out of the box. Having emptied the box, the stranger tightly closed the kettle with a massive metal lid, then firmly twisted the thick wire around the whole contraption several times. Now he thoroughly puttied all the cracks. Only two long insulated wires, thickly coated with tar, stuck out of the puttied and tied lid of the kettle. All this was so enigmatic and incomprehensible that I could no longer contain myself, and asked, "What do you want to do, citizen?"

"The same thing you do," the stranger answered coolly.

"Nothing of the sort, I came here to catch Grandmother!"

"And so did I!"

"But surely you're not planning to fish for her with an electric bell?"

"Very simply, with an electric bell," the stranger answered me, looking at me over his spectacles with a sly glance, in which contempt was also visible.

He turned away and, paying no attention to me, started to tie the kettle to the end of the long pole.

"Excuse me, citizen," I addressed him, "but if you start ringing the bell underwater, you'll scare Grandmother away from me."

"I beg your pardon, citizen," the stranger answered me in a reserved tone. "There is a question here: who is going to scare Grandmother away from whom—you from me with your flintlock, or I from you with my bell! It's most likely that *you* will scare her away! I'll tell you frankly: you won't accomplish anything here with a gun. There have been people here no less intelligent than you who've tried the same kind of rehearsals. All kinds of people have shot at the old lady, but not one has attained his object. I advise you to abandon this enterprise!" And with these words the stranger started to undress.

I tried to explain to him that I had killed pike with my gun many times before. I displayed my harpoon and the rope stowed on the shore, and I mentioned the optical illusion that occurs when one looks at objects located under water.

"Don't give yourself airs with me," the stranger replied. "A pike is one thing; a carp is something quite different. I've watched for many years as all kinds of riffraff have been shooting at that Grandmother. I'm simply overcome with pity when I look at such unserious people! I'm a hunter too myself, and believe it or not—not a single person here has killed as much game as I have. But to shoot at Grandmother . . . forgive me for my frankness, but I've never succumbed to such ignorance!"

"But permit me to ask what you intend to do with your bell?"

"Forgive me for my frankness, but it's my pougasse."[2]

"Pougasse?" I asked.

"Yes, an ordinary pougasse."

"And what is that?"

"An ordinary demolition bomb. I will quite officially blow up Grandmother with electricity. Here's the push-button . . . here are the battery cells, here's the cast-iron shell, and in it four and a half pounds of gunpowder. When I push the button, the bell will start to shrill, it will set off a spark—and Grandmother is kaput! Understand?"

"What are you, an electrical engineer?"

"Excuse the expression—no."

I was crushed. I had never in my life heard that an electric bell could be put to such a use. By all indications the stranger was a sensible and clever fellow. He possessed an indubitable gift of inventiveness. In any case, he did not seem to be a dilettante. I felt an involuntary respect for him and understood that the harpoon I had invented probably was inferior in originality to the stranger's conception of a homemade "pougasse."

"But look here," I said to him, "if your pougasse misses fire, then *I* will shoot Grandmother, and she won't get away from me."

The stranger smiled contemptuously and lovingly inspected his contraption.

"You won't get Grandmother. It's official: the battery cells are completely in order."

He got completely undressed. With imperturbable calm he raised the long pole with the "pougasse" attached to it over the water, then slowly lowered it into the pond near the root. Having finished doing that, he rolled a homemade cigarette, adjusted his spectacles, and sat down by the edge of the pond, pensively contemplating the green water. In his hands he held the push-button with its green wires. I climbed up on a high alder tree and took up a position on a branch sticking out over the water.

We both preserved complete silence, and as we watched the water, every once in a while we would steal glances at each other. One could feel that we were rivals, and in such cases silence is the best means for avoiding unpleasant conversations and perhaps conflict. Both of us had come here with a single goal. Both of us had brought our own inventions here.

Battle had been joined. Whose gadget would turn out to be the best? Who would win: the harpoon, the "pougasse," or the old Grandmother?

The "pougasse" inspired a lively interest in me. Sacrificing my passion for hunting, I decided to let the stranger try his venture first, so that in case he failed, I could immediately pierce the back of the hundred-year-old carp with my sharpened harpoon.

We sat by the water in complete silence for a good half hour, and each of us was plunged in meditation about the old Grandmother, who had lived for a century on the bottom of the old pond.

Suddenly there was movement in the green water next to an alder bush. The stranger went on his guard. He carefully took hold of the end of the long pole and began barely noticeably to move his "pougasse" toward the bush.

And now, just like yesterday, the tip of a huge dorsal fin appeared above the water, and the huge, broad body of the ancient fish began to be vaguely outlined. With beating heart I aimed the barrel of my gun under the dark shadow. At the same moment in the depths of the water a muffled explosion resounded: the water near the bush swelled into a hump for a moment, and countless bubbles gurgled up.

At that instant the stranger turned up in the pond. He looked around in distraction, searching for Grandmother. An enormous yellowish streak appeared on the surface of the water, three paces from him. It was Grandmother's gigantic belly. Like an otter the stranger jumped on her and tenaciously grabbed hold of her slippery body with both arms. He was choking from the water and from excitement, and his eyes were rolling wildly.

"I got her!"

The triumphant inventor lifted his prey with difficulty, tail up, and dragged it to the shore. He had hardly stepped onto dry land, however, before the stunned monster suddenly came to life. It flapped its powerful bronze tail with unbelievable force and, having inflicted a mighty blow to the stranger's face, tore itself out of his embrace and disappeared into the green depths. The blinded electrician helplessly waved his arms and fell into the water. After a moment he was already on his feet and rushing onward.

"Where? Where?" he cried in a frenzy, wiping his eyes.

Meanwhile from the tall alder tree for one instant I perceived the dark shadow of the departing carp.

At that second my good flintlock glided like a fly under the dark shadow, and I pulled the trigger . . .

I had correctly allowed for the refraction of the light. My long rope, coiled up on the shore, unwound with lightning speed, emitting a whistle all the while. Its ninety yards uncoiled in an instant, and after a few seconds the thick stick to which the harpoon rope was attached flew into the water . . . The harpoon reached its mark . . . I too had conquered!

The stranger convulsively seized the stick, and Grandmother, rushing under the water, pulled him into the pond.

"Let go! You'll break the rope!" I shouted to him, clambering down from the tree.

"After me!" he shouted and began running headlong toward town. His callused bare feet slapped against the trampled path. I could hardly keep up with him.

We flew like a hurricane to the "town" side, where the market women were already starting to gather. They were quite amazed and frightened when they saw a man running along the shore, whose entire simple costume consisted of a pair of spectacles on his nose. Paying no attention to the frightened market women, we galloped to the dock, jumped into a boat, and flew like an arrow over the pond, searching for the stick that was floating among the waves.

Only an hour before, the stranger and I had looked at one another as enemies. Now we were no longer rivals, because we had been united by the same passionate desire to finish off Grandmother. Without a word being spoken, a close bond of friendship had been formed between us. I suddenly felt something like kinship for my rival, a feeling that bordered on fervent sympathy.

No less than half an hour had passed before the stranger and I finally dragged the utterly exhausted ancient monster out of the water with our combined efforts.

The fish was more than three feet long, and its broad back was covered with moss. The bronze-colored fish was covered with large, uneven scales. Some of the scales were the size of a child's palm. Next to the dorsal fin we could see old scars from the shot of hunters who had been unsuccessfully shooting at Grandmother for many years. From one of the monster's gills protruded a metal ring covered with silt and mud.

We were excited. The stranger firmly shook my hand and said, "Let's introduce ourselves. I'm Semion Semionovich Bochonkin, an official hunter and amateur."

"Khvoshch." I gave my name and shook his hand firmly in return.

"I didn't think you were such a special marksman," my new acquaintance declared with a smile.

"Accuracy has nothing to do with it," I answered. "The trick is in understanding the optical illusion. You shouldn't aim at the fish, but beneath the fish."

"I confess," Semion Semionovich noted, "that I thought you were simply a boaster; but now I see that you're a real optician! Take your Grandmother . . . she's really fat!"

"By no means!" I answered. "Your pougasse surpassed anything I have ever seen. You have a correct approach to grandmothers, and you succeeded in stunning the old lady. I beg you to take her for yourself."

12

"But after all I miscalculated a bit: in the first place, I was foolish to lift her with the tail up, and if I'd used six pounds of gunpowder instead of four and a half . . . Believe me, if you hadn't shot at Grandmother . . . That's official!"

"I'll gladly believe you and therefore I give her to you!"

We argued for a long time, exchanging pleasantries and compliments. It ended with our deciding finally to consider it our common catch and to demolish it together.

The demolishing of the fried and boiled Grandmother was the final seal of our intimacy. Some of Semion Semionovich's friends, who also turned out to be hunters, were invited to join in demolishing her. My new friend acquainted me over the feast with many interesting citizens, and while dining on Grandmother we told each other many interesting things. We spent a whole three days eating Grandmother, since she turned out to contain about fifty pounds of meat.

The ring we found in one of her gills was made of gold. We deciphered an engraved inscription: "Ring inserted in 1787."

The old lady was over a hundred and forty years old!

We donated the ring to the local Museum of Regional Studies, and apparently it is still there today.[3]

This event was registered by the local press. In the newspaper *Red Voice* an amusing little article appeared: "One hundred forty years under water." There our whole adventure and our life stories were described in detail.

Thus perished the ancient Grandmother of the pond . . . But in perishing she gave birth to a close friendship between two passionate hunters, who are friends and companions to this day. After catching Grandmother, Semion Semionovich and I understood that we deserved each other. From that time he and I lived through more than one exciting and thrilling moment.

Shchadilov Pond

IT WAS AFTER 1 A.M. Semion Semionovich and I were heading toward Shchadilov Pond and had already passed our little town of B., which was plunged in peaceful sleep. In the distance the rattle of the night watchman could be heard. A gentle night breeze wafted the fragrances of spring towards us. The full moon shone brightly for us and illuminated my companion in all his hunting splendor. He was wearing an old dark-green jacket, a gray cap, and stylish riding-breeches, which sank into his clumsy wading boots. The moonlight played on his spectacles and on the steel of his absurdly large gun.

"Well, you've really got a cannon!" I said in amazement, looking at Semion Semionovich's weapon.

"In the old style, Vladimir Sergev . . . It's a very special gun; one might say it's a puntgun. You won't be able to find such a gun today in Tula itself."

"It must be heavy, I guess."

"Seventeen pounds."

"You don't say!"

"There's nothing surprising about it: it's an eight-gauge barrel. And the barrel is forty-two inches long."

"What do you need such a machine for? You're just burdening yourself with extra weight."

"But on the other hand, it has a long enough range to reach across the whole Shchadilov Pond. Officially, I load it with a triple charge of powder and shot."

"So it must have a hell of a recoil?"

"A little bit . . . if you're not used to it you won't stay on your feet."

"And will it really reach across Shchadilov Pond?"

"Believe it or not. With shot it officially functions to a distance of 200 paces, and with buckshot one might say it will carry twice as far. It's a dirigible, not a gun."

"So, are there ducks on Shchadilov this year or not?"

"A depot!" Semion Semionovich snapped out curtly.

14

"That is, er, what do you mean 'depot'?" I asked uncomprehendingly.

"Quite simply—a depot . . . You'll see for yourself."

I had heard of locomotive and firehouse depots, but duck depots . . .

"Vladimir Sergev! Whether we're going to kill anything today—I don't know, but that we're going to shoot—is a fact. There are ducks this year like in a depot. The guys from Lomovka have been banging from dawn to dusk."

We approached Shchadilov Pond, located about two-thirds of a mile from town. This pond was well known to the townspeople. In summer young lovers liked to stop by here to seek solitude under the shade of the dense trees and bushes that grew by the tall reeds across from the old dam.

In May poetic natures (and there were quite a few such natures in our town) would come here. They were attracted by the beautiful, fragrant lilac bushes that grew in wild profusion near a little old farmhouse not far from the pond. Throughout that month, melodic nightingales and resonant cuckoos would be on constant duty at the service of the poets.

In autumn little boys would come running here, because on the hill that rises beyond Shchadilov Pond, young apple trees grow bearing large fruit, the kind I myself once was fond of stealing.

At the beginning of spring, in April, serious people—that is, hunters—would come here. They were led here by a passion for those strong sensations they would experience right next to the water, among the old willow trees that fringe Shchadilov Pond on two sides.

We quietly approached the dam and even more quietly crept up to our reed tent, already built by the experienced hand of Semion Semionovich the day before. We settled down and each rolled a cigar while waiting for dawn to break.

The moon flooded the surface of the quiet pond and the bushes on the opposite shore with bright light. There, right next to the water, a light unexpectedly flared up.

"Semion Semionovich, we're not alone here. It looks as if someone else is lying in wait for the ducks. Over there—somebody's smoking on the other side."

"That's not a serious person. I know him—it's Mishutka from Viazovka."

"How do you know?"

"What's not to know! His place is under that bush. He always sits there, many years now. But he's not serious: his gun always misfires. He's no threat to us, because my gun officially will reach the other shore with buckshot, and while Mishutka is messing around with his misfires, I'll take his ducks from here."

"Well, are there any serious people here?"

"There aren't many serious people . . . Maybe just Pal Mikhailov . . . The others are, you know . . . riffraff!"

"Semion Semionovich, it's starting to get light in the east! Where's your famous depot?"

"Just wait a bit, Vladimir Sergev! As soon as they start to bang in the direction of Lomovka, then in six and a half minutes you can expect ducks on Shchadilov. From here to the Lomovka dam it's six miles, and as soon as they scare away the ducks from there, they fly here, and it officially takes them six and a half minutes. Every year that's the way the rehearsal functions."

At that moment somewhere to the left of us we could hear the loud quacking of a wild female duck. We pricked up our ears.

"She's woken up, the rascal," Semion Semionovich whispered, adjusting his spectacles and peering in the direction of the duck call.

"Well, Vladimir Sergev, shouldn't we have a bang at that same duck? Let's sneak up."

"What are you saying, Semion Semionovich? You can't kill females in spring, only drakes."

"Stop it, Vladimir Sergev! Here on Shchadilov we don't reason that way. If it's not us, then some other guy will surely sneak up to that duck. I've observed such facts already many years here."

"You bring her down, Semion Semionovich, but I can't reconcile it with my conscience."

Semion Semionovich adjusted the percussion cap on his muzzle-loading dirigible and started crawling in the direction of the quacking that continued to resound. Out of curiosity I quietly followed him.

After covering some distance, we saw the black silhouette of a wild duck, so familiar to every hunter, on a bright strip in the water. It was quietly swaying on the waves not far from the shore. Semion Semionovich carefully cocked his gun. And then . . . just as he was ready to take aim, someone else, a stranger, forestalled my companion. Ahead of us a bright light flashed, a shot followed, and small-shot whistled past not far from us . . .

All our attention was focused on the duck, who nevertheless continued to peacefully sway on the waves, and strangely enough, was now without a head; only its neck stuck up out of its body.

Our amazement didn't last long, for at the next moment loud cursing rolled passionately over the mirrorlike surface of Shchadilov Pond.

"Bastards! Why did you ruin my decoy? Who invited you? And they're hunters, too!"

A dark figure emerged from a bush and pulled the ruined duck decoy on a rope to the shore.

"Pavel Mikhailov," Semion Semionovich quietly whispered. "Let's go back without a sound—he's a serious person."

16

The victim wouldn't quiet down: "Can't you see that you're shooting at a decoy, you irresponsible idiot?"

"And why are you luring people with a duck call? I suppose you're responsible, huh?" someone's taunting voice could be heard.

"What do you mean 'why am I luring people,' when a loudly calling drake has been sitting here in the reeds since evening. I'd think you'd understand what was going on."

Semion Semionovich and I quietly retreated to our former place.

"I'm amazed," my companion reasoned, "that they give hunting licenses to such riffraff! I would deprive all irresponsible people of the right to hunt."

"But you yourself wanted to kill the duck! You know you're not supposed to."

"But I wanted to responsibly, because that's the only way on Shchadilov Pond. You yourself see what's going on here . . . It's shocking!"

We had hardly made it to the tent before we heard several shots in the distance, which made a faint sound in the transparent morning air.

"The Lomovka guys have started banging," Semion Semionovich whispered. "Look at your watch: in six and a half minutes the ducks will be here, that's official."

Shchadilov Pond became stock-still and seemed to go on the alert, awaiting the arrival of the Lomovka ducks. Everything all around took on an expectant air. The minutes seemed endlessly long.

"Take a look at your watch—has a lot of time gone by?" my impatient companion asked.

"Exactly six minutes."

"Get ready, they should be coming now."

In fact, only a few seconds passed before the characteristic intermittent whine of flying ducks could be heard over our heads.

Eight wild ducks with their long necks stretched out were flying high over the pond. Something strange occurred: the hunters hidden in tents and bushes, of whom there unexpectedly turned out to be a whole detachment, started furiously trying to lure the ducks with duck calls of all sorts and nuances. Each hunter wanted to lure the ducks closer to himself. A bizarre, unheard-of concert began, in which the quacking and vociferous horn of Semion Semionovich could be distinguished most clearly of all. He played it so loudly it seemed as if he wanted to frighten everyone and everything away from himself.

But the ducks . . . Oh, the foolish ducks! Having described a circle or two over the pond, they descended and, paying no attention to the cacophony of duck calls, flew right over the water with the clear intention of alighting.

But the wild ducks did not succeed in settling on the water. Contrary to the predictions of Semion Semionovich, the gun of Mishutka from Viazovka did not misfire this time, for a loud shot resounded out of the treacherous Mishutka's bush. The ducks instantly took a sharp turn upwards, which served as the signal for a unanimous but fruitless volley from the Shchadilov hunters.

The shot whistled in all directions and rustled through the bushes.

"That bastard Mishutka always mucks it up like that," Semion Semionovich said, lowering his monstrous gun. "That man has no conscience, but he tries to be a hunter! Let's have a smoke, Vladimir Sergev."

"You know, Semion Semionovich, this hunt is rather dangerous: before you know it they could knock out your eye with shot."

"That would be quite simple. Three years ago on this very spot four pieces of shot hit me in the mug. I went to Doctor Nikitskii. He's a very special doctor. He pulled out three bits! The fourth one fell out by itself."

Semion Semionovich pointed to his chin, on which white scars could be seen.

"So who was it who decorated you like that?"

"None other than Mishutka from Viazovka . . . But he won't admit it, the bastard."

I was filled with involuntary respect for the courage and stoicism of Semion Semionovich, who, although he had been injured on this very Shchadilov Pond, still came here every year to subject himself to new dangers.

But now we could again hear in the clear air the faint sound of distant, rapid shots. Six minutes and thirty seconds later the same eight ducks came flying to us. Again the symphony of duck calls, again the shooting, again the ducks take off into the heights and disappear in the direction of Lomovka. Several minutes later the sound of distant volleys reached us, and the ducks came flying to us a third time, completing their journey with mathematical accuracy in six minutes thirty seconds. But now there were only seven ducks.

Semion Semionovich exclaimed: "Those Lomovka bastards! They knocked one off after all. Okay, townsmen, let's give it to them!"

Bang, bang, ba-bang . . .

And the ducks fly away . . .

It became a kind of game of lawn tennis between the Lomovka hunters and the hunters from our town, with wild ducks being flung back and forth instead of a ball.

But now, when the town hunters had for a fourth time repulsed the attack of the wild ducks on Shchadilov Pond and had started to have a smoke, counting on their lawful thirteen-minute rest—at that moment, completely unexpectedly, six multicolored pochards came flying in and nonchalantly settled on the water in the middle of the pond opposite the dam.

The hunters froze. Although it was tempting to shoot at a flock of ducks sitting on the water, "there's many a slip twixt the cup and the lip"—it was a long way from the pochards to the nearest hunter, about 180 paces.

It was time for Semion Semionovich to act.

He wiped his spectacles in a businesslike fashion, adjusted his percussion cap, took aim, and made such a boom with his monstrous gun that it seemed as if the entire vault of heaven had crashed to the earth. Four ducks flew adroitly away. One that had been wounded was floundering in the water, raising columns of spray, and one had been killed outright.

"What did I tell you?" Semion Semionovich said triumphantly. "It's a dirigible, not a gun! It reached so far!"

The risen sun illuminated the hunters crawling out of their refuges.

"There's Semion Semionovich for you! Good going!"

"Ivan Ivanovich . . . my respects."

"Hey, Piotr Nikolaev, why're you shooting so bad today?"

The hunters greeted each other. About fifteen or twenty of them had gathered.

The dead duck, carried by the waves, was slowly floating toward the shore. The wounded one was diving and disappearing for long periods under the water.

We shot at it for a long time, but the nimble bird would disappear so quickly under the water that we had no hope of finishing it off. Gathering its last strength, the duck flew heavily away over the dam and disappeared from sight.

"It flew to the town pond to die," someone said.

"That's official," Semion Semionovich confirmed. "It doesn't have anywhere else to die."

The dead pochard was pulled out of the water. On the old dam it was inspected and examined by all the hunters who had gathered.

"Boy, it's a fat devil!"

"A real gander!"

While the hunters smoked and shared their impressions, one of them by the name of Ivan Ivanovich opened up a grimy bundle, and right there on the dam he began a peculiar trade in percussion caps, cartridge cases, shot, extractors, and other supplies.

We returned home.

"Vladimir Sergev, let's go to the town pond to finish killing the pochard."

"Thank you no . . . I'm going home to sleep."

I don't like to finish off wounded birds. My lodgings are not far from the town pond. As I was falling asleep, I could hear the sound of shots for a long time. Semion Semionovich was finishing off the stubborn pochard.

———

About ten years had passed since the first time I visited Shchadilov Pond in the spring. I had not been in our little town for a long time.

One day chance again brought me there. It was an early April morning, and the sun had not yet risen when the Elets train, very behind schedule, rolled me up to the station.

I had hardly managed to exit the train and take a few steps along the platform before I heard distant shots in the direction of the village of Lomovka.

"The Lomovka boys have started banging," flashed through my mind.

I looked at my watch: it was 2:30 A.M.

I set off for the town on foot, and as I was approaching the house of Kobiakov, I could hear the "battery" on Shchadilov Pond start to speak.

My watch showed with mathematical accuracy the time of 2:36.30.

And I thought: "There are unshakable, immutable, universal laws . . . Decades may pass by. Our old, ancient world will see many changes . . .

"And the earth? It will continue as before to complete its path around the sun in 365 days.

"And the ducks?

"The ducks . . . maybe even in fifty years, when they start banging in the morning in Lomovka, you may be assured that six minutes and thirty seconds later they will bang on Shchadilov Pond."

I tell you that officially.

A Trap with a Triple Rehearsal

IT HAPPENED IN the year 1919. The entire Russian Soviet Federated Socialist Republic, and along with it our little town, was without yeast, matches, firewood, and sugar.[1] In a word, everyone was suffering a crisis of provisions, and those citizens who had false teeth had nothing to use them on. Nevertheless, we were sometimes given small quantities of matches and sugar with ration cards, but as far as firewood was concerned—the district commissioner ordered that a parcel of the town forest be allotted, on which our townsfolk could cut down green little aspen trees for themselves. Although it was difficult, all the same the citizens could manage to get a little of this and that. Only one thing was impossible to get, namely: hunting supplies. Even if some hunters managed to dig out a little powder from the cartridge of a military rifle, they weren't given a pat on the back for such things.

"Vladim Sergev, let's be politically conscious. It's easier to destroy than to build. Let's not dig around in a military cartridge!" Semion Semionych said to me, when I expressed the feeble impulse to get a little powder by this means.

"Semion Semionych, I've gotten terribly sick of living without hunting. Besides, you can eat hares, and for a fox hide the speculators will give either a little flour or some kerosene."

"That's correct, Vladim Sergev. You are saying official things, but to dig around in a military cartridge—that's an uneducated attitude. You can catch hares with a rope trap and foxes with an iron trap."

"But we don't have any traps, Semion Semionych!"

"That's not important. What's important is social development. Don't you think we can make a trap? Just wait, Vladim Sergev, let there be a little more snowfall, we'll get us some foxes!"

From that day we began manufacturing fox traps, and meanwhile the snow just kept heaping up. When winter had firmly settled in, wolves appeared right near our town. There were three of them, the most impudent gray beasts you can imagine. It was as though they sensed that in this difficult

21

time people didn't have time for hunting. The three wolves became so brazen that once they got to the outskirts of town and killed a dog in the yard of one of the outlying houses. I personally saw their tracks in the vegetable gardens right near the town. They were constantly roaming around our town, and several of the townsfolk saw them directly. The wolves were making a nuisance of themselves. The rumors about their escapades, as always, were exaggerated, and it got to the point that many of our old-time residents no longer dared to go outside town in the evenings, while the hunters sat idle with no powder.

All this induced Semion Semionych and me to occupy ourselves with the wolf question as well. My friend set to work perfecting the fox traps, and finally invented an intricate triple-action trap that weighed about fifty pounds. The construction of this device involved iron runners from a broken sled, an old oven fork, a poker, and a piece of rusty roof iron. The local blacksmith Gavrila Komarov (whose nickname was "Mr. Bronze") helped us in this work with his forge and anvil. With his help we made devilishly strong springs and two terrible sharp-toothed clamps. When the device was completely finished, Semion Semionych looked it over lovingly and said: "Now there's a trap! We made it first-class! Now if some gray one sets his foot here—he's finished: he'll never be able to get out, because the thing has turned out triple-action. One may say: it's a beast-killing device with a triple rehearsal: all at the same time it grips the paw, and hits the head with the poker, and crushes the beast with a log from above. In a word—it's a beast-killer, not a trap."

My friend's invention was in fact most terrifying to look at. Everything was so arranged and fitted out that the wolf had only to barely touch a large round plate with its paw in order for it to immediately jump off its little hook and turn on a spindle. At the same time, the strong springs would straighten out with a crash, and the two sharp-toothed clamps would instantly bang shut with a sinister click. Simultaneously the poker, pulled back on a spring, would come off its hook and go into action, striking the wolf full force in the muzzle. At the same moment a rope fastened to a heavy log would be stretched out. Breaking away from its support, the log was to turn the trapped wolf into a flat pancake.

All this had been devised for a reason, because Semion Semionych and I knew that wolves who fall into ordinary traps often chew off the paw that has been caught and walk away on three legs. My friend's invention ruled out such a possibility. It was to work without fail.

Semionych was radiant. I was in ecstasy, and we ardently began to track the brazen wolves.

We followed the wolf tracks for days, trying to determine their invariable routes. After a week we had figured out that their staff headquarters was in the forest not far from the village of Bolotovka. From there they would go hunting almost every day, almost always keeping to the same route—through the town forest. In one place they had a constant passageway, namely near the forest edge, where they would come out to their own old track and walk along it for a while past a gnarled birch tree. Then they would walk single file, following the track, and each time they would carefully place their paws in their own old footprints, so that it would seem as if only one wolf had passed here instead of three.

We were very careful and kept as far as possible from the wolf tracks, observing them from afar so that the wolves would not suspect that they were being tracked.

Finally, when we had precisely established where the wolves' constant travel took place, we decided to set up the triple-rehearsal trap on their track, and we chose as our site the gnarled birch tree, because it would be easy to hide the heavy log there.

The wolves were amazingly bold. The line of their regular crossing was not more than a hundred paces from the boundary of the plot of land marked out by the district commissioner for the needs of the townspeople. During the day it was noisy and well-frequented here. Our townspeople would come here in whole families to fell trees. At night the wolves would appear here.

But it was very difficult to set up the triple-rehearsal trap. It was a hellishly laborious business! Our slightest omission could ruin the whole thing. It was bad that in setting up the trap we would leave our own footprints in the snow, and this would frighten the intelligent beasts away. We had to destroy any hint of our presence. We worked with small wooden shovels.

Right by the birch tree we cut away a large square piece of snow with the mark of a wolf's paw on it. In its place we put our famous trap, then covered it on top with the same piece of snow containing the wolf print. We assiduously smoothed out all the rough spots and filled up our own footprints with snow, carefully making them level with the surrounding snow cover. We worked like artists. The rope attached to the log was beautifully camouflaged, and it seemed as if everything indicated that we would have complete success.

Very close to this spot we found a fox crossing. We set up an ordinary anchored fox trap on it and took the same precautions as we had with the wolf trap.

We worked in the evenings with great secrecy, after the townsfolk had left the forest. It would be a pity if one of the townspeople who was there to get wood was able to get hold of a trapped beast before us.

Having set our fox and wolf traps, we returned home full of the brightest hopes. From that time we would go to the town forest every day on the sly to check our traps.

About two days later, while following a fox track, we noticed that the fox had gone to its usual crossing and headed for the trap. Overjoyed, we hurried to it. Imagine our disappointment when we saw that nothing had been caught in our trap. From the prints we read as if in a book what had happened: the fox had scented something wrong. It had only to make one more step in order to step on the camouflaged trap, but it had suddenly made a huge leap to the side and had evidently taken off at full speed away from the dangerous place.

"Man, those foxes have good noses!" Semion Semionych marveled. "And you and I are fine ones: we didn't stop to think that the trap would smell of humans. Oh, Vladim Sergev, we should have rubbed our hands and the trap with pine needles so as to remove the human scent."

We had to perform the whole operation again from the beginning. Fortunately for us, there was another fox crossing not far away, and the wolves for some reason had not yet passed this way along their own old track. Apparently they were still sated. Thanks to this we had the possibility of correcting our mistake. Now, before setting up the trap, we first rubbed our shoes with fresh horse manure, and before setting to work we rubbed the traps and even our own hands with pine needles.

The next day, as usual in the evening, we set off for the town forest. We had a gun, loaded with the only charge of small-shot we had left. We took the gun with us "just in case."

A little snow had fallen overnight. It had barely sprinkled the bushes and trees. Festive and motionless, they greeted us with mysterious silence. The town woodcutters had long ago returned to town, and now there was not a single human soul in the forest.

It was getting dark. The blue evening shadows lay softly on the ground. The forest preserved its mystery. What was it preparing for us today?

We came out to the fox crossing.

Hurrah! We had had luck: the fresh track of a little vixen was distinctly imprinted on the snow. It went in an even, neat little chain into the bushes.

"Well, Vladim Sergev, now it's in the bag," Semion Semionych said confidently. "One might say—we've earned enough to buy flour."

We rushed to the thicket.

"She's caught!" my friend cried joyfully.

Behind the bush a trapped little red vixen was struggling. When she saw us she began writhing with all her might, trying to pull her black front paw out of the trap. She flashed angry eyes, full of hate, at us.

"Don't shoot, Vladim Sergev, save your shot! Let me whomp the beast with a log!"

Semion Semionych took a hearty swing, and the little red vixen ended her thievish existence.

"Good hunting, Semion Semionych!"

"Good hunting, Vladim Sergev! Now there's a little flour for you, a little kerosene! Well, wasn't I right, that there was no need to dig around in military cartridges?"

We freed the vixen and stroked her warm, soft fur, experiencing great satisfaction. We hadn't had an easy time catching her.

"Now let's see how things are with the wolves. Oh, I can sense we've caught a beast there as well! The wolves haven't come out to their crossing for an awfully long time. It's high time they did!"

The old wolf crossing was to the side, so we walked straight to the gnarled birch tree under which our infernal triple-rehearsal trap had been so sinisterly secreted. We walked in a bright and cheerful mood, discussing our success. Now we could see the gnarled birch . . . another step—and I stood rooted to the spot:

A dark, indistinct mass was lying under the birch.

"Look, Semion Semionych, we've got a catch here too! A wolf!"

"It's a fact that it's a wolf! Wait, Vladim Sergev: it's a wolf . . . but for some reason it has something of the kangaroo about it!"

Indeed, a wolf of a very strange sort had been caught in the trap. Its fur seemed unbelievably fluffy. The oncoming twilight made it hard to see it properly.

"Semion Semionych, it doesn't exactly look like a wolf!"

"Then what is it? It's not a bear! We don't have bears here. Vladim Sergev, don't get near it! What if it's still alive? Give me the gun. Just to make sure I'll hit the beast with a little small-shot. Although small-shot won't kill the beast, nevertheless after the shot the creature will have to give itself away: is it alive or has it croaked."

It was not more than thirty-five paces to the birch tree. Semion Semionych aimed and fired small-shot at the strange wolf.

What happened next we could never have expected. In answer to the shot, from under the birch resounded a real-life woman's voice, loud and piercing:

"Help! They've killed me, oh, they've killed me, the accursed Herods! H-e-e-lp!"

"Vladim Sergev, what kind of rehearsal is this? This kind of thing doesn't happen in life," Semion Semionych babbled with a changed countenance.

"Semion Semionych, it's time to get used to the fact that everything happens in life! Instead of a wolf, alas, it's a downright woman who's run up against your triple rehearsal . . . It's a lucky thing that she's still alive!"

We rushed to the gnarled birch. On the snow, pinned under the log, lay our acquaintance the widow Chistozvonova. One of her feet was clamped in the trap. We immediately set to work freeing her from the grip of the infernal snare.

The widow moaned, interrupting her moaning with unbelievable cursing.

"Ooh, you bandits, you murderers! That's what they gave you freedom for—to kill defenseless widows half to death? Oh, I can't stand it: all my bones are cracking! Torturers without a conscience! Where is your conscience?"

"I'm sorry, citizeness, we thought you were a wolf . . ."

"Haven't you mocked me enough? I'm an honest woman, and not some mangy creature that you shoot a gun at!"

"Citizeness, you must be more politically conscious. Why ever did you get into a wolf trap? Who asked you to do that? Why were you silent when we approached you?"

"Why was I silent! I was crying and shouting for two hours! I'd begun to lose my reason! I shout and shout, I plead—no one comes to help me. I wore myself out and didn't have the breath to shout any more. I got weak. Oh, don't touch my shoulder, you monsters!"

We completely freed the tormented widow and seated her in the snow. Her situation was in fact an unenviable one. Apparently when the log came away from its brace it broke her collarbone. The poker had adorned her forehead with a very large lump, almost the size of a fist. Thank goodness the widow's head was wrapped in a thick warm kerchief, which had to a certain extent protected her skull. On her leg the skin was flayed off. The small-shot had also done its work: now the widow could only sit sideways.

From her fragmentary explanations we understood that she had come to the forest on horseback to saw wood. The widow did not want to content herself with aspen. She got greedy and tried to cut down the only gnarled birch that existed in that part of the forest, and since that birch was growing outside the boundaries of the assigned plot, the widow decided to act on the sly and without witnesses. She waited until all the other woodcutters had left the forest. That's why no one came when she cried for help. The widow's greed had been cruelly punished. We tried to explain this to her.

We found the widow's horse and carefully laid the widow on the sledge. This wasn't so easy to do: despite all the crises, the widow's carcass weighed no less than 200 pounds.

Despite all our correct behavior, despite our attention and nursing, the widow would not calm down and refused to make it up with us. She announced that she would make a complaint against us and that the case would end up in a tribunal.[2]

Semion Semionych and I gloomily followed her sled, listening to her threats and curses.

"There's going to be trouble now," Semion Semionych whispered, sadly shaking his head. "I know this old hag very well. She'll get her way. And you know what times these are. They'll deal with us with all the severity of the revolutionary era! And what got into me to shoot at her with small-shot! Now just try and prove that I'm not a murderer! It officially turns out that I'm a killer with vile motives!"

"It's all right, Semion Semionych, don't lose heart. We'll get out of this fix somehow or other. The worst they can do is send us to forced labor. After all, we are bringing the widow back alive."

"It's a fact! Boy, what an organism this old hag has! Nothing gets her: not the poker, or the log, or the shot! One might say that a wolf would have been flattened like a pancake, but her—she's not bothered in the least! Okay, so she broke her collarbone a little bit. Vladim Sergev, say what you like, but this widow is a thing that clings to life! And nevertheless the triple rehearsal functions conscientiously. All three triggers worked completely up to snuff!"

What could be better? What more can I say?

We conveyed the widow to her lodgings and immediately ran to Doctor Nikitskii with an invitation to visit the patient forthwith. After frankly telling the doctor everything that had happened to us, we asked him not to tell anyone about this ticklish business.

Doctor Nikitskii was a hunter himself. He understood us perfectly and promised to keep complete silence. He set our minds at ease, saying that medical ethics would not permit him to expatiate upon the causes of the widow Chistozvonova's illness.

We accompanied the doctor to the widow's lodgings. Upon saying goodbye to him, Semion Semionych seemed to have trouble speaking:

"Excuse me, doctor . . . a little comradely request . . . In view of the fact that at the present time we have a crisis with shot, could you please . . ."

"I don't have any shot myself," the kind doctor interrupted my friend.

"I know that you don't have any shot . . . that's not the point . . . the point is that my gun shoots a lot of shot at once . . . understand?"

"So far I don't understand. Tell me directly what exactly you want me to do. Come on, speak, don't be embarrassed."

"Well, you see, doctor, of course shot—it's a ticklish thing, but because my gun shoots so much shot at once, I imagine that you'll collect nearly a whole charge of small-shot out of the widow's haunch. No matter what, you'll have to pull all that shot out of her. It would be a pity if it just got thrown out. You yourself understand that we're in a crisis, and you can't get small-shot anywhere no matter how much money you pay. Well, that's why I have this little comradely request of you . . ."

"I understand," the doctor said with a smile. "Whatever I collect, I'll give back to you. Word of honor!"

We firmly shook hands with the kind old man.

The next day I dropped in to see my friend. He was occupied with skinning the fox we had caught in the trap the day before.

"Well, Semion Semionych, did you go to see the widow?"

"Yes."

"Well, how does she feel? Has she finally calmed down?"

"What are you talking about? She's still raging. She's writing a statement about us to the authorities."

"Hmm! This is turning out to be really tiresome. What are we going to do?"

"Vladim Sergev, I think we'll have to make a present to her of this fox hide. Maybe after that the widow will cool off a little bit. Other than that we don't have anything to give her."

"Go ahead, Semion Semionych. Bring her the hide today."

The fox hide didn't make matters any better. The widow was unshakable in her resolve to bring us before a tribunal. I didn't know what to do. All this could have ended tragically.

Semion Semionych found the solution. Not for nothing did he have the mind of an inventor. He invented a sure means of rendering the energetic widow harmless.

About three weeks later Doctor Nikitskii and I enjoyed ourselves at the wedding of Semion Semionych and the widow Chistozvonova, the estimable Matriona Andreevna. Among the invited guests was the hairdresser Ulybkin. Slyly winking at my friend, he asked insinuatingly:

"Tell me, my dear fellow, just what did you catch in your celebrated triple-rehearsal trap?"

"A she-wolf, and a real mature one!" my friend answered with a sigh. "She officially weighs about 200 pounds."

We smiled slightly, and Semion Semionych leaned over to the men and said quietly, "If it weren't such times as these, I never would have gotten married. Denikin and Kolchak are to blame for everything."[3]

"What do Kolchak and Denikin have to do with it?"

"It's very simple. If only there were no Denikin and Kolchak, there would be no crisis, and if only there were no crisis, citizenesses wouldn't be coming to the forest to get wood themselves, but would buy it at the market. Also, if only there were no crisis of powder and shot, Vladim Sergev and I wouldn't have set traps, but would have officially shot with our guns at foxes and wolves. In a word, if only there were no Denikin and Kolchak, I never in my life would have signed the registry book with Matriona Andreevna."

The hairdresser said with a subtle smile, "If only, if only beans grew in my mouth, then it wouldn't be a mouth but, excuse the expression, a whole plantation."

We did not dwell any further on this touchy subject.

I don't know to what extent Kolchak and Denikin were involved in this affair. I only know that Semion Semionych's marriage to the widow Chistozvonova turned out to be a firm union, as a result of which a whole generation of young Bochonkins is now growing up.

I Got the Fox!

HAS IT EVER happened in your life that you come upon a streak of failures and bad luck? Everything's going well for you until suddenly something is broken off and spoiled, and from then on nothing you undertake works out right. If you hit such a streak, don't despair, have patience: after all, it's only a "streak." I give you my word that sooner or later you'll pull out of it. Have the firm belief that some day (perhaps even very soon), your life's path will intersect with a "lucky streak" too, full of successes and good luck.

That year it seemed as if I had hit just such an "unlucky streak." For a hunter this is always especially palpable. Despite wonderful weather and an abundance of game, that year I simply had no luck at all: either a mortally wounded fox would run into its lair right in front of my nose, or a hare I had grazed would be torn to pieces and eaten by my own dogs, or for some unknown reason my favorite hound would go lame, or the firing-pin on my gun would break during the hunt. In a word, I had hit a terribly unlucky streak, but firmly convinced that it would come to an end, I decided to interrupt and break it no matter what—and I stubbornly continued to go hunting.

On the day this story took place, for some reason I was sure that I had finally gotten out of the ill-starred streak of failures. I was in such a good mood!

It was one of the first snows, which are so dear to hunters and which they remember for so long.

Already on the road to the Kibenskii forest I shot an uncommonly large gray hare right out of its lair, weighing about twelve or thirteen pounds. In such hares the fat alone weighs a pound, and no sooner had I entered the forest than my hound Dokuka had flushed another one.[1] The second hare turned out to be what we call "literate," and led me and Dokuka a merry chase before ending up in my sights and, finally, hanging over my back. At this point my indefatigable hound ran onto a fox, and our fun began again.

The fox was also an experienced one, who had seen more than one hound in its foxy life. No matter how I tried, for a long time I couldn't get anywhere. The fox cleverly fooled Dokuka and me many times that day.

Dokuka would be hot on its heels, and the fox would suddenly turn and go back along its own track right toward the dog. Hiding behind a thicket of bushes, it would suddenly make a huge leap to the side and let the excited dog run right by it. Dokuka is an old, experienced hunting hound. In her doggy life she has chased down more than a few dozen foxes, and you might say she knew them inside out. Of course she would soon figure out what was going on and get back on the right track.

The fox was circling and crossing in the thicket, not wanting to come out into the clearing. Dokuka was pressing it. The fox made up its mind. Now it unexpectedly appeared before me, about sixty paces away. At that moment, when my gun was nimbly bobbing up and down, trying to get up on my shoulder, at that moment the beast's green eyes met mine. It was only a moment, maybe a tenth of a second, but it was quite enough to make me miss the sly deceiver: it seemed to be rushing to the left, but in fact it went right, into a thick aspen grove, having deceived me with its fluffy tail.

About five minutes later I saw it already behind me. It was breezing through the open field, heading for the nearby Aleksandrovskii forest. It went with funny, unhurried leaps, stopping continually and looking back to see if it could see the dog, lifting its sly little muzzle high in the air. Dokuka figured out what was what and rushed through the field after the fox, furiously barking in her melodious alto.

I went to the Aleksandrovskii forest. The fox circled around there for about an hour and a half, and circled in such an expert fashion that I couldn't do anything with it.

Now the fox and Dokuka rush back to the Kibenskii forest. I run there too. The dead hares make their presence known, and the straps by which they're hanging on my back cut my shoulders painfully. The fox is going in little circles in the very densest thicket. It is beginning to tire. Now it comes out into a fir grove. Now I finally understand its tactics. I crawl into the thicket and lie down, aiming my gun into a narrow glade. I lie like that for about a half hour in the wet snow, never taking my eyes from the narrow little corridor between the fir trees. Now I know that all I need is patience, and my patience is rewarded: the exhausted and worn-out fox appears soundlessly from the side. It places itself in the sights of the already aimed gun, and all I have to do is pull the already cocked trigger, which I do.

The fox has been killed. It is a magnificent full-grown male, a splendid specimen for whose fur I will undoubtedly get a large price.

Dokuka and I are pleased and satisfied. It's not easy to kill a fox with a hound. Just go try it, and if you've never hunted with hounds before, I guarantee you—you won't be able to kill a fox no matter what: it will deceive you without fail, no matter how you've studied this kind of hunting in theory. Yes, it's flattering to kill a fox with a hound, and especially such a beauty as I now had in my hands. I came to the forest edge, to where the bushes were sparse. On my back were full-grown hares, and in my hands—a full-grown fox.

Enough! The hunt had been very successful. I could make my way home, especially since it was starting to get dark, and it was a fair piece to my house. The damned fox had led us around for more than half a day, exhausting both me and Dokuka.

The fox was heavy to carry. In order not to burden myself, I decided to skin it, and in order to do this I sat on a stump, got out my knife, and intended to begin the operation. But nothing of the sort: Dokuka, who suddenly began squealing, caused me to throw the catch on the snow. Priceless Dokuka! She had begun chasing yet another beast.

Would I really knock off yet another creature? Well, this day was really turning out well! I could hear my dog turning into a gully, and it became clear to me that I was about to shoot at another beast. I ran to head them off. It was still light enough to shoot, and I peered out, expecting to see a rushing hare . . . I could see something rushing along the bottom of the gully . . . What is it? Another fox! What luck! It was flying at top speed, as if stretched out on the snow, beautifully extending its huge tail.

Bang! And this one was dead. I went up to the killed fox.

What a fox! A female of long experience. It must have been the spouse of the male I killed—she was a real match for him. What a beauty!

So, two foxes, two hares. All four of them—full-grown. Not bad. For our neighborhood that was extremely not bad. One might say, rare, phenomenal luck! Hunters remember such occasions for a long time.

Only one thing was unpleasant: during the last chase I lost my knife, and now I had nothing with which to skin the hides. I would have to carry the bag on my back. I gathered my trophies and hoisted them onto myself.

But just try to carry such a company on your hump! You hoist two full-grown foxes and two hares onto your back after a whole day of running through soft snow. Now take your good old two-barreled gun in your hands. Can you feel it? The bag alone weighs more than fifty pounds! Now take a walk in that condition. After a couple of miles you'll get into such a sweat that you'll curse the whole hunt.

I knew that I couldn't walk home this way. And I suddenly realized that the railroad halt No. 63 must be somewhere near here. Although the only passenger train had passed through in the morning, I decided to try to get over to the halt. Maybe I'd be lucky and some freight train would come through on its way to the town, and the conductor would understand my plight and allow me to ride on the brake platform for just one stop.

I turned toward the halt and started slowly trudging along. I walked for a quarter of an hour—and collapsed on the snow in exhaustion. I was completely worn out, but my spirit was light and happy.

"Well," I thought, "now I've gotten lucky. My wife will be happy. Oh, how happy she'll be! First of all, the foxes: about seventeen rubles or even twenty rubles apiece for the hides—that's already about forty rubles. So all right, I'll give my wife twenty-five or thirty rubles, and the rest of the cash is mine. Semion Semionych and I will have a drop to drink. And the hares? Again: they're tasty, and substantial, and there are a lot of them. My wife will be happy. She won't have a leg to stand on any more when I disappear for days hunting. The main thing is, the fact is clear: my bad luck has come to an end from this day!"

I was approaching the halt. With my trophies hanging off me, I could hardly climb up on the platform. As soon as they saw me the chief of the halt and the watchman exclaimed. They surrounded me with questions and praise.

"That's something I understand—a good little hunt!"

"Aha, you caught the one that carried off my chickens," the watchman said joyfully, stroking the dead fox. "Ooh, it's so sleek—it always had good grub to eat."

They were also delighted with Dokuka.

"What a dog . . . Now I really understand—it's a Saint Bernard!"

I asked whether there might by chance be a freight train going to the town, and whether I could ride on it.

That day I was really lucky. It turned out that a freight train was already standing on the siding at the semaphore and was about to set off.

A hunter covered with game is always a heroic figure, and everyone sympathizes with him.

"Run as fast as you can to the train. See the headlights over there. Hop up on the brake platform without talking to anyone about it, and in forty minutes you'll be home."

Stumbling, I rushed in the direction he indicated, leading Dokuka on a leash. From out of the fog the silhouettes of train cars unexpectedly emerged. On the brake platform of the last car was the black figure of the conductor. This callous man turned out, however, to be a great formalist and refused to let me onto the platform. I argued and insisted, and time was passing. The conductor's whistle sounded, and I rushed ahead with the intention of getting on the next brake platform.

It was only about three or four cars away. A person was standing on the little platform.

"Hey, citizen, help me to get up on the platform with these hares and foxes!"

"A hunter . . . Well, come on, climb faster. The train is moving," resounded the low bass voice of the stranger.

"Take the hares!"

"I got the hares!" the black figure said in his bass voice, deftly taking the game from me.

"Take the fox!"

"I got the fox!" the unknown citizen again boomed.

The train was starting to move slowly off.

"Take the other fox!"

"I got the other one!"

All my game was now on the brake platform.

I grabbed Dokuka with both arms and raised her in the air.

"Well, now grab the dog by her collar. Hurry up, take her."

"The dog? But it's going to bite!"

"Nothing of the sort, she's tame. Take the dog! Come on, hurry."

"What are you talking about, citizen? Do you think I'm some kind of fool, who'll drag your dogs around?"

The train was putting on speed. I was walking along with the car. I tried to squeeze the loudly howling Dokuka to my side with one arm. With my free arm I grabbed the iron handle. Dokuka was squealing and squirming. But the stranger suddenly barred my way.

"Where are you going, citizen? Do you really think you can get on here with a dog? Clear off!"

"Throw the foxes back! Hurry up, throw them!" I screamed desperately at the departing train.

"Best of luck!" the dark figure of the scoundrel boomed, disappearing into the fog, into which soon also disappeared the whole train, carrying my bag away to unknown towns and lands . . . Its mocking red lights had already floated off in the milky fog, and only the laughing wheels distinctly tapped out: "Idiot-dolt, idiot-dolt, idiot-dolt."

"But where are your foxes and hares?" the chief of the halt greeted me.

I explained.

How he guffawed! How the watchman laughed! Fools! They were literally falling down laughing. Clearly, it was boring to live at a railroad halt.

My story of the departing foxes and hares had introduced a great deal of variety into the drab life of little halt No. 63. The chief forced me to tell him everything from beginning to end twice. He was so pleased that he ordered for the samovar to be put on.

Worn-out Dokuka lay gloomily in a corner, licking her wounded paws, that had gone through so much that day. She looked into my eyes with bewilderment.

She understood everything, but fortunately she didn't know how to curse.

During tea the kind chief telegraphed to the next station, but they answered that there were neither hares nor foxes on the train that had arrived, nor any suspicious citizens who speak in a bass voice. Where they disappeared to, I will never, ever, find out.

Dokuka and I made our way home on foot late at night, exhausted to the limits of human and canine possibility.

My wife cursed me . . . How she cursed! She didn't believe a single word of my tale and announced to me that all my life I had brazenly lied.

And not just my wife! Semion Semionych didn't believe me either, when the next day I told him everything down to the slightest detail.

"Do tell, Vladimir Sergev!" was all I heard from him.

I don't know whether you'll believe me, reader. But just ask the watchman and chief of halt No. 63. I think they're still hanging around there. Ask them. They'll tell you whether I'm lying or not . . .

The Death of the Dirigible

Sing and sigh, obedient sail!
Ripple beneath me, gloomy ocean. . . .
—Pushkin

WHEN OVER THE haze of deserted autumn fields the first caravans of wild geese float by in the distant deep-blue heights, and their voices reach the hearing of people on the ground, every person who owns a gun inevitably thinks: "Hey! If only I could bag just one!"

That is how people with guns think. But the geese know it . . . . Yes, they know well the thoughts of the people in whose hands are the strange sticks that hurl thunder and lightning; that is why it can be so hard to bag a wild goose during the autumn migrations.

From under the ancient dike of our old town pond flows the shallow little stream Uperta. The little Uperta humbly flows over tiny pebbles past our steppe settlements and villages. Only in the village of Ivlevo, where once upon a time some clever miller barricaded the humble stream with a stubborn dam, the stream thought for a moment and finally flowed out into a whole lake in the middle of the village itself. It was here that the wild geese came to settle after completing their spring and autumn migrations. Semion Semionych and I had long been aware of this, and when in September we heard the first geese setting out for the south, we conceived a *burning* desire—and we decided to bag some of these beautiful, unapproachable birds at any price.

It was not the first year that Semion Semionych and I had been trying to succeed at this, but up to now we had had no success—those gray birds were very cautious and unapproachable. We would crawl up to them right on the field when they were feeding on stubble. We would watch for them by the water, where they usually flew by in order to alight on the lake. By moonlight we tried to sail up to the geese in a boat; we would hoist a dark-colored sail and approach them in complete silence . . . No! the geese were unattainable. But meanwhile Semion Semionych possessed his monstrous puntgun, famous for its long range, which the local hunters had nicknamed "the dirigible."

Wild geese are intelligent birds: sometimes you'll see a shepherd in the field, walking right by some feeding geese, and they let him pass because

36

they're assured of his peaceableness: the shepherd has no gun. But just try to approach them with a shotgun—you won't get anywhere near them!

At that time it happened that Semion Semionych and I had exhausted all our stores of shot, and since things like that were not sold in our little town, we naturally started trying to dream something up. My wife gave us an idea.

On the other side of the town pond rose an enormous old building—a crumbling palace in which landowner-Counts once lived. The Counts had disappeared, but in the attic of the old house remained all kinds of trash no one was interested in. According to my wife, in that attic there was an old broken hanging lamp, and in the lamp—there was some shot. Our inspection of the attic offered brilliant results: we counted up no less than twelve pounds of excellent large shot. But when we were getting ready to leave the gloomy attic, Semion Semionych called to me: "Vladimir Sergev! Look over there—what a pan!"

By the wall stood a strange object: a washtub but not a washtub . . . a pan but not a pan . . . a washbasin? Yes, something like a washbasin, but of enormous size and without handles. The strange thing was about three feet in diameter and was painted bright green.

"Did the Counts really boil their jam in this vat?" my friend asked in amazement.

"No, that couldn't be . . . it's made of tin . . . and it's painted . . ."

"So what's it for? Did they maybe wash their clothes in it?"

"No, that can't be either . . . They bathed the Counts' children in it!" I guessed.

"No, come on—children! What all didn't the bourgeoisie dream up . . . Bathing children in a pan! Would some kid really allow himself to be crammed into such a piece of junk? Just think!"

"Why not? First nanny puts a piece of candy in his mouth, and then she bathes him in a little warm water. It's pure pleasure . . . Oh yes, I remember now. My wife told me: yes, the Count brought this thing from England and bathed his children in it, and in English it's called a 'tub.'"

"A special thing," said Semion Semionych, slapping the tub on its dirty bottom.

He inspected it long and carefully from all sides.

"Vladimir Sergev, what if we put this 'tubby' to use with regard to the geese?"

"What do you mean? What are you talking about, Semion Semionych!"

"It's very simple! We'll have goose-meat now. That's official!"

"I still don't understand what you want to do with this thing."

"Here's what: this 'tubby' is a green thing . . ."

"So?"

"We'll put it in the water, stick sedge, reeds, and various twigs in along the edges. It will precisely turn out to be a natural object in the manner of an islet. Understand?"

Semion Semionych smiled broadly.

"What, you mean you want to get your gun and get into this thing instead of a boat and sail up to the geese?"

"That's official."

"But can it hold up? It'll go to the bottom!"

"Nothing of the sort. Let's give it a try."

I liked my friend's idea. After all, geese know perfectly well what a boat is, and it's impossible to camouflage it. But the Count's washbasin, made up to look like a reed-covered islet, would fool any goose, if only it would bear the weight of a man.

We immediately set to work dragging out our find from the attic, and in about five minutes we had launched the strange vessel on the waters of the town pond. Our vat turned out to be watertight. Rocking on the waves, the thing didn't look bad at all. We moved it to a shallow spot, and as a precaution Semion Semionych took off all his clothes, down to his spectacles.

O miracle! The pan bore the weight of my friend. It's true that it sank almost entirely into the water, and that now its sides stuck up from the surface only two or three inches, but this was precisely what made it possible to camouflage it perfectly.

I tried out the pan next after Semion Semionych. After sailing for half an hour I was convinced of my friend's inventive genius. Our practice sail demonstrated to us that you had to sit cross-legged, right in the center of the pan. The smallest incautious movement threatened catastrophe. But after all, there's no such thing as success without risk.

The means of propulsion was a little awkward: you had to push off with a long, thin pole, which would be highly inconvenient while hunting for geese. Here too my friend found the solution: he quickly ran home to get his wife's umbrella, and using the wind and the umbrella instead of a sail, our vat turned out to be capable not only of sailing with the wind but of tacking sideways.

We took turns sailing on the town pond all day, studying seafaring technique. The town idlers took notice of us. With the speed of lightning the rumor spread through the town that wonders were taking place on the pond—people were sailing in pans with umbrellas for sails!

Toward evening the whole town had gathered on the bank of the pond, marveling and feasting their eyes on the daredevil who was skimming over the pond under an umbrella, seated on God knows what, and picking up pretty good speed at times. Indeed, when the wind got stronger, the "tub" left a long, seething, watery trail, like the wake of a transatlantic steamship.

The local town hunters got especially excited. When they recognized me and Semion Semionych, they piled into two boats and persistently followed the pan, greeting each of its passengers with loud shouts of approval. In the crowd on shore there were some photographers, who preserved for posterity Semion Semionych's brilliant invention. He, however, did not lose his sense of dignity. Maintaining utter imperturbability and sangfroid, he continued proudly foaming up the waves of the town pond, paying not the slightest attention to the rejoicing crowd of spectators.

The spectators had something to rejoice about! I guarantee you that there never was anything of the kind anywhere in the world, and that our town pond was without a doubt the only body of water on earth that carried on its waves such a vessel and such a passenger! It is enough to look at the attached photograph (taken by the local hairdresser, Ulybkin) to understand the daring nature of my friend's undertaking.

Having made a smart turn, Semion Semionych moored the vat to the dike, and as we dragged our vessel onto dry land it was already getting dark. The crowd of townspeople immediately clustered around us. The policeman on duty asked the crowd in the properly formulated words not to push and shove, and declared to us that we should no longer disturb the peace with our actions. He kindly suggested that we choose some other body of water for our seafaring practice. But although the lips of this conscientious keeper of the peace were speaking rather sternly and even sharply, in his eyes was shining complete sympathy with our plan.

Like two heroes we carried our tub through the streets of the town, accompanied by a rather large crowd of sympathetic citizens. Everyone sympathized with us. Only Matriona Andrevna (the helpmeet of Semion Semionych) did not display any joy and, on the contrary, even seemed to be out of sorts. When her husband returned home, she met him with a stream of unfriendly, undeserved, and even insulting reproaches.

But we had no time for Matriona Andrevna. We set about discussing and thinking over the further improvement of the tub. We assumed that with some string wound around the sides of the tub we could fasten a whole fence made of tall reeds. The weak point in the whole scheme appeared to be the umbrella, which, for one thing, could scare the suspicious geese, and for another, would undoubtedly get in the way of the shooter's view. After thinking a bit, Semion Semionych solved this problem too: he suggested painting the umbrella green and tying green branches to it. He also recommended cutting out two holes in the fabric of the umbrella, one above the other, so that one could stick the barrel of the gun through the lower hole and take aim through the upper. So the goose problem was solved brilliantly.

My friend immediately set to work carrying out our plan. Some green paint appeared out of nowhere, but when we had made the first stroke of the brush on his wife's umbrella, Matriona Andrevna couldn't stand it any longer: she declared to her husband that he was disgracing her, and himself, and their whole household; threw an iron at him; and disappeared from the house, slamming the door behind her.

"What lack of imagination!" Semion Semionych said, shaking his head. "My wife grudges the wretched umbrella, but the bullheaded creature doesn't think about the fact that she's going to get to eat goose meat! Well, isn't that a lack of imagination, Vladimir Sergev? No, it will be a long time before the masses develop a consciousness!"

The next day the weather had taken a serious turn for the worse. A west wind began to blow, bringing storm clouds with it. Matriona Andrevna's umbrella, painted the day before, had dried completely overnight, and we set off for the village of Ivlevo, planning to use our new invention for hunting wild geese that very evening.

We had to walk about seven miles to get to Ivlevo. It was pouring rain, but we were beautifully protected from its streams. We covered ourselves with the tub and walked without feeling the slightest dampness. The horses pulling the carts we met couldn't figure out what we were, and as soon as they saw us they shied away. And it wasn't only horses: even the people we met took on a look of utter astonishment when they saw four human legs covered by a single monstrous green hat from which streams of water poured.

I was walking in back. Ahead of me Semion Semionych picked his way, carrying Matriona Andrevna's green umbrella and his muzzle-loading dirigible, with its gigantic forty-two-inch barrel, fraught with goose death, pointing downwards. We walked as if under a roof, listening to the rain drumming on the bottom of the tub.

O sovereign Count! Former proprietor of the tub! What would you think if by chance you could see us today on this muddy road? And the tub? You stylish English tub, product of the fantasy of the pampered bourgeoisie! You were once created for the carefully tended little body of a small but rich do-nothing child . . . O tub! Stylish English tub from London! Whither are you going now along a muddy autumn cart-track? Whose heads are you saving from the streams of rain? Tell me, O stylish tub, when you were with your former master the Count, did you ever think the day would come when over the waves of rivers, lakes, seas, and oceans you would carry bold, experienced hunters on the trail of wild geese?

You're not a "tub" any more . . . You're just a tubby!

Meditating thus, we finally reached the village of Ivlevo. Toward evening the sky cleared, and the setting September sun began to play on the surface of the Ivlevo Lake. In its very center sat a flock of wild geese who had just flown in from feeding.

We approached the water in such a way as to have a favorable wind and began to camouflage our vessel before lowering it into the water. A small group of curious peasants who were very interested in the imminent hunt crowded around us. They were giving us advice. The local teacher Pamvin appeared out of nowhere with a pair of binoculars. He occupied a position on a rise in the ground. Surveying the surface of the lake from there, he began to report to us as if from a battery observation post:

"Twenty-nine, thirty . . . thirty-two geese . . . wild . . . the ones near the shore are domestic . . ."

The tub was ready. On one of its sides we had managed to fit a kind of support for the heavy "dirigible." We drew lots to see who was to sail first. The lot fell to Semion Semionych. In stern silence he set about loading his "dirigible," cramming in the maximum charge. The blows of the ramrod resounded solemnly in the silence. The copper percussion cap was installed in its place, everything was checked and inspected, and Semion Semionych settled down cross-legged in the tub.

"Let's go!" he commanded tersely.

I shoved the round thing off from the shore . . . But at this point we realized that there was something we hadn't taken into account: the weighty barrel of the seventeen-pound "dirigible," when stuck through the hole in the green umbrella, caused the tub to tip dangerously. The tub took on a little water. In order to preserve equilibrium, Semion Semionych had to move his seat to the very back. Now the sides of the tub stuck out of the water no more than two inches.

"Let's go!" Semion Semionych commanded a second time, and Matriona Andrevna's umbrella, catching the wind, slowly carried my friend out into open water.

Now he's thirty paces from the shore. A brilliant ruse! Now the tub is completely indistinguishable from an ordinary reed-covered islet. Exactly the same kind of islets are sticking up from the water here and there over the whole lake. The gun is absolutely invisible. Success is guaranteed! Semion Semionych holds his course straight for the geese. The wind has died down, and the tub moves slowly forward. However, this slowness is an undoubted pledge of success, for the treacherous green islet will approach the birds gradually and unnoticeably.

The crowd on the shore fell silent. With great anxiety we watched the hunt without tearing our eyes away from the tub. The teacher Pamvin on the hill, binoculars to his eyes, froze like a statue; he was completely lost in contemplation. Semion Semionych was sailing up to the flock . . . Now he's within the firing range of his long-range gun . . . Semion Semionych is using his cunning . . . Amazing self-possession! He wants to get even closer . . . to make sure. The geese don't notice him at all and are performing their ablutions in the water as if nothing were wrong.

But what's this? The treacherous green islet is suddenly enveloped in a thick cloud of white smoke: the "dirigible" has begun to speak!

"Bu-ukh!"—the terrible detonation booms out. The densely gathered flock erupts in unbelievable alarm. An uncommon shot, monstrous in its results . . . But where is the islet? Is it behind the smoke? But there's no smoke left . . . On the water there are only dead geese.

I pounced on Pamvin and grabbed the binoculars from his hands. What I saw made my hair stand on end under my forage cap!

On the smooth surface of the lake floated about ten corpses of wild geese, and in their midst the end of the forty-two-inch barrel of the "dirigible" stuck out of the water in lonely isolation!

A thin stream of white smoke was still coming out of the eight-gauge barrel. A little further on floated Matriona Andrevna's green umbrella. There was no Semion Semionych. The binocular lens sought him in vain. He and his invention had been swallowed by the waves. The stylish English tub could not withstand the monstrous recoil of the "dirigible"! The product of pampering could not survive such a shock.

The teacher's binoculars fell from my hands. We dashed in a crowd into the cold water . . .

Note at end of story:
Don't be sad, reader! Semion Semionych has not perished, as you perhaps think. He returned to life, although he was stricken by a serious illness. "Psycho-Curiosities of Semion Semionych"—that is the name of the next story dedicated to the adventures of our heroes Bochonkin and Khvoshch, which our readers will find in *Pathfinder* No. 1 for 1928.

Psycho-Curiosities of Semion Semionovich

SEMION SEMIONYCH'S HEALTH was slowly restored.

He didn't perish. Only the "dirigible," his famous gun, perished. It was trampled into the silt at the moment my friend was saved.

We pulled a lifeless Semion Semionovich from the bottom of Ivlevo Lake, where he had lain underwater no less than five minutes, covered by his own invention, the huge tub in which he had sailed so boldly up to the geese.

For more than half an hour we tried in all possible ways to resuscitate the lifeless body of Semion Semionovich, and we massaged him with home brew. When our last hope of bringing this hardened hunter back to life had disappeared, he unexpectedly smacked his lips, thereby giving us the first sign that he had not yet perished. Heartened by this, we began to pump and massage the numb hunter with new energy, and finally we pumped him so hard that he lost his patience: he drenched us with a whole fountain of water spewed out of his mouth, and flung such a bad word at us that many of the rescuers then lost the desire to take any part in reviving my dear companion.

What didn't I experience in those minutes! But I consider it superfluous to expatiate on this. It should be quite clear without this.

So Semion Semionovich did not perish. His last goose hunt, his last masterly shot, which killed eight wild geese on the spot, produced a sensation in the whole town, and there wasn't a single citizen who didn't know about it.

For a whole week the town's hunters came to Bochonkin's lodgings to ask about his health. They would look with envious eyes at my friend and the eight wild geese killed with one terrible shot from his dirigible.

The hunters thirsted to know the details.

But Semion Semionovich expatiated on his catastrophe only with reluctance.

"There was a shock, and after that an impromptu," was his terse explanation of his misfortune, which was the result of putting too big a charge into the dirigible. The gun recoiled more strongly than usual, so strongly that the shooter's torso reeled back, and his legs were thrown upwards, which caused the instantaneous destruction of the ingenious sailing vessel. The tub over-turned and covered my friend. In a word: "there was a shock, and after that an impromptu."

Semion Semionovich seemed to have recovered completely. But after what he had experienced, from time to time he behaved strangely. He became taciturn and somehow depressed. He complained that "a sheep is chewing its cud in my left side." At times he would develop an annoying belch "like after drinking methylated spirits," although he did not ingest any methylated spirits at all. And then for some unknown reason he developed a kind of gramophone murmur in his stomach, which greatly disturbed his wife at night. In short, Semion Semionovich was depressed.

Despairing of a cure, he went to see Doctor Nikitskii, bringing me and his spouse Matriona Andrevna along to bolster his spirits. In our little town Doctor Nikitskii had the reputation of a very special doctor.

The learned Aesculapius cast an experienced eye over the patient and began to drum on his stomach in all possible ways with a little metal mallet. Then he listened through a tube, which the little old doctor applied literally to all the parts of Semion Semionych's body, trying to detect something suspicious with his experienced ear. We followed his movements with tear-filled eyes and bated breath. But the doctor did not detect anything suspicious and declared that all of Semion Semionych's organs were in the best possible condition.

"It's simply a curious case of psycho-neurosis caused purely by nerves in the aftermath of a shock."

Such was the diagnosis of Doctor Nikitskii.

"But how can we treat him now, Doctor?" Matriona Andrevna and I asked in unison.

"Only with a regimen! And no medicines at all. The patient is nervous. First of all he needs a change of scenery. He needs to be amused."

We began to think up what kind of amusement we could arrange for Semion Semionych in order to cure his ailment. Doctor Nikitskii proposed:

"Take him to Moscow! Let him see the sights of the capital: new impressions will dispel the psycho-neurosis, and soon your hunter will again bring wild geese home to us."

"What are you saying, Doctor!" Matriona Andrevna said, waving her arms. "You think I'm going to let Senia anywhere near the water now?"

"Well, that's none of my business," the doctor smiled, and gaily slapping Semion Semionych on the shoulder, he went off to the washstand, saying, "The most curious case of psycho-neurosis caused by nerves . . ."

When we came out, Semion Semionych looked at me sadly and asked, "Vladim Sergev, have you ever heard of such a sickness: 'psycho-curiosity,' caused by scurvy?"

"Not psycho-curiosity but psycho-neurosis," I tried to reassure him, "and not caused by *scurvy* at all, but by *nerves*. It's nothing."

"Now I get Moscow!" my friend suddenly roared with flashing eyes.

"You'll get it," I winked at him and firmly shook his honest hand.

Semion Semionych had never been in Moscow. He had never shown his face farther than Epifan, Efremov, and Elets, and therefore you will of course understand how interested we were in my friend's upcoming trip to the capital.

In view of the fact that I had had occasion to be in Moscow before, Semion Semionych insisted that I accompany him. I readily agreed; incidentally, I had relatives living there.

For about a week Semion Semionych regularly visited the tailor Svinolupov. And this Vanka Svinolupov was a real specialist! He knew that he was making a suit jacket not for just anybody, but for the famous hunter Semion Semionych Bochonkin, who had become the hot topic of the whole town after the doctor ordered him to go amuse himself in Moscow.

Svinolupov knew that now the capital would see his work. That is why he worked such a fashion miracle—a double-breasted green-checked jacket and jodhpurs of the same material—devilishly fashionable indeed!

The tailor Svinolupov did not rest here. Somehow he managed to obtain for Semion Semionych green headgear of a type never before seen in our town, made not exactly out of a gourd, not exactly out of seaweed—a kind of helmet or bowler hat made of hard loofah. This hat was called a "how-d'ye-do-g'bye," and had two bills, in front and in back.

Now add to this whole costume an unbelievably large metal badge of the All-Russia Union of Hunters, which Semion Semionych had ordered specially from the local jeweler Tetelbaum. My friend wanted to make a good impression when he appeared in the capital.

Judge for yourself what a picturesque sight Semion Semionych was when he appeared at the station before the train's departure, surrounded by a crowd of hunters seeing him off!

At the sight of her husband dressed to the nines, in his splendidly fitted suit, Matriona Andrevna's heart skipped a beat and she was suddenly overcome by jealousy toward the ladies of Moscow.

The train departed to the rumble of the warm parting words of our companions and the dramatic protestations of the wife reminding her husband that she would not tolerate infidelity . . .

We arrived in Moscow early in the morning and came out onto the platform of the Kursk Station, stunned and confused by the unaccustomed bustle. Because of the early hour we had absolutely no idea where to go.

Semion Semionych finally decided to call on his old aunt, who lived in the Khamovniki neighborhood, and I decided to take a drive down Tverskaia Street to visit my relatives.

At about 7:00 I put my friend on the "B" tram and explained to him how to get to Khamovniki. We parted with the understanding that we would meet at the apartment of Semion Semionych's aunt at about 1:00 and then go together to look around Moscow.

It was already after 1:00 when I rang at the entryway of an unprepossessing little house in one of the Khamovniki lanes. Semion Semionych's aunt herself opened the door and was greatly amazed at my arrival. She became even more amazed when I told her that I had come for Semion Semionych. "He hasn't been here; he had no intention of stopping in here."

The old lady and I became seriously alarmed. More than six hours had passed since the moment when the figure of Semion Semionych had disappeared from my sight, leaving the Kursk Station on the tram. My friend was in Moscow for the first time in his life, and who knows what might have happened to him!

For about half an hour the aunt and I discussed how to find her nephew now, and finally I decided to go to the police station to report the disappearance of a man in a green-checked jacket and a hat of the style "how-d'ye-do-g'bye."

But I only managed to go out onto the street and walk a few paces along the sidewalk before I saw the familiar green figure of my friend with his "how-d'ye-do-g'bye" on his head. Semion Semionych was extremely agitated. The glasses on his nose gleamed defiantly.

"Vladim Sergev!" he cried out to me from a distance. "It's an outrage! An official outrage! You won't be cured of a psycho-curiosity here; no, excuse the expression, on the contrary: you'll acquire two of them!"

"What happened?"

"I'll tell you straight to your face: it's not the letter B, but robbery!"

"You were robbed! A pickpocket got to you? Oh, Semion Semionych, but I asked you to be careful in trams and to watch out for pickpockets!"

"Who's talking about pickpockets! It wouldn't be so bad if someone had tried to pick my pocket—I would have shown him! No, the point is that no one tried to pick my pocket, but three and a half rubles are gone just like that!"

"But who cleaned you out?"

"Forgive me for my frankness—the ticket collectors!"

"I understand, you lost your ticket. But the fine for that is only a ruble."

"Nothing of the sort! I didn't lose any ticket, but I was officially fined three times for a ruble each, and I have no idea what for!"

"That's very strange! How could that happen?"

"Very simply: I'm riding on that B . . . I bought a ticket for eleven kopecks, I look out the window . . . The city is truly of the most official sort! We travel for a long time—we just don't arrive. I look: it's the Kursk Station again! I think, what kind of rehearsal is this? And then, all of a sudden, that same ticket collector pops up: 'Your ticket, please, and a ruble, please; your ticket, he says, has expired long ago—you went around the entire ring.'[1]

"'Excuse me,' I say, 'I didn't go around any rings, but I'm honestly and uprightly traveling to see my aunt in Khamovniki.' And he says, 'Don't make a disturbance, please, but pay your ruble and ride in the opposite direction.' What are you going to do? I pay a ruble note; I get on another B and make my way in the other direction. Well, I think, I should be getting to Khamovniki soon. Nothing of the sort! I look: again my B is approaching the Kursk Station, and that same ticket collector is pushing his way into the car. 'Give me another ruble,' he says. I say, 'Citizen, excuse me, I already paid you a ruble note, here's your receipt, why are you being so insolent and again asking me for money? What do you think I do, manufacture it?' 'That's not my affair,' he says. 'Pay or I'll call the police.' 'But when,' I say, 'are you going to get me to Khamovniki, and how much is it going to finally cost? Tell me right now.' 'It will cost only fourteen kopecks.' I paid him a ruble and fourteen kopecks, received a receipt, and continued on my way. And on the streets I see so many people! People! And all those automobiles pushing in! Well, well, I think, Moscow! And there I look, and I don't believe my eyes: there on the square— stands the Kursk Station! What kind of rehearsal is this, I think—there's just no end to this Kursk Station! I had hardly taken it into my head to get off, but don't even think about it: the ticket collector was right there on the spot. He was so serious; he suddenly stopped the tram and pushed his way through the whole crowd to me: 'Pay,' he says, 'another ruble and scram out of here in- stantaneously.' And I say: 'Forgive me, citizen, here are your two receipts, and now tell me: where is your conscience? I'm a sick man, moreover from the provinces, I came to Moscow to be treated for psycho-curiosity, and you have put me in an interesting position. I'm not giving you a ruble! I've paid you plenty of money. I beg of you, convey me to Khamovniki for my money—oth- erwise, give back the two rubles twenty-five kopecks . . . that's up to you!'

"Well, there really are some people without a conscience! I look, and that same ticket collector stops the whole letter B and says, 'Pay a ruble and get out of here—the car is not going any farther.' I say, 'Nothing of the sort,' and he calls a policeman. I messed around with him for half an hour; they were about to drag me to the police station . . . I ended up having to give them another ruble note! No, Vladim Sergev, say what you will, but in those Bs of yours—the devil himself wouldn't be able to understand either B or M! Well, I think, that's it; if I go on the B, no amount of money will be enough, and I won't get to my aunt's in the next week. I ended up having to hoof it, and it was so much simpler: I walk at my own pace and ask people the way from time to time—that's how I made my way here."

Semion Semionych spread before me three tram tickets and three receipts for the total sum of three rubles thirty-nine kopecks.

He was tired and hungry. We went to his aunt's place to set the old lady's mind at ease.

Adventures at the Zoo

SEMION SEMIONYCH AND I stayed two days in Moscow. During that time my friend's illness vanished as if by magic. We visited many interesting spots, but the one we were most interested in—the Moscow Zoo—we intentionally left for last. We planned to end our epic Moscow journey with this visit.

Because it was Sunday there was a huge crowd, and we had to stand in line a long time to buy our tickets.

The first beasts we saw turned out to be the most ordinary hares. Some sort of "specialist" was leading a big crowd of people and, having stopped in front of the hares, was explaining to the tourists the concept of animals' protective coloration. The gray hare has fur whose color resembles the color of the fields in which he feeds and sleeps. The white hare turns white in the winter so that it is hard to see him in the forest amid the snowy bushes and tree stumps. All this has been intentionally arranged in nature so that the little hares can escape the indiscreet glances of their innumerable enemies. According to the "specialist," almost all wild animals have protective coloration which serves either for defense or for hunting.

The zoo hares turned out to be just hares, and couldn't amaze such experienced hunters as us.

"I say, what a wonder! They're displaying a hare! We've carried more interesting things than that on our backs," Semion Semionych growled. Knocking about the zoo with the tour group seemed a little boring to us, so we set off independently.

We walked among the beasts and were amazed at every step: wolves, bears, pelicans with large crops—all this was real, alive, intelligent, and "did everything but talk." But one of these animals did talk, in pure Russian. It was a big green parrot.

Passing by his cage, Semion Semionych asked, "What kind of bird is that?"

Unexpectedly the bird introduced itself: "Little priest, dear little priest," it said, affably nodding its head.

Semion Semionych stepped back in amazement and looked around at me perplexedly.

"Did you hear?" he asked me.

"I heard. Well, what's so surprising? Didn't you know that parrots talk?"

"Although I read about it in *Robinson Crusoe,* forgive my frankness, I didn't believe it. Now I see that Robinson Crusoe was right."

Semion Semionych boldly entered into conversation with the parrot.

"Hey, you winged creature!" my friend addressed the parrot. "Although you're an insect, still you know how to think a little bit. Tell me, who am I?"

"A fool!" the bird cried.

"I beg of you not to swear! Just look who I'm hearing this from! But which of us is the bigger fool is still not clear," my friend said indignantly.

We set off further and unexpectedly found ourselves in front of the lion's cage.

Semion Semionych had heard a lot about this king of the beasts, but he had never yet had occasion to see him. My friend and I stood there for a long time. The iron grille separated two lions from each other. One was a natural lion. The other was Semion Semionych! One had a covering of yellowish-brown, the other of green check. On the head of one was a mane. On the head of the other was a "how-d'ye-do-g'bye." But all the same, both of them were lions, both were the terror of the animal kingdom. Now they looked each other in the eye in stern silence and experienced many emotions.

This wordless picture was long engraved in my memory: Semion Semionych and the lion looking at each other!

The kangaroo was also favored with our attention. Semion Semionych had never even heard of this animal. But when he learned that the kangaroo has a pocket on its breast for carrying its own children, he noted significantly: "A special beast."

We passed by a fenced-off meadow. Behind the fence stood a big shaggy animal. It looked at us with an unusually proud and disdainful air, lifting its long neck high in the air. The animal was chewing something.

"Llama. Do not tease," we read on the sign.

"Ooh, she's a proud one," Semion Semionych noted, examining the llama carefully. "But after all, it's a beast like any other. There's nothing interesting about it. Chew to your heart's content, you fool," he said to the animal.

I don't know whether all llamas understand human speech. In any case, this llama understood perfectly that she had been called a fool, and the proud creature considered herself insulted. She answered Semion Semionych with a well-aimed gob of spit in the nose.

Semion Semionych was rooted to the spot.

"Oh, you slut! You miserable hooligan!" he cried, wiping his face.

"Tfoo!" the llama repeated and adorned my friend's checked waistcoat with a new gob of spit.

"Oh, you accursed spitter!" Semion Semionych flew into a rage.

My friend was seriously angry, and I hastened to calm him down.

"Stop it, Semion Semionych! Let's leave here. Why do you want to get mixed up with all kinds of cattle."

Here I too caught it from the llama, because the word "cattle" apparently also displeased the intolerably arrogant creature.

We were forced to retreat. Semion Semionych was covered with spittle and continued to grumble for a long time.

"The beasts have put on airs. A little while ago a winged creature swore at me for no reason at all, and now Mrs. Llama has covered me with spittle from head to toe. They've gotten awfully proud—you can't say a word to them! What kind of business is that: the slightest little thing happens, and you start spitting. Well, did I really order a new jacket from Svinolupov so that all kinds of short-legged creatures could cover it with spittle?"

At that time an employee of the zoo had come into step with us. He heard my friend's complaints and turned to him with a smile: "Did the llama spit on you? Well, I congratulate you, citizen! Now you're going to stink for a whole week."

"Vladim Sergev, come on, smell me, do I smell?"

"And how!" I answered my friend, after sniffing his fashionable suit.

"I'd better wash up somewhere, Vladim Sergev. Maybe I'll take a bath in a pond."

"Would that be proper, Semion Semionych? After all, we're in the capital."

"But what else can I do?"

We were entering the terrarium. Here were exhibited all kinds of snakes, frogs, and turtles. One of the turtles was very strange looking. It was a rare specimen found in Lake Kanka, that had been brought here from the region of Ussuria. The turtle looked like a large flat shell. It lay motionless on the bottom of a large aquarium filled with water.

Semion Semionych looked around. There weren't many people here. Semion Semionych instantly took off his hat, got on his knees, and without a second thought, ducked his head in the aquarium in order to wash away the stinking llama spittle. At the same moment, out from under the turtle's shell a small head on an unusually long neck thrust itself forward. From the side I could see perfectly well how the long neck of the turtle quickly stretched out toward my friend's face. I didn't have time to warn Semion Semionych before he suddenly jumped away from the aquarium and began to moan. Water was streaming from his physiognomy, his lower lip was swelling, and a drop of blood appeared on it. Semion Semionych snorted.

"Ooh, the irresponsible parasite! Ussurian plague!" my friend moaned, covering his wounded lip with his hand.

"Semion Semionych, maybe this is a poisonous turtle?" I asked him with alarm.

"He's as poisonous as hell! I don't understand why they want to exhibit such a nasty thing to the public."

We hastened to leave the terrarium and its unattractive inhabitants.

We set off through the zoo to find the hippopotamus. We were directed to a big building that stood on a hill. There was a line at the door.

We got in line, and just in case we asked whether the hippopotamus lived here. It turned out that the hippopotamus really did live here, and therefore we confidently moved forward. In the spacious building a multitude of people of both sexes and all ages and professions had gathered. They were all making their way and pressing to one side of the building, standing on tiptoe and looking over one another's heads. We energetically pushed forward and occupied a place in the first row above the pool. There was no hippopotamus. At our feet the water was agitated, terrible waves were rising, and the people said that these waves were coming from the hippopotamus.

We stood for a few minutes and finally we saw a sort of small pink object appear above the surface of the water.

"Look, look, he's appeared! There he is, the hippopotamus himself!"

We hadn't imagined it this way. We had expected to see something huge and unwieldy, and here we're shown a little pink bump.

Nevertheless we surmised that the trunk of the hippopotamus was under water, but we couldn't tell which part of its body it was showing us now. I was inclined to think that the visible bump was the animal's front end. Semion Semionych thought precisely the opposite.

"It's the front," I maintained.

"It's not the front, but the other way round," Semionych maintained.

We argued for a long time. One of the citizens in the crowd expressed the opinion that the pink bump was the hippopotamus's nostril.

"It's the nostril," he insisted, "see—it's blowing bubbles!"

"But where the bubbles are coming from is still in question," Semion Semionych retorted.

"Vladim Sergev, enough! Let's leave this disgraceful scene!"

We left the building somewhat disappointed, but our disappointment quickly passed when we saw a real, enormous elephant strolling about behind a fence. Here was a beast being displayed without any deception. We stood still by the fence, extremely satisfied and pleased.

It was a female Indian elephant. With amazement we read a long list posted by the fence which indicated all the foods the elephant consumes in a day. It turns out that the elephant devours hay and carrots and bread and sugar, and washes it down with twenty buckets of water. I don't remember precisely how much this beast eats. In any case, an unbelievable quantity.

The elephant was approached by the same tour group which we had met not long ago by the hares' cage. The same "specialist" was leading the tour.

He began to tell about the elephant and declared that the elephant is a forest animal found in the eternally green tropical forests.

"Excuse me," my friend interrupted the "specialist," "but why isn't the elephant green?"

"What do you mean 'why'?" the "specialist" asked in amazement.

"You say it's found in green forests . . . Where is its protective coloration?"

The "specialist" was obviously taken aback and didn't know what to answer, and Semion Semionych, smiling smugly, nudged me with his elbow.

"Didn't I cleverly cut him off?" he asked me quietly.

At the same time the elephant had slowly approached the fence, slyly looked at Semion Semionych, and, sticking its long trunk through the bars, with a melancholy look picked up Semion Semionych's green hat, made of seaweed in the style "How-d'ye-do-g'bye." The elephant lifted the green seaweed hat high above its head and in a leisurely fashion directed it into its mouth. The animal smacked its lips with gusto. She had probably gotten rather bored with hay, bread, carrots, and sugar, and a hat made of seaweed was more to her taste.

The crowd exclaimed loudly, and Semion Semionych . . . not for nothing had he belonged to a physical training club for a whole year—in the twinkling of an eye surmounted the high fence and found himself in the elephant's cage. Holding its trunk with one hand, he boldly stuck his free hand into the very mouth of the enormous animal. I don't know how this daring and desperate attempt would have ended. A zoo employee who came flying at Semion Semionych like a whirlwind ruined the whole thing. A bizarre scene took place between them. They seized hold of each other. The crowd went wild. Everyone was shouting. One woman went into hysterics.

"Give me back the hat!" Semion Semionych roared.

"You have no right!" the employee howled.

I rushed to help my friend. The frightened elephant made off for a far corner of the enclosure.

We failed to save the hat. It perished forever in the elephant's monstrous maw. We were taken to the police, and the crowd followed us.

Semion Semionych walked proudly with his head held high. He did not lose his dignity. I was agitated.

"Vladim Sergev, don't be afraid," my brave friend whispered to me. "Nothing will happen to us. Rely on me."

At the police station we were greeted sternly. The interrogation began. Who are we, where are we from. The business seemed to have taken a nasty turn. They clearly suspected us of malicious hooliganism. Unexpectedly my friend asked for paper and pen. He began to write. I leaned over his shoulder and worriedly followed what he was writing. Here is what Semion Semionych wrote:

To the Moscow Police,

DECLARATION

by Citizen Semion Bochonkin

Taking into account my working-class origins and the fact that I was officially covered with spittle by a llama, which will cost no less than 16 rubles (for which I have a receipt from the tailor Svinolupov). In addition 4 rubles 50 kopecks for a hat which was eaten up by an Indian she-elephant. I ask that you recover 20 rubles 50 kopecks from the Moscow Zoo, and that you annul myself and Citizen Khvoshch from custody, in view of the fact that we did nothing unprintable, but on the contrary we came to Moscow with the educational purpose of restoring my health.

Semion Bochonkin.

Attachment: Citizen Svinolupov's bill.

Semion Semionych was a real shyster! He presented the declaration calmly and imperturbably to a stern man clothed in a policeman's uniform. The more the man read, the more his stern face brightened up. O, miracle! From a terrible executor of duty the policeman suddenly turned into the nicest and most cheerful fellow. After asking us two or three questions, he suddenly declared:

"Hey, guys . . . What got into you to mess with that Indian she-elephant?"

"And my hat?" my friend interrupted the policeman.

The policeman smiled, waved his hand, and said, "Get the hell out of here!"

On happy feet we rushed out of the police station. When we found ourselves on the street, Semion Semionych caught his breath and said testily:

"Vladim Sergev, after all it's a beastly thing, the zoo!"

The Recovery of the Dirigible

IT WAS A cheerful April morning. Semion Semionych and I were sitting in a cramped hunting tent made of reeds on the shore of Shchadilov Pond and had our eyes glued on a small flock of wild ducks. Their black forms were visible on the open water about 150 paces from us. Turning their wide bills in our direction, they swayed on the waves and seemed to be saying to us, "And you can't get us—we're too far away!"

"Oh, Vladim Sergev, if only I had my 'dirigible' gun with me right now, I'd shoot from here and, say what you will, I'd knock off three of them! Well, what can you do with a popgun like this!" and Semion Semionych scornfully rapped his finger against the barrels of his light flintlock.

"Can you believe it, Vladim Sergev—no matter how many guns I've tried after the dirigible, they've all turned out to be trash: pop, pop—and nothing more. Oh, I used to load my dear dirigible with a triple charge, and boy, would I blast!"

"Semion Semionych, why recall the past! Your dirigible has perished. Since last fall it has lain dead on the bottom of Ivlevo Lake. It's time to get used to the thought that you no longer have a dirigible. Don't disturb yourself needlessly. Wait—it looks like the ducks are swimming toward us."

We fell silent. The ducks indeed were quietly approaching us. We waited for them a very long time. The flock was already about ninety paces from us, when suddenly the birds for some reason changed their minds and turned back, slowly moving away from us.

"Vladim Sergev, let's blast at them once. Aim at the center . . . Ready? Okay, one . . . two . . . three . . ."

We shot simultaneously and showered the whole flock with shot. The ducks instantly took off from the water and flew away. Only one duck had been wounded. Quickly flapping one wing, it swiftly swam away from us and immediately got out of shooting range.

"No, Vladim Sergev, say what you will, but with guns like this, it's not hunting but official personality corruption. Being without the dirigible is like being without hands. Without the dirigible it's as if I don't even exist."

The morning's results were lamentable. Many ducks were flying, but we took only a pair. My friend became sad.

"Vladim Sergev!" he said. "I'm starting to lose all my appetite for life, and I'm also hunting without any appetite. It's boring without the dirigible. It's boring without its dear booming. Let's get it from the bottom of the lake!"

"My dear fellow, have you lost your mind? In order to extract the dirigible from the depths of Ivlevo Lake, you will probably have to hire deep-sea divers. It would be cheaper to order Tula craftsmen to make a new gun in the style of the dirigible."

"Vladim Sergev, you can't get a gun like that made today no matter how much you pay for it. The late dirigible is an antique gun, and it was made by a famous Turkish craftsman. They say that gun cost a lot of money. Remember how last year I knocked off eight wild ducks with one shot? We have to get the dirigible."

"Madman, but how are you going to get it? You're talking nonsense!"

Semion Semionych sighed deeply and fell into profound thought.

Spring was at its height. Semion Semionych had become completely apathetic and stopped going hunting. I was forced to go hunting alone. When on returning from the hunt I would drop in to see my friend and share my impressions with him, I almost always found him bored and pensive. My friend's gloomy mood was nothing other than longing for his beloved lost gun.

Summer arrived. Sadly I oiled my gun and secreted it in its dusty case, in order to pull it out only on the eve of August 1, when hunting season would begin. And then, when only about three days remained until August 1, I went to see my friend to find out whether his mood had changed. I wanted to propose that we open hunting season together and go to the neighboring district, which abounded in snipe.

Semion Semionych wasn't home, and his estimable spouse was in an abominable mood. She announced to me that her "accursed" husband now was absent from home for days at a time.

"Senia has gotten completely out of hand and out of the house. First he's going to see Doctor Nikitskii for some reason, then he's running to the pharmacy, and he's always secretive about something."

"Maybe he's ill?" I inquired.

"He's healthy as a horse. Do sick people really act like that?"

At that moment we heard steps in the entryway, and Semion Semionych himself came into the room.

"My compliments, Vladim Sergev! I haven't seen you for a long time."

My friend smiled gaily and firmly shook my hand. He was in an animated mood and for some reason had a triumphant air.

"Semion Semionych, I came to see what your plans are for August 1. Shall we go hunt snipe?"

"It's very simple—we're going to hunt ducks."

"So your splenetic mood has passed? I'm very glad."

Semion Semionych winked gaily and glanced around at his wife. She was standing with her back to us and energetically wiping dirty dishes. My friend quickly bent over to me and quietly whispered: "Vladim Sergev, tomorrow morning, come to the city pond. I'll be waiting for you by the cove. I need you desperately . . . there's some business afoot."

I looked at Semion Semionych in amazement. He didn't let me speak.

"Shh," he whispered and, raising his finger to his lips to silence me, looked eloquently in Matriona Andrevna's direction.

I was filled with curiosity. I really wanted to ask my friend what the secret business was that he was hiding from his wife, but Matriona Andrevna stubbornly hung around in the room the whole time, and it was impossible to ask him in her presence.

I got ready to leave and was saying goodbye. Semion Semionych accompanied me into the entryway and while shaking my hand reminded me again:

"So it's agreed, tomorrow about nine in the morning I'll be waiting for you by the cove."

"Semion Semionych, why this mystery? Tell me what you're up to."

"Vladim Sergev, you'll find out tomorrow."

At nine in the morning I approached the small cove of the city pond, not far from the high school. On the shore lay Semion Semionych's boat. He was sitting in it and with a businesslike air was nailing to the bench some kind of wooden shaft with supports. This boat had at one time been knocked together out of "the materials at hand" by my friend. Into its construction had gone boards from crates, an old fence, and even some rusty roof iron. At one time Semion Semionych had dreamed of installing on this boat a motor he had himself invented. For this reason my friend had even named his boat the *Automotor*. The scheme with the motor didn't succeed for some reason, but the fine-sounding name *Automotor* remained attached to this strange vessel.

Semion Semionych was very cheerful.

"Well, Vladim Sergev, let's get to work!"

My friend quickly jumped out of the *Automotor*, ran over to a broom bush growing nearby, pulled a bag out of it, dragged it to my feet and shook its contents onto the ground.

First of all I saw a large rubber ball of the kind children play with. The ball was an ordinary one—striped blue and red. Then I noticed two quite ordinary bricks with a pair of old sandals tied to them. Nearby lay a bicycle pump, a long rubber pipe, and a shovel.

While I inspected these objects with curiosity, Semion Semionych had time to quickly undress. He unexpectedly appeared before me in the same guise in which he had appeared on planet Earth. Then he took the rubber ball. Here I noticed that there was a piece of an old rubber inner tube attached to it. My friend raised the ball over his head and with an effort pushed his head into the wide piece of inner tube. I shuddered: out of the striped ball the sly eyes of my friend unexpectedly looked out at me. Slightly squinting, these eyes looked at me through two round lenses that had been skillfully inserted into the thin walls of the ball. Semion Semionych's neck was firmly squeezed by the piece of inner tube.

"Semion Semionych, what does this mean?"

Semion Semionych didn't answer. With a swift movement he firmly wrapped a long, wide oilskin bandage around his neck over the inner tube and fastened it with a shoelace.

"Semion Semionych, come to your senses! You've gone out of your mind!"

My friend paid not the slightest attention to me. He took a seat on the grass and nimbly put on the old sandals with heavy bricks tied to them. At this point I became seriously frightened, convinced that I was dealing with a man who had clearly gone insane.

"Semion Semionych, goddammit!" I cried in a frenzy. "Stop playing the fool, stop frightening me, or I'll run away from you right now!"

"Vladim Sergev, don't be a child!" the voice of my friend hollowly resounded out of the striped ball. "Take the pump and pump it gently."

Semion Semionych shoved the bicycle pump into my hands and then boldly headed for the water, clumsily shuffling in the old sandals tied to bricks.

"Come on, pump it, pump it, do you hear me?" the sound of a suppressed, impatient voice was carried to me.

I noticed that a long rubber pipe extended from the bicycle pump. It ended in the ball that Semion Semionych had put on his head. I mechanically began to pump and with horror noticed that Semion Semionych had suddenly disappeared under the water. In the place where his striped head had dived, bubbles now quietly gurgled. With heart pounding, I continued to pump . . .

A horrible minute passed—Semion Semionych did not appear. Only little bubbles as before gurgled now and then in the green water. Another minute passed. No sign of my friend. This was more than I could bear. I quickly threw off my shoes and was just preparing to dash into the pond when a round striped head suddenly appeared out of the water. It uttered hollowly and reproachfully:

"Vladim Sergev, where is your conscience? How can I rely on you? I ask you to do something, and you deprive your friends of air!"

I stood as if struck by lightning, and Semion Semionych came out onto the shore and began to take the striped ball off his head. When I again saw his kind face and was assured that he was alive and well, the gift of speech returned to me.

"My friend!" I said with restraint. "In fact, how am I to understand your conduct? What do these magic tricks of yours signify?"

"Wet suit!" Semion Semionych answered, shrugging his shoulders and panting.

"Wet suit?" I asked in bewilderment.

"Yes, an official wet suit. It's time you knew that a wet suit is an outfit for deep-sea diving!"

"No problem—an outfit! And may I ask what the hell you need it for?"

"Vladim Sergev, after all you gave me the idea yourself last spring when you said that the only way to find the dirigible would be to hire deep-sea divers to come here. Well, I thought: why hire deep-sea divers?"

My friend had carefully thought out all the details. It turns out that he even obtained a little electric lantern in the pharmacy in order to illuminate the depths of the lake. The lid of the lantern was tightly covered with wax so that the interior of the lantern would be protected from moisture. Semion Semionych told me that in recent days he had read a lot about divers and had cut out all newspaper articles that reported the work of Japanese divers in recovering treasures from the sunken English ship *The Black Prince*.

Semion Semionych proposed to devote this day to practicing diving in the town pond, so that right away tomorrow he could go to Ivlevo Lake and find the dirigible there, come what may. My friend well remembered that before its last benefit performance before the geese, the dirigible had been conscientiously smeared with thick oil, and so there was the hope that its barrel had not been too corroded by rust.

Foreseeing all eventualities, Semion Semionych had fitted out his *Automotor* as a diving vessel. A ladder had been attached to the stern. The diver could descend on this ladder to the bottom of the lake and ascend from the bottom back to the *Automotor*. In case of a mishap, I was to pull the diver up to the surface using rope reins tied under his arms. To facilitate the lifting, Semion Semionych had set up a winch with a massive crank and flywheel.

Semion Semionych had worked out an original system of signals, which he immediately forced me to learn by heart. On the side of the *Automotor* there was a bell taken from an alarm clock. A long string extended from the bell, the end of which was attached to the diver's waist. Pulling on this string, the diver could ring the bell. The signals were the following:

One ring: "Pump more quickly."
Two rings: "Pump more slowly."
Three rings: "There's a problem; turn the winch."

Four rings: "Give me the shovel."

When I had learned this system of signals to perfection, Semion Semionych decided to have a dress rehearsal. We got into the *Automotor* and, having sailed to the deepest spot in the town pond, we dropped anchor. My friend put on his "wet suit" and his belt, and wrapped the reins around himself. During this time I lowered the ladder over the stern. With imperturbable calm Semion Semionych climbed over the side, took hold of the ladder, and deliberately began to descend.

I worked the pump evenly and slowly. Minute after minute passed. Somewhere deep below me my friend was scouring the bottom of the pond.

"Give me the shovel!" Semion Semionych rang. "Pump more quickly!"

I carried out his orders precisely. Suddenly three sharp rings striking against my nerves conveyed that a misfortune had happened to my friend. I rushed to the winch and turned the handle with all my might. I felt the rope reins becoming taut under the water. The winch began to creak. The *Automotor* pitched. I worked as hard as I could, but suddenly the alarm-clock bell began to ring madly, often, and in protest. Not understanding what the problem was, I leaned on the winch with even greater energy, and after a few minutes I heard something soft strike against the bottom of the *Automotor*. It was the striped head of my friend. I pulled him into the boat with terrible difficulty.

"What happened?" I asked him in terror.

"You're awfully quick, Vladim Sergev! For the sake of rehearsal I gave you the distress signal, and you almost killed me in earnest. I banged my head on the *Automotor*—and all because of you! Can you really pull up a diver so roughly? Didn't you hear my protest?"

"What protest are you talking about?"

"Oh, come on, didn't I ring: ding, ding, ding? Didn't you hear?"

"I heard some kind of pealing, but I didn't understand what it meant."

"It meant: 'Vladim Sergev, can't you pull more slowly—you'll crack my head!'"

"You didn't warn me about that signal. Well, how did you feel in the deep?"

Semion Semionych took off the "wet suit." He was breathing heavily. His teeth were chattering, and his whole body was shaking. He quickly put his clothes on, sat at the oars, and began rowing quickly in order to get warm. The glorious *Automotor* took off like an arrow.

The day of August 1 turned out to be unusually fine. The *Automotor,* which we had carefully loaded onto a cart, arrived early in the morning, safe and sound, at Ivlevo Lake. Semion Semionych left home in total secrecy. Already the day before he had entrusted me with the bag containing the diving paraphernalia. Semion Semionych was concealing his bold undertaking from his wife.

We arrived at the lake happy, full of the most cheerful hopes.

The *Automotor* was lowered into the water and the "wet suit" was tested out. We cast anchor at the very same place where the terrible drama of the dirigible had so unexpectedly been played out the previous fall. This was a spot we well remembered!

Semion Semionych dressed in his diving suit with impressive speed and immediately slipped into the water.

It had been a rainy summer, and the level of Ivlevo Lake was much higher this year than last.

About fifteen minutes passed. During the whole time the alarm clock on the *Automotor* only once asked me to pump a little more air. I didn't receive any other orders. Soon I understood from a light bumping against the stern of the *Automotor* that Semion Semionych was returning.

Now his striped head appeared, then the chilled, trembling body of my friend climbed out . . . No dirigible.

Semion Semionych danced a kind of unbelievable dance in the *Automotor* in order to warm up, and again plunged to the bottom. This time we had sailed about twenty feet farther down. Three minutes had not passed before the ringing of the alarm clock informed me that my friend had stumbled upon a discovery. Semion Semionych was asking for the shovel. I lowered it over the side on a line. After about five minutes I heard three sharp rings—the distress signal. I started madly working the winch. A strange object appeared out of the depths of Ivlevo Lake—a kind of rusty metal wheel. I seized it and with an effort pulled into the *Automotor*—a completely rusted machine gun. After a second Semion Semionych himself appeared with the spade in his hand.

"Congratulations, Semion Semionych! Apparently over the winter your dirigible made a career for itself. Now it's turned into a regular machine gun. Heartfelt congratulations!"

"Vladim Sergev, this is no time for joking! This popgun had to have fallen in here during the Civil War. We have to turn it in to the District Military Commissariat. Let's see what Military Commissioner Seriukov will say to this! It's completely official that for recovery of an enemy machine gun they'll give us a reward. Now let's return to the old place. I'll try to dig up the whole bottom with the shovel. This machine gun had gotten completely stuck on the bottom. I accidentally bumped against the end of its barrel with my foot, and I could hardly dig it out of the mire."

No matter how Semion Semionych dug up the bottom of Ivlevo Lake with his spade, the dirigible was nowhere to be found.

After a few hours of work my friend had gotten very weak and was trembling like an aspen leaf. Nevertheless, he had no desire to give up and stubbornly insisted on continuing the search. And now, during his tenth trip to the bottom, I suddenly saw a boat sailing toward me over the lake. In it was sitting the watchman of the Ivlevo Regional Executive Committee, Mikhailo Zashchipkin. I immediately recognized him by his red beard and greeted him from a distance.

"Where is Semion Semionych?" he asked me as he sailed up.

"He's here, not far away," I answered evasively. "Do you need him?"

"Yes . . . I have a little business with him. Our chairman sent me to find him. We saw you on your boat fishing the other day. The chairman said to me then, 'Mikhailo, get in your boat and take Citizen Bochonkin his gun.'"

"What gun?" I asked in amazement.

"The same gun that Semion Semionych sank here last fall."

From amazement I nearly capsized the *Automotor.*

"How did you get it?" I exclaimed.

"Back then, in the fall, soon after you were here . . . Vanka Busharov got it. He's a real demon for diving! He's our best lad. He just dove about twice and in an instant he got your gun. Well, the chairman of course took the gun away from him and wrote to Semion Semionych at the Union of Hunters that the gun had been found safe and sound. From that time the gun's been lying in our regional office. We were wondering why Semion Semionych was taking so long to call for it. Could the chairman's letter have been lost in the mail?"

"Mikhailo, you dear man, give me the gun right now!"

"My pleasure . . . Well, I must be going . . . I have some other business to attend to. Good luck."

Mikhailo handed over my friend's famous puntgun, turned his flat-bottomed boat around, and quickly sailed toward the shore.

I was in unspeakable ecstasy and immediately wanted to pull Semion Semionych out with the winch in order to make him happy as soon as possible. But then I had the amusing idea of arranging a pleasant surprise for my friend.

We had our guns and ammunition with us. In my friend's bag I found his percussion caps. I quickly loaded the dirigible with a triple charge. After performing this simple operation, I quickly hid the dirigible on the bottom of the *Automotor* and covered it with a bast sack. I had hardly finished when Semion Semionych, blue with cold, climbed out from the bottom of the lake. Wearily he removed the wet suit and sank sadly and exhaustedly onto the bench.

"Well, Semion Semionych, not having any luck today?"

Semion Semionych kept silent.

"Okay, my friend," I continued. "Get dressed right away. You're completely frozen. Put my coat on."

Semion Semionych didn't move. He was limp and apathetic.

"Semion Semionych, there are so many ducks flying. Let's have a blast at them. Well, come on, why are you so bored today? Just imagine that you have your glorious dirigible in your hands. There's a duck sitting on the water—take a shot at it."

Semion Semionych waved his hand hopelessly.

"Look, look: a whole flock is flying!"

A small flock of teal was flying toward us. With a swift movement I pulled the dirigible out from under the bast sack, cocked it, and shoved it into my friend's hands.

"Shoot, shoot! You have the actual dirigible in your hands, word of honor!"

My friend mechanically put the dirigible to his shoulder, took aim . . . and blasted away at the departing flock as if a thousand devils had begun bellowing at once.

It was a remarkably effective and masterly shot! The teal fell from the sky like hail. The whole flock had been killed, and not a single little duck was fluttering. Yes, it was a marvelous shot!

The dirigible had again begun to speak.

"Vladim Sergev! Vladim Sergev!" my friend babbled incoherently, inspecting his treasure. A tear welled up on Semion Semionych's eyelashes.

In a few words I told him everything that had happened during his last dive. Having finished my short account, I rowed up to the dead teal and began to pick them up.

"Oh, Semion Semionych, it turns out you tortured yourself for no reason! What the hell did you need that diving suit for?"

"Vladim Sergev, don't be a dullard! Not to mention the machine gun I fortuitously found, just think how useful the wet suit can be! I tell you officially: *the wet suit—is for science!* Will you really refuse to work with me on scientific underwater research?"

"Semion Semionych, I will never refuse you anything for as long as I live!"

And our hands merged in a firm clasp . . .

The Wolf Hunt

WHEN THE BAREFOOTED little daughter of Semion Semionovich came running breathlessly to my place and announced that her daddy was waiting for me, I immediately understood that my companion was summoning me on hunting business. My premonition did not deceive me.

"It's a notice again . . . about the wolves," was how he bluntly addressed me instead of a greeting.

My friend was apparently agitated. The notice he had received had been typed on the letterhead of the district executive committee of the Party and looked extremely impressive and official. It read as follows:

"To the Chairman of the Hunters' Union:

"In view of the increasing number of victims both in the form of cattle and of people, we hereby propose that you take urgent measures for the liquidation of wolves in the district; I also hereby caution you, that if there are any more human incidents, the entire responsibility for this will lie with its full weight on you."

After I read the notice, I too became agitated. We began to hotly discuss the contents of the notice. It emerged that two days before, three wolves had chased a female schoolteacher who was traveling from the village of Dedilovo, and she escaped only thanks to the speed of her horse, which got her to the nearest village at full gallop. Apparently this incident was the reason for the chairman of the hunters' association to receive official instructions. Semion Semionovich, however, did not want to admit guilt and responsibility for this incident.

That evening the two of us talked for a long time about the wolves, which had multiplied into a particularly large population that year. We remembered that before 1914 there had never been more than two wolf litters in the entire district; at the present time Semion Semionovich had reliable information about twelve litters in our region.

We calculated that if there was an average of ten wolves for every litter, including yearlings, then there must be no fewer than 120 wolves marauding in our district. Semion Semionovich estimated on an abacus that in order to feed this company, it would require a contribution from the district of no less than 2,500 sheep or about 2,000 calves and foals. In fact, the peasants in the villages were raising a regular howl as a result of the devastation caused by the predators on their herds. There were also isolated incidents of wolves attacking people. In one of the subdistricts a little boy had been torn apart by wolves.

At that time there were no properly organized hunting brigades. True, a month before this Semion Semionovich had received a notice from the provincial administration, ordering him to refrain from organizing any hunting in our woods prior to the arrival of the so-called "provincial shock detachment of wolf exterminators." This detachment did in fact arrive under the command of a mustachioed technical expert, who gave himself out to be a former master of the Grand Duke's hunt.

The provincial wolf exterminators carried themselves with great style and in their conversations with us tried to demonstrate that they were great experts in their field. But the detachment did not prove itself in action: in the course of two weeks the detachment exterminated a huge quantity of homebrew; in the Kazan subdistrict these brave lads killed one small wolf cub, and in another subdistrict they wounded a full-grown peasant beater.

This ended the detachment's activity, because the peasants in true shock-worker fashion beat both the head expert and his entire shock detachment to a bloody pulp.[1]

The detachment made a hasty retreat, and the wolf litters, disturbed out of their lairs by the hunters, began to play even dirtier tricks as they roamed about the entire district.

That evening Semion Semionovich and I parted with the agreement that the very next day he would convoke a general meeting of the local hunters for the purpose of discussing how to organize wolf battues as soon as possible.

The meeting was stormy. Many people argued and got hot under the collar. We were finally able to convince the representative from the District Executive Committee who had been invited to the meeting that neither we nor our chairman were to blame for the wolves' outrages, and therefore we declined all responsibility in case the wolves took it into their heads to again regale themselves with human flesh. We secured a loan in the sum of thirty rubles from the executive committee for organizational expenses, and we entrusted the universally respected hunter Pavel Mikhailovich with the task of immediately tracking and verifying any litters that had not yet been disturbed from their lairs; we had decided to kill them, in order, on the one hand, to ease the laborers' lot, and on the other, to cover ourselves in new glory.

Pavel Mikhailovich went on reconnaissance that very day. Two days later Semion Semionovich received a telegram from Pavel Mikhailovich informing him that he had found wolves in the Gnilushi woods, about sixteen and a half miles from town. The hunters were to gather in the village of Tychok.

Starting in the evening we began filling cartridges with buckshot, and on the very next day we set out in four carts for Tychok.

It had been resolved to recruit only experienced hunters and good marksmen to this serious hunt, but there were so many people who wanted to participate and who might be offended that neither Semion Semionovich nor Pavel Mikhailovich could find in themselves the courage to deny the people who should have been denied.

In fact, it is very hard to tell a person who lays claim to the title of hunter that he is a worthless shot or that he just won't do for a serious hunt.

And who *didn't* show up for that hunt! There were fourteen of us in all. There was the locksmith Adamov, and little old Doctor Nikitskii, and the joiner Struev, and the tradesman Iuriev, and the inspector of finances, and finally, armed to the teeth, the hairdresser Ulybkin. This last fellow had brought along a five-chambered revolver-carbine of the Browning type, a revolver of the Bulldog type, a large quantity of cartridges, a Caucasian dagger, a camera, a compass, and opera glasses. Later it turned out that the provident hairdresser had also not forgotten to bring along a one-and-a-half-liter bottle of pure alcohol. By the way, Doctor Nikitskii too had a suspicious-looking travel flask dangling at his side, which compelled the reflection that doctors are lucky people, because sometimes they manage to get hold of pure alcohol "for medicinal purposes."

On the way we learned that the hunt would be joined by the director of the Mikhailovskii alcohol factory, the German Spiller, who was traveling to the place of assembly on his own. As it turned out, a couple of the hunters had invited the esteemed director not without ulterior motives.

It was a jolly trip. It got jollier when we got to Tychok, where Pavel Mikhailovich met us and announced that he had verified the presence in Gnilushi of eleven undisturbed wolves, including the old, the young, and the yearlings.

In Tychok the hunters were divided up into two groups: the center of one of them was the hairdresser Ulybkin with his one-and-a-half-liter bottle; the center of the other was Doctor Nikitskii with his travel flask. Since the hairdresser's vessel was much larger in scale than the doctor's, it goes without saying that the hairdresser's group was also more numerous. But even apart from his vessel the hairdresser aroused interest in himself, since he constantly took photographs and looked through his opera glasses, which he offered to the others too. He also shot his revolver at a bottle at ten paces and sometimes hit it, to general enjoyment. Doctor Nikitskii didn't do any of this, but just recounted a lot of entertaining and not uninteresting cases from his long medical practice.

Semion Semionovich and I joined the hairdresser's group. As evening came on, however, without telling the others we appealed to Pavel Mikhailovich to take us into the forest to hear the wolves howl at sunset. Pavel Mikhailovich, who was maintaining neutrality and had not joined either group, agreed, and we left the village without attracting anyone's notice.

Gnilushi is a small, mostly planted oak forest. This forest has a far from primeval, not at all vulpine look to it. The oaks are planted in regular rows. There are no bushes or thickets at all.

In the center of the forest stands a lodge which is abutted by a small but overgrown planted fir forest. The little firs form a dense thicket and occupy a space of no more than three acres. It was here, right by the lodge, that the old she-wolf had given birth to her babies and safely lived through the whole summer with them. It was also here, a few steps away from the wolves' lairs, that the forest watchman's calf and piglet peacefully grazed and his chicken wandered by the very edge of the fir grove as if nothing were wrong. One could hear peasant women calling back and forth to each other, ending their raking of leaves. It was hard to believe that wolves—those sworn enemies of humanity—could have found refuge here. Apparently the wolves had multiplied so greatly that they could no longer be choosy about their lodgings, and there weren't many forests in our steppe area. It is known that wolf families avoid settling near each other, and as long as wolves keep to their lairs, each family has its own area for finding food.

The watchman's gray dog met us with a hoarse bark. Apparently he too could get along with the wolves. The watchman, a young lad with a simple-hearted physiognomy, came to meet us.

"Do the wolves really not hurt you or touch your livestock?" Semion Semionovich asked him.

"Now, why would they want to hurt their neighbors? It's not in their interest. The wolf knows how to think too. Just ask the people in Tychok. My wolves don't damage their livestock either, because Tychok is only a mile from here, and it's not in their interest to hurt the Tychok folk either. Now the villages that are a little farther away, like three or four miles, now there our wolves get really cheeky."

We marveled at the wolves' powers of reasoning and sat down on a big log right by the fir grove. This close to the wolves, we involuntarily wanted to speak in a whisper so as not to frighten them, but the watchman spoke without lowering his voice, and we had a smoke. The watchman told us that this was the third year in a row that the wolves had had litters in this same fir grove. In all that time they had never dared to steal even a chicken from him. Every day at sunset they would howl right by the lodge. The old wolves were about the size of a calf, the young ones the size of a dog.

"So that's it," said the watchman. "This year's wolves are ordinary, but now three years ago there was a terrible big wolf living here. The size of a cow, and a mane like a stallion . . . And when he'd howl the glass in the windows of the lodge would tremble . . . That's how strong that wolf was," the watchman said, getting carried away by his story.

It quickly got dark, but there were still no wolves. We were overcome by impatience, and we even had a sneaking suspicion that there might in fact not be any wolves here. I, at least, had never encountered wolves in such peaceful circumstances, nor had I observed such close cohabitation of irreconcilable enemies.

When it had become quite dark and the tops of the trees were barely outlined against the dark, cloudy sky, Pavel Mikhailovich could no longer contain himself and addressed us: "Well, lads, you sit here, and I'll go to the edge of the grove and howl like a yearling." Pavel Mikhailovich moved off, and in a few minutes we heard him uttering a long drawn-out howl at the edge of the grove. Pavel Mikhailovich was a master of howling. He had hardly finished before a full-grown she-wolf began to drone in a low bass voice about thirty paces from us, in the depths of the fir grove. We shuddered . . . and then the young ones took up the howl in their thin yelping voices. At first they joined in lightly, but then more and more loudly, and finally in a deafening, unpleasant tone. The forest echo took up the wolves' howl, and it seemed as if the entire forest had suddenly been filled with the voices of the wolves.

I had never in my life heard this terrible, melancholy song in such immediate proximity. Even though you know the wolves will not touch you, it's still so eerie and frightening that your flesh creeps and your heart starts to beat faster.

The wolves broke off their eerie song all at once, and complete silence came over the whole forest. But the forest . . . the peaceful, planted forest, wrapped in the darkness of night, now seemed terrifying and ominous.

Yes . . . it's unpleasant to hear wolves a few paces away. But when they cease their song, you want them to sing it again and again. This song is beautiful in its eerie and painful melancholy.

Pavel Mikhailovich returned to us happy and somewhat excited. He sat down next to us and soon after that we heard the real head of the wolf family howl ominously in his bass voice at the edge of the trees, after which his family again repeated its savage song.

We returned satisfied to Tychok. Here in a large, roomy hut we found our comrades. Both centers, the doctor's and the hairdresser's, had now merged into a single company. In our absence the director of the alcohol factory had arrived, and what he brought with him definitively united all the hunters.

We sat drinking for a long time, telling each other interesting stories and joining in choral singing, until we finally fell down to sleep.

Some of the hunters had already started snoring, but the eerie night song of the wolves was still resounding in my ears. From the far corner, fragments of conversations were carried to me: the hairdresser and the inspector of finances were arguing on the subject of the national economy.

"Take the potato," the inspector of finances argued, "it's a useful thing, but 150 years ago no one in Russia had ever heard of the potato, until they brought it from abroad."

"Nothing of the kind," the hairdresser objected. "The potato was discovered by Robinson Crusoe. I read myself how he and his parrot traveled around an island and dug up potatoes."

"But your Robinson never existed!"

"How could he not have existed, when they write about him in books! If you, an educated man, haven't read this, that doesn't mean that Robinson never existed."

"Oh, you Robinsons! It's time to sleep," someone grumbled.

And we soon fell asleep.

By six o'clock in the morning we were in the forest. Pavel Mikhailovich had been carefully studying the forest for two days, determining the beasts' possible tracks and choosing the appropriate places for the shooters to sit.

A whisper was going quietly among the hunters saying that the best and most reliable places should go to the good, already tried marksmen; but as always happens in such cases, the business ended with drawing lots. Pavel Mikhailovich poured fifteen little numbered tickets into his cap; each hunter pulled out a ticket, the number of which determined his place.

Finally everything was ready. About thirty peasants came from the village, who had volunteered to participate in the hunt as beaters.

Pavel Mikhailovich led us to our numbered places and repeated to each of us the rules of the hunt: not to leave our number until he personally removed each hunter from his post; not to shoot along the line of hunters; not to smoke; and to shoot only at a wolf.

The hunters took their places with serious faces. My number was the very last. To the right of me, about eighteen paces away, I saw my neighbor, Doctor Nikitskii; to the left, through the trees, I could see the winter field.

Pavel Mikhailovich went to lead the beaters beyond the lairs, and was himself to guide them to the line of shooters.

In the forest all was quiet. A fine October rain was drizzling as if through a sieve. Brown autumn leaves could be seen here and there on the bare trees. It was cold standing in one place; I desperately wanted a smoke. But now in the distance I could hear knocking and the sound of squelching feet. The battue was beginning, and my heart started beating faster.

In such cases one gets doubly excited. On the one hand, you simply get excited as a hunter who anticipates catching sight of and shooting at a large beast of the kind that one seldom gets a chance to shoot at. On the other hand, one is excited by the presence of companions: if you miss, they'll laugh at you and tease you, and you'll be to blame, and even a good marksman is never guaranteed not to miss.

As the sounds of the driving-in came closer, our excitement intensified, and finally I reached such a state that I started to think, "If only the wolf doesn't come out toward me," while at the beginning I had dreamed of just the opposite.

I was standing in a little spur of a deep ravine whose opposite slope was clearly visible to me. My vision and hearing were strained to the utmost. Suddenly my eye caught something gray and living, which vaguely flashed on the other side of the ravine among gray tree trunks. My heart contracted painfully . . . The next moment disappointment set in: into a clearing jumped a hare frightened by the sound of everyone shooting at once. It waited for a moment, listening, then with a crazy air it dashed headlong right by my feet.

I didn't keep watching the hare. My eyes were fixed on the gray-brown thicket of the forest. Bang! . . . A short, dry shot resounded far to the right of me, striking on my nerves. Someone had killed a wolf. This was clear, because a second shot did not follow. My excitement increased; any moment now a beast would come out. A bush at the top of the ravine was particularly suspicious. For some reason I thought that a wolf would come out precisely there, and suddenly I distinctly made out a huge beast which had stopped far to the right of the bush.

The beast was that strange color that only wolves have: not quite yellow, not quite gray. Maybe even brown—greenish brown. In the zoo they are quite different than in the forest for some reason.

I was suddenly overcome with a passionate, powerful desire to kill. My consciousness said that the wolf would first pass by the doctor and would not avoid his shot. Oh, if only the doctor would miss! I squinted at the doctor without losing sight of the beast. The doctor noticed: he made himself small, bent over, and froze. Now he took aim, keeping the beast in his sights; the wolf was quietly descending into the ravine. It seemed huge; now it finished its descent and set off past the doctor at an unhurried trot . . . Bang! . . . The wolf hunched over, spurted ahead and took off at a broad gallop. Bang! The doctor bashed him for the second and last time. The wolf rushed past me and succeeded in leaving the forest for the winter field. Now he was fifteen paces from me. My gun sight was fixed on his brown fur in front of the shoulder blade. My heart and my index finger felt it: now! My finger made its familiar small movement . . . my ears didn't catch the rumble of the shot . . . The wolf fell heavily to the grass. Its back leg twitched and trembled, his jaws gaped open. Dead outright. A sigh of relief . . . the vise let go its grip on my exhausted heart.

But the hunt was not over.

Bang-bang-bang-bang! could be heard to the right. It was clear that the hairdresser was shooting his revolver-carbine. There was no doubt that it was him, because after the gun shots one could hear the revolver shots from his "Bulldog." "Idiot!" flashed through my head; but I didn't care, because I was deeply satisfied and happy: fifteen paces away from me the beautiful brown mass of my trophy had become motionless.

Two more shots rang out. The driving-in was over. Opposite me the beaters appeared. Seeing the dead beast, they ran up to it, overtaking each other, and surrounded it in a tight circle.

Pavel Mikhailovich congratulated me on a good hunt. The doctor came up to me. He was displeased and envious. He also said, "Good hunt, Vladimir Sergeevich!" and smiled artificially.

We went up to the wolf. It was a large male yearling, as big as a full-grown wolf. Almost the entire charge had hit him under the left shoulder blade. It was a good shot. The wolf was cleanly killed. I restrained my joy. Pavel Mikhailovich and I went to relieve the marksmen from their numbered posts.

We approached the inspector of finances—he hadn't seen any wolves. The next number—the locksmith Adamov, had seen a she-wolf with her young. She came out near the hairdresser. The result was unknown. We walked farther and caught sight of the hairdresser. Gesticulating excitedly, he was talking to the beaters who had approached. In his hand was his revolver-carbine. He was covered with cartridges, binoculars, holsters, and daggers.

"Did you shoot?"

"Yessirree."

"At what?"

"At a mama and her children, sir."

"Well, did you kill them?"

"Crisis!" answered the hairdresser, shrugging his shoulders.

"You let a she-wolf and cubs get away. Oh, man! And you had the best spot . . . and you have a revolver-carbine!"

"It seemed like I grazed one of them with my revolver," the hairdresser guiltily tried to vindicate himself. "I could tell because one of them seemed to start limping."

Pavel Mikhailovich made a hopeless gesture with his hand. We reached Semion Semionovich. He was standing under his tree with an affectedly indifferent air.

"Did you shoot?"

"A wolf cub."

"Is it dead?"

"Behind the bush."

We went up to the bush. There lay the watchman's gray dog, with its head shot through and buried in the grass.

"Semion Semionovich, what have you done? Look who you killed!"

"Oh, hell! The damned rain . . . my glasses fogged up. Oh, you devil! The damned crocodile!" he cursed.

A beater approached and explained that during the driving-in he had seen the watchman's dog in the forest and threw a log at it; it took off with its tail between its legs right toward the line of shooters.

The last number—there stood the joiner Struev. This master craftsman had a true eye. A dead yearling wolf lying not far from him served as proof of this.

The hunters gathered at the lodge. They animatedly shared their impressions and experiences with each other. The hunt was not a very successful one. Out of eleven wolves only two had been killed. Everyone blamed the hairdresser. He tried to justify himself and explain how he shot at the whole litter with its mama at once out of his revolver-carbine.

"So I set my sights on the gray ones, and I keep banging: bang, bang, bang . . . I think I've got to graze one of them . . ."

"You don't say! You 'grazed' it," Semion Semionovich interrupted angrily, terribly out of sorts after the misunderstanding with the watchman's dog.

"And you, my dear sir, whom did you shoot today?" the hairdresser said with a sly wink.

"Me? I shot a dog. But I didn't miss. And you and your toy pistol spoiled the whole hunt for us. To take dolts like you along on a hunt means making a mess of the whole business."

"Sorry—*I'm* a dolt? Excuse me, but who was lapping up my liquor yesterday evening? I'm a dolt, you say? *Merci très beaucoup.*"

Beautiful Mecha

"VLADIM SERGEV, I'M sick of our old spots. It would be good to take a hunting trip somewhere a little farther away."

"You're right, Semion Semionych: I'm bored! We've made a thorough study of every little bush here. I propose to you that we make for Beautiful Mecha. We haven't been there even once, and they say there are some pretty good duck-hunting spots there. What do you say?"

"Well, why not, let's try it, let's go!"

The river Beautiful Mecha (or, as some call it, Beautiful Mech) originates in the Ogariovsk region of our district and flows about twenty-five miles from our little town. I had long planned to take a look at this river, which was mentioned in Turgenev's *Sportsman's Sketches*.[1]

On the first fine day Semion Semionych and I went to the market, tracked down a cart from the Mecha area, and hired its bearded owner to take us right to Beautiful Mecha, to the village of Buchan.

This bearded peasant was a gloomy and taciturn person. On the way he answered our questions so reluctantly that it seemed to be costing him a great effort.

"Are there many ducks on the Beautiful Mecha?" we asked him.

"Na-a-a-h . . . few . . ."

"And do you have a lot of hares?"

"Na-a-a-h . . . few . . ."

"And what about foxes?"

"Few."

"It appears you have few of everything. What do you have a lot of?"

"Moonshine. We have a moonshine factory."

"A factory! Ah! Who is it who's so enterprising?"

"The miller Kasian."

I simply leaped out of my seat: "What?! Kasian?! It can't be! The same Turgenevian Kasian from Beautiful Mecha? So that's what he's doing with himself now!"

The bearded one blinked in bewilderment.

"Vladim Sergev, do you mean to say you're acquainted with the Buchan village miller?"

"Of course, I know him from Turgenev's *Sportsman's Sketches*. And the whole U.S.S.R. knows Kasian. They probably know him abroad too."

Semion Semionych and the bearded one looked at me mistrustfully. Finally the bearded one spat and said with an effort: "Everyone in our village is named either Kasian or Mikita."

At this point I realized that the Buchan miller Kasian and Turgenev's Kasian were a simple coincidence. I remembered that Turgenev's Kasian was a poetic soul who caught nightingales. He wouldn't be likely to engage in such a prosaic business as manufacturing moonshine with the aim of making a profit. Besides, already in Turgenev's time he was an old man, and Turgenev himself had died almost fifty years ago. A lot of Kasians had lived on the earth since then, and particularly near Beautiful Mecha. I again addressed the bearded one: "So your miller has opened a moonshine factory. How does your regional commissioner tolerate such a scandalous disgrace?"

"He's a drinker himself."

"Well, well, well! We've really come to the backwoods. It's clear that your village is far away from all the centers. So I guess you're boozing all the time around here?"

A profoundly thoughtful silence.

"Your miller Kasian probably makes a good profit on this business?"

A deep sigh and a sideways spit instead of an answer.

"Well, old man, I see you're a talkative type. It's impossible to get bored with you."

A crack of the whip over the emaciated back of the gray gelding.

Semion Semionych and I stretched out in the jolting cart and also fell silent. My thoughts soared into the distant times of Turgenev. I thought about this and that . . . Well, isn't it strange? Many decades ago the writer Turgenev was returning from the hunt in a jolting cart. Along the way he conversed with the coachman and met Kasian from Beautiful Mecha . . . Today I'm going hunting in just such a jolting cart, I converse with my driver, and perhaps I too will meet Kasian from Beautiful Mecha . . . And meanwhile how far we have come since Turgenev's times! Kasian from Beautiful Mecha—then. Kasian from Beautiful Mecha—now: what an abyss!

So if Turgenev lived in our day, would he write a story called "Kasian from Beautiful Mecha" in which he would offer a vivid artistic image of a retrograde miller-kulak who gets the laboring masses drunk on moonshine?

An ungreased wheel squeaked piteously beneath me, and the twenty-five-mile road, meandering through endless black-earth fields, seemed to us to be a devilishly tedious way to kill time.

"Hey, come on out," the gloomy bearded one shook us awake. We rubbed our eyes and saw that we had come to a small village. Tall old willows grew in front of huts with straw roofs. Under the trees extended a wide green meadow. In the distance was an azure river with a dam.

It was late to go hunting, and we accepted the bearded one's invitation to spend the night on the hay in his barn and meanwhile to have tea.

The little village of Buchan apparently was a godforsaken backwoods. Not for nothing was it located away from the main roads. Our arrival created a big sensation. As we were climbing out of the cart and pulling out our guns, almost the entire population found out about our arrival. We were instantly surrounded by a crowd of locals. They pointed their fingers at us, and the little kids exchanged their impressions of us in a loud voice.

"Ooh, look how tall he is. Man, what a beanpole," one says, pointing at me.

"And look, that guy has some kind of little pieces of glass on his eyes. And look at that gun, ooh! I bet it can really shoot."

"And where might you be from?" the grownups asked us. "Why did you come here? Are you some kind of commissars?"

"We're hunters . . . from the town. We came here to shoot wild ducks."

"Hunters? So tha-a-a-t's it! Hunters have come . . . Hey, Kasiashka, Nikitka, Pashka, come here and look, hunters have come!"

The crowd grew. Every newcomer had to ask us who we were, where we were from, and what in fact we wanted here. We answered each one that we came from the town to go hunting. Our answers evoked bewilderment and even mistrust. It was strange for the local inhabitants to hear that hunters from the district capital itself could appear in their midst.

While we drank tea in the bearded one's hut, a huge crowd of people pushed their way in. They all wanted to look at us and our guns. That evening we fell asleep only after answering for the twentieth time the question: who are we and why did we come to the village of Buchan.

We got up early and after a quick breakfast set off for the river. A young lad accompanied us. The evening before he had been present at our tea. His father owned the only boat in the whole village. The lad kindly allowed us to use it and told us that a mile and a half below the dam there was a long cove overgrown with sedge. Wild ducks were always to be found there. According to the lad, there weren't any ducks anywhere else.

We had no choice, and we got into the little boat and sailed off down the river. This boat looked more like a coffin than a vessel. It was barely big enough for two people and was so old and full of holes that the water came in through the rotten bottom in little fountains. While one of us rowed, the other constantly pumped water out, and it was hard to say who was working harder.

The famous Buchan cove did not justify our hopes, and its size had been greatly exaggerated. We traveled its length and breadth, frantically slapping our oars against the sedge to flush the wild ducks. After an hour of fruitless effort, we finally managed to flush one old duck and three ducklings that were hardly able to fly yet. Semion Semionych killed one of them. This nestling had a repulsive, plucked look about him.

"Vladim Sergev, it's a shame to shoot such a bird! Apparently it's a late brood, and there aren't any more broods around here. Again our wives will have a fit—we're going to come home with empty hands."

"What are we going to do now?" I asked my friend. "What fools we were to come dragging here, twenty-five miles from home, in order to kill this mangy duckling!"

"Vladim Sergev, say what you will, but this was your idea. What got into you to want to see this, excuse my frankness, Beautiful Mecha . . . There's nothing the slightest bit interesting here, but on the contrary, it's just a wasteland of dullness."

Semion Semionych squeamishly took hold of the repulsive duckling by the tip of its little wing and flung it into the sedge.

"It would be better to come home with empty hands than to drag that filth twenty-five miles with us, so that the whole town could laugh at Bochonkin!"

We were in a bad mood. My friend grumbled terribly, and this was a rare thing with him. Almost quarreling, we made our way out of the cove onto the middle of the river. On the other bank was sitting a gray-haired old fisherman in a faded shirt of an indeterminate color. Like a statue he was frozen motionless over his long poles, waiting for a bite.

I felt somewhat guilty towards my friend for enticing him to go hunting at Beautiful Mecha. I wanted to make up for it and find some kind of wild game. Perhaps this old fisherman could help me? I turned toward the bank and put in next to the old man. He had an amazingly patriarchal and dignified appearance.

"What kind of people are you? Where are you from? Why did you come here?" the same eternal, tiresome questions pelted us. We had no choice but to answer.

I explained to the old man that we were hunters from town looking for wild ducks. The old geezer clearly didn't believe me. He remembered that about thirty years ago a real hunter had in fact come from the town to Buchan. That hunter had a very strange name (the old man had even forgotten it). That hunter had a shaggy dog, and he killed a lot of ducks. But we didn't have a dog—what kind of hunters could we be? It was not nice of us to try to deceive old people.

"So now who are you?" the loquacious old man asked me all over again.

I had gotten so thoroughly sick of this question by now, it was so stupid to keep answering the same thing, that finally I couldn't control myself and answered with a certain irritation: "We? We're agitators in the struggle against moonshine. We came here to pinch your miller Kasian and his moonshine factory."

"Oh, you're lively ones!" the old man drawled out, and after a pause added: "Well, that's a good thing to do. We should maintain sobriety in the peasantry, but our old Kasian is probably not such a fool as to get mixed up in such doings."

"Oh yeah?"

"Yes, yeah," the old man mimicked me. "So I guess you've got a detachment traveling with you, or are you working just so, without a detachment?"

"With a detachment," I answered the old man confidently. "Our lads are going to make it here from the city today. We'll quickly sniff out who's trading in moonshine. Well, and meanwhile, tell us, grandpa, whether there are any wild ducks and where they can be found?"

"Wild ducks? We have as much as you like of that kind of goods. Just get yourself to the swamp . . . There are ducks swimming in whole herds over there."

"And where is this swamp? Is it far?" we asked, overjoyed.

"It's probably about a mile and a half from here. Over there beyond those vines there's a little path. Just go along it and it will take you right to the swamp. You see the forest on the mountain? It's that black spot over there. Well, the swamp will be about a third of a mile before you get to the forest. There are a lot of ducks there."

We immediately went on shore and tied our boat to a bush. The old man began to reel in his fishing poles in a leisurely fashion.

"Well, grandpa, I guess it's clear that whoever angles for fish will wind up with nothing?" joked Semion Semionych.

"Well, you whippersnappers, we'll see what you wind up with," the dignified old man answered, and taking his long poles with him, he solemnly and leisurely began to walk toward the village.

"Vladim Sergev, you really fooled grandpa with those stories about moonshine. Now they're going to have a hell of a lot to talk about in the village!"

We laughed. The old geezer had given us new energy, and we cheerfully set off to find the duck swamp.

After we walked along the designated path through the meadow for about a mile and a half, we in fact saw a tiny little lake. We walked all around it in no more than ten minutes and determined that there was no wild game on it of any kind.

"What a rehearsal!" Semion Semionych said. "Is this really the right swamp? Where are the ducks? Maybe the old man was talking about a different swamp?"

"It can't be. Here's the forest nearby, and there's not even a puddle anywhere else around."

"That damned old man, to hell with him! There's nowhere here where ducks could live. Just look: all the grass has been mowed flat . . . the old geezer really fooled us. You lied to him about the struggle against moonshine, and he spun an even taller tale. The old bastard must have figured out that you were making fun of him."

The sun was unbearably hot. I wanted to sit down on the grass to rest, but Semion Semionych resolutely announced: "There's no use in our cooling our heels here any more. The hell with the whole place, your Beautiful Mecha! Let's go to the village and figure out how to get home as soon as possible."

I reluctantly got up, and we dragged ourselves back to the river, silent, upset, and extremely discontented.

Our holey boat was awaiting us in the same place where we left it. We pumped the water out of it and set off for the dam in deep silence. We felt really awful: twenty-five miles to Buchan, and the same distance back. And for what? What were our wives going to say?

We sailed for a long time. We still had about two-thirds of a mile to sail to the dam. Nearer to the dam the river gradually got narrower.

"Vladim Sergev, look over there on the right—it looks like a dead fish," my friend unexpectedly broke the silence. "It is, and a really big one!"

Near the boat a large chub was floating belly up.

"Semion Semionych, he's alive! Look: he's breathing. And he just barely moved his tail. Pull him into the boat!"

My friend bent over the side and pulled the beautiful, barely alive chub out of the water.

"Now why did he get it into his head to croak? Of old age, was it? Vladim Sergev, look over there: there's all kinds of dead small-fry floating around!"

Indeed, all around us we could see white fish bellies. There were roach and small perch and chub, and all kinds of other trash.

"A strange rehearsal. But they're all alive! The damned things are breathing! They're breathing in the most official manner!"

We sailed about another twenty-five yards.

"Now there's a big one. Look, it's the most official perch, he's easily four pounds. Damn it, there's another one!"

"And another one . . . And there . . . there, look what's going on!"

We got excited and kept pulling barely living fish out of the water. We took only the big ones, paying no attention to the small-fry.

"Semion Semionych, did you ever think that we'd become fishermen? With this catch we don't have to be ashamed to go back to the town or to show ourselves to our wives. I bet even that old fisherman who just fooled us about the ducks never in his whole life got so many fish on his pole!"

"It's very simple . . . well done, Vladim Sergev. Well, this Beautiful Mecha is an interesting little river! The only thing that's strange is that when we were here this morning there was nothing of the kind. Maybe someone here is poisoning the fish with some kind of drug. I've heard of such tricks."

"It's possible. But who here would occupy himself with such a business? There's not a living soul visible on the riverbanks. Besides, we've hired the only boat in the whole village.

"Strange business . . . Well, let's get that there fish too. Oh, it's a heavy one—it'll be six pounds!"

The big fish lazily moved its tail, dove from time to time and then swam up to the surface, turning onto its side. Soon we began to notice that the fish floating belly up were becoming somehow more lively, as though their drugged state were beginning to pass.

"Hey, Vladim Sergev, the fish are starting to figure things out. Pull more quickly, before they come to."

We energetically set to work. And we got so many fish—a boat full of large, beautiful specimens.

"Semion Semionych, we'll have to hire a cart to get to the town."

"I've got it all figured out. We'll sell them to the town fishwives at the market: we'll be able to pay for the cart, and make a little pile of money, and eat some good fish."

We worked until we had no more room to put the catch. Meanwhile the fish soon came to their senses completely and stopped showing their white bellies.

We came to shore not far from the dam and walked up to the mill. On the dam we saw the old fisherman who had recently sent us off to shoot nonexistent ducks. He was looking inquisitively into our faces and even seemed to be waiting for us.

Thanks to our unexpected success, all our animosity toward the old man who had fooled us had passed. I addressed him gaily: "Well, grandpa, did you catch a lot of fish with your poles today?"

"I caught about five or so. And you, did you shoot a lot of ducks?"

"It didn't work out with the ducks, but anyway we brought home a boat full of game."

"Oh yeah? And just what kind of game did you get today?"

"We got fish too . . . a whole boat full. If you don't believe me, just look. Something very strange happened to the fish today: all of them were floating belly up. You could just take them with your bare hands and pile them in the boat. Can you believe it?"

"Were the fish really floating belly up?" the old man asked somehow uncomfortably. His face had taken on a strange expression, and he bowed his head low.

At that time a young peasant came up to us. Paying no attention to us, he addressed the old man directly: "Hi, Kasian Nikitych. I've come to see you . . . How are you doing with that *thing*? Can I possibly get a couple of bottles?"

The old man quickly looked around and blinked his eyes: "What the hell are you blabbing about! What *thing* do you want? No, brother, anything else, but I don't have anything to do with that thing!"

The peasant looked at the old man in amazement. The old man gave a barely perceptible sideways look at us, and both peasants suddenly fell silent.

"Tell me, grandpa," I asked the old man, "do you know where we could hire a cart here to go to the town?"

"When do you want to go?"

"We'll go right now. We don't have anything more to do here."

The old man looked at me in bewilderment.

"Now just where are you from?" he asked me.

I broke out into delighted laughter.

"Oh, now, again it's 'where are we from'! I told you, we came to carry on the struggle against moonshine. Now we've done our job, and it's time for us to return."

The old man suddenly changed expression. All his dignity immediately disappeared. He suddenly turned crimson and screamed furiously: "You're crooks and nothing more! Parasites! Get out of here! Go back to where you came from! Who asked you to come here, you damned devils?"

"Grandpa, couldn't you keep it quieter? What are you shouting for—we're not deaf!"

The old man wouldn't calm down. In one minute he belched out a stream of such unbelievable curses that we had trouble answering him in the same spirit. Semion Semionych finally gave up with a wave of his hand. With a final "Same to you!" flung at the old man, he walked away from the dam, pulling me along with him.

"Well, there's some old man! Did you ever see the like?"

"Yes, a very rare specimen. It's as if a wasp stung him on the tongue. And he got so red, it's a real marvel!"

We walked quietly, talking about the old man. After a minute the young lad who had been conversing with the old man in our presence caught up with us. The lad was very amused.

"Well done, guys," he said to us. "You did a good job of scamming our miller. It serves the old bastard right. He's drunk our blood!"

"What happened, what miller are you talking about? We didn't see him."

The lad laughed at the top of his voice: "What do you mean, you didn't see him! You were just talking to him. He's ready to throw himself into the river out of fury. He lost a lot of money today on account of you!"

"What do you mean? Talk sense."

"Well, of course . . . An hour ago he sank his whole moonshine factory in the river . . . ho, ho, ho, you must have really scared old Kasian!"

The lad was bursting with laughter. We laughed too.

"Now did he really have a factory?"

"A whole factory! All fitted out with equipment. He supplied the whole province with moonshine, several barrels at a time. Oh, I can't take it! And today our Kasian himself sank his goods in the river; more than a hundred buckets of moonshine, and about a hundred and fifty buckets of distillery waste under the dam. And the main thing—the old devil lost all his equipment today. He sank it all. Ha, ha, ha! You need a cart to get to the town? I'll take you. You're good guys."

While the lad was harnessing the horse, Semion Semionych and I returned to our boat.

"Semion Semionych, now do you understand why the fish were floating belly up today?"

"I got it. The fish had a little party today. Fish probably like to have a spree too and try Kasian's moonshine for free. The perch and the chub—they were all sloshed to the gills. What a rehearsal!"

"Yes, Semion Semionych, this isn't how I imagined 'Beautiful Mecha' before. Apparently a lot of water has flowed out of the Beautiful Mecha since Turgenev's times."

"It can't be denied: the river's gotten quite shallow. But that's not important. What's important is that today without any slander or scandal we did a good deed: we were able to strike a blow for sobriety."

"Yes, Semion Semionych, moonshine is a terrible evil."

"It can't be denied: a poisonous thing! But incidentally, fish can be caught with it very specially."

The Aggitator from the Mississippi River

THIS YEAR TURNED out an amazingly unlucky one for our little town and for our whole district. Misfortunes seemed to pour one after another onto our poor heads, and it began with the fact that in the village Viazovka, right near the town, several farmsteads burned down in a single night. After that, fires started to happen so frequently in the town that our famous town fire brigade was constantly on alert. It got so sharp that it began leaving for a fire with the speed of lightning, two or at a maximum three hours after the alarm . . .

Besides fires, we suffered from unprecedented heat and drought, and we watched in horror as the peasants' harvest perished at the root from the lack of rain.

The misfortunes did not stop there. On the railroad bridge over the little river Uperta, not far from the town, a freight and passenger train traveling to Moscow was wrecked, and some people were even killed in the accident.

Immediately after this sad accident a new, terrible calamity came to our town—thieves. Not a day passed without some thefts, which bore a rather strange character. For some reason they mostly stole domestic ducks and geese from the town pond. I myself had a pure-bred gosling pinched there. Citizen Kobiakov's bay mare was stolen from his yard, and the hairdresser Ulybkin, who lived on the shore of the pond, had a piglet swiped by the unknown thieves.

All these calamities were assuming such proportions that our little newspaper had to set aside a whole page for the "Incidents" department, and once there appeared there a witty little article under the headline, "Policeman, tighten your discipline." But with all impartiality one must state that our police, headed up by an energetic chief, were on top of the situation. The police were doing their utmost to pinch the thieves, but the thieves were so skillful that they remained elusive, and every morning some housewife or other found either a pair of ducks or a gander missing on the pond.

Now when our esteemed citizenesses would meet, instead of the usual greetings they would utter completely different words, like for example, "Did you hear? Marya Nikolavna is just weeping and wailing! Last night the crooks swiped a second goose from her!"

Or: "Mrs. Shurup, the poor thing, has been sobbing bitter tears since morning. Her drake disappeared last night. It's just terrible what's happening!"

After such greetings the housewives would usually begin to moan and curse the police, but meanwhile two vigilant police sentries, posted by the authorities on the shores of the pond, kept their eyes open all night and keenly followed the movements of any citizens who appeared.

Your average citizen is a strange creature. Haven't you ever noticed that in civic or even personal misfortune, your average citizen is for the most part inert? He loves to whine, snivel, and wail, but he has small capacity for displaying energetic initiative, until somebody gives him a good shaking-up.

Our kind police chief had correctly taken this circumstance into account, and issued an eloquent appeal to civic consciousness in the newspaper. The police chief cast into the thick of the average citizenry two beautiful slogans:

ALL AS ONE PERSON—INTO THE STRUGGLE WITH THE PARASITES!

IT'S TIME TO OVERCOME NARROW-MINDEDNESS AND SLOPPINESS!

After reading this notice, Semion Semionych and I decided that the police chief was on the whole completely right, and his appeal found a lively response in our hearts. We were hunters, and tracking down game has a lot in common with tracking down crooks.

We decided to act on our own initiative, and we began working out a plan of action. The town pond was again to be transformed into our arena, on which this time we were to appear in the capacity of noble heroes of a crime drama.

First of all we established precisely the ducks' favorite corners of the pond where they usually spent the night. The main body of ducks and geese spent the night on the water in a corner of the pond on the town side near the dam. Another group gathered for the night by a little cove near the high school. Now there were police sentry posts set up at both of these places for the night. How a thief could go undetected into the water over his knees and pinch a vociferous duck without any commotion was truly incomprehensible!

"Vladim Sergev, this is not some ordinary thief at work, but a highly qualified one," said Semion Semionych. "Most likely he undresses in the park at night on the other shore and goes into the water there. From there he quietly swims up to the sleeping bird, takes it carefully by the leg, makes his way back with it, and that's all she wrote."

Semion Semionych's supposition was well founded. Of course, no thief would risk going into the water from the town side in full view of a policeman. Therefore we decided to place under observation the opposite shore, where an ancient, neglected park from the time of the Empress Catherine was spread out.

When it began to get dark, we set off there, taking along lanterns and guns loaded with small-shot. The policeman on duty, smiling condescendingly, followed us with his eyes. On the other shore we determined which spots would be most convenient for the thieves' nocturnal operations, and each of us chose a zone of observation.

Night came on swiftly. A full moon shone brightly from the heavens, reflected in the quiet water. From the town we could hear the rattles of the night watchmen and the sounds of distant concertinas. Their cascading arpeggios, mingling with the echoing calls of the pond frogs, pleasantly caressed the ear.

I got bored and was overcome with a desire to sleep. I cheered myself up with the knowledge that I was laboring for the public good, but after midnight, when the town concertinas began to fall silent and the town on the other side of the pond was plunged into deep sleep, I felt that if I were only to sit down I would inevitably fall asleep. In order to chase sleepiness away, I decided to go see my friend for a minute and pick up at least a bit of alertness from him. I set off in his direction and soon caught sight of his dark figure. He was standing in the shadow of a tree and, gun at the ready, was looking in my direction, undoubtedly taking me for a thief. It was evident that my friend was more vigilant than I.

"Semion Semionych, please lower your gun, otherwise you might injure your best friend," I said to him under my breath. "I came to see you for a minute. Is everything all right with you?"

"Oh, Vladim Sergev, is this really the way to lie in wait for highly qualified thieves! Turn around and go back to your place immediately. One might say that the most official thieves' hour is approaching, and you leave your post. Throw away that papirosa, you're ruining the whole operation with it! The thief might see you and run away."[1]

With irritation I flung the half-smoked papirosa into the pond. It fell into the water near an old fallen willow tree, the thick trunk of which hung low over the water. Hardly had the ignited tip of the papirosa hissed away in the dark water, when suddenly some large and heavy being noisily tore away from the trunk of the old willow and plopped heavily into the water, raising a fountain of spray.

"There he is!" Semion Semionych and I cried in one voice, rushing to the bent-over tree, the top of which was sunk in the water.

"He dove, the accursed one!" Semion Semionych said. "Well, just wait, you're going to have to come to the surface, and you won't get away from us again!"

But the thief did not come out, and the surface of the pond again shone as an imperturbable smoothness.

"Vladim Sergev, come on and move a little to the right, and I'll scoot over to the left. The thief must have swum away underwater."

We ran along the shore of the pond, expecting to see the surfacing thief, but he seemed to have gone to the bottom.

"Vladim Sergev, light the lantern. The thief had to have taken his clothes off somewhere around here. We have to at least be able to find his clothes. That'll be evidence, anyway."

We lit the lanterns and began furiously seeking the daring thief. No matter how we searched, how we rummaged under the bushes—there were no clothes, no evidence to be found anywhere.

"He's a sly one! He's a sly one!" Semion Semionych kept saying. "And his work is so clean—you can't get at him!"

"Semion Semionych, but you're also a fine one. The thief was sitting ten paces from us, and you missed him. Aren't you ashamed?"

Semion Semionych defended himself energetically.

We stayed on the alert right through until morning. Nothing more of interest happened during our watch, and we left our posts when the town was beginning to wake up. Worn out, we made our way home. The yawning policeman by the dam announced to us that the night had passed peacefully and without any incidents.

We came home, immediately fell into a deep, peaceful sleep, and when we awoke, our wives informed us that the previous night Pavel Mikhailov's goose and a duck belonging to the wife of the inspector of finances had disappeared from the pond. Moreover, that morning at the market, Doctor Nikitskii's purse with three rubles and his identification card had been pinched.

We were staggered.

The next night we again found ourselves on the shore of the pond, and we took up our old posts, skillfully hiding in the shadows of the ancient trees.

I was listening keenly to every nocturnal rustle, never taking my eyes from the water, when suddenly the soft crack of a breaking twig caused me to shudder and turn around. I firmly gripped my double-barreled gun in my hands.

"Vladim Sergev, don't be afeared . . . it's me," I heard the choked and breaking voice of Semion Semionych.

The next instant he appeared before me on the path.

"What happened?"

"Vladim Sergev, *he's over there . . .*"

"Where?"

"In the same place as yesterday . . . he's hidden near the trunk of the old willow."

"Semion Semionych, why didn't you apprehend him? He's going to get away!"

"Vladim Sergev, he's not going to get away. He didn't see me. I went quietly around him. He's been sitting there for a long time."

"But where did he come from?"

"Out of the water."

"What?!? Out of the water?"

"Word of honor, out of the water. I saw completely officially how he crawled out of the water onto the toppled trunk and started crawling along it. Now he's sitting right there."

"But after all, why didn't you apprehend him?"

"Vladim Sergev, *he's not a person.*"

"What? Well, then, what is he, he's not a water sprite, is he?"

"Vladim Sergev, it's rather awkward to say just what he is."

At this point I noticed that my friend was trembling from agitation. His gun was simply jumping in his shaking hands. Semion Semionych's agitation was soon communicated to me.

"Semion Semionych, I beg of you, don't torment me. Tell me immediately who you saw."

"Vladim Sergev, forgive me, but I don't even dare to speak of such things. Go look for yourself. Let's crawl over there together. But quietly, or else we'll scare him away."

We carefully crawled forward. I was seized by a terrible curiosity. Now we could see the old toppled willow. Its top was sunk in the water. Another few paces and . . . My hair stood on end. My heart stopped beating in my chest. On the thick old trunk the long, gleaming body of a beast was hiding itself. The moon brightly illuminated a monstrous, bottle-shaped maw and the long, powerful tail of a lizard! Its round eyes looked into the distance with an eerie fixedness.

I gave myself a painful pinch and was convinced that this was not a dream. My heart had begun beating so hard in my chest that I was close to fainting. My thoughts were all confused. Only one thing was clear and indisputable: *in front of me was the most authentic, huge, live crocodile.* One could clearly see the pulse beating in his hideous neck.

"Semion Semionych, what is this?" I babbled in horror.

At the sound of my voice the crocodile raised its head in alarm and moved its clumsy paw.

I decided to shoot at the beast, and with shaking hands I raised my gun.

My movement was awkward. A broken twig crackled under me. At the same moment the crocodile flapped its tail and threw itself noisily into the water. The spray flew in various directions, the water became agitated under the tree, and the monster immediately disappeared from our view. For a long time, large ripples emanated from the spot where the monster had disappeared.

At this point I couldn't help but remember a story I had recently heard from two of our town "young ladies," who while swimming in the pond that summer had been frightened by a huge black fish the size of a log. I remembered that at that time I had had quite a bit of fun at the expense of the nervous young ladies. Now I came to understand their fright. They had undoubtedly seen the crocodile. I also understood the disappearance of birds from the town pond: they were serving as food for the terrible predator.

The fact was staring us in the face. A crocodile had taken up residence in our town pond. A *crocodile* in the Tula region!

"How did he get here?" I asked myself out loud.

"Vladim Sergev, it's very simple," Semion Semionych explained. "The crocodile appeared here because of the heat. This summer is terribly hot and dry. The water in the pond became as warm as milk fresh from the cow. Well, so crocodiles appeared. Such a thing can happen completely officially."

"No, Semion Semionych! Such a thing cannot happen. It's true, this year's hot summer has created favorable conditions for the crocodile to live in our climate, but crocodiles do not appear all by themselves. Undoubtedly this crocodile was introduced here by one of our citizens, but where did he get it from—that's the question! Not only are crocodiles not found in Europe, but a live crocodile costs a hell of a lot of money, and in the U.S.S.R. you certainly can't buy one for any amount of money. Yes, Semion Semionych, we are confronted by a terrible and insoluble enigma."

"Vladim Sergev, did this mammalian animal really pinch Doctor Nikitskii's purse and identity papers yesterday? What the hell did it need them for?"

"Semion Semionych, in the first place, a crocodile is not an animal but a reptile, and in the second place, the doctor's purse was of course pinched not by the crocodile but by an ordinary thief. The ducks are another matter. They're being carried off by the crocodile."

Semion Semionych and I did not sleep all night, conversing animatedly about the enigmatic crocodile, coming up with a thousand suppositions. We calmed down only toward morning, having firmly decided that at all costs we would catch the monster dead or alive.

"What's the matter, comrades?" the police chief greeted us when Semion Semionych and I appeared in his office in the morning.

"We know who's stealing geese at night," I announced confidently.

"Point him out!" the energetic fellow said tersely.

"It's a crocodile!" we answered in unison.

The police chief thought for a minute, as if taxing his memory. Finally he said, "The personage you have named is unknown to me."

"It's not a personage, but a mammalian reptile," Semion Semionych explained.

Interrupting each other, we began to tell the chief about the events of the previous nights. The chief listened attentively to us for a long time and finally interrupted us impatiently: "Here's the thing, lads, don't try to stuff my head with nonsense! I thought you came to see me with serious business. Get your butts out of here! And if you come here to make a disturbance again, I'm warning you: I'll converse with you in a different way!"

We looked at each other and, shrugging our shoulders, hastily left the office, since the chief's face had suddenly become very serious.

"All right, my dear chief, we'll see how you change your tune when we present you with a live reptile!" my friend whispered as we went out onto the street.

During the day we prepared for the coming hunt. Semion Semionych proposed that we catch the crocodile with a rope trap. For this end we got some new strong rope and stocked up on several massive iron spikes. We knew the favorite spot of the monster. We knew that sooner or later the crocodile would again crawl out onto the old willow trunk.

We worked energetically all day without tiring. Along the whole length of the thick trunk of the fallen willow we fastened about ten strong rope nooses, nailing their ends to the trunk with the long iron spikes. A terrible, powerful paw was sure to get caught in one of these nooses. We skillfully camouflaged the nooses with thin green willow branches.

We worked in this way until evening and returned home only in order to fortify ourselves with supper. No matter how we hurried to eat, it was already almost dark when we left home.

The red disc of the rising moon, like the glare of a conflagration, was swimming out from the horizon. We walked quickly along a path in the park, heading for the old willow. Now we went around a bend; now we passed a ruined old water tower . . . But where was the old willow? It wasn't there!

We stopped, completely dumbfounded, and looked inquiringly at each other. What kind of devilish illusion was this? Who was playing such evil and nasty tricks on us? Only half an hour ago we had been working here, pounding iron spikes into a strong tree, and now not even a trace of that tree remained. You could only have taken it away from here on a cart, and there was no hint of a trace of any wheels in the vicinity. Moreover, there wasn't a single broken twig visible on the ground!

Semion Semionych was the first to break the silence: "Vladim Sergev, I congratulate you on the hunt!"

"But why?"

"Very simple, because our reptile got caught."

"How do you know that?"

A triumphant smile lit up my friend's face. Instead of answering he pointed to the pond. By the light of the risen moon I could see a long willow trunk fifty paces away from the shore. Its branchy top was quivering and swaying on the water. Someone unseen was slowly towing it.

A loud "hurrah" burst from my throat.

"Hurrah!" Semion Semionych caught up, throwing his striped cap high in the air.

"Hurra-a-a-h!" we cried, choking from ecstasy.

Undoubtedly our "hurrah" could be heard even on the town side of the pond. Undoubtedly our honest town housewives could hear it. The poor things—they still didn't know that this shout was proclaiming to them a victory over their terrible enemy! They still didn't know that from this moment their geese and fat ducks would no longer be subjected to mortal danger. The town had been delivered from calamity!

Yes, it was a beautiful moment!

All night my friend and I sailed around on his own boat, which he called the *Automotor,* chasing the floating willow that was being towed by the crocodile. He turned out to be an unbelievably strong rascal. At times he would stick out his ugly bottle-shaped mug and bare his terrible teeth. He flapped his tail in a monstrously furious manner, raising fountains of water and uttering a threatening growl. The crocodile was executing such desperate and intricate movements that we were afraid to sail close to him. The beast seemed to be indefatigable.

"Listen, Semion Semionych, how much longer is this performance going to go on! Isn't it time to finish off the beast with a charge of buckshot?"

"What are you saying, Vladim Sergev! By no means! We must present the chief with the living fact in relief. Scare him with the oars, don't let him rest. Let's wear the nasty beast out. A crocodile isn't a machine!"

We slapped our oars against the water with such effort that we wore ourselves completely out.

Only toward morning did we notice that the crocodile was weakening. He beat his tail less and less often. His movements became listless. Finally we sailed right up to him and stuck an oar into his side. The crocodile protested sluggishly. Then we took in tow the old trunk with the beast tied to it and slowly came in to the town side of the pond.

It was growing light. The animal was so exhausted that he allowed us to put a rope collar on him without any protest. The crocodile was loudly panting like a blacksmith's bellows. We were struck by the colossal dimensions of the beast and by his hideousness. After we freed the crocodile's left leg from the noose, we drove him into the town. Semion Semionych walked in front and led the crocodile behind him on a rope. I drove him from behind, using a large cudgel. We moved slowly, because the crocodile was just as slow and awkward on land as he was swift and agile in the water.

We slowly walked out into the marketplace. A strange thing: the crocodile did not grumble. He had ceased to fear us and seemed completely tame. Moreover, I soon became convinced that the beast had undoubtedly been trained. I had only to touch the crocodile's shoulder with the cudgel for the beast to begin twirling as if he were dancing a waltz. And when I poked him in the neck, he would click his teeth in a hilarious way.

"An attractive subject," my friend said, watching the crocodile's tricks.

It took us about two hours to make our way to the police station. We tied the crocodile to the gate and burst into the duty room. The policeman on duty was so stunned that for three minutes he couldn't say a word. When his stupor finally passed, he ran like a shot to wake up the chief.

There was such a stir in the police station! There was such a stir in the town!

Despite the early hour, the interesting news flew through the town at once and roused almost the entire population. The police station was besieged by a crowd. The chief interrogated us in a reserved tone, entering our testimony into the minutes. In carefully official terms he asked the townspeople not to get excited. He ordered that no one besides us be allowed into the courtyard. An exception was made only for old Franz Ivanovich Ellers, the teacher of zoology at the high school. The learned man carefully inspected the beast from all sides and confidently proclaimed: "Alligator Mississippiensis . . . an alligator from the Mississippi River."

Here Semion Semionych had the bright idea of demonstrating the alligator's training.

"Hello, hello, aggitator . . . get a move on!"

The good-natured animal conscientiously danced a waltz and clicked its teeth. It was a great success. Even the imperturbable chief couldn't restrain a smile and offered us papirosas.

"What do you say, chief, isn't that a real bas-relief?"

"Thank you, comrades," the chief replied and invited us to proceed into his office. After politely offering us a seat, he addressed us:

"Friends, please forgive me for my sharp words yesterday. Last night I discovered that you were right. The crocodile found its way into our pond a month ago, having come along the river from the railroad trestle. Here's how it happened."

Here the chief pulled a newspaper clipping out of his briefcase and gave it to us:

DETAILS OF THE CRASH OF A MIXED FREIGHT AND PASSENGER TRAIN

According to the latest information, among those who perished in the train crash near B. was the well-known tamer and trainer of alligators, Ernesto Manetti. The deceased had recently arrived in the U.S.S.R. with his famous alligator Giovanni. Manetti was traveling to Moscow, where he was to make several appearances. Alas, this trip proved to be a fatal one for him! So far nothing is known about the fate of the alligator.

Having listened to this report, Semion Semionych became pensive and, nervously drumming his fingers on the table, said:

"Well, so that means the aggitator has lost his master. Poor, poor little beast."

Several days later in the major newspapers there appeared the following advertisement, which perhaps you may have happened to notice:

FOUND: CROCODILE. Gender unknown. Coat: dark green, with scales. Wart over the right eye. Small scar on the tail. Length: sixteen feet, three inches. In three days I will consider it my property. Town of B., Pervomaiskaia Street 18. S. S. Bochonkin.

The Black-White-and-Tan Skewbald Dog

'Tis time, 'tis time! . . . The horns resound,
The dogs are leaping on their leashes. . . .
—Pushkin

THERE WAS A hard, bracing frost. The red ball of the rising
sun slowly emerged from behind a knoll. The village of Ivlevo was smoking
from all its chimneys at once. The smoke rose in thin columns and disappeared into the pale blue heights, presaging a quiet, marvelous day for
hunting.

"Hey, you hunters! Do you by any chance need a hunting dog?"

Thus did the Ivlevo peasant Mikhailo Zashchipkin hail Semion Semionych and me as we were passing his hut with our hounds.

"Thanks, we're satisfied with our own dogs," I answered. "But where
did you get a dog?"

"It followed me from the woods and has been living with me for more
than two months now. It chases hares damn good. Wait a minute, I'll show
you."

With these words Mikhailo disappeared into the yard.

"Tell me, Semion Semionych, did you, as chairman of the Hunters'
Union, receive any notices of a lost hunting hound?"

"There weren't any notices, but I know all the hunting hounds in our
district personally. I'll know right away whose dog Mikhailo found."

In the yard resounded a dog's desperate howl, and at that moment
Mikhailo appeared before us. He was leading a large, multicolored dog on a
rope and was energetically shoving it along from behind with his knee.

At the sight of this dog Semion Semionych and I couldn't help but burst
out laughing, and our hounds—Sobber, Dokuka, and two of Dokuka's children, wiry young hounds—all at once started furiously pulling on their
leashes, bristling their fur and raising their tails in a challenging pose.

"Hey, Mikhailo! Aren't you ashamed to show off such trash! Your dog
isn't going to live another day. It's terrifying to look at her."

In coloration Mikhailo's dog did in fact resemble a hunting hound of an
Anglo-Russian breed, but what a repulsive appearance it had! I have never

92

had occasion to see such a worn-out dog. It was a skeleton covered with skin; you could easily count all its ribs and vertebrae. The dog had a drooping rump, its back had an unhealthy hunch in it, and it seemed to be staggering from weakness. To top it all off, it was hopping on three legs and carried its fourth, sore paw tucked up under itself.

"Let's go, Vladim Sergev," said Semion Semionych. "There's no use wasting time here. The day is short. We're not going to bag much today. So long, Mikhailo! Send your cholera-ridden doggy as far away as possible. She's not even worth a load of shot!"

"Hey, hunters!" Mikhailo called after us. "Wait a minute! You're making a big mistake in knocking this dog! First give her a try at hunting, and then you can abuse her. I'm telling you straight: it's a damn good dog!"

Semion Semionych waved his hand dismissively, and we quickly set off in the direction of the Kustrovatyi forest. This young forest was famous for its abundance of hares, of which, in Semion Semionych's words, there was a whole "depot."

"There are all kinds of idiots on this earth!" Semion Semionych reasoned. "This, you'll excuse the expression, dog was probably driven out of the house by its former owner on purpose so he didn't have to feed it for nothing, and here Mikhailo has the gall to try to foist her off on us and get us to try her out. Clearly he's got a shortage of conscience."

We turned off the road and took a beeline for the forest. The dogs were sinking up to the neck in loose snow. It was especially deep at the edge of the forest. We let the dogs loose, and they immediately penetrated into the young forest, making a path for themselves with difficulty. This kind of hunting demands a huge amount of endurance and energy from the dogs.

Semion Semionych and I sat down opposite each other on some little stumps and lit up as we waited for one of the dogs to give voice. Indeed, after about five minutes Dokuka yelped from the midst of some young oak trees. This meant that she had found the trail of a hare left overnight. Dokuka began deliberately following the trail "gropingly," occasionally giving voice.[1] Soon we could hear the intermittently sounding voices of the other dogs. The whole pack was following Dokuka "gropingly." The dogs had not yet reached the hare's lair, the hare had not yet been roused; apparently it had managed to leave quite a trail in the young forest over the course of the long, frosty night.

Suddenly, quite far ahead of the place our dogs had reached, an excited barking resounded. Some dog had raised the hare from its lair and was chasing it. But it was not our dog. Its voice was ringing, deep, and desperate. One could sense that the dog was chasing with an unusual enthusiasm. Some of the notes in its voice sounded downright gripping. Gradually rising, the barking turned into a furious, triumphant howling.

"It's music and not a chase! But who the devil is hunting here besides us? What nonsense!"

Our hounds joined the unknown dog. The whole pack was chasing together. The Kustrovatyi forest began to ring from the chase. The voice of the unknown dog stood out from the whole pack in its strength and beauty. The hare apparently had turned toward the edge of the forest. Stumbling and overtaking each other, we hurried there and arrived at the forest edge at the very moment when the quick, long-eared hare jumped out into the open field and came rushing toward us like a bullet.

"Bang-bang," our guns cracked in the frosty air. The big old hare took a huge leap and plopped into the snow dead. Only grey bits of fluff from its fur seemed to hang in the motionless, frozen air. We went up to the hare. The dogs' voices were coming closer. Soon the bare branches crackled and, hot on the hare's trail, there appeared the head of the unknown hound. What marvelous music that head was producing! The dog was rushing with all its might. Far behind it, our famous dogs were trying to catch up.

"Semion Semionych, look: it's Mikhailo's dog!"

"It can't be!"

"It's a fact!"

There was no doubt. Choking from passion, wriggling its whole body, sinking into the deep snow at every hop, the dog, emaciated as a skeleton, came flying. All powdered with snow, it had been transformed. Its eyes were bulging. It was in a kind of ecstatic state.

Apparently she had broken from Mikhailo's hands and followed us, unable to resist the temptation to give chase. The sight of our guns and dogs had a seductive effect on her.

Seeing the dead hare, the dog understood that the tragedy was finished. She immediately quieted down and stopped in her hunched pose, tucking her bloody, sore paw up under her. Out of the bushes appeared the triumphant Sobber and Dokuka with her children. After jumping around the dead hare and rejoicing with their masters, our dogs began to make the acquaintance of the multicolored dog. They took turns sniffing her, they wagged their tails welcomingly, and finally they made it known to the stranger that they had nothing against her. Only my dog Dokuka seemed to be in a bad mood, sensing that the multicolored dog was a rival.

Semion Semionych and I looked at the multicolored dog and couldn't believe our eyes. How could a dog who looked as if she was barely alive, beaten down, lame, and utterly worn out, chase with such a fiery temperament in these impassable snowdrifts?

"And where does she get it from? She's nothing to look at, she's dog's death warmed over! But what a heart in that multicolored creature!"

Meanwhile the "multicolored creature" had again disappeared into the bushes. Not three minutes passed before she again gave voice, attracting our dogs to follow her.

What an unforgettable day! We chased one hare after another without a break until sunset. The whole hunt was directed by the multicolored dog, and her skill eclipsed the mastery of Dokuka and Sobber. Our hounds seemed to acknowledge her superiority and followed her lead.

When we were hunting the last hare, something strange happened: our dogs were chasing through the whole forest, but the voice of the multicolored hound suddenly began to sound from a single place. When the last hare had been killed and our tired hounds came to us, the multicolored hound was still giving voice from the same spot, as if she had been tied to a tree. The dog did not appear at the sound of our horns. Then we went towards her voice ourselves.

What Semion Semionych and I saw then definitively won our hearts. The multicolored hound was lying on the hare's trail. She had finally reached her breaking point and was so weak she couldn't get up. Her traumatized, bloody legs refused to serve her, but mentally she was continuing to chase the hare. Her emaciated body was trembling convulsively, her eyes were wandering, she was desperately barking, but she could no longer get up and seemed to be dying at her post.

"Is she dying?"

"No . . . she's just famished. That conscienceless Mikhailo probably didn't feed her."

Semion Semionych cut off the hare's paws and threw them to the unfortunate dog. She greedily grabbed them and swallowed them at once. We gave her bread and the hare's innards. Looking at the hungry, gobbling dog, Semion Semionych said affectionately:

"Go ahead, creature, gobble to your heart's delight! You are a thinking, sensible creature!"

The dog licked herself and asked for more.

"Oh, you insatiable gobbler! An official gobbler!"

The dog wagged her tail.

"Well, so that's who she is, Gobbler."

Fortified by the bread and entrails, the dog jumped to her feet and took off chasing along the hare's trail on which she had been lying.

"Did you ever see such a devil! Vladim Sergev, it's not a dog but a fire!"

It was already getting dark. We hurried to catch Gobbler and did so only with difficulty. Semion Semionych and I had never seen such a desperate hound. We admitted to each other that she was better than our celebrated dogs—and, by the way, hunters never admit such things. It would be a crime to let such a good worker out of our hands, and we decided on the spot to buy the multicolored Gobbler from Mikhailo.

The deal was struck that very evening. The dog was acquired for three rubles. Neither of us wanted to cede the dog to the other, and so we decided that Gobbler would belong to both of us. At that time I had moved in next to Semion Semionych. Our dwellings were divided by a common yard, and so it turned out to be possible and even convenient to own a dog in common.

"What a monster! How disgusting! Get it out of here! Are you out of your mind?"

That's how our wives met us. They were peacefully having tea when we returned from the hunt and led the lame multicolored dog into the room. Our wives said many bitter and unkind things to us on the subject of our purchase of Gobbler. In their opinion, it would have been much more useful to spend several rubles on ladies' shoes than on the purchase of a half-dead dog. Our wives categorically announced that they would not feed Gobbler and that they would not tolerate her presence indoors.

Gobbler took up residence in the yard. She was so lacerated and worn out that we didn't take her hunting. But hunting season soon passed. We fed her well with boiled horse meat, and the dog put on weight. We gave her our respect, tasting in advance the hunting joys that she would provide us in the coming season.

Spring came. Semion Semionych, in his capacity as chairman of the local district branch of the Hunters' Union, received official notification from headquarters that in two weeks the provincial dog show would take place. All districts were asked to send their exhibiting dogs to the show. Although our district boasted many fine working dogs, we did not have any that were particularly beautiful or of good pedigree. Semion Semionych and I were discussing this and trying to decide which dog in our district had the best pedigree. As we were talking I happened to go up to the window. The newly plump Gobbler was basking in the sun before my eyes.

"Gobbler!" I called to her through the window.

The dog got up lazily, stretched, yawned, and wagged her tail in greeting. In the course of two months she had become unrecognizable. I had never looked at her from the point of view of breeding. Seeing her from day to day, I had become too used to her. Now I began to try to ascertain her defects and suddenly discovered that she had none. Gobbler suddenly appeared extremely beautiful to me. I was struck by her lovely large head, fiery glance, powerful ribs, chest, muscles, her ideally placed tail, impeccable paws, and her particular, purely hunting dog's bearing. The dog was impeccable. Moreover, I suddenly realized that standing before me was an unusually beautiful specimen of a dog of the Anglo-Russian breed.

"Semion Semionych! Come here . . . Look: that's who we're going to present at the show!"

"Oh, come on, Vladim Sergev! But you know . . . Well, hell! Must be from the good grub . . . You wouldn't recognize her. Factually, she's turned out to be an official hound!"

We went out into the yard and submitted Gobbler to a detailed inspection. That very day Semion Semionych wrote to the center that our district would present a female hunting hound of the Anglo-Russian breed at the provincial show.

Dog shows are exciting for the dogs. They're even more exciting for the dogs' masters. If the dogs are excited by the mere presence of a multitude of their peers, with whom they want to fight for some reason, their masters are excited by questions of self-esteem and the official solemnity of the situation.

Already during the veterinarian's inspection of the dogs on the eve of the opening of the show, Semion Semionych and I began to get nervous. Every hound that appeared caused us anxiety: what if this is the one that will put Gobbler to shame?

The provincial show was set up in a very solemn fashion. A great multitude of people had gathered for the opening. Expert judges had been invited from Moscow. A catalogue of the show had been printed. Reading this catalogue was a strange experience. There in black and white was written:

No. 32. Anglo-Russian hunting hound Gobbler (black-white-and-tan skew-bald).[2] Parentage unknown. Owners: S. Bochonkin and V. Khvoshch.

It was pleasant to read our names, printed in a beautiful gray booklet. We were agitated by the strange official expression "black-white-and-tan skewbald." It was clear right away that this was a very serious business and not a joking matter at all.

"'Black-white-and-tan skewbald!'" said Semion Semionych, looking pensively at Gobbler. "What language! 'Parentage unknown!' So I guess you and I are responsible for the dog . . . Vladim Sergev, what if they make fun of us for our 'skewbaldness'?"

Our further reading of the catalogue agitated us even more. There were eighty hounds being shown in all. For all these hounds there were only two prizes: one for the best male and one for the best female.

Eighty hounds! And what names there were! From the catalogue we learned that the company had been joined by a certain hound named Prey, who had once earned a big silver medal, and the famous Anglo-Russian female hound Hunting Horn, who had won the gold medal and first place at the All-Union dog show. In all there were five prizewinners included in the show.

We tracked down Hunting Horn. She was a proud, well-groomed dog who was aware of her importance. It turned out that she was housed next to

Gobbler. The two dogs were avoiding even meeting each other's eyes, such a hatred had they conceived for each other. Hunting Horn's master was a very unpleasant citizen with a haughty physiognomy and a serious graying mustache. He looked at us and our dog with deep disdain. We did not exchange a single word with him. His disdainful physiognomy and serious mustache annoyed us terribly. One would think that it was he and not his dog who had won the gold medal.

Many interested people came to look at Hunting Horn. They were all delighted by her points. No one looked at Gobbler. She had curled up cozily, and in this humble pose it was hard to distinguish her qualities. Only a single decrepit old man with the appearance of an experienced hunter came up to Gobbler and looked at her for a long time, smacking his tongue as if he were eating something very tasty.

"Oh, what a little she-hound!" he kept saying. "Very, very interesting!"

He was the only visitor who paid any attention to Gobbler.

The experts' examination of the hounds began. They were divided according to breed. First the male hounds of Kostroma breed were brought out into the ring, then the females. After the Kostroma hounds came the Anglo-Russian dogs, and finally it was Gobbler's turn to be led out. She was together with a group of seven others. Our hearts skipped a beat when our number 32 was called.

A crowd of about a hundred spectators was gathered around the ring. At the command of the Moscow expert, the masters and their hounds began to walk around the ring. Seeing herself surrounded by unfamiliar dogs, Gobbler bristled up, and the devil knows what she was doing with her white tail. She looked like an infuriated tigress, and Semion Semionych could hardly hold her back.

The judge kept silent for a long time, looking at the strolling dogs with piercing, predatory eyes. Then he pointed his finger in Gobbler's direction and commanded: "Stay!"

"Now they're going to kick us out," flashed through my head.

But no. They had no intention of kicking us out. The judge began to call the dogs into the center of the circle one by one. He carefully inspected every part of their bodies and noted something down in his little book with a look of such solemnity as if he were performing the most majestic act of state.

Gobbler was the last to be called. Could she really be worse than all of them? The Moscow judge looked at her for a long time with keen, impassive eyes, and finally said:

"Hunting Horn, stand next to Number 32."

Hunting Horn's master led his dog into the center and placed her next to Gobbler. The dog judge began to circle around Hunting Horn and Gobbler. He looked at them from the front, from the back, and from the side. Finally the judge stopped, and his face took on a solemn expression. A deathly silence came over the crowd of spectators. I felt my heart begin to beat more rapidly. Hunting Horn's master suddenly turned as white as a sheet. What was he going through? What were we going through? What were our dogs going through?

Finally the judge announced in an impassive voice:

"Number 32 is the best of all!"

Oh, how the unpleasant physiognomy of Hunting Horn's master fell! His cheeks colored deeply. Semion Semionych and I exchanged a barely perceptible glance, but we didn't lose our composure, despite the storm of feeling that had suddenly seized us.

"Excuse me!" Hunting Horn's master protested. "My dog won the gold medal at the All-Union show. She is the daughter of the famous Bother and Gather! On what basis do you give preference to some obscure dog whose parentage is completely unknown? Allow me to ask whose daughter she is?" he turned to us, pointing at Gobbler.

"She's the same daughter of a bitch as yours," Semion Semionych answered with dignity.

There was laughter in the crowd.

"This is a disgrace! I protest! I will not let this matter rest here!" the mustachioed man said in agitation.

The Moscow judge shrugged his shoulders indifferently and said coldly:

"You can protest all you want. The question is settled: Number 32 is the best."

Thunderous applause shook the building where the show was being held. Hunting Horn's master hurriedly led his dog away; Semion Semionych and I were immediately surrounded by the crowd.

"Now *that* I understand—what a dog!"

"I noticed right away that she was the best hound!"

"And I predicted yesterday that she would take first prize!"

What lies these people told, trying to prove that they were experts! We were deluged with questions, people wrote down our address and signed up on a waiting list to receive Gobbler's future pups.

In the evening we were ceremoniously presented with the first prize—a silver hunting horn and a beautiful certificate "for the awarding of the gold medal to the female hound of Anglo-Russian breed Gobbler (black-white-and-tan skewbald)."

Two days later our town hunters, notified by telegram, organized a gala reception for Gobbler and us at the railroad station.

From that day Gobbler took turns sleeping on my bed and on Semion Semionych's, and our wives did not dare to protest—such was the power of the certificate!

———

Five long months passed, and finally September 15 came—opening day of the season for hunting with hounds. How we had awaited that day! Our dogs were in ideal shape. But meanwhile circumstances had turned out for me in such a way that I could not go hunting that day: for business reasons I couldn't leave town. How I envied Semion Semionych! Before dawn he had already gone to the forest, taking both his and my dogs.

So while Semion Semionych was hunting, I was sitting in town all morning, occupied with business. For this reason I was in a disgusting mood, and I couldn't concentrate at all. The weather was amazingly good, and this irritated me still further.

At two in the afternoon I was done with my business. It was too late to go hunting, and besides I had no one to go with. I went out onto the street and headed for the market, thinking the whole time about what my fortunate friend was doing at that moment.

"The dogs are giving chase, of course," I meditated. "Of course Gobbler is out in front . . . Semion Semionych must be running to the ravine to intercept the hare . . ."

My imagination painted a distinct picture of a large gray hare leaping out of the very depths of the forest.

As I approached the market square, I fell to dreaming completely . . . Suddenly I stopped as if rooted to the spot, not believing my eyes: along Proletariat Street, coming right towards me, was rushing headlong a good-sized hare!

"I've lost my mind!" flashed the terrible thought.

I began shouting in a voice not my own and I saw the frightened hare turn sharply and rush back into the market stalls. All day I had been imagining various hunting scenes, and now I had reached the point that in the very center of the town I was having visions of hares . . . Yes, I was definitely losing my mind: now I saw Gobbler rushing by me, and after her all our hounds. They were howling frantically and knocking the passersby off their feet in their irrepressible, all-destroying passion.

What a fuss there was in the market! No, this was reality and not my imagination. A horse driven mad by fear rushed past me, dragging an empty cart behind it. In the stalls one could hear the desperate howls of the market women. They had all started wailing at once, as if at a fire. Howling, shouting, barking, and squealing—in a single moment the whole market had been set head over heels, and people were rushing in all directions.

Again the little gray figure of the swift-legged hare flashed by. He had gone completely mad and was rushing to Communard Street. The whole pack of dogs with Gobbler at their head turned to follow him.

"Vladim Sergev! . . . quickly . . . run and get your gun!"

I looked around and saw my friend. He was running out of the crowd of market women with his gun in his hand. Sweaty and panting, he looked like a madman. The market women shouted terrible things after him and shook their fists at him.

"Semion Semionych, are you in your right mind?"

"Vladim Sergev, officially . . . completely officially . . . Gobbler . . ."

"Well, what about Gobbler? What happened?"

"Let me catch my breath . . . Gobbler roused a hare in the town vegetable gardens. He leaped out onto the highway, and then Sobber and Dokuka turned him right into the town . . . What a lively one that Gobbler is! She won't let that hare go—she just hangs on his tail. I couldn't shoot. But run and get your gun and skedaddle over to intercept the hare at the corner of Proletariat Street and Communard Street. That's where the trail has to lead!"

"Semion Semionych, get hold of yourself! We're in the middle of the town. This is a scandal! Blow your horn, call the dogs off."

"Vladim Sergev, it's too late to call the dogs away: call them or not, either way there'll be a scandal, because not a single pot has been left unsmashed in the market. The dogs shattered every single thing there, it's a horrible sight! Can't you hear how the market women are wailing? Get over to the corner of Proletariat Street, take up your post there, and I'll move over to the town bathhouse—that's another official hare crossing! Hear how they're chasing him? So it is: the hare is taking them in a circle!"

And with these words Semion Semionych dashed off to the bathhouse.

I don't know what my wife thought when I flew into our apartment like a hurricane, grabbed my gun and ammunition belt, and ran out onto the street.

The corner of Proletariat Street and Communard Street was in fact a probable trail. Hares that are being chased have the habit of circling around and returning to the place they already passed. I took up a position not far from Ulybkin's hair salon, listening to the unceasing chase by the dogs. Now I too forgot everything on earth and gave myself up completely to the hunting passion, feeling as if I were in the forest.

By the way, it turned out that hunting with hounds in a town has its own characteristic features: well, for example, who could have foreseen that a hare overtaken by dogs would seek salvation in the very office of the District Executive Committee of the Communist Party! But that's just how it happened.

As we were told later, the hare rushed into the yard of the executive committee and before the very eyes of the executive committee guard, old lady Lukeria, scampered under the door of a little shed. The dogs surrounded the shed, barking furiously, and a crowd of curious citizens surrounded the executive committee headquarters. They immediately recognized our dogs. There were people in the crowd who had been injured by them at the market. These citizens began to demand that we immediately be punished. Other citizens, on the contrary, praised both us and our famous dogs. Work in the executive committee headquarters came to a standstill. The telephone rang, notifying the police that Bochonkin and Khvoshch were hunting hares in the middle of the town and committing atrocious acts. The mounted police were called out.

Meanwhile the guard, old lady Lukeria, decided to take possession of the hare. The energetic woman armed herself with a kitchen knife and bravely headed for the shed. She hardly had time to open the door before the whole pack of dogs piled into the shed at once. The gray hare had no desire to die; he screamed in a human voice and leaped out the window onto the street. Gobbler, Sobber, Dokuka, and her children immediately took off after him. They began to chase with the hare in sight, and again many citizens were knocked off their feet by our dashing dogs.

I still didn't know any of this, but could only hear the hunt suddenly take a turn toward me. Apparently the whole town had now found out that a hare had appeared on the streets. The curious came running from all directions. I saw Ulybkin himself pop out of his salon with his camera in his hands. His clients ran out after him, and among them a citizen with one cheek cleanly shaven and the other covered with a thick layer of shaving cream. Overtaking each other, they took off running towards the executive committee headquarters. The lathered-up citizen howled furiously:

"Hey, you goddamned hairdresser, get back here! Finish shaving my cheek, you curly-haired devil!"

But I had no time to think about the hairdresser. I could see the hare coming toward me from far away. With broad, dashing leaps he was tearing along Communard Street, his ears pinned back. From around the corner behind him appeared Gobbler, in an extremity of excitement. I cocked my gun and got ready. At that moment I could hear the clatter of many horses' hooves behind me, and I was nearly knocked down by a bay horse—a detachment of mounted police was heading for the executive committee headquarters. At the sight of the galloping policemen, the hare jumped up onto the sidewalk. This was right opposite the cooperative cafeteria. And it just had to happen that at that very instant the door of the cafeteria opened and the presiding magistrate of the People's Court himself came out! The hare instantly scampered through the open door and disappeared into the cafeteria.

Gobbler was the first to rush into the cafeteria. Sobber, Dokuka, and Dokuka's children jumped after her through the windows and the door. In a flash the cafeteria turned into a real hell. Tables, stools, customers, the manager himself—everything was overturned onto the floor. The clatter of dishes, barking of dogs, howls of the customers, the hare's mortal cry—Gobbler caught him! All five hounds sank their teeth into him at once. He was torn into five pieces.

People came running from all directions. The police dismounted. The figure of Semion Semionych unexpectedly surfaced out of nowhere right next to me. He was extremely agitated. Having waited in vain for the hare by the town bathhouse, he decided to join me at the more probable trail point. We approached the cafeteria at the very moment when the black-white-and-tan skewbald, the triumphant Gobbler, came proudly out. She was licking her chops.

"Gobbler!" Semion Semionych and I shouted in unison.

The people noticed us . . .

Now something happened that the citizens of our town love to tell about to this very day. As for Semion Semionych and me, we don't even like to remember it, let alone tell about it.

But if you absolutely have to find out how it all ended, then ask our presiding magistrate: he was a witness, after all . . . Or no . . . don't ask him, but read the September 16 issue of our newspaper *The Red Voice*. They published twice the usual number of copies of that issue.[3]

It was late autumn. The first snow had barely covered the muddy earth. We, of course, were hunting. Something absurd had happened with our hounds: they had roused a fox and a hare at the same time. Gobbler was following the fox's trail, and the other dogs went after the hare.

It's more interesting to knock off a fox than a hare, and Semion Semionych and I of course undertook to go after the fox, letting the other dogs go. The hunt took us the devil knows where—right up to Shchadilov Pond. We took up our positions, hiding in the yellowed reeds, and stared attentively into the thicket of osiers in front of us. We could hear Gobbler's passionate voice from there. Oh, how superbly she hunted that day!

Suddenly the thin ice on the pond cracked almost imperceptibly. I looked around and shuddered: the fox had appeared behind us. She had deceived us. She had carefully gone down onto the frozen pond. Apparently she sensed that the ice had not yet gotten firm, and she was stepping along it with extreme care. I was rather far from the fox. Semion Semionych could shoot from his place, but he hadn't looked around and seen the fox. I tried to hypnotize him so that he would turn around, but my hypnosis didn't work, and meanwhile the fox was getting farther away from him.

"Oh, I have to take a chance!" I thought. "Maybe my old gun will reach her."

I aimed and shot at the fox. The small-shot didn't hurt her, but the sound of the shot gave her a good fright. She jumped up, curled up her tail, and forgetting all her caution in her fear, took off along the ice at top speed, stretching out into a fiery ribbon.

The thin ice did not withstand the fox's desperate leaps. It broke under her with a crack in the very middle of the pond, and the fox tumbled into the water. She floundered, trying to get out onto the ice, but her front paws kept breaking the edge as soon as she tried to lean on it. Although the fox was out of range of our guns, she was now done for. She couldn't get away from us. Semion Semionych started running along the right bank and I ran along the left. The fox saw us and didn't know how to get out. It was a rare and interesting sight. Semion Semionych and I exchanged joyful exclamations.

"Vladim Sergev! Run over to the vines! Scare the fox over to me!"

"Watch out, Semion Semionych, don't miss!"

"Don't doubt a thing, Vladim Sergev! We won't mess up! That's official!"

At that point Gobbler appeared. She immediately saw the fox. The black-white-and-tan skewbald began to howl and after a running start leaped with all four paws onto the ice. Two or three hops, and the ice broke under her with a crack. Paying no attention to anything, the brave dog rushed toward the fox, breaking the ice with her chest. The fox had gone completely mad. She was furiously circling in the water.

Gobbler quickly came near her, and after a minute a desperate, mortal struggle began in the frigid water. The dog and the beast seized hold of each other's muzzles. A fountain of icy spray rose up around them. What a gripping and exciting scene! Gobbler was trying to seize her enemy by the throat, but every time she tried, water flowed into her open maw and she choked. Then the sharp teeth of the fox would sink into Gobbler's ear or lip. Gobbler was trying to crush the fox under her and drown her, but the fox was devilishly agile and resourceful. She defended herself valorously.

This went on for half an hour . . . Half an hour in frigid water amid floating ice floes—what suffering that must have been! Finally the two adversaries disappeared under the water. Judging from the gurgling, they were continuing the struggle even there. It was a terrible moment. It seemed that they had both perished. But now Gobbler's head appeared out of the water. She had conquered! Next to her floated the red body of a full-grown fox.

What feelings filled us to overflowing!

Incomparable Gobbler! No dog had ever caused her masters to experience such bright, unforgettable moments!

"Hurra-a-h!" Semion Semionych shouted. "Gobbler! Gobbler dear! Gobbler darling!"

The dog turned towards the bank. It was obvious that she had worn herself out. Breaking the ice with her front paws, now and then she would sink into the water over her head. She was breathing wearily and heavily. Wheezing burst from her bloody maw. She was sinking more and more often. Her movements became slower and slower. She was swimming toward me. Semion Semionych ran over to my bank. We wanted to jump into the pond and help the dog. But now she made a terrible effort and reached the bank. We bent over the water and pulled Gobbler out onto dry land.

How tormented she looked. Her ears were torn, her lips were bloody. The dog collapsed to the ground with a wheeze. Her whole body was trembling and twitching. We bent over her. She looked into my eyes with a strange, dimming glance, and then looked at Semion Semionych. Suddenly her multicolored body was contorted in a terrible convulsion, and she fell motionless . . . Her dog's heart could not hold out—Gobbler was dead!

Semion Semionych and I were struck as if by lightning.

"The black-white-and-tan skewbald has died . . . She must have hunted herself out! Vladim Sergev . . . How can it be? What's going to happen to us now? What do we do now?"

Tears choked us. Gobbler! Priceless, dear Gobbler!

"What do we do? There's only one thing left to do: let's bury her. We're not going to leave her to be eaten by foxes, are we? Let's ask for a shovel in that peasant hut near the dam."

Silently we buried our dog in the black, not yet frozen earth, and formed a neat little mound over her. Semion Semionych stood over the grave, took his gun, and cocked it.

"What are you going to do?"

"A salute! If we're going to bury her, then let's bury her with a conscience!"

Semion Semionych fired twice into the air. I followed his example. Then Semion Semionych took off the silver horn that Gobbler had won at the provincial dog show, and blew a prolonged blast.

Sobber, Dokuka, and Dokuka's children suddenly came running at the sound of our shots and the horn. They had probably caught their hare and were now looking for us. They were worn out and immediately sat down at our feet around Gobbler's grave. Semion Semionych sounded the horn again. Suddenly all four dogs craned their heads upward. The dogs' prolonged, heart-breaking howl resounded far into the distance over the earth powdered with snow. How they howled! It seems they understood everything.

Oh, you poor beasts! You won't see Gobbler again . . . You won't see your old friend . . .

"Vladim Sergev, we should leave some kind of official marker on the grave. For example, a stake with a little plaque, and an inscription on the plaque. Let the hunters who will hunt here read it and get some feeling for who our black-white-and-tan skewbald was."

I got a pencil and began to compose an inscription for the grave. It came out very long and ceremonious—just the way epitaphs are usually written. I read my composition aloud. Semion Semionych quietly shook his head:

"No, Vladim Sergev, it's no good: there's no soul in it . . . not enough feeling. Let me give it a try."

He took the pencil from me and, sniffling the whole time, took a long time to write something, frequently crossing out words and writing again. Finally he read me the following:

> The black-white-and-tan skewbald
> On Shchadilov Pond
> Officially strangled
> A full-grown fox.
> She passed away from her efforts
> After the demise of the fox.
> The burial took place
> Right here on the third
> Of November, the year 1926.
> Rest in peace, courageous bitch,
> Under the shade of the reeds!
> Let others take a lesson from
> How you hunted foxes.
> She gave chase briskly,
> But was a little humpbacked,
> Her voice was Italian,
> But she died on the feast of the Kazan icon of the
> Mother of God (according to the Julian calendar).
>
> Respectfully, S. Bochonkin and V. Khvoshch.

This poem, written by my friend out of the fullness of his heart, to this day adorns the humble little grave of the unforgettable black-white-and-tan skewbald dog Gobbler. All our hunters know it by heart.

Letters from Exile

Translator's Preface

VLADIMIR TRUBETSKOI wrote these letters from internal exile in Andijon (Andizhan), Uzbekistan, to his nephew Vladimir Golitsyn (who was also in exile). The letters were written between 1934 and 1937, the year in which Trubetskoi was arrested and shot. (The "Notes of a Cuirassier" were written during this same period and are alluded to in the later letters.) Trubetskoi's wife, Elizaveta Vladimirovna Trubetskaia (née Golitsyna, called "Elia" in the letters), was arrested in 1943 and died in Butyrki Prison in Moscow a month later. Following is a list of Trubetskoi's children, with birth and (where appropriate) death dates:

Grigorii (Grisha)	1912–75 (arrested in 1937; in prison camp for ten years)
Varvara (Varia)	1917–37 (shot three months after arrest)
Aleksandra (Tatka)	1919–43 (died in prison camp)
Andrei	1920–2002
Irina	1922–
Vladimir	1924–92 (lost a leg in World War II)
Sergei	1928–
Georgii (Egor, Gotka)	1934– (now a farmer near Moscow)

The letters are accompanied by a brief introduction by Vladimir Trubetskoi's son Andrei:

Several of my father's letters from Andijon to Vladimir Mikhailovich Golitsyn in Dmitrov and Gudauty have been miraculously preserved.[1] In them is vividly described our life full of cares, and our surroundings, and Father himself, a witty man of cheerful disposition and keen linguistic talent. It was impossible to establish the exact date of some letters; the ends of some letters have been lost.

1

May 1934

From beneath the very roof of the World—the Pamirs, dear Golyshka, I send you my broad central Asian greeting.[2] Although the greeting is from the Center, it is extreme, because it comes from a pure heart and an abundance of emotion. I long ago received your letter with the description of Klavdiia [the fiancée of Golitsyn's brother Sergei] and I laughed like a hyena while reading it. I think you have taken this incident too much to heart—the business isn't all that dramatic. I advise you to console yourself with wise old Russian proverbs. One of them says that love is wicked and one can fall not only for Klavdiia but for a smelly goat. Another claims that no one drinks anything (strong or weak) from a person's face, and therefore you can reconcile yourself to any physiognomy and even get used to it . . . in short, "you don't drink water from someone's face" [beauty is only skin-deep]. As for the fact that your *belle soeur* sometimes says "adventure" instead of "accident"—well, I personally am willing to forgive her such a mistake, because I know a number of most respectable and respected people who in some cases say "I beg your pardon" instead of "Sorry." By the way, I'd bet that you yourself have had occasion in recent months to run into a certain kind of personality whose linguistic mistakes are a hundred times worse than Klavdiia's . . . Well, enough about Klavdiia. I greet both her and Sergei in a central Asian way. Let's talk about central Asia. So I'm in it (that is, in that central thing itself). It's beautiful! I am in the Fergana Valley, surrounded on all sides by gigantic mountains. But let's begin at the beginning—first let's talk about *parandzhas* [face veils, Uzbek *paranji*], then about *aryks* [irrigation canals], camels, and other things Asiatic.

The *parandzha* is a wonderful thing! No husband has the right to fold back the *parandzha* from the face of his wife's girlfriend. Husbands cannot forbid their little wives to receive their veiled friends. That's the law, and just think, dear nephew, what marvelous opportunities and prospects this law opens up for enterprising Lovelaces![3] Under the guise of bashful female friends, shameless and randy young Uzbek men, picturesquely covered by the *parandzha,* visit the wives of their friends and cuckold them in the very best way . . . I'd like to buy myself an orange *parandzha,* but I'm afraid I missed my chance—Aunt Elia has come . . . And my height is also a problem: Uzbek women are petite, and it wouldn't be hard to expose a daring beanpole in a *parandzha* and at the same time stick a jealous little eight-inch blade between his shoulder blades or into his navel, *ad libidum* (as is the custom here near the Pamirs). The overwhelming majority of women here are still covered by *parandzhas* and only a comparatively few advanced women have thrown off their veils and shown themselves to an astonished world.[4] Indeed, these "advanced" women have turned out to be pretty and there are a few real darlings

1. Vladimir Sergeevich Trubetskoi in the dress uniform of
Her Majesty's Life Guards Cuirassier Regiment, or
Blue Cuirassiers, 1912

2. Elizaveta Vladimirovna Golitsyna (later Trubetskaia)
in costume for a masquerade ball, 1910

3. V. S. Trubetskoi and E. V. Golitsyna, betrothed couple, summer 1912

4. At the Golitsyn estate Zhelezniaki, 1913. From left: E. V. Trubetskaia, her mother Sofia Nikolaevna Golitsyna, her father Vladimir Mikhailovich Golitsyn, her sister Tatiana Vladimirovna Golitsyna, Vladimir Sergeevich Trubetskoi.

5. In front of the house at the Trubetskoi estate Menshovo, 1910. From left:
E. V. Obolenskaia, Praskovia Vladimirovna Trubetskaia (mother of Nikolai and
Vladimir Trubetskoi), Nikolai Sergeevich Trubetskoi (the future linguist), Vladimir
Sergeevich Trubetskoi (in his navy uniform); members of the Gagarin family.

6. In front of the house at the Trubetskoi estate Menshovo, 1913. At far left is
E. V. Trubetskaia, next to the horse is V. S. Trubetskoi, the others are unidentified.

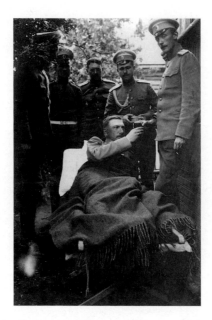

7. A scene from camp life at the maneuvers of the Guards
regiments, 1912. At far right is V. S. Trubetskoi.

8. Taking a break on maneuvers during "patrol exercises," 1912. At far left is
V. S. Trubetskoi, in the center is the regimental commander, P. I. Arapov.

9. From left: E. V. Trubetskaia, V. S. Trubetskoi with their daughter Tatiana on his lap (Tatiana died of illness in 1917, in St. Petersburg), Nikolai Sergeevich Trubetskoi, Praskovia Vladimirovna Trubetskaia. Photograph taken in 1914 before Vladimir's departure for the front, at Menshovo.

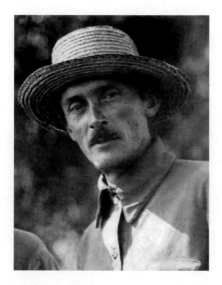

10. V. S. Trubetskoi, Sergiev Posad, 1920s

11. The addressee of Vladimir Trubetskoi's letters, Vladimir Mikhailovich Golitsyn, and his wife Elena Petrovna Golitsyna (née Sheremeteva), 1923

12. V. S. Trubetskoi hunting. Winter, Sergiev Posad, 1920s. Next to him is his dog Palma. According to Vladimir's son Andrei Vladimirovich, this dog was distinguished by unusual intelligence and charm, and would pull fighting children away from each other by the seat of their pants.

13. V. S. Trubetskoi hunting in the neighborhood of Sergiev Posad, 1920s

14. The family of Sergei Nikolaevich Trubetskoi. From left: Sergei Nikolaevich, Vladimir, Nikolai, Praskovia Vladimirovna, Mariia. Menshovo, 1904.

15. V. S. Trubetskoi in costume for a masquerade ball at the Glebovs, 1900

16. At the Trubetskoi estate Menshovo, 1910. From left: Nikolai Sergeevich Trubetskoi, unidentified, Praskovia Vladimirovna Trubetskaia, Vladimir Sergeevich Trubetskoi, Mikhail Osorgin (the father of Mishanchik), Mariia Sergeevna Trubetskaia.

17. "Vladim Sergev," V. S. Trubetskoi hunting, 1920s. Drawing by
V. M. Golitsyn for the hunting stories of V. Trubetskoi

18. V. S. Trubetskoi, 1907

19. V. S. Trubetskoi hunting with the writer Mikhail Prishvin, Sergiev Posad, 1920s

20. The family of Sergei Nikolaevich Trubetskoi, mid-1890s:
Sergei Nikolaevich and Praskovia Vladimirovna with (*from left*)
Mariia, Vladimir, and Nikolai

21. V. S. Trubetskoi doing a test run in a large metal washtub on the Bogoroditsk pond, 1920. He is holding a pole for steering the "boat" and an umbrella (serving as a sail). This real-life incident serves as the subject of the story "The Death of the Dirigible."

22. Grand Duke Nikolai Nikolaevich, 1910

23. The patroness of the Blue Cuirassier Regiment, Empress Mariia Fiodorovna.
Portrait by Genria-fon-Angeli, 1874.

24. Scene from the parade of the Blue Cuirassier Regiment in the presence of the
regimental patroness Empress Mariia Fiodorovna, 1900s. In the carriage are
the Empress and the Grand Duchess Mariia Pavlovna, surrounded by members
of the Imperial suite and officers of the regiment.

25. The standard platoon of Her Majesty's Life Guards Cuirassier
Regiment in dress uniform, 1900s

26. The commander of Her Majesty's Life Guards Cuirassier Regiment (from
1899 to 1901), Major General Baron Rausch von Taubenberg, in dress uniform

27. The officers' club of the Blue Cuirassier Regiment in Gatchina

28. Grand Duke Nikolai Nikolaevich

29. Tsar Nicholas II. Portrait by E. K. Lipgart, 1900

30. Vladimir Sergeevich and Elizaveta Vladimirovna Trubetskaia
after their marriage, 1912

Герб князей Трубецких

31. "Gerb"—coat of arms of the Trubetskoi family

among them—swarthy little sweeties. They wear multicolored trousers and draw their eyebrows into one line with black dye, and from under those brows they shoot piercing glances from little eye-pistols. These darlings braid their raven hair into fifteen or twenty little plaits, which to my taste looks better than our hairdos like the "fox-trot." A modest and silent little flirtation started up between me and one of these babes who lives in our lane (Uzbek women don't speak Russian at all, and so far I've managed to learn only "bulbul," which means "nightingale," and "yakshi kizinka"—"beautiful girl"). The flirtation so far consists of the following: when I walk by my darling I silently give her a papirosa, and she, with a pensive smile, confers upon me a crimson rose. This all seemed poetic to me until one time when my darling, after taking the papirosa from me, blew her nose on her little fingers and wiped her snotty hand on her multicolored little trousers. This gesture somewhat grated on my poetic feelings and I no longer make an effort to treat my rather dirty lady friend to a papirosa.

The bashfulness of the women here is amazing. For instance, the city has two lines for buying bread—a male line and a female line. If on a stifling day outside the city you meet a group of Uzbek women walking from the bazaar with their *parandzhas* folded back, as soon as they catch sight of you from about 150 paces away, all the girls, old and young, as if on command, turn their backs to you, squat down, put their goods on the ground, and hasten to cover themselves with the *parandzha*. In this position the girls let you go by, and only when you've gone a good distance do these untamed women finally come out of their state of petrification. I tried, under cover of cornstalks, to let some of these girls get within five paces of me, and then I flew out at them face to face . . . and what do you know? Not a squeal, not a scream, not a smile! My little savages turned their backs on me quickly, but with dignity, and squatted down, covering themselves with the *parandzha*.

Until lately a man had to marry a girl "in the dark," so to speak, because he didn't have the right to look at her until after the wedding. Now times are changing and before registering civil marriages in the local *zags* they require that the bride fold back her *parandzha* and show the groom her mug.[5] It often happens that after looking at his bride in the *zags* the groom refuses to marry her. This happened a few days ago to one of my Uzbek friends, who almost married a one-eyed, pockmarked woman.

Well, enough about women! . . . The *aryks* are also interesting. I'll tell you briefly about the *aryks* and I'm even planning to send you a whole article about them for the journal *The Young Guard*. The rich, fertile Fergana Valley turns out to be the cradle of artificial irrigation, which has been used here for thousands of years, and perhaps even earlier than in Egypt. The entire complicated irrigation system, millions of cubic meters of excavations needed to dig the *aryks*, has all been done and continues to be done with the most primitive aboriginal tool—the mattock, with which the Uzbeks still dig around in the earth, preferring it to the spade. This slave labor is rewarded a hundred-fold . . . You stroll along the bank of a rushing natural river that winds under a high cliff, and you can't figure out how a deep and powerful *aryk* came to be flowing along above the river at the height of a church steeple. There are no hydraulic towers to be seen. Sometimes such *aryks* flow in parallel, one above the other, three to five stories apart. *Aryks* have been built and dug for dozens and hundreds of miles from streams, and ramify into hundreds of branches; you encounter them at every step, they furrow the whole country. Huge fields, miniature kitchen gardens in the *kishlaks* [central Asian villages], city and country yards—all are irrigated, all are filled with the talkative sound of running water. There are no wells anywhere. Every little heathen boy imbibes the art of irrigation with his mother's milk, knows where to dig an *aryk*, and can irrigate an entire field in a trice without a watering can, damming up his little *aryk* now here, now there for a half hour at a time, knowing how to manipulate the level of water. The fields are divided into horseshoe-shaped, spiral, straight, and crooked plots, between which the water flows, and to our eyes this has a very curious appearance. I met an irrigation engineer here who is nicknamed "the water god." He told me the most astronomical figures on the number of cubic meters of excavations for irrigation. This engineer is adorned by a beautiful scar on his forehead—a souvenir of a *basmach*'s saber.[6] He told me lots of marvelous stories about the Uzbeks: in order to irrigate a certain region or field, Russian engineers first carry out complicated surveying and calculations and only then do they begin excavating. The old illiterate Uzbeks do the whole job without any surveying and *never* (!) make a mistake in choosing the most advantageous direction for an *aryk*. They walk out onto the field, bend down to the ground a time or two, looking off into the distance—and it's in the bag: they have it all figured out and determined with amazing accuracy (and this has been verified many times). There are many curious traditions and genuine historical facts concerning water that have been passed on by the old men. Water is *everything* for the Fergana Valley. And how wildly fertile is this grayish, clayey soil, furrowed with *aryks* lengthwise, crosswise, and obliquely! The whole valley is just a luxuriant garden. We climbed the big hills near the city . . . and what do you think . . . the whole city with a population of about 100,000, situated in the foothills, was *completely* invisible, so hidden were its buildings by the trees. It seemed as if there were not a city beneath us, but a dense forest.

The abundance of ditches in the country has influenced the type of vehicle used. The carts here have the hugest wheels—higher than my head—in order to cross the *aryks* more easily.

Well, enough about irrigation! Write and tell me whether this sketch would be suitable for the journal. I can also write about silkworms. I wanted to write you a very long letter today, but it's so hot—I'm getting exhausted. There are a lot of strange things here, but every day you get used to your surroundings and aren't struck by anything any more. I've gotten sick of camels and don't find them a proud sight any more. Just think—what do they have to be proud of!—there's a rope through his nostrils, his coat is shabby. They're big tall fellows, but they follow so submissively on their rope behind the tiny little ass, who is very simple and nice and isn't proud at all, but matter-of-factly drags behind him on the rope a single file of thirty camels, called (who knows why) the "ships of the desert." What kind of ships are they, when even little kids beat them for no reason at all! No, our old Russian nags are prouder in my opinion, especially when they neigh. A nag begins to stamp her hooves, and her shoes ring against the pavement until sparks fly! . . . But a camel just shuffles along soundlessly, as if he's wearing felt boots without soles—no chic, no brilliance. Only his mug is contemptuous. Squinty eyes, sagging lower lip, stick a lit cigar in his mouth and he'll look just like a diehard conservative English lord.

I'm glad for your Mashenka for refusing her admirer. By the way I also sympathize with the poor "parachutists."[7] You know . . . (but I beg of you, don't say anything about it yet)—my Varia also got the idea of refusing her admirer and says that over the last few months her admirer had shown himself to be unworthy of either love or respect! Aunt Elia and I are secretly glad of this, although on principle I scolded my little daughter: what did she see in him earlier?! Strictly speaking, I find that maidens who accept a proposal and then reject it are not quite in the right—mainly from the point of view of their rich and distant relatives, who hardly succeed in congratulating them and sending the whole Torgsin as a dowry before they receive notification that the wedding's off.[8] Now our rich relatives will be wiser, and I'm afraid they'll stop succumbing to our matrimonial blackmail and sending money for such dubious affairs. For purely "Torgsin" considerations we'll have to invent something different. For example, we could send overseas a sad epistle like the following:

Letter No. 1
"Dear relatives, alas, alas! Uncle has died. Immediately send us some bucks for Uncle's coffin and prayers for the repose of his soul. We are with you in spirit."

Upon receiving the Torgsin notice from our relatives we can write our dear ones a joyful letter with the following content:

Letter No. 2
"Dear relatives, hurrah, hurrah, hurrah! Uncle is alive and had no intention of dying, but was just indulging in a two-week-long lethargic sleep . . . What

haven't we endured! . . . Greetings. We're with you in spirit. Uncle sends you a kiss."

By the way, dear Volodka, please don't think that I personally intend to engage in blackmail. I have cited these invented letters only because of my conviction that "Letter No. 2" differs very little in essence from our letters announcing the broken engagements, and must inevitably produce exactly the same feeling in our relatives, causing them both annoyance and regret over money spent in vain. No, say what you will, although I sympathize with the pretty but vacillating young ladies, at the same time I condemn them for so unwarily promising to marry such not very attractive suitors. Did they really not have enough spirit to reject a begging and pleading enamored bore? (and what must be the state of the latter!). I personally, as the father of my daughter, am ashamed and feel terribly awkward vis-à-vis my dear distant relatives, who responded to our important family event and sent money for the wedding . . . I know very well that money does not come at all easily to these distant relatives right now (you can write to Linochka about this).

Well, I'm done. I'm tired. Have you heard what happened to my Irinochka when she got stuck in Samara? All thanks to the petty-bourgeois mentality displayed by my dear family! While they were passing through Samara, they sent the unfortunate little kid out of the train to get boiling water. The little kid toted a whole teapot full to her brothers, sisters, and mother. Then they discovered that the rusty tin lid of the teapot had disappeared. They yelled horribly at the little kid and sent her onto the platform to look for the lid at the terrible moment between the conductor's whistle and the answering whistle of the locomotive. The thing that had to happen happened: the train started off without the lid to the teapot and without my beloved little shock-worker kid, whom my family had the pleasure of observing out of the window of the train-car as she ran with all her little might with the lid in her hands, dropping hot tears on the cold railroad ties, following the train as it moved away.[9] None of my idiots had the sense to pull the emergency cord. Grishka was sent back to Samara from the next station to get Irinochka. Grigorii didn't send a telegram and the family arrived in Andijon without the lid, without Grishka, and without Irinochka, who had disappeared without a trace for more than two days. On the third day I got nervous and was already starting to equip a new rescue expedition to Samara. In short, the terrible drama of the rescue of Nobile was about to be repeated, in which the role of Nobile was played by Irinochka, and the role of the doomed Amundsen was played by Grishka.[10] I was already preparing to send my own *Malygin* and *Krasin* to save Nobile and Amundsen, when they both announced themselves, having arrived in Andijon with the train *Maksim*. The reunion was very emotional. Irinochka appeared before us with the rusty bent tin lid in her hands, for which she was awarded the title of "meritorious family little kid" and promised a new outfit . . . By the way, congratulate us—along the way my family ran over a camel and enjoyed the sight of his entrails, which got so thickly wound around the wheels of the locomotive that it was stuck for a quarter of an hour. Continued on postcard. [Postcard No. 1 with a view of the cotton bazaar in the old town. On the picture side of the postcard is written: "The arrow indicates not sacks, but the backs of women wearing face veils. Can you feel how hot it is here?"]

I am sending you views of the old and new towns of Andijon. The new town does not differ from any other town. But the old town! . . . On the second postcard is a picture of the street where my "garden-restaurant" is located, in which I play every day without a day off from 6:30 in the evening to 2:00 A.M. I earn a fair amount of money, but I get exhausted. My garden-restaurant is a marvelous little spot. The little tables are set up right under cherry, apricot, and pear trees, and the garden is full of blooming roses. The clientele is decent and even well-dressed, with some good-looking babes. Moscow could envy such a garden. Our repertoire is Muscovite. In general it's a lively city. There's a circus, an operetta, clubs, a theater, a wonderful amusement park, three restaurants with good music. [Postcard No. 2 with a view of the main street, Lenin Prospect, and the District Party Committee building.]

I am expecting a letter from you, and please write to the *post office*, general delivery (poste restante), because letters addressed to my address in the neighborhood Kzyl-karvan get lost. Well, so long . . . I press your hand.

I *really, really* hope you will come visit us. But the devil take it, get your idiotic leg healed finally! How I regret that I don't know how to paint. Everything here just begs to be painted, and in watercolor. I looked at your blacksmiths—there's nothing particularly interesting about them. I warmly greet all your relatives.

2

[Postcard addressed to Dmitrov, Moscow District, Semeniuk Street, No. 26, Golitsyn family. On the postcard is a picture of a combine with the slogan, "A machine in good repair will ensure a harvest of good quality!"]

12 June [1934]

My dear ones!

Miracle of miracles, tra-la-la
My old lady gave birth to a son [Georgii]!
Despite her 45 years
She's given birth again.

He was born near Andijon.
We'll call the kid African.
The fifth Trubetskoi boy,
Very big and fat,
Was born in burning heat.

The heat here is African and therefore we had to name the kid African, although it would be more correct to call him central Asian, but there is no such saint in the calendar, no matter how we and the priest searched for it. The birth was quick and easy. Elli feels well but is grumbling. But for me it was like water off a duck's back, and I'm very happy although I was hoping for a little girl: all sons—as a rule—are loafers and good-for-nothings . . .

Your Uncle Vetov-Pamirskii

3

1 September 1934

Dear Vladimir,

I haven't written to anyone for a long time, since I simply haven't had the strength in this hellish heat, which we have been suffering without a break all through July and August. Today is the first bearable day. Remember how hot it was in Astrakhan? But even then I was able to write feuilletons for the Astrakhan newspaper. Here it's much hotter—I'm roasted through and through. It hasn't been less than 36° Celsius [97° Fahrenheit] in the *shade*. It has reached 40° [104° F] in the shade, and it's hard to describe what it's like in the sun. At noon you can't even think of going barefoot. You can fry eggs on the roof, and under the roof human blood and brains turn into carpenter's glue. Sweat pours off me in rivers all day. Night brings no coolness. The charms of the southern nights have been praised, in my opinion, by idiots. It's the same thing as finding charm in a dark, heated-up bathhouse or kitchen. The only difference is that in the kitchen there are no frogs, but here the rascals not only croak but whistle like policemen all night from the *aryks*. We sleep completely naked in the courtyard. The whole country does the same. In Mangyshlak it is hot but dry. Here in the Fergana Valley, cut off by the mountains from the deserts and sands, it is hot and humid. It's strange for us to look at the eternal snows of the Pamir Mountains (the Alai range); we get nothing out of the nearness of that mass of snow and ice except picturesqueness, and you get sick of that fairly quickly. In general the subtropics are an acquired taste. Take, for example, the tropical mosquitoes—what torment for the newcomer! The mosquito is hardly visible to the eye and bites very softly so that you don't even feel it, and as a result the newcomer's whole body experiences an unbearable itching and is covered with purulent blisters similar to small-pox. Arms, legs, chest, face—all one scab. It's still pitiful to look at Aunt Elia. The children and I have already gotten over it—the organism has adapted. Because of the mosquitoes we have suffered all summer from mosquito fever—"pappataci." A 40° [104° F] fever without chills that lasts for three days. Then utter weakness and apathy for two weeks. Loss of appetite and sense of taste for the same period. We all experienced what one might call subtropical diarrhea as well—but it's better not to write about such nasty stuff. I also had occasion to be subjected to yet another powerful subtropical plea-sure—a scorpion sting. (We've already found six scorpions in our apartment since we arrived.) This serious bastard usually crawls into your towel, night-shirt, or underpants at night while they're hanging on the wall, and bright and early it stings the honest worker in whatever part of the body it comes upon—stings him so badly that the honest full-grown worker rolls on the floor for two or three hours and, with no fear of God, howls unprintable words. This hap-pened to me personally once in the morning, when after washing I started to dry my neck with a towel in which a scorpion had hidden . . . Some time try screwing a red-hot poker onto your neck for two or three hours. Then you'll have a perfect idea of the pleasure that a scorpion's stinger can offer.

Besides these purely subtropical pleasures there are also universally human joys here, and the main joy for us is fruit. Mountains of red, juicy, big, fragrant, and, most important, *cheap* fruit.

Peaches of all sorts—5 kopecks apiece
Watermelons—25 k./kilo
Grapes (marvelous)—80k./kilo (they say they'll get even cheaper)
Melons (heavenly)—35 k./kilo
Fresh figs—75 k./kilo

Pomegranates, walnuts, almonds, etc., etc. Every day at dinner we eat moun-tains of fruit—a regular *nature morte* of the old school! It's pleasant to look at and to gorge oneself on. Right now the local bazaars are nothing but fruit. It's really worth painting the appetizing picture in watercolors: on the carts, under the carts, on the ground, on the tables, in the stalls—piles, hills, mountains of yellow, orange, green, red, and purple fruit, and all around donkeys, camels, and Asiatics in multicolored robes under an astounding cloudless sky.

I haven't written any stories yet and it's not because of laziness. In the daytime it's too hot for my brain, which has turned to mush. In the evening I play piano in the outdoor restaurant until 2:00 A.M., and in the morning I work until noon in the Uzbek State Theater, where to the sounds of my piano a dar-ling ballerina, sent for specially from Moscow, teaches the Uzbek actors eu-rhythmics, ballet steps, the polka, and the fox-trot. Actors in robes, actors in trousers. Not artists but wild animals—they can neither talk nor move in a European way, but my darling ballerina has been ordered to introduce them to European culture. After you watch this for a while, your belly would burst from laughing if it weren't so hot. I saw her force the actors to try the fox-trot for the first time. The cavaliers stubbornly refused to hold the ladies close. Finally they were persuaded to do it, but after three minutes some of the actors turned pale, started to shake, and began breathing heavily. Two actors, very embarrassed, categorically demanded that they be excused from the fox-trot, since it was too exciting. They were very ashamed, but they could not vouch for themselves—after all, they're living men, not sticks! And it was too hard (simply impossible) to restrain their feelings. All this was completely serious! The Uzbeks have devilish temperaments, and it seems there's a reason why they form two lines in stores—one for women and one for men—it's because of the Uzbek temperament, which makes it quite impossible for a woman to stand in a common line with Uzbek men. Now you understand the deep significance of the *parandzha*.

The Uzbek theater in Andijon is very good. It is considered the second best in central Asia after the Tashkent theater. The winter and summer stages are beautifully equipped with turntables for scenery changes. The budget is a little less than a million (the government subsidy alone is 400,000 rubles). There are 180 employees. The productions are by Uzbek authors and directors, but now that a Russian director and ballerina have arrived we are starting work on some European productions in the Uzbek language. This is unbelievably hard. There is material for short stories here. I've long been planning a little book called *Memoirs of a Soviet Musician*. There are tons of material . . . But when can I write? In the morning the theater, in the evening and at night the restaurant. After lunch it's hot and your uncle, who's starting to grow old, needs to rest. I want to write stories, but it's both scary and a shame to give up my salary in the theater, since there's no guarantee that anyone will publish me. After all, I alone have to carry an entire huge family on my powerful shoulders. Grisha has gone to work in the mountains for reasons of climate and health, and his salary is hardly enough to feed himself. He's working in the little town of Gulcha on a Pamir road not far from the Chinese and Afghan borders. By the way, he saw that very Chinese general and Chinese detachment of Mauser riflemen who had to be interned in the U.S.S.R. because they were being pursued by Chinese government troops (they wrote about this in the major newspapers). In general, Grisha is living in a wild area and sees a lot of interesting local color, and I envy him. In the mountains his asthma disappears completely, but all he has to do is to descend into the Fergana Valley and the terrible illness begins to torment him again. I am sending you some rather interesting clippings from the local newspaper *Pravda of the East*. Aren't these good subjects for short stories? Work and heat have not permitted me to go hunting yet. But now there is supposed to be some beautiful fall weather and I will soon set off to hunt wild boar. There are a lot of them in a place about thirteen miles from Andijon, where people lie in wait for them at night in rice fields and vegetable gardens. We will be very happy if Seriozha and his wife come here. Workers in his field are needed here.

I send you my love. I kiss Elena's little hands and send warm greetings to all your family.[11]

Uncle

Do you plan to come here and when? How is your leg? I'm waiting for a letter. Oh, of course the children lost the interesting newspaper clippings . . . Just try to write short stories!

4

[end of 1934]

Dear Vladimir,

Forgive me for taking so long to answer your last postcard. A few days ago I received a kind letter from V. A. Popov asking me to work on the journal *Pathfinder of the Urals*.[12] I'm very glad that this dear journal is being reborn and of course if it will be the kind of journal it used to be, I will work there with pleasure. I am, however, somewhat disturbed by the fact that the *Pathfinder* will now be *of the Urals,* and as Popov writes, will be filled mainly with Ural motifs. This is too bad. I don't know the Urals and only crossed them twice on a train, looking out the car window. Popov asks me to write Bochonkin and Khvoshch of the Urals. As I understand he's talking not about one or two stories but about a whole *series,* and purely relating to the Urals, and this is not at all easy for me. As a beginning I can offer only central Asian stories: the *Pamirs* (in particular the Pamir border guards), *the hunt* (for tigers, leopards, boars), *the silk master, scorpions, the struggle for water, the basmach phenomenon* (which is still fresh in people's memories here and the echoes of which are still being felt), *the subtropical institute, earthquakes,* and other central Asiatica. Will this suit the new *Pathfinder* . . . or will it maybe suit some other journal? Write to me how much they're paying per page now. I'm sick of the local theater and quit my job there, so now I have time to write stories. This is an adventurer's land and I think that hardly any other place in the Soviet Union is so full of adventure as right here. Now I'm working as a musician in the best restaurant, located in the best hotel, and every day I see all sorts of adventurers (in the good sense of this word, with a purely Jack London orientation). There are various engineers who have just come down from the Pamirs, or doctors who have stopped in here from the desert for a few days, gold prospectors, scientists returning from expeditions, finally a border guard with a fresh scar, or a public prosecutor come to investigate a fresh crime. All these people are stuffed with quite warm adventure tales, and when they end up in Andijon, they head for my tavern, where the old pathfinder Vetov [Trubetskoi's pseudonym] spreads his nets and over a bottle of wine catches fresh new themes. They all still remember Vetov, because they all read the *Pathfinder* and therefore they're glad to talk to *Vetov* about pathfinder themes. Now I've begun to write a story about the local silk craftsmen and about a sorcerer who heals with scorpion poison. It's an adventure story. It's hard to write. I've gotten out of the habit. After all, I haven't written anything for four years. I'm afraid I may have forgotten how to write. As soon as I finish the story about silk I'll start a little story "à la Maupassant," the plot of which is based on a real event narrated to me by a public prosecutor. Here's the essence of the story.

Two years ago an expedition down the Amu Darya River was made on a *kaiuk* [large Uzbek boat] by a group of people assembled by chance: the public prosecutor, a bookkeeper, his assistant, a Red Army soldier, a botanist, and an unattractive factory mechanic along with his wife Sonechka (a bold little babe). The group put in to shore for the night. They have a bite to eat. Moonlight. Suddenly—*basmachi.* A whole hullabaloo. They tie up the men and get ready to dissect them alive, but the leader of the *basmachi* takes a real liking to Sonechka. He tells Sonechka that he is going to keep her as his concubine. At this point my babe suddenly tears herself away and rushes toward the Amu Darya. The head *basmach* follows her. There's a terrifying cliff over the abyss. Sonechka says, "Not another step or I'll throw myself into the whirlpool." The leader tries to talk her out of it. They bargain. The babe agrees to stay with the *basmachi,* but only under the condition that the leader immediately frees all the captive men and lets them go. The enamored leader agrees. They let the men go and they start rowing with all their might to the next town. Sonechka's husband, a puny and ill-favored laborer, is beside himself: he suffers, wrings his hands in despair and moans, "Save my Sonia!" . . . The *kaiuk* arrives at the town. The prosecutor kicks up a fuss. They immediately send a detachment, which in the course of a week captures all the *basmachi* and saves the captive woman. They ceremoniously convey Sonechka to the town. They recommend her for a decoration and in honor of the heroic babe they arrange a ceremonial banquet. There are a lot of speeches and toasts glorifying the selfless babe who sacrificed herself for the salvation of Soviet citizens . . .

The real zest of the story is at the end: After the banquet, remaining alone with the babe, the prosecutor expresses his rapture at her resoluteness and exclaims: "Sonechka, *what* a sacrifice you made! . . . and where did you get such courage and bravery?" And the babe laughs and replies:

"I don't understand, what bravery are you talking about? And what exactly did I sacrifice? You saw the *basmach* leader, didn't you?"

"Well, of course I saw him . . . So what?"

"What do you mean 'so what'? That guy was *great!* . . ." And Sonechka slyly gives the prosecutor a thumb's-up sign.

This is all true from beginning to end. I just think I'll make the mechanic a hairdresser and make Sonechka a townswoman. Would this little story suit some journal?

I'm thinking of putting together a whole little collection of "Central Asian Stories," which could also include our old Caspian adventures "The Siege of the Lighthouse," "The Gift of Suleiman," and "Between Land and Sea."

Yes . . . today is your papa's name day. I congratulate him on his saint's day and on Linochka's engagement.[13] I know the groom to be a very upright and decent lad. You don't hear anything bad but good about him. Of course, he's not a very clever fellow and he won't set the world on fire, but why set the world on fire? To hell with it! Decency and honesty are more durable than fire. I'm sincerely glad for Linochka and ask you to write her that I congratulate her and am sorry that I won't be able to dance at her wedding.

We're doing well. For the October holidays the last rose bloomed in our little courtyard. During the day it's still warm, but at night there's frost. The sky is cloudless. I go hunting for little hares, which can be found right outside the town. Our boar hunt fell through; you have to go for three or four days, but they won't let me off work for that long. Too bad. I content myself with small game. The problem is that I don't have a decent gun, and my friends in Moscow keep fooling me. In June a driver from Zagorsk was living with me here, and I gave him money to buy me a gun in Moscow and send it to me. Of course the driver ripped me off. He writes that he loves me very much, but he doesn't say anything about the money and the gun. I sent 110 rubles to another Zagorsk friend, the jurist Ialovetskii, well known for his probity. This Ialovetskii himself offered his services to Aunt Elia to buy a shotgun and send it to me. Now this guy writes that he received the money, but it's been three months and he hasn't sent the gun. I sent money to the musician Raevskii with a request to buy and send me strings and catgut for my violin bow. He writes that he received the money, but doesn't send the strings. How tedious and irritating this all is. Can you really not trust anyone?!

Oh, by the way, when Zhenia Durnovo visited us we sent fifty pounds of melons for you, Uncle Vovik, and for Niks.[14] Did you receive them? Write and tell me.

Listen, little nephew, are you planning to visit us? Please come, best of all would be in March or April, but be sure to come.

Warm greetings and so on.

Regards to Elena and all your family. Write to poste restante.

Uncle

5

26 December [1934]

Dear Vladimir,

Happy New Year!

I got your letter. Please write to us about the incident with Mashenka, Olia, and the architect. We already know about the Moscow announcements.[15]

    I am sending you my story "The Silk Master" by registered mail. Everything I write in this story about scorpions is true. I intended this story for *The Pathfinder,* but Popov wrote me that he needs exclusively Ural stories—how tedious! My story is long—it was intended for a thick journal (about 8,000 words). Where can it be published? Do what you want with it. Now I'm going to write about the adventure on the Amu Darya with Sonechka and the *basmachi.* I'll try to make it shorter and in a different, non-*Pathfinder* style. When you're in Moscow, call the violinist Anatolii Andreevich Raevskii—cuss him out for me. I sent him money long ago so that he would buy me a slide flute and a little jazz trumpet, but he of course swindled me. Tell him to send them immediately. In general he's not a bad guy and we were friends.

    We're still waiting for winter. Grisha, Varia, and Tatia are still sleeping in the courtyard under the awning, although it gets cold at night. But it's warm during the day. It's dry and dusty on the streets. I'm wearing my summer coat. The old-timers say that if there's no snow by January 10, there won't be any winter this year at all. Snow has attempted to fall only twice—but both times it just barely powdered the ground and melted all away in an hour.

    I'm suffering without a gun. I've been swindled by a driver from Zagorsk and a certain jurist named Ialovetskii (also an inhabitant of Zagorsk) to whom I sent money to buy me a gun in September. Well, so long. I'm expecting a letter. We really appreciated the incident with Academician Pavlov. Greetings to your family, I kiss Elena's hand with feeling. Happy holidays.

Your Uncle

Come visit us with Elena.

6

12 January 1935

Dear Vladimir,

Tomorrow is our birthday. Happy Birthday.

> Expecting winter, nature waited—
> Only in January the snow,
> Night of the second, started flaking.
> Next day Uncle Vetov, early waking,
> Saw through the window, morning-bright,
> Roofs, flowerbeds, and . . . the *duval*. . . .[16]

That was Jan. 9, on "Bloody Sunday."[17] Snow suddenly started to fall and continued without stopping for forty hours. It piled up fourteen inches deep. When it cleared, I went hunting gray hares with a certain Andrei Timofeich. The local hares had been so stunned by the deep snow that they hadn't left their lairs for three days and had been fasting. There was not a trace of them. Virgin snow everywhere.

In one of the vineyards right outside the city I notice a huge pile of brushwood frozen together. Just in case, I nudge the pile with my foot and I happen to notice at the very edge just one tiny little trace of a hare's paw the size of a five-kopeck piece. It's clear—there's a hare under the pile. Timofeich and I start shouting and kicking the pile—it doesn't come out! We climb up on the pile and start dancing and jumping on it, howling obscenities—it won't come out! Now I crawl into the pile with the greatest difficulty and shake the brush. No matter how I shake—the hare won't come out! Suddenly I see: a meter and a half away from me, two hares are sitting next to each other! I enter into negotiations with the hares and propose that they come out—they don't listen! I can't crawl any farther—the brush is too thick. I can't turn around. I talk loudly, start the cusswords going—they don't listen! The hares look at me, blink and snort steam from their nostrils. Timofeich advises: "Break off a twig and tickle the hare under its tail." I follow the advice. The hares kick, but don't come out. "Tickle them more energetically! Stick the twig up his asshole, don't be shy!" I stick it in his asshole—it makes no impression. Timofeich himself crawls in. From opposite sides of the pile, lying on our bellies, we try to persuade the hares to come out. If I could just stretch my hand out another ten inches—I could grab the hare by the ear, but I just can't do it. We mess around like this for about an hour and a half. There's already a whole crowd of Uzbeks around the brush pile. They're all giving advice. Finally with the greatest difficulty I manage to stick into the pile my gun that Prishvin sent me the other day.[18] I place the muzzle against the hare's very temple and for the last time I ask the hare to obey. The hare is silent. I pull the trigger. Misfire. Five misfires in a row. At every misfire the hare blinks like a human being. It's creepy! Finally the gun fires. I choke on the smoke. The hare has been liquidated. The Uzbeks run for an axe. We cut off a hooked stick with which we extricate the hare from the pile. He looks as if he's been put through a meat grinder. The second hare meets the same fate. We walk away from the pile. We wander around the vineyard. Under a grapevine powdered with snow sits a third hare. Threatening and inflexible, we approach him. We propose to the hare that he immediately leave his lair. Instead of jumping up, the hare presses himself to the ground and stretches out at attention. I find the idea of shooting him revolting. Timofeich shoots point-blank and cleanly knocks off the hare's head. We grimly carry three bloody hares into the city. We too are covered with blood . . . *January 9—Bloody Sunday!* Brr . . . No, that wasn't hunting, it was God knows what! Never in my entire life as a hunter have I encountered such strange and stubborn hares as they have here in central Asia.

Before January 9 we didn't have even a hint of snow. They were plowing the fields. There was dust in the city, and my three eldest children were sleeping in the courtyard all the time. Only today (Jan. 12) did Grisha and Varia move into the house to sleep. Tatka is being stubborn and still spends the night outside. Did you get my story "The Silk Master"? I kiss you, greet you, congratulate you!

Uncle

7

[A postcard with the slogan: "Each ruble deposited in a savings bank hastens the victory of socialism." Stamped by the Dmitrov post office February 27, 1935. Address: town of Dmitrov, Moscow District, Semeniuk Street No. 26, V. M. Golitsyn. Return address: Andizhan, Central Asia, Post Office, Vetov.]

Dear Vladimir,

I received your letter long ago. If they accepted my story, you can send the honorarium to the poste restante. I'm finishing a second story, "Sonechka from Turt-Kul." I'll send it in a few days. Winter has long been over here. It began on January 9 and ended with a pouring rain on February 1. Just three weeks of snow and frost. Now it's warm. My children are running around barefoot and naked (and this is instead of the frosts on Sretenka!).[19] Geese and ducks have been flocking here from India and Afghanistan for a week already—they nest on the *daryas* [rivers] and local lakes (from here to the bor-

124

der of India it's 250 miles as the crow flies. To Afghanistan it's even closer, and to China it's 155 miles). Come visit with Elena in April-May. Call Raevskii and cuss him out for deceiving me. I'm waiting for news from you. They're predicting an earthquake here. We've gotten ready to shake—it'll be a real laugh!

Love, Uncle

8

13 and 14 March

Dear Vladimir,

I'm sending you "Sonechka from Turt-Kul." I don't know whether it's a success. It seems to me that the Maupassant manner doesn't suit me, and no matter how I try to invent it, it all comes out in the *Pathfinder* style. I had Sonechka go bathing in order to create a mood that emphasizes her power to affect men sexually, and then, it seemed to me, it would be understandable why the *basmach* chief falls in love with her with such lightning speed. I don't know how it came out from the ideological point of view. I limited myself to the prosecutor's words: "Soviet power knows whom to reward and whom not to reward . . . We'll sort it out." I'm sending you my proxy for receiving the honorarium. Fill in the blanks yourself. I doubt very much, by the way, that my stories will be accepted. In my opinion there is no journal for them yet. But I don't feel like writing without encouragement: the times aren't right. My Varia has started writing quite well. She wrote "Sonechka from Turt-Kul" in her own way and without my influence. It came out not bad at all, but she's embarrassed to send her manuscript because she thinks that my version is better. I described the Amu Darya and the *kaiuks* quite correctly. Going upstream they are towed by horses. It's not good that too little space is allotted in the story to the Turkmen—not a single positive character—probably it shouldn't be this way.[20]

Our weather has been summery all along, like the end of May. The trees started to turn green, flowers and frogs appeared. Today it suddenly turned cold and started to rain and hail.

On February 28 I went duck hunting and fishing eight miles away, to the Kara Darya. It was really hot. There weren't many ducks and they were flying so high that I couldn't get a shot. The migrating flocks of ducks have passed by our region. I had more luck fishing. We waded in the backwaters of the Kara Darya with our dragnet in water up to our necks and caught about fifty pounds of small carp, barbel, and *marinki*, and one big sheat-fish weighing about ten pounds. In the place where we were the Kara Darya is very picturesque and unusual. It's about as wide as the Oka and wider than the Syr Darya.

By the way, on local maps I can't figure out where the Syr Darya ends and the Kara Darya begins. If you have a good atlas, please draw me a map of Andijon, Kara Darya, and Syr Darya. I really miss having a camera. There are some ravishing spots here and they're so unusual that they simply beg to be photographed.

Are you getting your Torgsin coupons regularly? We haven't gotten any from anyone yet this year and this has really sapped our strength, despite the fact that I'm making a pretty good living on my music. Apparently there are some misunderstandings here in the Foreign Trade Bank, which lost our new address. We sent a statement there on March 3, but I don't know whether that will be enough.

Have you ridden on the subway? If you have, write me your impressions.

The news of the death of S. Istomin really hit me hard. I didn't even know that he was in Asia too. If possible, send me his mother's address or at least Ksenia's: I want to send them my condolences.[21]

If you see Olga Zvegintseva, give her my heartfelt greetings. I was very friendly with her first husband. By the way, I saw that husband (that is, Petrik) in 1931 at my sister's. He inquired whether I knew anything about his first wife (that is, Olga) and asked me to find out about her. On the same occasion I saw her son, a very nice and modest young man. Olga Zvegintseva herself had in her day the reputation among high society of being a very frivolous woman. The reputation was deserved, because she put out for everyone left and right, without paying the slightest attention to rumors, gossip, and talk. In a word—she was a wild babe, 100 percent. (Ask her where the friend of her youth, Liuba N., is.) You keep writing about the games you've invented. We're really interested in them. Be sure to send them to us.

I send you all a warm greeting and hope to see you and Elena in our exotic clime this year. Love, Uncle.

Maybe the story "Sonechka from Turt-Kul" should be called "The Last Gang"? Do whatever you want with it and write me your impressions of it.

9

[30 June 1935]

Dear Vladimir,

Since winter I've had no news of you. How are you? How is your leg? What are you drawing? What amusements are you inventing? We're now in the season of heat, fruit, and diarrhea. Cucumbers are ten kopecks a kilo, and as a result—universal trots.

There's no news in particular. I acquired a decent dragnet and on my days off I go fishing with my boys. Not long ago I went fishing with a friend and my sons in an automobile. We got completely lost and ended up in a god-forsaken place—the region of the so-called drainage waters, i.e., the place where they drain the used waters from the whole irrigation system. The whole area is unusable salt marshes. The soil is white as snow and it's a huge area of swamps, lakes, reeds—and billions of mosquitoes. A ghastly backwoods. Here and there among the swamps are old sandy hills on which little *kishlaks* are huddled, villages not marked on any maps, with completely savage inhabitants who live like Africans in reed houses. All this against the background of grandiose distant mountains. Masses of wild game. The inhabitants are so cut off from civilization that they don't recognize the new money. They have only a dim idea about the collective farms and in general they don't do a damned thing. Their cattle graze all on their own somewhere in the salt marshes. Again I was sorry I don't have a camera—everything there is so unusual and original. The little overgrown lakes are stuffed with carp, pheasants, and snakes. Unfortunately the lakes are so overgrown with swamp grasses that you can't even think of fishing with a net. The inhabitants catch tons of carp with fishing rods. After a sleepless horrible night, spent in constant battle with the mosquitoes, at dawn we heard hundreds and hundreds of pheasants calling to each other from all directions. We couldn't even believe that there could be so many of them in those reeds. We also saw innumerable traces of pig hooves. In places everything had been dug up by boars. To my great annoyance I didn't have my gun with me, but I firmly resolved to return to this little place (if only I can find it again) at the end of July or in August during the full moon in order to lie in wait for a boar. By the way, this isn't so simple: boars come out of their thickets only in certain spots that you have to know. I'll have to live there among the mosquitoes about three or four days in order to get to know the boar's ways out. It seems to me that I've discovered an untouched place. Around Andijon, and especially in the Fergana Valley, they've killed off a lot of the game everywhere over the last few years, but in this spot there's still tons of it, and apparently no hunter with a gun has yet wandered in there. I'll have to hurry, or the other hunters will sniff it out—and it'll be all over.

In town news, the biggest event is the rout of the local prostitutes . . . As a restaurant musician, I've had the daily opportunity to make close observation of these dear but fallen creatures, so I could now write a whole little book about wh[ores], but a funny book . . .

In that same restaurant the old cashier (an exiled criminal) is a former madam from Omsk, where she had her own "establishment." The cashier hired herself an errand boy and through him kept in constant contact with her "girls." As soon as some group of revelers with money appears, our old lady sends the boy to get the girls. Everyone's happy: the revelers, the girls, and the cashier—because she also gets a "commission" from the girls. One day in the old town the violinist and I met our wh——s and they invited us to a name-day party of a certain Maruska. We went. In an old mosque in Maruska's comfy little room about half a dozen wh——s had gathered, along with the cashier and us—that is, "our crowd." The refreshments were excellent. Everything was done quite properly. The cashier, sitting at the samovar, was incomparable, recounting to us her memories of the "good old days" in Omsk, when she had her own considerable establishment. And how she loved her "girls" and *how* the girls loved her! And how mischievous some of them were! I told the company about the little Paris brothels and the taverns of Montmartre. The girls just gawked and sighed: "Oh, that's where life is! That's where I'd like to go!" And the cashier would add: "It's so pleasant to have a chat with cultured and well-informed people and to unburden one's heart" (the cultured one—that's me).

And once the following curious thing befell me: some of our Pamir friends on a toot arrived at the restaurant. They were carousing with the girls. Finally, when everyone had already gotten drunk, the company demanded cognac. There wasn't any cognac. The wh——e Valka volunteered to go get cognac. They gave her sixty rubles for this purpose. Valka disappeared with the money and didn't come back. Everyone was indignant. They closed the restaurant. I went home. Suddenly I see Valka walking ahead of me in a white blouse, dark blue skirt, with a white men's cap on her head. Well, I think, now I'll catch the thief red-handed. I quickened my pace, and at that moment the electricity went out. Having gone about fifty paces, I see my Valka sitting on a bench, apparently waiting for a "john." . . . I stole up to her quietly from behind in utter darkness and—grabbed her by the scruff of the neck. "Oh, you hooligan!" I shouted in a loud voice . . . and suddenly (what a terrible mistake)—I had grabbed by the scruff of the neck not Valka, but a resting policeman in a white cap. He jumped up and turned his Nagant revolver on me.

"Forgive me," I said in embarrassment, "I thought you were a wh——e . . ."

"What kind of wh——e am I to you! Let's go to the station."

I didn't end up at the station. The policeman turned out to be a good guy, he understood my mistake. Now when he meets me he always shakes my hand and says, "My compliments to comrade musician!"

Well, that's enough about wh——s. Now that doesn't exist any more. Not long ago the Criminal Investigation Department imprisoned a whole bunch of wh——s. The remaining ones either disappeared or laid low and now behave like "decent women." Yes, you get to see a lot of things, working for years in taverns!

They say that Popov has deviated from the Urals program in the *Pathfinder.* Can you send him my "Silk Master"? In his last letter your father wrote that you're thinking of leaving Dmitrov. I approve of this idea. I recommend our region.

Well, so long. I send warmest greetings.

I'm waiting for a letter from you, but better not write about the news from the sea.[22]

I'm with you in soul,

Your tavern uncle

10

[Autumn 1935]

Dear Vladimir,

I received your letter. You ask how my boar hunt went—very unsuccessfully. Another hunter (a certain Gartman) and I ended up in that same remote area that I already described to you. Toward evening as we were wandering through *dzhudovnik* [central Asian bushes] with our guns, Gartman suddenly cried out in a terrifying voice: a snake that had concealed itself on a branch had bitten him . . . in the *nostril,* from the inside. Apparently this was the snake known as the "arrow," which is distinguished by its unusual speed of movement and its ability to leap into the air. It has a very narrow head. At first the snake hit him in the glasses with its head and then instantly repeated its strike right into his nostril. Gartman broke out into tears from pain, flung the snake away with his hand, and began to sneeze furiously, which seemed funny to me at first. This all happened so fast that Gartman didn't even have time to see what kind of snake it was. In five minutes his whole head began to itch horribly, and no more than twenty minutes after that his body was covered with bright red spots. He began vomiting, he became terribly weak and had pain in his stomach and legs. Now I got really frightened, because I couldn't help him in any way. After all, you're not about to suck snake venom out of your neighbor's nostril! The poor fellow's pulse became terribly weak and quick, and his legs refused to work and he lay prone. I managed to procure some milk, which I gave him to drink, after which the vomiting let up. Toward morning I got the wounded man to the town, with terrible difficulty. There they treated him in the hospital (a blood transfusion and injections of some kind of medicine). He was sick for four days and then got well, but they say he still feels weak. There's your boar hunt for you! I haven't been to that area since then—it's very far away—you can't get there on foot. In general there are a lot of snakes around here: all sorts of "racers," moccasins, vipers, "arrows" [sand snakes], and snakes called "efa" [saw-scaled vipers], which are extremely poisonous. Fortunately rattlesnakes and cobras have not been observed in the Fergana Valley. My sons and I often go fishing with a net, and when we're fishing we always encounter two or three brown snakes near the water. On these fishing trips we have amusing encounters with Uzbeks in the *kishlaks,* who are very open-hearted and hospitable, invite us in and feed us to the point of puking with huge melons. To eat and drink in an Uzbek home is pure punishment. There's no society in which there are so many "Chinese" ceremonies and stupid procedures for every type of viands, and it is impossible not to observe these rules of propriety—either you'll offend everyone or you'll revolt them with your gaffes. Not long ago on a fishing trip in a remote *kishlak* the Uzbeks served us pilaf. You have to eat it with your hands in such a way that you don't drop a single grain of rice, since to drop rice on the floor is sinful and unseemly. When your fingers are unaccustomed to this it just doesn't work—so we started to eat with spoons we had brought with us. Looking at us, the Uzbeks roared with laughter and called some ancient old man to look at how we were eating. The worldly-wise old man looked at us for a long time, then said to the people around: "I've already seen Russians eating rice with spoons, and that's nothing, but just imagine: I knew a Russian in the town who was such a pig that when he 'went to the outhouse' he wiped himself with paper! . . . yes, just imagine—with clean paper! . . . instead of wiping himself with a clump of dirt, as decent people do. Russians in general are amazing freaks."

The old man's story had an amazing effect on the Uzbeks. They shook their heads and kept asking us: is it really true that there are such strange people among the Russians, and who are they? The Uzbeks really do always wipe themselves with dirt, and in old Andijon near the public toilets the old beggars to this day hand out little dry lumps of dirt to the visitors. An Uzbek will relieve nature in front of anyone without embarrassment, but always hides his bare bottom by lowering the hem of his robe in back—then everything is decent, because a bare bottom is the most shameful, disgraceful, indecent, and offensive thing on earth. Even in the bathhouse an Uzbek will wash either in his underpants or with a rag covering his bottom. (Homosexuality is very widespread here—much more than in the Caucasus—the direct result of the isolation of women and of the *parandzha.*)

The Uzbeks in the town have nevertheless acquired a little culture, but the inhabitants of the *kishlaks,* despite their open-heartedness, are terrible beasts. We have sworn never to let our daughters go outside the town alone. It's simply impossible here! Our Varia worked on a collective farm outside town—she was attacked three times by the nomads. Once an Uzbek policeman chased her and she barely escaped from him. Another time on the collective farm an Uzbek attacked her and started to choke her, so that bruises from his fingers remained on her neck for a long time. The third time on a deserted path three Uzbeks attacked Varia at once, and she escaped by throwing herself into an *aryk,* where she lay fighting them off with teeth, hands, and feet, so energetically that she pulled the ligaments in her legs and was on sick leave, bedridden, for twelve days. She was saved by the fact that she screamed madly and people came running in time to help . . . But the state she was in when she returned to us—horrible! All cut up, wet, covered in silt . . . and lame. Tatenka was also chased at night right in town, but Tatenka didn't lose her head, and after letting the Uzbek come up close to her on a little bridge over an *aryk,* she shoved him into the water. That's what kind of country this is, where the mere sight of a woman not covered by the *parandzha* stuns the village dweller to the point where he loses his reason. The local newspaper *Pravda of the East* is dotted with accounts of rapes or brutal murders of women out of jealousy or because the wife, neighbor, or sister removed her *parandzha.* Just a few days ago in the center of Andijon, across from the post office, in broad daylight and in front of people a woman was knifed to death for taking off the *parandzha* . . . and this in spite of the fact that the local authorities are waging a cruel battle against such crimes and the court gives no mercy, which is very well known to all.[23]

In general the future of my elder daughters depresses me greatly. They are both rather pretty and a horde of low fellows (all sorts of Petkas, Kolkas, Lenkas, and so on) are dangling after them, extremely vulgar, endlessly democratic, uncultured, and poorly educated. It will end with my having the type of son-in-law that would be a disgrace to display to any decent person . . . There is not a single appropriate suitor in all of Andijon, and my girls, who never see decent men, may be enticed by the indecent ones, which would be quite natural.

Varia, of course, was until recently studying in a school for parachutists. Fortunately they ignominiously expelled her the other day for the same reason they expelled Andrei from the ten-year school. By the way, Andrei's case has not yet moved forward. I submitted a statement that said that I am *Vetov,* and my books have not been withdrawn from school libraries throughout the U.S.S.R. to this day, and that Soviet children are even given my books as prizes in school (*a fact*), at the same time as my own children are driven out of school.[24] On the basis of this statement the local municipal department of public education made an inquiry to the Tashkent Commissariat for Education, and an answer is expected in the next few days.

You keep suggesting that I continue to occupy myself with literature—for some reason I don't feel like it: my characters are either ideologically inconsistent, or exaggerated to the point of caricature and parody, my style is old-fashioned, and today people find it insipid and "lacking vivid imagery." Apparently I haven't kept pace with literature. As for my memoirs . . . after all, memoirs have above all to be truthful, and in order for my memoirs to be published—I would have either to lie, or to keep silent about a whole series of interesting things that played a major role in my life. All the same, I'm very grateful to you for bothering with my most recent stories, and it's good that you sent "The Silk Master" to Popov.

Grisha asks whether it's possible to buy a bicycle of a recent model from one of our factories in a Moscow store and, if so, how much it would cost. Well, so long. I look forward to a letter from you. Uncle

Your mother asks, what is pappataci? It is a mosquito-borne fever from which we are all suffering here. It's a vile, exhausting illness caused by mosquito bites. Pappa-taci—are Italian words [*febbre da pappataci*—sandfly fever]. The illness lasts two weeks.

11

7–8 August 1936

Dear Nephew,

I received your letter today and I hasten to answer it today, taking advantage of my day off, since on workdays I don't have time. I'm working a lot—mornings in the Model Railroad Cafeteria until 2:00, and in the evenings in the restaurant, also until 2:00 (but now A.M.). I've started earning a better salary, but it's terribly boring! I have no private life at all and I come home during the day or at night only to sleep. I'm going crazy from all the fox-trots, blues, tangoes, and bostons, which seem to be turning me gradually into a quiet idiot. From your letter I was pleased to gather that they're not going to cut off your leg, and that you will after all be able to walk without crutches. We are placing great hopes on your coming operation. A local surgeon I interviewed here told me that your bone condition can be cured without difficulty and even without operations. In the autumn I'm also going to have an operation, they're going to cut out my beloved bump under my chin (remember, on the right side of my neck?). Over the years it has grown a lot, and thanks to it I've stopped having success with chicks, babes, and broads, which is rather sad, and besides everyone scares me by saying that this bump (if it's not cut out) can turn into cancer. I've recovered from hemorrhoids. Apparently Saint Suleiman was touched by my sincere repentance for my tactlessness, and has forgiven my sinful butt, which insulted his beloved holy stone slab on the Osh cliff.[25] I won't do it again! I read in the newspaper, and your letter confirmed it, that you're having an unheard-of heat wave (35° [95° F] in the shade). You lucky people! We've reached 39½° (103° F), but fortunately this only lasted three or four days, and they write in the newspapers that this summer is very cool for central Asia. In fact, last year and the year before last were worse. This year at least you can breathe, and this is the second day we've felt a little coolness and even seen some rain, despite the fact that the beginning of August here is the hottest time of year. Nevertheless the climate here is really obscene. In the summer everyone gets sick. Our Andrei contracted the worst kind of tropical malaria and turned into a kind of skeleton covered with skin. Egor never gets over his diarrhea. At night no one sleeps because of the mosquitoes, and we all do nothing but scratch ourselves. The mosquito is a real bastard. It's almost invisible, completely inaudible, and you don't feel its bite, but it causes desperate itching. The other night Varia was bitten in the calf by a scorpion, and her whole leg hurt up to the groin, and not long ago in the courtyard where our Egorka plays my boys caught and killed a real viper that was starting to slither toward my bed near the door (in the summer we sleep in the courtyard). Also the other day in the garden a stagehand I know was bitten in the butt by a *falanga* [spider], and on the third day after that his butt began to turn brown and they had to cut a big chunk of meat out of the stagehand's ham. A student friend of Tatka's was bitten near Andijon by the spider called the *karakurt* (have you ever heard of this bastard?). The doctors just barely pulled the student through, and only because he had been bitten through his clothes. In a word, we're sick to death of the "climate" here.

I'm already thinking quite a lot about what we should do when I finish my enforced residence here. This will be in about two and a half years. We don't want to stay in Andijon. If we're still alive, we're thinking of making our way to some place on the sea—some kind of Makhach-Kala, Derbent—or the shores of the Sea of Azov in Berdiansk, Genichesk, or something like that.[26] The Sea of Azov is closer to us [at home in Moscow]. Maybe you have some practical advice in this regard. I need the sea, good fishing, hunting, and . . . *taverns*—profitable taverns, where I can earn money to feed my family. Advise me—you probably have a lot of acquaintances in various editorial offices, who've been at various seasides.

Aunt Elia has undertaken the trouble of getting them to pay her, as the mother of a large family, 2,000 rubles a year for Egor. They will probably grant her application, and we decided to put 1,000 rubles of that money into a savings account every year, so we can move to the seaside.

Alka Bolduin wrote to me in the last year I was in Zagorsk, and she wrote to me here in 1934. Even then she wrote that her husband was going to get rich any minute. For some reason I doubt it! But is it true that Alka has inherited the manners of her great ancestress?—that's what it means for a young babe to marry an elderly husband.[27] After all, Filipp's over fifty now. Write her that I greet her, remember her, and sympathize with her. I won't write myself. Write to us more often. We haven't received any letters from anyone for a long time and we've completely lost the thread of family news. Find out from Lina and write me whether my aunts are alive: Agrafena Mikhailovna Paniutina, S. N. Glebova, Aleksandra Vladimirovna, etc. If they're alive—*be sure* to send them greetings from me.

How and where are my nephews Sashka and Alioshka? What happened to Alioshka's wife? Aunt Vera wrote us once that it would be good for him to make his way to us. I think he could manage this, and we personally would set him up somewhere here with pleasure and joy. Send us his address if you know it.

We lead a very boring life, for some reason. Our recent sensation was the unheard-of flash floods caused by intense thawing in the mountains. The Darya and *sais* [tributaries] overflowed terribly; several railroad bridges collapsed, the neighboring town of Sharikhan, into which the wild Sharikhan-sai flows, was turned into an island. Thousands of people struggled against the high water day and night and tried to defend the town of Andijon, which was also under threat since the capricious Darya suddenly changed course and approached the Andijon-sai (a wild little river that flows through our town) at a distance of only a few meters. Through heroic efforts they were able to turn the Darya aside with the help of *sipais,* which were constantly being knocked over and carried away by the current (a *sipai* is a huge wooden tripod that is lowered into the water to direct the stream). If the Darya were to join with our *sai,* we would be flooded. In the mountains there was a gigantic avalanche which dammed up the *sai* to a height of 660 yards, thanks to which in a few hours a huge lake was formed here, which also threatened to break through and cause a disaster. The flooding has long been over, but nevertheless a lot of cotton and rice was ruined because of it. The other sensation was the procession through Andijon of the automobile race Gor'kii [Soviet Union]–Khorog [Afghanistan], with new streamlined limousines "GAZ"-"Ford."[28] They were met by the whole town with music, banners, and speeches.

Well, so long. Warm greetings, and wishes for success. *Write!*

Uncle

[On a separate sheet is a translation of several Uzbek curses, followed by: "I just cannot get my sons to tell me what 'senninske' means. They say it's so obscene that they're ashamed to say it."[29] On the other side of the sheet: "Receipt. I have received from the theater box office . . . ," crossed out, and Trubetskoi's signature underneath.]

12

[January? 1937]

Dear Vladimir,

I received your letter. Thank you for the greetings, and forgive me for wishing you a belated happy birthday. We spent that day, as is our custom, with drinking, eating, and music. I haven't written to you for a long time, because I've been terribly busy. I work day and night in various places, and recently I took on a job in the local *Academic* [*sic!*] musical theater to write incidental music for Schiller's *Kabale und Liebe,* so I haven't had ten free minutes in a day and I'm totally exhausted.

The writing of my memoirs is going slowly. In the autumn I could still snatch a little time to write one or two pages every day. Even that got difficult in the winter, since my restaurant work begins a whole two hours earlier in the winter. And on my day off, I'm seized with an irresistible impulse to chase after bunny-rabbits. In the spring I'll have more free time and I'll again apply myself to my memoirs. I've conceived them in four parts: *Part I—"Memoirs of Youth"* (this part ends with my service in the navy). *Part II—"Memoirs of a Cuirassier"* (this part ends with my evacuation at the end of 1914). *Part III—"Memoirs of a Man in the Trenches"* (my service in the war in the administration of the governor-general of Galicia and on the General Staff of the army, Romania, etc.; this part ends with the Revolution). *Part IV—"Notes of a Musician"* or *"Memoirs of a Musician."* I'm afraid that I won't be able to write the last part after all (for various reasons). All four parts will be under the general title *Memoirs*. I've begun writing with the second part, because it seems easiest to me. I'm writing a very detailed account, since this period of my life has been impressed in my memory especially distinctly. I feel that I have a defect common to all memoirs, namely, there's a lot of the *personal,* which is not always interesting to the general reader and is interesting only to my descendants. I devote a lot of attention to everyday life, to regimental and cadet mores. That's all right. The [description of the] Krasnoe Selo camps and in general everything about Krasnoe Selo is successful. Here I describe and touch on aspects that it appears have not yet been illuminated in the literature (in particular in memoirs). It's hard not to embellish, but I am trying to adhere to the *truth.* I know that the late S. D. Evreinov before his death wrote his memoirs about our Galician occupation.[30] Since I served once under his command in Galicia, I would really like to read these memoirs (compiled by him according to his diary) before starting work on the third part of my memoirs. I don't know whom to get them from—unless it would be from O. I. Raevskaia (she's the sister of Evreinov's wife). By the way: Is O. I. Raevskaia still alive, and do you know her address? I want to write to her. So far I have written not more than 40,000–48,000 words of the second part, and I've only gotten up to my promotion to cornet. As soon as I've amassed 60,000–80,000 words, I'll send them to you for criticism, without fail.

We're leading life quietly, without interesting events. I'm making a fairly good living with my music (900–1,000 rubles a month), but the cost of living is so high here and our family is so big that even that isn't enough. Grisha is working in Sherikhan, but my eldest daughters are here, and the amount they earn (about 150 rubles) is only enough to buy them shoes and clothes. I'd like to know, how much do musicians earn in Gudauty? Maybe I really will move there in about two years. By the way, what are Gudauty exactly? What's their real Christian name? I mean, what were they called before?

I recently went on an interesting hunt on the flood-lands of the river Sherikhan-sai. It was in the beginning of January. It was 15° below zero [–5° F] and there was over a foot of snow. I ran across a snipes' wintering place near some warm marshes that never freeze. There are no snipe here in summer, but in January I encountered hundreds of them in the space of a few acres. In the same place I flushed two woodcock. In general, though, the hunting here is rather poor. Every year the tractors conquer new tracts of wild undergrowth and reeds for cotton cultivation, so the wild game have nowhere to hold their ground, and no game can live in cotton fields. Judge for yourself: after the cotton is sown, they hill it up three times, then in summer there are six or seven waterings, then they harvest it and immediately plow it and again lay it out for irrigation for the whole winter. People are constantly working on these fields. How can there be any game there?! Even the rabbits have all moved to the gardens and backyards of the *kishlaks*. But pheasant love thickets and run from cultivated areas. Boars are the same. In the fertile Fergana Valley people live so bunched together that one *kishlak* stands on another and even the jackals have all disappeared, because in recent years lots of Uzbeks have become hunters.

My authoress-daughter sends you her greetings. She is constantly having some kind of emotions and enthusiasms. All autumn and winter she wore a Red Army uniform, with riding breeches and boots, because she joined an Osoaviakhim [Special Detachment of Aviators and Chemists] detachment where she took cavalry courses, learned how to hack with a saber, had shooting lessons, groomed horses, did orderly duty in the stables, and has now passed as a "Voroshilov horseman" and is listed as a junior commander in the reserve.[31] Similar extravagances are constantly floating into her head. She also went to parachutists' school, but luckily the doctors pronounced that her heart was too weak for parachuting. Well, all right. Goodbye for now. We're waiting for a letter from you. I envy you for being by the sea, but I hope the time will come when I will join you somewhere on the seashore.

Uncle

Greetings to Elena.

(As an illustration to this letter I am including on the next page the Certificate issued to Varia by the Andizhan Osoaviakhim.)

CERTIFICATE

[Seal in two languages with the date 16 January 1937, No. 52]

This certificate has been issued by the Andizhan Regional Municipal Soviet of Osoaviakhim to Comrade VARVARA VLADIMIROVNA TRUBETSKAIA, who has passed the theoretical and practical training for passing the standard test of a "VOROSHILOV HORSEMAN" in 1936, and who upon examination showed the following results:

1. Care and protection of horse	Good
2. Grooming and feeding of horse	Good
3. Horseback riding	Satisfactory
Task No. 1	Satisfactory
Task No. 2	Satisfactory
Task No. 3	Satisfactory
Task No. 4	Satisfactory
4. Tactical training	Good
5. Marksmanship	Satisfactory
6. Mastery of sidearms	——
7. Equestrian vaulting	——
8. Use of gas mask	Good
9. Political training	Excellent

According to the decision of the selection committee, Comrade TRUBETSKAIA V. V. has the right to wear the badge "VOROSHILOV HORSEMAN" No. 13616, having passed the standard tests given by the Osoaviakhim of the Uzbek S.S.R. for a "VOROSHILOV HORSEMAN," as certified by the Andizhan Municipal Regional Soviet of the Osoaviakhim.

Chairman of the Andizhan Gorraisovet OAX	[Zbrodov]
Chief of Battle Training	[Kuchkov]
Chief of Cavalry Manège	[Karpenko]

[Round seal]

13

1 April [1937]

Dear Vladimir,

I am sending you seven chapters of the *Memoirs of a Cuirassier.* I would have sent them earlier, but I suddenly discovered that mice ate a whole half-notebook and I had to copy them over again. Don't read this piece all at once, read no more than two chapters a day—otherwise it'll be monotonous. I gave it to the only cultured person in the city—a certain professor—to read. He says it's very interesting and compares it to Shulgin, but doubts that it will be published, since he finds that the author is biased and sympathizes too much with what he's describing.[32] The final, seventh chapter is particularly dubious—the end, which has a lot of analysis and opinion.

In the following chapters will be: maneuvers, my promotion, the Borodino celebrations,[33] marriage, Mikhail Aleksandrovich's affair with Mrs. Vulfert and Olga Aleksandrovna's affair with Kulikovskii, the Romanov celebrations,[34] equestrian competitions, horse races, [Grand Duke] Nikolai Nikolaevich, a duel, mobilization, East Prussia, the death of Herbert Viktorovich Briummer and his funeral in Friedland (this episode should come out particularly well). Remember, I told you about this "Vralmann" Briummer[35] and his adventures that always ended in the same way: ". . . the next day a doctor friend of mine called me on the telephone and said, 'Herbert Viktorovich, come quickly . . . an amusing case,'" and so on. In general—I regard the *Memoirs of a Cuirassier* as excellent material for a historical novel, material that could be offered to a real writer of fiction, because several events and personalities are described with photographic accuracy.

So. We're having an abundant spring—the best time of year: apricots, peaches, almonds—everything is in luxuriant blossom and the wood splinters are trying to climb up onto each other.[36] The town is going wild over bicycles. I have never seen such a quantity of bicycles as in Andijon. I too bought a bicycle, on which my entire family runs around from morning till night, or rather did run around, since the bicycle is now in need of major repairs because the other day Tatka ran into a truck, dragged her poor face along the truck's body, and crushed the front wheel, frame, and handlebars as flat as a pancake, and there's no one to fix it, since hooligans knifed the bike repairman in a nightclub two days ago. In general they really like to knife people in Andijon. The other day a certain Armenian lost 5,000 rubles to another Armenian, and, of course, knifed the winner right on the street. The murderer's wife took poison so that the ancestral vendetta would go no further. They sang the prayer for the dead over the wife and imprisoned the husband, and the whole town is impatiently awaiting the trial, because both Armenians are well known to everyone. Characteristically for Andijon, an innumerable horde of townspeople and idlers buried the murdered gambler with music (!). The typical Russian youth in Andijon: cloth cap at a 45° angle, blue T-shirt under which one can see the tattoo on his chest, a bicycle in his hands, in one pocket a switchblade, in the other a half-liter bottle, he's called either Kolka or Lenka and he has a minimum of three to four protection rackets in stores and offices. In the summer he replaces the cap with a multicolored Asiatic *tiubeteika*—with a tassel, of course.[37] He wouldn't dream of dancing the tango or rhumba in a nightclub or restaurant without a papirosa between his teeth. He's evading alimony payments. So. Write soon. Greetings to your dear little wife!

Uncle

14 (last letter)

June [?] 1937

Dear Vladimir,

Finally I got a little letter from you! What is this new trick of treating your leg with rotten fish?! In all the years I've lived on this earth, this is the first time I've heard of such a trick. If you only knew how I envy you for living by the sea amid such beauties. I can just see the surroundings you describe: a Turk at the helm, beautiful girls, a wineskin, cheese, shooting at dolphins, and nature.

We don't have anything of the kind. I have made a thorough study of Andijon and I'm desperately sick of it. It's especially repulsive in the summer, precisely because there is no waterscape. The farther you go into the continent, the more you miss the sea. Besides all the other local charms, now we're having all kinds of difficulties finding food. There's not a damned thing to buy in the market or the stores. The cost of living has gotten much higher this year. Even fruit, which we always have heaps of, is quite scarce this year because of unexpected spring frosts that suddenly fell after blossom time.

I've lived through some most unpleasant moments recently. I was in the city hospital, where they operated on me: they cut out a huge lump under my jaw (a cyst). It was incredibly nasty—this lump had grown together with the muscles and blood vessels. For a long time they tried to tear it out "by blunt means," and the doctor grasped it and ripped, tugged, and pulled the thing until he shit his pants. Finally he lost his patience and cut it out with a lancet. Then it turned out there was a second lump hidden behind the first one. Here we go again! What a delight. Even now I have pain and can't shave.

While I've been writing you these lines my youngest son Egor, who was given a little wooden ship as a gift today, has peed a little puddle and put the ship in it. His older brothers are shouting at him, and he is now roaring and cussing his brothers out in Uzbek: "Ooh, senninske! Dadayni arvayge ske!!"[38] What a kid! He's three years old, walks around completely naked, and in this state makes independent excursions to the main street, to a big, swiftly rushing *aryk,* and to the neighbors. At home Elia is always in a panic. The other day we found him by the *aryk* in the company of two dead-drunk Uzbeks, with whom he was eating snacks, conversing, and using obscenities. He has a rich imagination. In the evenings he prays to God: "Lord, save and have mercy on Papa, Mama," then he enumerates his brothers and sisters and always adds the following in his own words: "Lord save and have mercy on the gramophone and records." A gramophone is the dream of his life.

I have rattled off three years and three months here. There are one year and nine months left [in my sentence], and if they count preliminary detention—then it's just a year and a half. Then I'll go live by the sea without fail. If only I can find decent work. I'm still writing my memoirs little by little, but that goes slowly. As soon as I accumulate another five or six chapters, I'll send them to you. I'm very glad you like them.

The hooligans in Andijon continue to stick knives in everybody right and left. The other day in the restaurant at 11:00 P.M. they killed our waiter Misha (our best waiter) with one blow to the heart. They knifed him while he was working and so deftly that no one noticed! Honest to God! It was in the little garden where there are some tables. They caught these hooligans about two days later. They confessed that they killed Misha only because they had no money to pay, and they had gobbled and drunk up forty rubles' worth. About two days after that they knifed a teacher on the street and left the knife in her side. They knifed a little boy, they knifed the husband of a bank teller, and a few other people—that's Asia for you! and all in the course of a few days.

Lately I've been working in the restaurant as a jazz percussionist. I play thirty instruments and thanks to this I'm very popular and successful. I'm enclosing actual notes that have been passed to me through the waiter. How do you like the style?!

Well, so long. Say hello to Elena and the kids. I'm expecting a letter from you, but I ask you to remember that they're strict with me. Say hello to the dolphins.

Uncle

Our Grisha, who is now a pretty good sound engineer, set up a wonderful tube radio with a loudspeaker for us. Every evening we listen to broadcasts from India (Delhi and Bombay)—enchanting fox-trots and wild Indian music.

[Letter from Elizaveta Vladimirovna Trubetskaia to her sister Vera in England]

30 January 1935

Uz.S.S.R. Andizhan

Post Office. Poste Restante.

My dear Vera, you can't imagine how happy I was when I finally got a letter from you! After all, you haven't written to me for six months, and I sent you three letters and you apparently didn't get them, I wrote to you in detail about the birth of little Egorka and about our life in the summer. Finally I got terribly worried about you and through Misha I learned that you are alive and well. And finally your letter; and the next day I received a letter from Alka with a photograph of her boys. Thank you too for the photograph of Elenka, at last we see how she has turned out and we like it. Continue to write to me at "City Post Office. Poste Restante," because although we are firmly settled in the old town, our address is too complicated and the postmen often don't manage to deliver our letters. But one of us goes to the post office regularly every day.

We are alive and well, we live quietly; we have two Uzbek one-room houses, with earthen floors and clay whitewashed walls; in our large room, where our five (!) sons, Vladimir, and I live (alone among all the men!), we have put a cooking range and oven; in the small room where the girls live there stands a little iron stove. Before Christmas there was no snow and the weather was beautiful and clear, in the daytime the sun was quite warm; then the snow started and it snowed for three days and we started to have the same kind of freezing weather we have in Russia, and now we have real winter, but they say that in March it will be warm again and we can sit out in the garden. Vladimir is working as a musician in a restaurant, the salary is 300 rubles and besides that he makes good money from special requests, sometimes he brings home up to 35 rubles in an evening, in Russia he didn't make that kind of money. Varia worked all summer taking care of rabbits on farms and kolkhozes, but she's gotten very tired of this and quit to become my right-hand woman for housework. Grisha is working as a projectionist. Tatia was working in the Uzbek theater, but she soon quit that job, which made us, her parents, very happy: there's a disgusting atmosphere there and all the actors suffer from syphilis (!). The other kids are in school, except Seriozha, whom we just couldn't place, and who's been playing hooky for a year; in August he'll be nine years old. If you could only see how big they've all grown; all of them, including your godson Andrei, who's fourteen years old, have already outgrown me; even Irinka is already catching up to me. A few days ago our Volodia returned from a sanatorium, he's gotten well, he has good color, he's gained weight, and we must hope that his illness will disappear. How glad I am for you that you've made it out of your seclusion and ended up in a place where you see people and even your fellow countrymen. Is Artemii really coming to see you? I saw him in Moscow and it was so pitiful to see him on crutches; now he probably has an artificial leg.

Now and then I hear from our relatives, everything's fine with them. Misha is feeling not bad, although in winter it's worse than in summer. Vladimir is making a very good living inventing board games for children; Niks and Vovik don't write to me at all, but I know they're both working.

I'll end this letter because I'm going to bed, in the evening I'm not good for anything since I get very tired during the day and towards eleven o'clock I'm already asleep. I send you and Elenka warm kisses; now we'll write to each other again.

Your Eli

[Letter from Elizaveta Vladimirovna Trubetskaia to her brother V. V. Golitsyn]

12 May 1937

Dear Vovik,

I received your letter and haven't yet answered because I was waiting for something definite to emerge regarding Sasha's working here. So far there is nothing definite, but I am writing to you anyway since you are probably wondering why you've had no answer yet. We have no theaters; all we have is the Uzbek State Theater, where they have their own directors. There are clubs and drama circles, there is the Uigur Theater, and Vladimir dropped in a word there, but there is no answer yet. Then there is one definite proposal: they need a cultural director in a big 600-person resort. It's not in Andijon but in the town of Osh, thirty miles from here, on a bus line. The pay is very high (I don't know how much), along with full room and board. Besides which, every week there are new elegantly dressed babes (this is information contributed by Vladimir). That's the information we have so far. As soon as we learn anything more I'll write to you immediately. By the way, the Osh resort has sent Sasha an inquiry about his agreement to come here, since they were looking for a cultural director and Vladimir gave them your address.

Everything here is fine, but not long ago we experienced great alarm: on April 12 our little Gotka came down with measles, for the first few days the illness took a normal course, but then something strange appeared in his lung, and at the doctor's insistence I went to the hospital with him and stayed there ten days. On the 29th they discharged him and we went home. He got very sick and I almost lost hope of pulling him through, they gave him a blood transfusion, took my blood and transfused it into him and after that he started to quickly get well. This is the new method of curing measles and in my opinion it's a very good method.

On May 20 Varia will probably leave us to visit you in Moscow; she's going completely "on spec" and if she can't get herself settled somehow she'll return here again. She has saved up money for the trip and for the first few days in Moscow, and after that she'll see; they'll keep her job for her here since they have a high opinion of her as a secretary and typist.

Well, that's all our news. I send you a big kiss. If there's something else for Sasha, I'll write.

Eli

[Note by A. V. Trubetskoi: "This letter was written a little over two months before the arrests. From this letter it is apparent that our parents didn't have any suspicions about what was to happen. This is also apparent from Father's last letter, No. 14."]

Notes of a Cuirassier

Chapter One

Choosing a Regiment

MY FRANK CONVERSATION with my uncle Aleksei Kapnist was decisive for me and turned my whole young life upside down.[1] In fact up to then I had thought about my future in an unforgivably frivolous way. In my dreams about the future everything fit together—my ship, interesting sea journeys abroad, everyday life on board ship, so dear to my heart; all this fit right in with a deeply beloved wife and a family life full of "cloudless stormy happiness." These dreams had lasted for years, and now all it took was a single frank talk with my uncle, a little common sense, to smash all my rainbow-colored plans. With my infinite optimism I had never thought seriously about what our family life would turn into when I became a sailor, or how it would be for my sweet little wife to sit on the shore of the blue sea, constantly parted from me. At the same time my feelings for my fiancée were growing steadily, turning into a kind of cult, and I had terrible difficulty enduring any separation from her, no matter how long or short. It was hard for me not to see her and be near her even for a month . . . but how would it be when the ship would constantly keep us apart, and for long months at that! Indeed, my wife and I would be able to live together only sporadically. A good sailor must be at sea. A good husband must be on shore at the family hearth. It is impossible to combine the sea with the family hearth, and it's impossible to take a sweet little wife onto a battle cruiser. There's a reason for the proverb "*Femme de marin—femme de chagrin*" ["The wife of a sailor is the wife of sorrow"].

No, I had to decide on one or the other and weigh my beloved girl on the scales against my beloved sea. There could be no compromise here. But the very thought of scales in this regard seemed to me to be base. I could not waver: our feelings had gone too far—my fiancée and I were too close—and I renounced the sea.

Yes, it was hard. But my fiancée must not know of it. She might be grieved by the thought that I was sacrificing for her everything I had so doggedly striven for since childhood. On the other hand, I was tenderly moved by my own behavior: "Look what an amazing love I feel and what a remarkable cavalier I am, who sacrifices that which is most dear for the sake of a beloved woman." I was enraptured by my own feelings and, strangely enough, my sacrifice not only did not cause me any irritation toward my fiancée, but only intensified my ardent love for her. For her part my fiancée understood and appreciated exactly what I was doing without any explanations.

But how strong was my affinity for everything connected with the sea! Even today I constantly catch myself thinking and daydreaming about warships. On sleepless nights I spend long, painful hours remembering Tsushima, vividly imagining the tragic destruction of the Russian ships in that battle.[2] I still love to think up designs for unbelievably powerful warships with the most advantageous disposition of artillery and armor plating. Even now I still follow with interest the new inventions and refinements in the area of naval materiel, and I eagerly read the specialized maritime literature, easily memorizing the data for various ships, always interesting to me: their displacement, capacity of the engines, speed, thickness of armor plating, caliber and number of guns, radius of operation, etc.

So I was done with the sea—I had to enter the military service on land. I consoled myself with the thought that even on land one could just as honorably and truly serve the ideals that had been firmly established in my consciousness and that could be reduced to the elementary formula "for Tsar and country." I had to immediately choose an arm of the service, and without hesitating I settled on the cavalry. I won't conceal that I very much liked the handsome, elegant cavalry uniform, the mellow chime of spurs, the particular dash and spirit of the officers, always smart and dandified.

It was a great consolation that one could become an officer in the land forces more quickly than in the navy, since the army required much less specialized knowledge. I could get married only after I had become an officer; my mother insisted. She would often say to me, "First become a person, stand on your own two feet, then think about getting married." "To become a person" meant to attain a certain position in society, to acquire a certain specific gravity in the world, and in this respect the military route was the easiest, most pleasant, and quickest to execute. An officer was indisputably already a "person," while a student of something or other could not be considered as such.

The following plan was sketched out: a year at a lower rank in a cavalry regiment as a volunteer of the first class, officer's examination in the military school, promotion, and, finally, marriage—that is, the attainment of complete happiness.[3]

It's true that my mother, as a well-educated woman and also the widow of a great scholar, of course wanted to see her sons be first of all educated people in the highest sense of the word; me, however, she had given up for lost, convinced that I had no enthusiasm for scholarship and was a poor and reluctant student who stuck to the phrase "I don't want to study for life, I want to get myself a wife." My mother was consoled by the fact that my brother Nikolai loved scholarship and was remarkably successful in it, showing great promise.[4]

It was spring. I had to hurry and pick out a regiment. But what was to guide me in choosing one regiment or the other? In society, people would say a certain regiment was good but another was bad. For example, civilians said for some reason that the Sumskoi Hussar regiment, quartered in Moscow, was a bad regiment. What was good and what was bad about regiments I did not really understand at the time. My mother was still in London, and I didn't know what to do. It seemed to me that I should choose a regiment that had its quarters in a big city and that had one of the more handsome uniforms. In the store of the General Staff on Prechistenka Street I bought color plates of all the uniforms of the Russian cavalry regiments. There were so many I was dazzled. They were all handsome, but I liked the hussars most of all. (One of Kozma Prutkov's aphorisms aptly says, "If you want to be handsome, join the hussars.")[5] I showed my fiancée the plates with the gaudy uniforms, and the two of us performed divining rituals over them, unable to decide until Mama arrived from London and immediately directed the discussion of my choice of a regiment into the proper channel. For her it was completely obvious that if one was to be a military man, he should of course be in the Guards. The Guards gave one a "position in society." There were more career prospects there. But the main thing was that the Guards were very selective and accepted only the nobility. A Guards officer was considered to be well-bred in society's eyes. But in the army there could be no such guarantee. The chic of the army cavalry was of course not to my mother's liking, precisely because it was chic. If it was chic, it must be in bad taste (my mother hated the very word "chic"). Perhaps the Guards regiments also had a certain chic, but it was more refined and "noble," and that of course was also not quite right.

Only two regiments were in my mother's eyes totally separate from chic and thus truly respectable—the famous and historic Preobrazhenskii Life Guards Infantry Regiment and the Chevalier Guards.[6] They had a kind of super-chic that consisted in the total absence of chic. This was a kind of refined essence of gentlemanliness.

My mother of course had never been interested in regiments, and in fact didn't know any but the two mentioned above, living as she did almost always in such a "civilian" city as Moscow, and receiving as guests either scholars or Moscow boyars, the vast majority of whom were civilians. But in her youth, when she was still an unmarried lady and going out into society in St. Petersburg, my mother belonged precisely to that select circle in which most of the cavaliers were either Preobrazhenskiis or Chevalier Guards. My mother's father, my grandfather Prince Vladimir Andreevich Obolenskii, was a Chevalier Guard in his youth. My other grandfather, on my father's side, Prince Nikolai Petrovich Trubetskoi, was a Preobrazhenskii in his youth. The husband of my mother's sister Countess M. D. Apraksina once commanded a Chevalier Guards regiment, and my mother's cousins, the Obolenskiis and the Ozerovs, also served in those regiments. Both of these regiments accepted the flower of high nobility society. These were truly exclusive aristocratic regiments that were particularly selective in accepting officers. To bear a famous old noble name and have wealth and court connections was far from sufficient to assure entry into one of these rarefied regiments. Only an impeccably well-bred young man, about whose reputation and conduct that regiment gathered thorough information, could hope to get in. And the Chevalier Guards in some cases even rooted around in the genealogy of a young applicant, checking his grandmothers and great-grandmothers for several generations back to make sure that no *madame* with an unsuitable background had wormed her way in and thus spoiled the genealogy. After all, she might have passed on plebeian traits to her posterity. Here no patronage could help you. It was not unusual for sons of ministers and high dignitaries to be rejected upon application to these regiments.

So my mother wanted me to enter one of these, so to speak, family regiments. Having an impeccable genealogy, a famous name, and the suitable upbringing, I had everything I needed to become a chevalier guard or a Preobrazhenskii, but I myself categorically refused to enter the Preobrazhenskii because I wanted to serve in the cavalry. With respect to the Chevalier Guards, my mother herself started to have doubts. It was one thing to be a bachelor chevalier guard. For this one did not need particular wealth, because the Chevalier Guards conducted themselves modestly (without showy chic). It was another thing to be a married chevalier guard, a family man. A bachelor could live with an auntie or in a bachelor apartment. He could be satisfied with a single footman or valet. But a married man had to have not a nook but a decent, nice apartment in the capital and enough money not to fall short of the demands of the level of social life generally accepted in the regimental milieu, moreover in the conditions of a capital city. My mother was afraid that she would not be able to give me such means. She did not want her son to content himself with only the minimum necessary for a married chevalier guard. According to her I should have somewhat more. On the other hand, my mother was worried about my youth, light-mindedness, and inexperience. She was afraid that there would be temptations for me and my wife, that we would forget about prudence, that I would begin to live beyond my means and run into debt.

My mother turned for advice to her relative, Uncle Kolia Miller, a confirmed bachelor and retired military man, and also to her Uncle Mitia Lopukhin, an officer of the General Staff who at that time was commander of the Bug Uhlan regiment (later he took the Life Guard Regiment of Mounted Grenadiers and as the commander of that regiment was killed at the beginning of the World War). Both uncles reassured Mother and pointed out to her that besides the Chevalier Guards there were some quite "appropriate" Guards regiments with excellent traditions. Several of these regiments were quartered in the outskirts of the capital, in nearby towns such as Gatchina, Tsarskoe Selo, and Peterhof, where the way of life was naturally more modest than in the capital. Her uncles assured Mother that she could safely send me to any of the Guards regiments.

But the decisive role in my selection of a regiment was played by the former governor of Grodno and Tula, my uncle Mikhail Mikhailovich Osorgin, who was that very year arranging for his eldest son Misha to do his military service with the Gatchina Blue Cuirassiers (officially Her Majesty's Cuirassier Regiment of Life Guards).[7]

Uncle Mikhail Mikhailovich himself had been a page in his youth and then a chevalier guard, and if he was now arranging for his Misha to spend a year with the Blue Cuirassiers, it was only because that regiment was in the command of his old friend and regimental comrade General Bernov. Bernov assured Osorgin that in his regiment Misha would be as safe as in his mother's arms. Uncle Osorgin proposed that my mother send me to the same regiment along with Misha. Now he wrote from his Kaluga estate, where he lived all the time with his whole family, that General Bernov was an excellent man and that because of my youth it would be very good for me to live in the same quarters with his well-behaved Misha. This Misha was already twenty-seven years old. Thrifty, pious, and modest in all respects, he would have a beneficial influence on me and would hold me back from all kinds of bad temptations and frivolous acts.[8] When she received this letter my mother remembered that in Gatchina her cousin once removed, Prince Denis Obolenskii, was quietly living out his life, hidden away from society because of his deformity. The prince was completely deaf, completely blind, and hunchbacked into the bargain, none of which prevented him from having a reputation as a very practical, lively, and energetic person. My mother immediately sent a letter asking this old man what one heard in Gatchina about the Blue Cuirassiers, and Cousin Denis answered that one heard nothing but good things about the regiment. My cousin would be happy to have me visit him in Gatchina.

My fate was decided. I was content. The Blue Cuirassiers had a very handsome uniform. But what made me happiest was that these cuirassiers had a reputation as remarkable cavalrymen-athletes who nearly always emerged the victors at *concours hippiques* [equestrian competitions] not only in St. Petersburg but even abroad. For example, at the international competitions in London and Vienna, the cuirassier officers von Exe and Pleshkov, whose names were well known throughout Europe to all those interested in the sport at that time, won first place every year. I knew personally and well only one officer in that regiment, the young cornet Prince P. Urusov, a very merry fellow who had recently graduated from the Pages to the regiment. He often visited Moscow, where his mother and his sisters Ara and Ira, former friends of my fiancée, then lived.

And so, after being examined by the military doctor and taking all the necessary documents from the university, one fine day in May 1911, that well-behaved cousin Misha Osorgin and I left for Gatchina to present ourselves to the cuirassiers and their commander General Bernov.

I liked Gatchina immediately. Amazingly tidy, with scrupulously neat, beautifully paved little streets, clean little houses, a huge, exceptionally well-kept city park in which lakes gleamed picturesquely, the town looked festive and cheerful, not in any way reminiscent of the Russian provinces. In those days it was a typical palace town, in which quite a few people lived who were connected with the palace and the court in one way or another. In Gatchina the famous and very expensive Imperial Hunt was quartered, with an enormous staff of huntsmen who lived in the Huntsmen's Settlement. This was also the site of an astounding menagerie that occupied a huge area, where noble deer and wild goats grazed and wandered in complete freedom, and golden pheasants were bred. The exemplary stables of the palace administration were also kept in Gatchina. The magnificent palace built by Emperor Paul, drowning in greenery on the shore of a beautiful lake, made an inevitable impression with its proportions, its grandeur, and its gloomy elegance, which lent the entire town a special, ineffable tone of gala smartness and respectability that I particularly liked. When we arrived in Gatchina, the Empress Mariia Fiodorovna, the most august patroness of the Blue Cuirassiers, was living in the Gatchina Palace.[9] On the occasion of her stay in the city, one could see on the streets a large number of smartly turned-out police officers with a highly respectable and worthy appearance, and officials of the special palace guard with twisted green braid instead of shoulder straps, who were jokingly called "botanists." Mere cabbies, policemen, even ordinary residents of Gatchina—everyone looked respectable, seemly, worthy, and a little festive.

A respectable and seemly cabby drove us straight from the Warsaw Station to the quarters of the commander of the Cuirassier Regiment of Life Guards, located in a comfortable and stylish building that was formerly the palace hunting lodge.

Major General Bernov of His Majesty's Suite greeted us very simply in his elegant study, carpeted with the hides of bears that he himself had bagged, as he explained to us.[10] There was something exaggeratedly general-like in Bernov's appearance. He was a downright caricature. Short, round, and unusually potbellied, with thick greasy light-brown whiskers exactly like those of a walrus, he had a very important, haughty, and pointedly stern air, but in the small and slightly bulging bright-blue eyes blinking through his pince-nez one could see a good-natured stupidity and inoffensiveness. In spite of his impressive whiskers, the general's rosy physiognomy had something womanish or even childish about it. Later we learned that no general in the Guards had as many humorous nicknames and sobriquets as the young Guards had conferred upon the potbellied Bernov for his unusual appearance and intellectual qualities: "Walrus," "Auntie Votia," "Boob-nov," and finally "Heh-peh-eh." The last nickname was given to the general because of his habit in official situations of solemnly adding the sound "heh-peh-eh" after every phrase he uttered. In fact this meaningless "heh-peh-eh," pronounced weightily with a feeling of enormous dignity, suited the general very well and emphasized his caricature-like nature. At regimental banquets he would orate: "I drink to the health of our adored patroness, heh-peh-eh." At exercises he would cry out, "Well done, lads of the Life Squadron! Heh-peh-eh!" or "Captain, be so good as to dress ranks! Heh-peh-eh!"

Bernov was so fat that it was hard for him to be on horseback long. Therefore whenever the regiment went to its Krasnoe Selo encampment it was invariably followed by a comfortable carriage into which the general often moved.[11]

On the whole, Bernov was a strange exception. Not a single other Guards regiment had such a commander. It was simply impossible to understand how the high command of the Guards, and especially the strict and demanding Grand Duke Nikolai Nikolaevich, could tolerate such a caricature at the head of such a distinguished regiment as the Blue Cuirassiers.[12] After all, at that time the Guards were considered to be the best, model troops. Special extra drill demands were made of the Guards, and any innovations in battle tactics or materiel were tried out first on the Guards during camp training. Undoubtedly Bernov was helped by the fact that the cuirassier regiment itself was above all an excellent drill regiment and passed all reviews with the highest marks, thanks to its excellent senior officers and very well-chosen sergeant majors. Bernov's regimental adjutant was a certain Lieutenant Pleshkov—an intelligent and outstanding young man who had a great influence on fat "Auntie Votia" and therefore on all regimental affairs. The commander's assistant in the line unit was Colonel von Schweder—the terror of the regiment.[13] He was a dyed-in-the-wool cavalryman-athlete and a mind-numbingly demanding officer who inspired horror in the lower ranks and terror in the officers. These were the people who moved the whole regimental machine. But I'm getting ahead of myself; I will have more to say about these regimental personalities later. And so, General "Heh-peh-eh" treated us, two young civilians, simply and kindly. After talking a bit about hunting, asking Misha about his papa, and reminiscing about the good old days when he was a dashing cornet in the Chevalier Guards, the general suggested that we take a walk with him to the regimental headquarters. He seated us in front of his desk in the regimental office, which was located almost directly across from the imperial palace, received the report of the regimental adjutant, and conveyed to him our documents and our applications for entry into the regiment. After signing the order of the day, he took us to breakfast at the officers' club. It was located across from the barracks in a large, new, elegant two-story detached house with large plate-glass windows. We passed through a sumptuous anteroom with a doorman in livery, a spacious hall with a grand staircase, a cozily furnished library, and the winter dining room, which boasted boar's heads and elk's heads on the walls and a massive carved sideboard on which various silver wine bowls and *surtouts de tables* [decorative silver vases] gleamed. The dining room looked out onto a splendid but rather tasteless grotto. We walked on through a huge white main hall with light-blue window blinds and a large portrait of Empress Mariia Fiodorovna in a golden frame, and finally we found ourselves on a long balcony where a large table had been set for breakfast, shining with a snow-white tablecloth and abounding with massive silver carafes, salt cellars, and other silver tableware and utensils. When Bernov appeared, everyone rose. About ten officers were having breakfast at the table. When Bernov appeared, they all jumped up at once with an accustomed adroitness, clinking their spurs with a martial sound, and stood at attention with impassive officerlike faces. From the adroitness with which this was performed, one immediately sensed that bearing and discipline were not taken lightly here. This was not the way they behaved in the navy when the captain appeared in the wardroom. The general muttered as if by habit, "Gentlemen, I beg of you, don't trouble yourselves," and introduced us, explaining the reason for our visit.

The general sat at the head of the table and seated me and Osorgin next to himself, as his personal guests.

Although the officers treated us quite politely, still there was a certain coolness and even distance in their manner. They involuntarily displayed the sometimes imperceptible antagonism that they felt toward civilians, and I felt that the black frock coat that I had donned for the occasion of an official visit was completely out of place here and inhibited me in this assemblage of smart military men. In those days a military man, and especially a young cavalryman, as a rule would treat civilians with a certain disdain and sense of superiority.

Only the good-natured "Auntie Votia"—"Heh-peh-eh"—in spite of his rank, continued to engage us in conversation, thereby displaying his true tact and good breeding. A loud and animated conversation was going on among the others at the table. After sitting back down in their places, the officers apparently were no longer constrained by the general's presence.

I listened to the conversations with interest and looked inquisitively at everyone there, trying to quickly understand and grasp the peculiarities and the general tone of that completely unknown society, in whose midst I was to find myself in time.

At one end of the table they were heatedly talking about the merits of a certain profitable mare that had just been bought by one of the cornets. At the other end, a lieutenant with a black mustache was talking about the summer racing season at the Kolomiagi Hippodrome and the coming equestrian competitions in Krasnoe.[14] A burly bald captain who was evidently not in his first year of commanding a squadron was recounting to his neighbor, a boyish staff captain, how and why his squadron always came in first in the regiment at marksmanship reviews. This kind of talk was completely new to me and had an enchanting sound.

Here at the table one got a strong sense of a special little closed regimental world of common tastes, interests, habits, settled views and relations, and also of their own little words and expressions. Many of them displayed in conversation an identical affected carelessness, an identical mannered way of speaking. There lay on them all the identical stamp of the regiment, and in particular the cuirassier regiment. Later I observed that every regiment had its own completely special stamp, invisible but strongly felt. Almost all of them had their hair combed the very same way, slicked down and glossy and parted down the middle. Almost all of them looked agile and lithe. Their single-breasted, high-collared jackets and riding breeches were all of an amazingly elegant fit which attested to the high skill of the tailors who cut them.

Looking at these dandified people, who continued ever so slightly to emphasize their superiority over me, I, young man that I was, could think of only one thing: quickly, quickly, as quickly as possible to become just like them, to become a *person* . . . Neither among professors, nor students, nor bureaucrats, nor even the civilian governors I knew had I seen such a dignified, self-assured air. I knew ministers of state, I knew high dignitaries—even they looked much more humble than these people whose every movement was accompanied by a marvelous ringing of spurs. And I thought: it would be wonderful to be a beautifully dressed man, a man of honor, a man always bearing arms—*a military man*—defender of his homeland.

With a feeling of great satisfaction I left Gatchina, planning to return there in the autumn to enter the regiment. But I must make one proviso. Our acceptance into the regiment, even as mere volunteers, depended in the last analysis on the decision of the General Assembly of officers of the regiment. We were to be informed specially of this decision. No one could be accepted into the Guards without a hearing. Such was the custom.

I remember that on the way back to Moscow I stopped in St. Petersburg at the home of my uncle, Prince Piotr Nikolaevich Trubetskoi, who at that time was a member of the State Council on Elections. His eldest son Volodia was then doing his military service in His Majesty's Cossack Regiment of Life Guards. (Volodia was attached to the Don Cossack troops because my uncle had estates on the Don.) He was just then finishing his officer's examinations as an external student of the Nicholas Cavalry School.[15] I too would some day have to take the same kind of examinations. According to my cousin, who had graduated from the university, these examinations were no laughing matter. The program of study was very extensive. One had to pass a two-year course on a multitude of special subjects. The school looked askance at volunteers and would flunk them at the drop of a hat. They demanded serious preparation, made difficult by service in the regiment, which took up a great deal of time and energy. Those volunteers who wished to become officers, who mostly came from rich noble families, were coached for the examinations by officers who specialized in this business and charged their students quite a lot of money. A certain Captain Basevich was particularly famous for his skill at preparing people for examinations. His service came "with a guarantee," but he charged an arm and a leg—up to a thousand rubles per student. One could, however, haggle with him. Volodia promised to arrange for this Basevich to be my coach.

The matter was complicated by the fact that I could not pass the examinations in a mediocre fashion. The school used the so-called twelve-point system, and you could be an officer in the Guards only if you received an average mark not lower than nine points. Those who received an average mark lower than nine could only become officers in the army. A mark lower than six in *any* subject was considered unsatisfactory, and anyone who received a mark of five failed outright. I remember that this seriously worried me, because I had been a poor high-school student and an even worse university student. This time, however, I showed good sense. Upon returning to Moscow I bought a lot of military textbooks in various disciplines, and for the rest of the summer I studied the most difficult ones, such as artillery, tactics, fortifications, and topography. Without a teacher this was rather hard. Nevertheless this timely preparation served me well later.

As usual, our whole family spent the summer at our estate near Moscow, Menshovo, where I practiced surveying, using a plane table I had acquired, and guided by Baron Brücken's textbook on topography.

Bearing in mind my coming service, every day during the summer I rode a bit on a horse I had bought from a Cossack who was in "His Majesty's Own Escort." It was a medium-sized but very fine bay steed which, in my childishness and longing to show off, I had given an idiotically Anglicized appearance by bobbing its tail and clipping its mane with my own two hands. To make things worse, I named it "Pif-Paf." On this mustang I made a dashing fool of myself and performed rather idiotic stunts and tricks, seriously imagining that I understood the very highest wisdom of the cavalry. On poor Pif-

Paf I jumped over all the local ditches and fences, and even some distant ones. My jumping was totally useless, but I did it with such enthusiasm and passion that I reduced the unfortunate little beast to utter exhaustion and nearly broke its front extremities.

Thus did I prepare for my service in the horse. My family, of course, began to consider me a remarkable cavalryman already. The old coachman Egor was of the same opinion, although he was very sad for the horse. I was just as friendly as I had always been with this nutty old man, who had served in our family for about forty years, and I was constantly in the stable with him. There he would tell me endless stories about "the old prince," my grandfather, for whom he had particular respect thanks to Grandfather's love for horses. And what horses Egor had bought for the old prince! And how the old prince trusted Egor! He also would tell how my uncles and aunties had done their courting in his carriage, and how he, Egor, would sit on the coach-box and listen to everything and just twirl his mustache, but never said a word to anyone, because "A word is worth a ruble, but sometimes a bit of silence will get you ten." He loved this saying very much despite the fact that he himself was exceptionally garrulous. He also liked to tell how, in his youth when he hadn't yet entered Grandfather's service and worked for some rich gentleman, he took part in the abduction of a bride for his master, and wore a beautiful troika of horses to death while being chased by the bride's brothers, who were rich but evil men.

The coachman Egor was one of the few people I had initiated into the secrets of my heart; I had told him who my sweetheart was.

"Well, will you get a big dowry with her?" was the first thing he wanted to know.

"I don't know," I answered candidly. "I am getting married not for the sake of the dowry, but simply because I like the princess."

"Oh, Pri-i-i-nce," Egor exclaimed, shaking his head in distress. "You mustn't reason like that. The way I see it, as long as the bride is rich—she can be a hunchback for all I care!"

In general, the summer of 1911 passed quietly for me, without incident. It was the last summer that I lived with my mother, and I did not leave Menshovo except for two trips to the Kaluga province to see my fiancée, whom I loved just as ardently as ever.

Ahead of me lay a new, quite independent life, full of enticing but hazy vistas.

Chapter Two

The Training of a Guardsman

AT THE BEGINNING of October my cousin Misha Osorgin and I arrived together to serve in Gatchina, where quarters had already been prepared for us.

On the very first day we set off for regimental headquarters and reported to our immediate superior, Lieutenant Palitsyn, who served as the head of the regimental training detachment to which all the volunteers were immediately assigned. First of all Palitsyn demanded that we order (at our own expense) a complete uniform at the regimental tailor's, and that this uniform not differ in the slightest detail from a regular soldier's uniform. Cloth, buttons, even the linings—everything must be exactly the same as the uniform of the simple line soldiers. We could report to the regiment only when dressed like regular soldiers. Only "in the city" and off duty were we permitted to dress a little more elegantly, but still observing the established forms of the regiment. I must admit, however, that even the regular Guards uniform was of quite high quality, quite handsome and fine. We were to wear black uniforms with gold buttons and brass helmets with grenade-shaped ornaments. We also had white dress uniforms, with cuffs, collar, and chest beautifully edged in yellow and light-blue stripes. These uniforms were called *kolety*. They had no buttons and were fastened by hooks, since in mounted formation one wore brass armor (the so-called cuirasses) over them. These uniforms were to be worn with gilded helmets, crowned by large gold double-headed eagles with outspread wings, and with "cuffs"—special white gloves with huge stiff tops almost to the elbow, like the gauntlets of medieval knights. We also had yellow double-breasted jackets and simple khaki shirts. Our ammunition belts were snow-white, like those of all the Guards.

Dashing lance corporals immediately took it upon themselves to teach us whom and how to salute. Our uniforms were quickly made for us, and about four days later, clothed in white dress jackets and having pulled on our heavy brass helmets adorned with eagles, we hired the regimental cabby Averian, who knew the addresses of all the officers, and set off to "report" to each of them separately, in accordance with the accepted custom. This was a whole procedure that required several rehearsals. We were rehearsed by a gallant sergeant major of the training detachment by the name of Maliar.

After all, we were merely soldiers—"the lower ranks"—and from the moment we put on a soldier's uniform, an enormous gulf opened up between us and the officers. Now, dressed just like soldiers, we could no longer speak frankly and behave naturally with a person dressed in an officer's uniform, even though we belonged to the highest court circles. We had to know how to present ourselves to an officer, how to appear "before his eyes" while holding broadsword and helmet, how to look into the faces of our superiors, simultaneously "deferential and cheerful."

A civilian is ludicrous when first shoved into a glittering military uniform. After all, in the old-time army, real military bearing was not easy to acquire and any civilian who dressed in a military way and wanted to imitate a military bearing was inevitably ludicrous and grotesque. It was easier for me, since I already had some experience in this area through my service on a navy ship. Misha Osorgin had no such experience and thus was very ludicrous, especially since he was a bit awkward and clumsy anyway.

Producing an unbelievable racket with our huge line-soldiers' boots, our spurs, and the enormous metallic sheaths of our broadswords, which hung unaccustomedly from our left sides and caught on everything as we walked, we would enter the officers' quarters marching in "goose step," which we did a poor job of. Presenting ourselves to our superiors, we would contort our faces into a "deferential but cheerful" expression, stand at attention like statues, and loudly shout in turn: "Your Honor, I have the honor to report to you on the occasion of enlisting in the Life Guard Cuirassier Regiment of Her Majesty the Sovereign Empress Mariia Fiodorovna . . . Volunteer So-and-so!"

We had to gallantly blurt this out in one breath. During this tirade the officer, no matter what his rank, would also stand at stony attention, then give us his hand, and then we would again fill his apartment with the loud and joyful cry, "To your health, Your Honor!" Some officers would limit themselves to this and let us go while the going was good. But others, after pronouncing the traditional, "For God's sake, don't trouble yourselves," would offer us a seat and try to enter into pleasant conversation, which never got going thanks to us, since we had fervently entered into our new roles as "soldiers" and tried to conduct ourselves with gallantry and discipline. Besides, we were simply unable to talk. Instead of "yes" and "no" we were required to say "yes, sir" and "no, sir," and had to either start or end every phrase with the form of address "Your Honor," or "Your Radiance" if the officer was a prince or a count. From lack of habit this was very inhibiting.

We were especially embarrassed by the brilliant Brigadier General Girard-de-Sucanton, former commanding officer of the Blue Cuirassiers, who belonged to the tsar's suite.[1] We noisily barged in on him as he was having tea with his family. To our embarrassment the general seated us at the table, and his daughter and his wife, a very fashionable and beautiful lady, began to treat us to tea. We were very well versed in how a well-brought-up young civilian should behave in such a situation. But the soldier's uniform and the consciousness that we were nothing but rank and file left us at wit's end in the presence of an officer of such high rank as a general, especially a general whose pretty daughter kept looking at us with a barely perceptible mocking smile.

After completing our visits and finally arriving home in the evening, we laughed at ourselves, reliving the impressions of the day.

The next day began our real service. It was by no means easy!

The sole privilege of volunteers was the fact that they were permitted to live not in the barracks but in their own private quarters. Early in the morning while it was still completely dark, Misha and I had already run across the Gatchina park, called "the Priorat" for some reason, to the regimental headquarters. In the barracks we would put on our yellow camel-hair jackets with black collars, and go in formation with the whole detachment to the stables, where we would clean, groom, and feed the horses by bright electric light.

The stables, which smelled like a circus, were kept in exemplary order, no worse than a good private home, and were remarkable for their splendid cleanliness. In the stalls stood the cavalry horses—huge beautiful chestnut giants—all of the best breeds.[2] These were the finest horses in the land, strictly screened by the remount commissions and selected for the Guards. These giants were supplied by the best stud farms, mostly in Poland (Drogojowski, Korybut-Daszkewicz, Manguszko, Zakrzewski, and other farms). The First Guards Division—the so-called Cuirassier Division, which included our regiment—was still considered, as of old, to be heavy cavalry (an arm of the service that no longer exists).[3] Therefore it was staffed by strapping men and the tallest horses—real monsters. You almost never see such horses these days. Their type has disappeared. During the World War and the Civil War they all perished either from exhaustion or on the field of battle. But even sadder is the fact that their thoroughbred sires and dams also died; they were, alas, not spared by the repeated mobilizations of wartime, which scoured the entire supply of suitable horses for the needs of both the White and Red armies.

A supply of thoroughbred horses is created only slowly and with great difficulty. It's true, even in today's cavalry one does see some fairly good horses, frisky and full of stamina, but in breeding, size, and beauty they are very far from those beautiful giants of the parade ground that used to be supplied to the Cuirassier Division of the Imperial Guards.

Oh, what steeds they were! But let me not get carried away by lyricism and digress from the description of our daily routine. It would begin for us with the grooming of the horses, carried out with the help of brushes and currycombs. To make the horse gleam the way the regimental training detachment required was not easy, and if after grooming the horse was clean but not *ideally* clean, you could really catch hell.

It was particularly difficult to groom those fiery and high-strung specimens who couldn't stand to be touched by the stiff brush, at the very sight of which they would begin to snort, tremble, beat their hooves, and kick in the narrow stalls, trying as hard as they could to bite you. An inexperienced person could easily be maimed by such a horse. You needed a special knack—the horse must fear and respect you.

When a certain amount of dander had built up on the comb, one had to carefully turn the comb over onto the floor and knock it with the handle of the brush, thus forming a neat little white square of dander each time. These little squares were arranged in checkerboard patterns in front of each stall, forming regular outlines on the floor. Just by the density of these squares toward the end of grooming the sergeant major could tell how thoroughly each horse had been polished. But he would not content himself with that and often would personally check the cleanliness of one horse or another, inspecting it in detail.

Our superior, Lieutenant Palitsyn, would order the sergeant major to give the volunteers the most difficult horses to groom, which was rather unpleasant. We were particularly afraid of the horse named Hebrew, from the Enisherlov stud farm—he was a real beast, high-strung, violent, and mean, who caused a lot of trouble in the stables. On the other hand, grooming the affectionate mare Widow—a dear, clever girl—was sheer pleasure.

By the way, grooming horses came more easily to me than to most. My friend the coachman Egor had once taught me this art in Menshovo. But some of the volunteers (there were seven of us in all) tried all sorts of stratagems for getting to groom a quiet horse, contrary to Palitsyn's orders, and for this purpose they would try to win Maliar over with tips. Maliar agreed to this reluctantly, because he was worried every day that the lieutenant himself would unexpectedly descend on the grooming session and give him hell. Everyone was mortally afraid of the lieutenant.

After the grooming we would go in formation to the barracks, where men were hurriedly drinking tea. We volunteers were immediately given the privilege of drinking tea with the sergeant major in his separate room, where we would treat Maliar to tasty sandwiches and jokes, which he loved. It was in this same little room that Maliar taught us the lore of the regiment. He, of course, was no fool and he became friendly with us.

After tea we worked on the leveling of rifles in the barracks, and got to know our rifles well. The lance corporal and the noncommissioned officers worked with each soldier separately on setting the rifle's sights. They worked efficiently and sensibly, by the individual method, preparing good riflemen.

By 8:00 A.M. everyone gathered at desks in a classroom. At the precise moment that the clock struck eight, the lieutenant himself would be announced. The sergeant major's cast-iron throat would bellow a thundering "Rise . . . Attention!" We would leap up and turn to stone. The orderly would dashingly and gallantly give his report. Then would come our superior's "Hello, lads," and the answering harmonious chorus: "Y'r h'lth, y'r H'n'r," shouted out loudly, "cheerfully and deferentially" in a particular accelerating rhythm. The lieutenant would remove his gray overcoat, which the orderly would obligingly catch, and in deathly silence he would attentively inspect with his piercing, stern, and all-noticing eyes the men, petrified like statues. After a pause he would order us to sit. He would himself sit down and begin lessons either in topography or the regulations. The soldiers had memorized these regulations almost by heart. Palitsyn would explain these subjects to the men in a remarkably sensible and clear way, patiently instilling in them an intelligent and thorough knowledge of the service. It could not be otherwise: the regimental training detachment was preparing the junior officer staff.

From 10:00 to 12:00 in the large and stylish regimental manège, the training detachment had riding lessons in rotation.[4] Then came lunch break. Here once again the volunteers enjoyed certain privileges and dined not from the common pot in the barracks but at our own expense in the officers' club, where they had allotted us a completely isolated room with a separate street entrance so that we had no possibility of encountering any officers. We were not given access to the officers' own rooms.

After "nap time" (which we volunteers almost never took advantage of, since we would have had to run home) right until evening we had lessons in gymnastics, infantry formation, acrobatics on horseback, fencing, and target practice. These classes were mostly conducted by Palitsyn's assistant, the young, acrobatic, black-haired and swarthy cornet Elvengren, of Finnish parentage—the idol of all the high school girls in Gatchina.

At all the lessons they vigorously scolded, hardened, drilled, tugged, and polished us, trying to create genuine soldierly bearing. In the evening we would return home exhausted and so tired that we hurried into bed. And so it went day after day for long months.

But the hardest of all were the riding lessons in the manège under the command of Lieutenant Palitsyn, who from the very first day gave us incredible hell and inspired panicked terror in all the volunteers. I can see him now with a whip in his hand, in an officer's ash-gray overcoat with gold shoulder straps and dark-blue collar tabs, in an irreproachably white cuirassier's cap with a turquoise band. Gaunt, extremely tall, blond, pale, with a long hooked nose and bulging gray eyes, he was the very model of military discipline, the personification of severity, exactingness, and *Zug*.[5] He was a line officer who deeply hated and despised everything "civilian" to the marrow of his bones. A former cadet of a famous cavalry school where *Zug* was taken to the status of a cult, Palitsyn was simply organically incapable of tolerating volunteers, seeing in them pampered, spoiled men who had accidentally gotten into the regiment from the civilian world. And how brutal he was with us, the unhappy seven volunteers, during riding lessons!

At first we had to ride without stirrups in order to adjust to the correct regulation seat. If you got a jolting horse, riding in formation without stirrups could be very exhausting. Of course the volunteers immediately caught on to this and by means of giving tips arranged to ride on calm, quiet horses. This could not escape Palitsyn's notice. "Volunteer So-and-so!" he would roar in a bass voice heard all over the manège, "you're riding a streetcar, not a horse! What kind of tip did you give the sergeant major for such a pleasure? Hey, sergeant major, starting today, give the volunteers only the roughest horses!"

I remember that after this order, to my unhappy lot fell the famous Hebrew—a horse that jolted insanely and would throw me out of the saddle when we were trotting in formation.

With no stirrups you had to keep in the saddle only by the strength of your knees, which you had to squeeze firmly on the saddle-wings, leaving free the part of the leg lower than the knee. At first I was bad at this, especially after the command "Field trot!" would resound.[6] Trying to achieve a more secure position, I would involuntarily start to press my lower legs to Hebrew's sides. The very fiery and nervous Hebrew couldn't bear this and would immediately speed up to a gallop, spoiling the formation and evoking Palitsyn's thunderous shout: "Volunteer, where is the proper interval? Get your legs back! Get your spaghetti-legs out of here, you pickled idiot!"

Biting my lips, I would dig my knees into the slippery saddle-wings with all my might, but I was too light, and Hebrew jolted too much, and again I felt that I was swinging in the saddle, calling forth new shouts from the lieutenant. After two or three days of riding like this, my knees were torn and bloody, I had scratches and very painful bruises. It couldn't continue like this. I went to see the regimental doctor in the dressing station. The junior doctor, Dr. Pikel, gave me some sort of ointment and excused me from riding for three days. The next day, as I was supposed to in such a case, I appeared in the manège without a horse and gave the lieutenant the doctor's note excusing me. "Well, all right, fine!" Palitsyn said calmly, smiling affectionately. "You've skinned your little knees, it happens sometimes! . . . You're excused for three days! . . . Well, that means you'll have three Sundays without leave . . ."

This was a blow. On the Sabbath we all usually liked to visit our relatives in St. Petersburg, and these trips were real holidays for us. I remember that the next day, in spite of my excuse and the skin flayed off my knees, I was again astride the hated Hebrew, hoping that Palitsyn would take it into account and forgive me at least two Sundays. In vain! I only hurt my cause by this: Palitsyn decided that since I wasn't making use of my excuse, I must simply be squeamish, and gave me extra duty out of turn.

During the trotting in formation, at the command "To the tail," the entire rotation was forced to swing their lower legs and bend their torsos forward and back while preserving the correct leg position, which was quite exhausting. Finally the long-awaited command resounded: "At a walk, at ease, put your dress in order, stroke your horse!" It seemed as if the longed-for minute of rest had come, when you could finally stretch your numb and sore limbs. But nothing of the sort! Palitsyn was already shouting in his bass voice to the whole manège: "Stand on your saddles!"

The soldiers would stand on the narrow, slippery, and swaying saddles and try to hold their balance by stretching out their arms. Palitsyn would indifferently let the plain soldiers ride by him without saying a word, but when the volunteers' horses went by him, he would begin, as if by chance, to softly flick them with his whip—this made the horses speed up, and the volunteers standing on their saddles would scatter like peas from their horses into the sawdust.

"Hey, volunteers!" Palitsyn would bellow, grief-stricken. "You'll be the death of me! You've grown so big and tall, but I have no joy of you! Back on your horses! Stand on your sa-a-a-addles!"

And again the flick of the whip and the inevitable somersaults by the volunteers, until the command, "Sit like human beings. Atten-shun," and again trotting without stirrups.

We also had a tough time during the lessons in horseback acrobatics, which we had to perform in full battle gear (that is, with rifle and saber). It was hard to be agile enough to leap up onto a huge galloping horse with one movement. At first there wasn't enough agility and strength in your arms and legs. The saber would get caught between your legs. Palitsyn would encourage the clumsy ones with his whip, which in such cases did, I have to admit, exert a most beneficial influence. Sometimes you would grab the end of the horse's mane on its withers with one hand, lean on the saddle with the other, and hang helplessly from the side of the horse, pushing your feet against the ground and trying vainly to fly up into the saddle. Suddenly you feel a sharp flick of the whip that seems to scorch the softest part of your body and . . . O miracle! All at once you somehow acquire the agility and strength—like a little feather you fly upwards, landing right in the saddle as you're supposed to, and Palitsyn is already booming: "Sorry, volunteer, I guess I got you instead of the horse by mistake!"

That whole time I only got a taste of the whip once. Its burning touch immediately taught me how to vault, but I could not forgive Palitsyn for a long time, and harbored a burning resentment and anger in my soul.

The other volunteers also tasted the whip, but it most often touched the pudgy and spoiled Sangovich, of whom I will speak later.

The manège truly became a kind of nightmare for us, even though most of us chose the cavalry out of love for equestrian sport.

Now the lance corporals and the soldiers excused from riding are dragging a stone wall into the manège. It is a massive wooden hurdle about three and a half feet high, painted to look like bricks and called the "coffin" for some reason. This hurdle is placed up against the wall of the manège. We hear the drawn-out command, "At manège gallop . . . forward march!" Palitsyn has the whole rotation ride past him over the hurdle without stirrups. A few bounds before the obstacle we have to drop the reins and put our hands on our thighs. This is done in order to train us not to hang on the rein or jerk the horse during the jump. This method helps people develop a firm and steady seat. But at the beginning, deprived of stirrups and having no other support than their own knees, many of the men would instinctively wave or spread out their arms during the horse's powerful flight over the hurdle, seeming to catch at the air with their hands. Palitsyn never forgives this convulsive gesture: "You're an airplane, not a cavalryman! Extra duty!" he cries after the offending party.

We understood very well why they made us jump precisely this way in the beginning. But it was another matter when Palitsyn forced the rotation to cross the hurdle facing backwards, with hands on hips to boot, and without looking behind us. This was, in essence, reckless, dangerous, and, I'm not afraid to admit, simply terrifying.

Here is the stone wall—the "coffin" by the wall of the manège. We're riding at a gallop. The advance rider is approaching the obstacle. Suddenly the command: "Scissors! Face backwards!" and we quickly turn and sit facing the horse's tail.[7] The pommel presses uncomfortably into your rear and reduces your area of support. "Hands on thighs! Don't dare to look behind you!" Now an awful chill begins involuntarily to creep into your heart—the anticipation of an almost inevitable fall. You pray to God for a second or two that it won't be painful. With anxiety you look into the muzzle of the huge chestnut horse galloping behind you, under whose hooves you will undoubtedly fall when you crash head first onto the ground. You can't repress the desire to look back at the hurdle, you sense its terrifying and swift approach with every bound. You want to dig your fingers into the horse's fidgeting croup. Too late . . . The horse flies powerfully upwards, the front pommel pushes your rear out of the saddle with an unexpectedly violent shove. You are thrown into space. Your arms are involuntarily flung upwards. You fly head over heels right under the legs of the horse galloping behind you. Luckily, horses possess one amazing attribute: while galloping they almost never strike a fallen person with their hooves, and in most cases they somehow instinctively gallop over him safely.

Leaping to his feet after his fall, the stunned man doesn't himself understand how he escaped unharmed. Scratching his bruises and spitting out sawdust, he runs, usually limping now, to catch his runaway steed.

There were cases of serious injury. Sometimes they had to send several men right to the regimental hospital with serious wounds or dislocated limbs, sometimes unconscious.

"Learn how to fall," the sergeant major would say to us. "When you fall, don't lose your head, roll tightly into a ball." Yes, there was a whole science to it. One of the volunteers broke a finger. Someone broke his collarbone, another broke a rib. Three or four men were even released from service entirely.

Luckily, soon after that Palitsyn put an end to the practice of jumping while facing backwards, which was supposed to develop "daring and fearlessness" in us. We found out later that the regimental commander's assistant in charge of line soldiers, Colonel von Schweder, noticed the growing number of injured men in the training detachment and reprimanded Palitsyn accordingly.

During rotation riding we spent a lot of time learning how to hack with our sabers. The regiment was famed in competition for its dashing swordsmen. Many young officers were keen on this activity and elevated it to a sport. One must say that they taught the soldiers to hack with great virtuosity. At a full gallop they could cut with their sabers a little potato hanging by a thread, plunge the saber through a narrow ring, dashingly cut off clay heads at full career; they could cut through thick straw plaits and vines while jumping over obstacles. They hacked beautifully, with style. Palitsyn would get very excited during saber practice. Woe betide him who while swinging the saber caught the rein with his left hand and jerked the horse, causing it to rush forward. Then you would inevitably hear Palitsyn's bass voice behind you: "Hey, So-and-so! Off to the sentry house at the same gait!" And the offending party would set off straight from the manège to twenty-four hours under arrest in the regimental guardhouse.

I myself was lucky and managed not to get arrested. To make up for it I was constantly being given extra orderly duty by Palitsyn. I had to be on duty both in the barracks and in the stables. I have to admit that I preferred the latter. It's true that after spending the night in the stables, your clothes were completely permeated by that special horse smell and stank of ammonia, but this was still better than the stench given off at night by Her Majesty's Cuirassiers after a heavy meal. Although our guards barracks was magnificent in appearance, the walls even decorated with genuinely valuable old engravings, the ventilation in these elegant, old-fashioned buildings left much to be desired.

In the regiment they emphasized "lance work" no less than saber handling. I was in the cavalry when they were still using wooden lances—thick, long, and very heavy, like those of medieval knights. Our lances were painted bright turquoise. The Yellow Cuirassiers had yellow ones, and the Horse Guards and Life Guards had red ones. On parade they were hung with fluttering multicolored pennants, which was very beautiful. Soon after, however, these awkward lances were replaced by light tubular metal ones that were painted khaki in all the regiments.

At our lessons in the manège we used our lances at a gallop to impale standing or lying straw dummies dressed in old cuirassier uniforms. We also learned how to thread the lance through little rings at full gallop, in order to develop the accuracy of our thrust. The whole rotation would gallop across the manège, making a "flanking movement" with our lances, that is, rotating the long shaft of the lance around the torso in a special movement that rendered the horseman invulnerable to an enemy blow during a hand-to-hand fight. Some cuirassier strongmen would rotate the lances in such a way that they literally hummed.

There was another exercise—throwing the lance up over your head. This was also done by the whole rotation at a gallop and simultaneously. You had to throw the heavy lance as high as possible. At first it often happened that someone's lance would fall on the ground, and this was rather dangerous. During my peacetime service I had occasion to find out what serious wounds this most ancient weapon could inflict. Once in a rotation of young soldiers (I think from the Second Squadron) the following tragic incident occurred. While the rotation was moving across the manège at a gallop, someone threw his lance up clumsily. It fell to the ground vertically, with its point up, and immediately began to tumble backwards. The rider behind didn't notice, because he was trying to catch his own lance and therefore was looking upwards. It turned out that he rode at a good clip right onto the falling lance point, which instantly pierced him through the chest and came a whole two feet out of his back. They immediately pulled the lance out and quickly took the wounded man to the military hospital, but they could no longer do anything for him. The poor man died two hours later in the arms of the regimental commander himself, who had hurried to the hospital when he heard what had happened. The entire regiment buried this soldier with great pomp and display. He was given a first-class funeral, and the commanders and officers raised several hundred rubles by subscription, which they sent to the family of the deceased.

From my description of the manège you might conclude that Palitsyn was a kind of soulless beast, but that would not be right. Much later, when I had become an officer, Palitsyn and I got onto the best of terms. He was an excellent, responsive comrade, and I became convinced that in essence he had a good heart. He loved the soldiers and knew each of his subordinates, with all his good and bad qualities, like the back of his hand. Despising everything civilian, Palitsyn respected the soldier precisely because he was a *soldier.* Deeply rooted in Palitsyn was the conviction that one had to develop in the soldier a martial daring and contempt for danger and for pain. In adoring stern military discipline and elevating it to the status of a cult, Palitsyn was only being logical as regards his own command. On duty he was a martinet. Off duty he was a completely different person. The soldiers liked him. They felt and saw with their own eyes that their superior was a man who truly knew his business. Palitsyn was an authority in their eyes, and therefore they respected him. The soldiers must have liked the way Palitsyn behaved towards the volunteers, i.e., us little noblemen: with us he was captious, but not with them. He would permit himself to make fun of us sometimes, but he never made fun of a soldier, and if he "gave hell" to a soldier, it was always with just cause. Palitsyn didn't limit himself to caring about his soldiers—he was interested in their lives and entered into their interests. He was witty and had a good sense of humor, which they liked. In essence he was a highly demanding, good line officer to the marrow of his bones. Officers like him were usually named to head regimental training detachments.

Palitsyn liked to go on a real spree every once in a while. He would time it to coincide with some especially festive occasion. For example, when he was awarded the medal of St. Stanislaus in the third degree for zeal in the service, he started drinking so hard to celebrate that he abandoned the lessons that day. He got drunk himself and treated the whole detachment, which celebrated along with its lieutenant.

Another memorable occasion was when some English naval officers were blown into our regimental officers' club by some wind I can no longer remember. According to custom, they were received with the regiment's inimitable hospitality and treated all night to a wonderful dinner, singers, trumpeters, and an ocean of champagne. The tipsy Englishmen began to brag about their ship's customs and to tell tall tales about the adroitness and training of their sailors. The Englishmen's boasting stung Palitsyn to the quick. It was already late at night when he made a bet with the English commodore that by sounding the alarm he could have his entire detachment formed up in six minutes in front of the club, with full ammunition and on horseback. No sooner said than done, and in the barracks embraced by slumber a telephone immediately began to ring piercingly.

I just happened to be on penal orderly duty in the stables. Suddenly at 1:00 A.M. a pale Palitsyn with bulging eyes comes bursting into the stable. He's in full field dress with a watch in his hands. I start to make my report, but from a distance he's already waving me away and howling in a panicked voice: "Ala-a-a-arm!" I remember that I was so stunned by the unexpectedness of it all that I took off running headlong down the corridor between the stalls, and, addressing the slumbering horses, I too started howling at the top of my lungs: "Alarm! Alarm!" There were no people in the stables except two orderlies asleep in the empty day-stall.[8] Only horses, blinking in bewilderment, looked around upon hearing my wild cries.

But a minute later the whole stable had been turned upside down. The doors were flung open noisily, spurs started jingling loudly, and about fifty out-of-breath cuirassiers who had just jumped down from their bunks came pouring into the corridor, overtaking each other. They were fastening their uniforms and hastily donning their ammunition belts while running. Palitsyn and the sergeant major, at opposite ends of the stable, were already energetically hurrying the men with strong language. In the twinkling of an eye, saddles flew from the shelves, the horses' bits began to rattle as they were bridled, and their hooves began to clatter resonantly as they were led at a trot out of the stables. This all happened so noisily and swiftly that I didn't have time to turn around before the stables were empty. While the detachment was galloping to form up in front of the entrance to the officers' club, Palitsyn, astride the mare Widow, rode up the staircase right into the front door of the club, passed at a trot through the entryway and the library and into the brightly illuminated hall, where he sharply reined in the gigantic mare in front of the chair where the stunned English commodore was sitting, saluted him in due form with his drawn saber, and gave report. The hosts and guests poured out into the street in a crowd, where the Englishman had to inspect a nocturnal parade.

That is how the lieutenant put the Englishmen to shame and upheld the honor of the Russian cavalry. Both the triumphant and the disgraced parties drank an *ocean* on this occasion. Our detachment's turnout in response to the alarm was remarkable. The next day the lieutenant relieved the men from morning classes and offered the detachment some rest and refreshment.

Night alarm drills were, in general, encouraged by the high command. But riding on horseback into the officers' club was clearly not part of the usual program. Some officers might not have gotten away with such a stunt. But the regimental high command was well-disposed towards Palitsyn. This time the colonel in charge limited himself to a "heart-to-heart talk" with the lieutenant and forced him to pay the bill for the damaged parquet in the club, which had fallen victim to Widow's hooves.

Besides Osorgin and me there were five more volunteers in the regiment: von Vittorf and Evreinov (inseparable friends who always stuck together), Sangovich, Iskander, and Speshnev. The last two intended as I did to take the officer's examinations in the Nicholas Cavalry School and be commissioned as officers in our regiment. But neither of them succeeded in becoming an officer—Iskander, because he failed the examinations two years in a row, and the bold and likable Speshnev, because he was unfortunately rejected by the officers' association of the regiment in his application to be commissioned as a cornet.

Strangely enough, they rejected him because before he entered the service he had been keen on the theater and had often appeared on stage as an amateur, sometimes acting along with professionals. The senior Colonel von

Schweder, who fastidiously and strictly guarded the honor of the regiment, regarded this as incompatible with the "high calling" of an officer of the Life Guards. A person who had appeared with professional play-actors and entertained the public from the stage, even without being paid for it and out of pure love of art, was, in the colonel's opinion, unworthy of the honor of being accepted into the society of regimental officers, despite the fact that Speshnev was from a rather good noble family, was well-off, and had graduated from an exclusive institute of higher education. The stubborn colonel could not be moved—he insisted that it would be unseemly to accept a "play-actor" as an officer of the regiment.

Whenever the officers' association of a Guards regiment rejected a young man who wished to enter the regiment as an officer, it was a heavy blow for the applicant. Anyone who was rejected by one Guards regiment would almost certainly not be accepted by any of the others. Sometimes they would reject people for trifles (as in the case of Speshnev) or because of some officer's personal antipathy. It was too bad that they did not keep a rejection secret, and people outside the regiment usually found out about it. Society would begin to look askance at a young man who had been rejected, as if he were a branded character, even though he might not have anything bad on his conscience. But I must confess that most rejections of applicants to a regiment had weightier grounds.

Speshnev became friendly with me and Iskander, whose brother was a staff captain in our regiment and commanded the Third Squadron. Those two brothers Iskander were legitimate children of Grand Duke Nikolai Konstantinovich, who was exiled to Turkestan in the reign of Tsar Alexander II, where he legally married some lady and had these sons by her.

At that time the reason for the grand duke's exile was little known to the broad public, and rumor even ascribed some sort of political basis to the story, which, however, never existed. I will tell you the story as I heard it from people who had important connections with the court at one time.

At the beginning of the 1870s, Grand Duke Nikolai Konstantinovich, nephew of Tsar Alexander II, became passionately infatuated with a foreign variety-show actress and had a stormy affair with her. Blinded by passion, the young duke went so far as to steal a rare piece of jewelry from his mother, Grand Duchess Aleksandra Iosifovna, and present it as a gift to his beloved. Of course the loss of the jewelry was discovered. This theft, which took place in the Marble Palace, and in the tsar's apartments to boot, was an unheard-of event and caused a big stir. The palace servants came under suspicion. The tsar summoned General N., the head of the police department, and ordered him to find the thief at all costs. Several days later General N. presented the grand duchess with the stolen object, but when she asked who the thief was, he categorically refused to answer. Only upon the emperor's firm insistence did the general finally reveal the terrible secret to him. The tsar was crushed. He regarded what had happened as a serious family disgrace. At a family conference one of the grand dukes proposed that the tsar reduce the guilty grand duke to the ranks, to which the tsar replied that he considered the title of soldier to be too high for his nephew, who had disgraced himself by such a shameful act. "I do not want to sully the title of Russian soldier!" he supposedly said. Soon a manifesto was issued in the tsar's name, in which the guilty grand duke was declared to be mentally ill but his crime was not mentioned, and then he was sent off to Turkestan forever. The actress who had captivated the grand duke—a foreign subject—was immediately deported from Russia.

I had little in common with the elder Iskander. He soon left the regiment by his own wish. But I served alongside the younger Iskander for a whole year. While he was in the regimental training detachment, in the spring of 1912 he was seriously injured in a fall from a horse and was relieved from the service. He was a morbidly touchy young man. He never spoke of his father, but in his room, decorated like a lady's boudoir in the form of a *bonbonnière,* there hung a large portrait of the disgraced grand duke in a frame with a golden imperial coronet. Iskander didn't receive his commission until the height of the World War, and at the front he proved to be a real daredevil.

Our most remarkable volunteer was Sangovich—a pudgy, sleek, and robust lad. This rather stupid, typical mama's boy broke all the regimental records for number of days held under arrest in the regimental guardhouse. There was no form of disciplinary penalty that Sangovich had not personally experienced, and more than once. It was seldom that any riding lesson ended without some scandal for this character. When on horseback he looked like a caricature, and he was a desperate, squeamish coward. Lieutenant Palitsyn simply couldn't stand him and claimed that he would faint at the very sight of Sangovich.

Sangovich was so afraid of horses, and especially of jumping over the hurdle, that he would fall off the horse ten paces before the obstacle. He couldn't be broken of this habit even by the lieutenant's wonder-working whip. Sangovich caught such hell in the regimental manège that he soon applied to the medical commission, asking to be completely relieved from military service. It would, of course, have been ridiculous to relieve such a big, strapping man from the service for reasons of health. So, while he was in the regimental hospital for tests, Sangovich resorted to a trick: he bribed a doctor's assistant for a very tidy sum, and the assistant got him some urine from a seriously ill patient whose kidneys were diseased. The analysis of this alien urine was supposed to decide Sangovich's fate in his favor.

To celebrate, Sangovich had a fit of generosity and at night in the ward he arranged a grandiose feast, in which the doctor's assistants, hospital orderlies, and all the soldiers who were not seriously ill took part. In the ward appeared a rich selection of snacks, a whole assortment of liqueurs, wines, and even champagne. They invited the regimental prostitutes, led by a certain Mashka the Jug, who was famous for saluting the regimental commander General Bernov himself, standing to attention just like a soldier.

Unfortunately, during this nocturnal orgy the senior regimental physician, Dr. Ivanov, came bursting into the hospital. There was an unbelievable scandal, since the doctor was a stickler for rules, and Sangovich and the doctor's assistant had to go from the feast right to the guardhouse lockup. The whole clever scheme with the urine was exposed, and as a result both the doctor's assistant and his ill-starred protégé were threatened with prosecution. All the officers were deeply angered, and the adjutant said that Sangovich was a disgrace to the entire regiment.

The business was turning nasty, and I don't know how it would have turned out for Sangovich if his papa, a respected admiral, the former commander of the imperial yacht *Polar Star,* had not intervened. The old admiral came in person to the regiment and begged General Bernov to somehow put a stop to the business. Out of consideration for the respected papa there was no prosecution, but Sangovich had to do sixty days under arrest—an unheard-of sentence, twice as long as the regulations prescribed to be in the power of a regimental commander to impose—an unprecedented case! But it was still better than being prosecuted and transferred to a penal battalion.

After Sangovich came out of the lockup they unstitched the tricolored volunteer's chevrons from his shoulder straps and transferred him from the training detachment to a noncombatant detachment as an ordinary private. He was lodged in the barracks, where he lived almost continually until the end of his term in the service. An incredible loafer, Sangovich managed to arrange a few more terms in the lockup for himself from time to time, even though he was in a noncombatant unit. Apparently he preferred the lockup to any kind of service.

From the very beginning Sangovich was a joke and an object of ridicule for us volunteers. We abused him in the most unbelievable way. Long before his amazing debut in the hospital, we used to beat him on the head with our spoons at dinner, calling him all kinds of offensive nicknames, of which the least obscene were "Count Gonorrhea-Snotnose" and "Assholich." Sangovich just took it all. When I asked him why he voluntarily chose to fulfill his military service precisely in the cavalry when he had the right to choose any arm of the service, he replied that he liked the helmet with the eagle, which he thought he looked very good in. The unfortunate clod could hardly have expected that that glittering helmet would turn out to be so heavy!

Chapter Three

Visits to St. Petersburg

THE QUARTERS I shared with M. Osorgin were located in a separate little gray house on Liutsevskii Street and consisted of four small rooms furnished, as they say, simply but sweetly, by whose efforts I no longer remember. In the so-called dining room there was a comfortable sofa, a round dinner table, and in the corner there stood in splendor a wonderful old clavichord made of mahogany, very stylish, but sounding as if it had a cold and sore throat, which didn't keep us from banging out all kinds of music on it when we had a free moment. Osorgin and I had chipped in to acquire this object for a pittance from an old resident of Gatchina. Each of us had a little separate room furnished according to our own taste. My apartment, of course, abounded in photographs of my fiancée, both hanging on the walls and standing in little frames on the table. But Mishenka's walls were adorned with icons in a more than sufficient quantity. For the first time in my life I was living on my own, which both amused and delighted me.

My cousin "Mishanchik" Osorgin had brought his own "man," a certain Evmenii, with him from his father's house. He was a footman of the Osorgins' who had served in their family for many years, an elderly and very good-natured fellow with typical footman's side-whiskers on his pale face. Evmenii was very devoted to the young lord, but he made fun of him a bit. He was the authentic type of the old servant from a "good house," a bit of a *raisonneur,* a bit of a philosopher. Evmenchik immediately introduced comfort and thrifty housekeeping into our quarters, simultaneously fulfilling the duties of a tutor, cook, counselor, and financial manager.

The Osorgin family way of life was distinguished by its exceptionally patriarchal nature, enhanced by high moral standards and religious devotion. The head of the family, Uncle Misha, being a man of especially strict principles, raised his sons in the fear of God and in a spirit that made impossible any light-minded excesses or deviations in the direction of loose morals.

Mishanchik and I had completely different personalities and tastes. Despite the fact that my mother raised us very strictly and tried to protect us from bad influences in every way she could, all the same I often felt a strong gravitation toward the pole of light-mindedness.

Now I experienced a break in my life. I had flitted out from under my mother's wing, I was becoming independent, I had finally become an adult and was striving with a certain degree of passion to taste as soon as possible the advantages and charms of independent life and to experience that which had been forbidden to me before.

Cousin Mishanchik was my complete opposite and sometimes irritated me greatly with his morality, especially when he would say to me in a groan, "Vovka, have the fear of God!" He was much older than me, more even-tempered, and it seemed to me that he was always trying to emphasize his moral superiority over me. Before bed he would put on a gray dressing gown and loved to play "old maid" with his servant Evmenchik. At such times he looked like a cozy old-fashioned painting. Before bed Mishanchik also loved to get comfy lying in bed while reading a book, sometimes of a religious content. Then out of a bratty feeling of protest I would sit down to read a frivolous dime novel.

There were occasions when the volunteers Speshnev and Iskander and I would organize jolly drinking parties. A couple of times these parties were held in our quarters, to Mishanchik's quiet horror. He was always shaken by this, and he would just repeat to me his usual groan, "Vovka, have the fear of God!"

On the other hand, Evmenchik was quietly radiant at these parties, and if I had occasion afterwards to go out into the town a little tipsy, Evmenchik would accompany me along the street with touching solicitude, "just in case something happens to our Prince . . ." I remember that once after such a feast Evmenchik and I wandered into the Priorat, where I demonstrated to the diligent servant my skill at the saber, damaging several young trees in the process, and he kept saying affectionately, "Prince, oh Prince . . . you really do hack beautifully, but permit me to put your little saber back in its sheath. God forbid your gentlemen officers should find you and me here!"

In essence, Mishanchik's personality was rather difficult. There were instances when he would turn from a man peacefully enjoying himself into a gloomy and depressed one, and would stop talking to me for two or three days. It was very easy to evoke such a mood in him, and out of brattiness and sinfulness I would sometimes do it deliberately and with relish. Once our good comrade and debauchee the volunteer Speshnev, after a "stormy night," found a pair of elegant ladies' underpants in his room. We brought them to our quarters with the aim of playing a joke on Mishanchik and evoking his favorite saying, "Have the fear of God!" And so at the very moment when Mishanchik, lying in his bed, started to read his book, we suddenly brought him the most secret item of a lady's toilette on the point of his own broadsword, saying, "Here's your standard! Kiss it and swear allegiance!" Then we tried to cover the dear boy with this nasty object. While doing this we brayed like jackasses (and in fact we were proper jackasses). We expected him to say his usual "Have the fear of God!" But this time the effect was astounding. Mishanchik became furious, started hitting us, and broke off all contact with us for several days. I'll admit that he had reason on this occasion to lose his temper, but in fact he would get angry and become gloomy over trivial incidents too. There was one instance in the spring when he wouldn't speak to me for two days, only because in his presence I accidentally stepped with my boot on a branch of an apple tree covered with tender blossoms. As a lover of agriculture and of rural idylls, Mishanchik saw in my action something deeply callous and immediately held me in contempt for a whole two days.

Despite his eccentricity, Mishanchik was still a good comrade, and after our quarrels we would get along well as if nothing had happened, until the next storm.

Of all the pleasant episodes of that period I remember the happy day when after a long parting my fiancée came to St. Petersburg from abroad, having made a trip to Italy with her mother and her sister Tania. Given advance notice by telegram, that morning I didn't go to clean the stables and completely missed grooming the horses, risking a severe punishment.

At 7:00 A.M. I was already under the glass vault of the Gatchina railroad station of the Warsaw line, waiting to meet the express train from the border, which had a three-minute stop in Gatchina. I remember how happily my heart missed a beat when in the turbid haze of dawn the lights and outline of the engine appeared. Closer, closer . . . and now with rumbling and hissing the train bursts in under the trembling vault, sharply slowing down. A young lady in a dark-brown traveling costume is standing by the open door of the international car. She is looking anxiously around, searching for someone. Can it be she? Oh, my God, of course it is! I run to her, but in the first instant she doesn't recognize me, apparently having completely forgotten that her fiancé is a soldier. But like a tumbler-pigeon I swoop down on her and clasp her in my embrace. For a minute we look at each other silently and with deep emotion, then we begin to utter simultaneous exclamations. We don't have a conversation, but some kind of idiotic, happy cries. This lasts a minute. Suddenly three sharp bells. I hurriedly help my fiancée to a seat in the car under the heartbreaking wail of the engine. The train starts off.

"You're coming to St. Petersburg today? Right?" she asks.

"I can't . . ."

"What do you mean you can't? Why?"

"I'm in the service!"

I'm running alongside the train-car.

"On Saturday, on Saturday," I shout sobbing after the departing train.

The train flies off quickly, constantly increasing its speed and dissipating like a vision in the foggy mist. Happy and renewed, I quickly set off in the direction of the regiment, going through back alleys so as not to be seen by a lieutenant . . .

On Saturdays all regimental activities ended by 12:00 noon. Then we had time off until Monday. All volunteers who were not doing penal duty were issued passes by Palitsyn, and we would hurry home to change clothes in order to go as quickly as possible to St. Petersburg, where we were allowed to go only after having learned to salute irreproachably, according to all the rules. Soldiers could appear on the streets of St. Petersburg only dressed impeccably, in a dandified way, and strictly according to form. St. Petersburg teemed with elegant military men. At that time Guardsmen were required to salute not only officers but every plain soldier. We saluted not only living people but monuments to the tsars and the grand dukes. In this respect there were particular strict requirements in St. Petersburg that did not exist in Moscow or in any other towns.

At the sight of an officer we were supposed to stop swinging our arms several paces before meeting him and start marching as if on parade—in goose step—that is, without bending the knee, to strike the whole foot firmly against the pavement and simultaneously to grasp the sheath of one's broadsword with the left hand in a particular gesture. Two paces before meeting any military man of a high rank, the soldier was to turn his head in an abrupt movement to face him, look boldly into his eyes, and simultaneously throw the right hand in its white glove energetically to the side, sharply bend the arm at the elbow at a 45° angle, place one's extended fingers to his cap, and then lower the arm forcefully. When meeting generals, members of the imperial family, officers of one's own regiment, banners, standards, and military funeral processions, one was to salute "standing at attention," that is, stopping and sharply turning the whole body in two movements toward the personage or banner. After letting the person or banner pass, one was to again make a distinct reverse turn in two movements, click heels, and then continue on one's way with a dashing step.

Walking on some streets, especially Nevskii Avenue, which teemed with military men, was pure torture—you couldn't relax your attention for a moment. You had to know how to salute while riding in a cab, how to salute when overtaking a general, and finally how to salute when your hands were occupied with a burden. There was a particular movement for each such case.

There was a whole science of how to carry oneself on the streets and in public places. There were special ranks of people who kept a strict watch on this in St. Petersburg, the so-called parade ground adjutants, who really loved to find fault.

We could ride only in third- or fourth-class railroad cars. We were not allowed to travel in our own carriages at all, in streetcars we could travel only standing on the platform without the right to enter the car, we were not allowed to smoke on the street, just as we were not allowed to enter not just any restaurant, but even the first- and second-class railroad station buffets. In the theater we were not allowed to sit in the loges or even in the orchestra, and had to be governed by the saying, "everyone should know his place." Yes, it was a science, and without studying it properly no soldier could set foot in the capital; that is why we were not allowed to travel from Gatchina to St. Petersburg for a very long time.

I remember a case in which all the regimental orders included a printed order by the commander of the Guards corps, General Bezobrazov, announcing his reprimand of the commander of one of the regiments because he, Bezobrazov, had noticed a low-ranking soldier of that regiment on the street with a papirosa in his teeth. I personally received two duty details out of order because, while seeing my aunt off to Moscow, I stepped into the first- and second-class railroad buffet for a minute. In a word, the rules were unbelievably strict, and only in the navy were they a bit more lenient; they did not put such pressure on sailors.

In St. Petersburg I most often stayed in the large pink mansion on Mokhovaia Street that belonged to my aunt, Princess Olga Obolenskaia, a very venerable eighty-year-old lady, the mother of my late uncle I. M. Obolenskii, the well-known governor-general of Finland. His family lived in the same house, and I was friends with his daughter Olenka. That year she was the fiancée of my great friend Petrik (also a Prince Obolenskii), who was then serving out his time in the Chevalier Guards. On Saturday evenings a small but gay young company would assemble at the Obolenskiis'; a certain brother and sister V. and L. Naryshkin, the chevalier guard Strukov, the Obolenskii betrothed, and I. After our austere and monotonous Gatchina service and the bachelor quarters that had palled on me, it was amazingly pleasant to relax and let down my hair in the company of two sweet young girls, laughing to our hearts' content at our silly young conversations in the cozy Obolenskii sitting room, where we so naively formed the most optimistic and alluring plans for the future.

What a contrast there was between the mood here on the Mokhovaia with the gloom and depression that reigned on Sergievskaia Street in the home of my young cousins Trubetskoi, where I also visited without fail every time I came to St. Petersburg. The reason for this depression lay in the terrible grief that had suddenly fallen on this family in the autumn, when the head of the family, good-natured Uncle Petia, beloved by all, had been killed by a revolver fired by our cousin V. Kristi. The court found that this senseless crime had been committed in a fit of temporary insanity, because of baseless jealousy of his flirtatious wife.[1]

This outrageous incident, which happened in the autumn at a family gathering, caused a great sensation; it lay like a heavy stone on the whole family and was keenly felt by all of us. Only thanks to her remarkable moral strength, tact, and knowledge of life was my widowed aunt, A. V. Trubetskaia, able to take all the family members in hand, inspirit them, and set their upset family life to rights, putting it back on its normal course in a home where no one had dared to pronounce the name Kristi, despite the extremely close family relations that had existed between the two families before this event.[2] At that time I was great friends with my cousin N. Trubetskoi and my female cousin Tatenka, but I could never bring myself to speak either to them or to any other member of the family about my late Uncle Petia, because I felt that it was *impossible* to speak about that subject on Sergievskaia Street. That is probably why an artificial, false note could be heard in our conversations on all other subjects for a long time, which was very painful.

During our visits to St. Petersburg, cousin Mishanchik often brought me along to dine in the General Staff headquarters on Dvortsovaia Square with his aunt Varvara Mikhailovna Zhilinskaia, the wife of the General Staff chief himself. She was an extremely affected and overdramatic lady, but at the same time a sensitive and affable one, and I enjoyed being at the Zhilinskiis'. I was already acquainted with General Zhilinskii, whom Mishanchik called simply Uncle Iasha.[3] Rather dry, sallow, a little slant-eyed, with gray hair and mustache, he was the most typical representative of the General Staff, the type of the pedantic armchair military strategist. Although he occupied one of the highest and most important posts in the army, at home Zhilinskii was very unpretentious and well-mannered, and I never felt any constraint in his presence of the kind I sometimes felt with the most insignificant cornet in our regiment. It was said that Zhilinskii's subordinates were very afraid of him, but he did not inspire the least bit of fear in me and even less in Mishanchik, and I was able to converse with him quite unconstrainedly.

I remember that that year we were present at Zhilinskii's departure for Paris, where he was going to "pay a courtesy visit," as they said in the domestic circle, to the French high command. There was a lot of idle talk about this trip by Zhilinskii's inane and garrulous adjutant, Staff Captain Panchulidzev, who was savoring in advance the Parisian amusements that awaited him, because this general's adjutant of course wanted to and could do in Paris all those pleasant and gay things that his dignified patron could not permit himself. Much later I learned that this very "courtesy visit" by Zhilinskii to Paris, where he went in such a seemingly modest manner, had enormous military significance. There in Paris portentous discussions were being held and opinions were being exchanged between the commanders of the Russian and French general staffs about a possible war with Germany and the attempt to coordinate the policies of the allied armies in such an event. The Russian and

French generals frankly laid their cards on the table. Apparently this was the only or at least the last such discussion between the representatives of the Russian and French commands before the World War. Even then the French were insisting on the most active operations by the Russians in the very beginning of the war, when according to French intelligence (later proved correct) Germany's first strike was to fall with full force on France.

During my Sunday trips to St. Petersburg I also visited my remarkable aunt, Countess M. D. Apraksina, who lived in her magnificent mansion on the Liteinyi.[4] My aunt was born in the 1840s. In her youth she was very beautiful, and Tsar Alexander II was acquainted with her and would come to visit her.

This remarkable aunt was famous for her enormous wealth (the Apraksins had an entailed estate) and for her complete ignorance of life, which was often taken advantage of by various people who hovered around her. The famous Apraksin market in St. Petersburg belonged to her, and it was said that my aunt contrived not to receive a kopeck of income from it, owing to the particular cleverness of her business managers.

This myopic and stern grande dame with the remarkably well-bred face of an aristocrat, always in a light-brown wig with side-curls and with a lorgnette invariably held to her squinting eyes, was disliked and feared by her nephews, because Aunt Mimisha herself treated young people rather coldly, without tenderness and raptures, and with frank naïveté would say things to young people that were not entirely pleasant for them to hear. Aunt Mimisha dressed in an old-fashioned way, was tightly corseted, and spoke French almost exclusively, and her nephews were required to address her with the formal "you" when she deigned to ask them a question.

Completely unexpectedly for me I suddenly became the favorite of my strict aunt, and—since at this period Aunt Mimisha played a certain role in my life—I would like to dwell in some detail on the personality of this original, eccentric, but essentially kind lady.

The story of my remarkable relationship with Aunt Mimisha began thanks to pure chance, to a misunderstanding, so to speak. This began back when I was serving as a volunteer in the navy, when our torpedo boat spent a long time guarding the imperial yacht *Standard*. At that time all the mail for the guard vessels was addressed to Peterhof. I remember that I was impatiently awaiting a registered letter from my fiancée, a letter that was very important for me. The letter had been sent to Peterhof, but our service in the guard had ended because the imperial family had returned to Tsarskoe Selo. Our torpedo boat arrived in Kronstadt, and on Sunday I went to shore, intending to travel to the Peterhof post office to get my fiancée's letter. After I arrived in Peterhof and obtained the letter, I intended to return immediately by train to St. Petersburg, but at the station I learned that passenger service had been stopped for two hours because of some kind of accident on the line.

I was faced with the dismal prospect of waiting for the train without being able to drop into a restaurant or buffet, since I was in my sailor's uniform. Then I remembered that in the summer Aunt Mimisha lived at her dacha in Peterhof, where my mother and I had visited her in the spring. Not knowing what to do with myself out of boredom and not having any acquaintances in Peterhof, I set off for my aunt's dacha and told the footman to announce me. Aunt Mimisha received me. She came out to me in her wig with a lorgnette at her eyes and met me with the usual phrase she addressed to everyone who visited her: *"Bonjour, bonjour . . . Veux-tu du chocolat?"* ["Hello, hello, would you like some chocolate?"] (My aunt had an old servant, the assistant cook Nikolai, who was famous for making amazingly delicious chocolate with whipped cream according to a recipe known only to himself.) *"Merci, ma tante Mimiche,"* I answered without ceremony, "your chocolate is so marvelous that it's impossible to refuse." Auntie squinted at me intently through her lorgnette, and I realized that I had made two gaffes: in the first place, I had replied in Russian, not in French, and in the second place, I had addressed her with the familiar "thou" when I should have used the formal "you." I was a little embarrassed, but I decided that it would be rather awkward to correct my mistake now, so after that I purposely said "thou," trying to conceal this familiarity with the most respectful behavior. "Nikolai, some chocolate!" Auntie ordered the waiting servant. "And you sit down and tell me why you've come to see me," she said to me in somewhat accented Russian. Not wishing to reveal to Auntie the true reason for my coming to Peterhof, since my engagement and correspondence with my fiancée were my secret, I started fibbing to her about how I had gotten leave and so on, and none of my relatives were in St. Petersburg just now, since they had all gone off to various places, and so I decided to call on my dear aunt and came to Peterhof specifically for that reason.

I started to tell my aunt about my ship, how the tsar held a review of our torpedo boat, and how he took notice of me during that review. In my simplicity as a still unspoiled eighteen-year-old lad I got carried away with my own story, showed Auntie some photographs I had with me of various episodes of naval life, and even made a present to her of a beautiful sea view that reminded her of Nice, completely forgetting that I was dealing with a strict and prim lady.

Over a cup of delicious chocolate a whole hour passed unnoticed as we conversed. Aunt Mimisha and I parted as friends, and as I left her I thought that in fact there was nothing frightening about Auntie at all. She's a lady like any other . . .

It turned out that my unexpected visit made a most favorable impression on the old countess. She was touched by my "family loyalty" (of which by the way there was no trace in me at that time). She was touched that for her sake (as she thought) I had made a whole journey. She was pleasantly struck by the simplicity with which I had behaved with her, although I never had before. To my mother's amazement, Auntie wrote her that she found me *"très distingué et avec beaucoup d'esprit* (!)" ["very well-bred and very clever"]. After that I didn't see Aunt Mimisha until my entry into the cuirassier regiment. But when she found out that I was serving in Gatchina, she wrote to my mother that she was surprised that I never dropped in to see her on the Liteinyi, since I was so devoted to my relatives. In a letter to me my mother reproached me for my unmannerliness and prompted me to make a visit to Auntie without delay.

I remember that second visit, which was very significant for me, as if it were yesterday. In the huge luxurious mansion of the Apraksins, which in its furniture and appointments looked more like a king's palace, Auntie for some reason received all her guests in a small, modestly arranged drawing room, where the furniture was rather simple and there were not even the carpets one expected to find in drawing rooms. When I arrived my aunt had about five elderly and imposing guests. She introduced me to the guests, after which I took a seat and preserved a respectful silence, not entering into the conversation with people who were much older than me, and only replying to the insignificant questions that were addressed to me. Auntie's guests were carrying on this staid and at the same time trivial conversation in French, as was proper in the drawing room of such a respectable lady. Having sat out the twenty minutes prescribed by decorum and having drunk a cup of chocolate, I rose, kissed Auntie's hand, bowed to her guests, and headed for the door. When I was already on the threshold of the drawing room, my aunt suddenly called to me in Russian: "Oh, Vladimir, wait! . . . I almost forgot . . . You know, I was in Nice in the fall . . . , and you know, they have wonderful hides there . . . oh, what are they called . . . *des petites choses en cuir* [little leather things]. Yes, leather things. And so I remembered that you like good leather and I bought you *un petit cadeau* [a little present] in Nice . . . a leather card case."

With these words my aunt rose, went to a writing desk, took from the drawer a small package wrapped in cigarette paper, and gave it to me.

"What nonsense," I thought. "Where did Auntie get the idea that I like leather!!!" Apparently I had never said such a thing either to her or to anyone else, and couldn't have said such a thing, since I am completely indifferent to leather goods. All the same, for the sake of propriety I pretended to be overjoyed, and after thanking my aunt for her consideration, I again took my leave of her.

"Be careful, don't lose it, it's very good leather . . . and it's a memento of me!" she called after me.

After quickly glancing at the quite ordinary leather card case, of the kind then used to hold calling cards, and sticking it in the pocket of my great-coat, I went outside with a feeling of relief, that finally I had performed my boring but obligatory number. In just a few minutes I had forgotten about Auntie and her leather, since I was setting off for more interesting people and pursuits. Only late in the evening when I was already sitting in the third-class carriage of the Gatchina train, by chance I put my hand in the pocket of my greatcoat, remembered Auntie's card case, and took it out into the light of day. It seemed as if something was contained in the card case. I opened it and uttered an involuntary exclamation—in each of its four compartments there was a beautiful 500-ruble banknote with a picture of Peter the Great . . . Now that was a *number!*

I had never in my life had my hands on such a large sum of money. Completely stunned, I couldn't believe my eyes, and when I came to my senses I even thought that this money had gotten into the card case by some misunderstanding, and that Aunt Mimisha in her absentmindedness simply forgot to take it out before giving me the gift. Could this really be meant for me? If there had been a hundred rubles in the card case, I could understand, but 2,000 (a very tidy sum of money in those days)! Such a generous gift was simply inexplicable. Why? For what? Really only because Auntie happened to take a liking to me? Apparently it was so. I recalled the particular intonation in my aunt's voice when she called after me, "Be careful not to lose it!" If she had thought that the card case was empty she wouldn't have said it in that special way. I was overcome by embarrassment. To accept this money from an aunt with whom I had so little in common was preposterous, but to return it would offend the venerable old lady. After returning home and thinking it over, I wrote a short letter to Aunt Mimisha in which in the most unaffected and, it seemed to me, fitting terms I thanked her for her gift, emphasizing how touched I was by her consideration, which I did not at all deserve.

From that time Aunt Mimisha adopted the custom of showering me with such gifts. It was seldom that I could visit her without receiving from her one, two, or even five thousand. (Auntie never gave less than a thousand!) And thus she continued right up to the October Revolution. She always arranged the bestowal of these gifts in such a way that it was impossible to refuse. Whenever I found her alone, she would never give me anything, apparently trying to avoid the possibility of my refusal. But when other people were visiting her, at the moment I was saying goodbye she would always pull some trifling gift out of the writing desk, like a hand-carved wooden egg, a leather cigarette case, a little casket or a small box of caramels. With the most innocent look Aunt Mimisha would give me the little thing with the words, "Here's a little gift I've stored away for you . . . *un petit cadeau* [a little gift] to remember me by. After all, you like cigarette cases, don't you? Well, *au revoir, au revoir,* go on, I'm not trying to detain you"—and my aunt would immediately turn to the guest or guests, continuing her conversation with them and making it simply impossible for me to refuse her little gift, so humble and trivial in appearance. I would get embarrassed, thank Auntie, and blushingly stick the thing in my pocket, already knowing for sure that thousands were hidden in that simple little egg or cigarette case. Sometimes when I found my aunt alone, I would ask her not to give me any more money, assuring her that it was simply unpleasant for me to visit her because of this, since I did not deserve such presents in any way, and I didn't need any money, so I was ashamed to accept it. Then my aunt would say that she wouldn't give me any more gifts, but I had only to come next time when she had some guest or other, and the old story would be repeated.

Despite her huge wealth, my aunt, as was often the case, was unhappy in her personal life. When she was quite a young girl she was married off to a cavalry commander, the rich Count Apraksin, who was no longer young and whom my aunt did not love. Her favorite daughter died in childhood, and her surviving son was mentally impaired and never appeared in public, so I never saw this cousin of mine. My aunt had no joy of her nephews either: fearing and avoiding Auntie, they never displayed any feelings toward her apart from an artificial deference. This perhaps explains her senile feeling of sympathy toward me, and the pleasure she took in spoiling me. At first I visited her only out of politeness, since she insisted that I do so. Later I came to sincerely love her because I understood her.

Once in my spare time, out of curiosity, I tried to calculate how much each of my appearances cost Aunt Mimisha, and I came to the conclusion that each visit cost her on average over a thousand rubles. Despite this and despite my youth, I still preserved a disinterested feeling toward her, which I realize is somewhat hard to believe.

In those years Auntie would often invite me to dinner. She had a fantastically good cook who was the talk of both capitals, and the dishes he prepared were true masterpieces of the most refined culinary art. I especially liked a certain dessert that was served only at my aunt's house—a dish consisting of huge stewed pears in rum sauce sprinkled with crushed pistachios, which were incomparably delicious.

My aunt always had five or six elite elderly guests for dinner, and at her table I was the only representative of the younger generation. Of the notable people who often dined at my aunt's house I remember the portly Baron von Knorring and the puny, gray-haired, ugly old man Ermolov, the minister of agriculture.[5] A great epicure and connoisseur of good wine, this apparently dried-out old man toward the end of the dinner would become a very witty interlocutor, displaying a great talent as an interesting raconteur. That year in my as yet unspoiled and naive simplicity I was not at all interested in the position occupied in society by the people I met. Thus for example I often met

Ermolov at my aunt's house, but it was only after a whole year of my acquaintance with him that I learned he was a minister. In this respect I was a typical Muscovite, and it was only after becoming an officer that I completely adopted the Petersburg psychology. Young people of Moscow society, if they happened to visit the home of some noble family, would do so without any hidden, ulterior purpose. Muscovites would visit whomever they pleased, without any considerations of self-interest, but simply because they wanted to and it was pleasant for them. But the high-society Petersburger, on the contrary, would often visit some boring salon purely because the hostess was intimately acquainted with some influential personage or other, whom one could meet in her salon and whose attention one could attract, or because the hostess herself could take an opportunity to put in a word, pointing out to the influential personage that this is a worthy and fine young man who deserves to be promoted.

Knowing neither life nor people nor the value of money, Aunt Mimisha often threw her money away for no reason at all, as in my case, for example. But there were also other cases. I remember how once in my presence Ermolov came to see my aunt in order to thank her for the 75,000 rubles she had transferred to his name for the aid of poor blind people, for whom the minister had displayed sympathy. Being very nearsighted herself and fearing that she would one day go blind, Aunt Mimisha loved to give patronage to the blind.

In general my situation had become rather strange from the time I became a volunteer. I had no rights at all. I could only get to St. Petersburg by traveling in a filthy third-class carriage. I had no right to sit down in a streetcar, and on the street I had to stand at attention before some insignificant army lieutenant, who could make an offensive or even insulting remark to me with impunity, but ten minutes after that I would be shaking hands with a high official or sitting next to a minister or general occupying a high post in the army, at an intimate dinner with Aunt Mimisha or at the Zhilinskiis'.

In that long-ago time and in the milieu to which I belonged simply by virtue of my birth, all this was considered quite natural thanks to the ancient way of life and customs of the gentry.

Time passed. The time for our officer's examinations was drawing near; we could only be admitted to take them after receiving the rank of noncommissioned officer in the regiment. This rank was given to soldiers of the training detachment after a review carried out by the regimental commander and a special committee of senior regimental officers. In view of the fact that such a review was under normal circumstances held only in the spring, and therefore there would not be enough time to prepare for the officer's examinations, with the consent of Palitsyn we four volunteers who wished to become officers formally petitioned for the immediate assignment of a separate review for us four. This petition was granted by the commander, and at the end of February, in the duty room of the officers' club, a committee chaired by Colonel von Schweder administered an examination on all the military regulations and on elementary topography, which we successfully passed. After that the four of us were tested on riding in the manège.

This is where we disgraced ourselves.

It's true, by the time of this review each of us had a fairly good seat, we could hack with the saber and wield the lance fairly satisfactorily, we could also jump obstacles tolerably well—but all this was not enough. To ride and do saber and lance exercises this well was acceptable in our regiment maybe for a rotation of young soldiers, but for noncommissioned officers, especially in such an exemplary regiment as ours, it was simply not good enough. We did not have the precision, or the necessary skill, or that machinelike polish and dexterity that were demanded of noncommissioned officers and that people could acquire only after long training. And of course, this could not escape the eyes of experts. The famous Staff Captain von Exe, who was serving on the committee, was especially displeased with our riding, and Colonel von Schweder categorically declared that he would not allow *such* riders to be promoted to noncommissioned officers, and that we had to continue our manège training right up until the general review of the whole training detachment.

Our failure was completely understandable. As riders we were insufficiently trained, premature, since five months of training in the manège is too short a period to be thoroughly schooled. One should also not forget that some of the best front-line soldiers came right from the cavalry squadrons into our training detachment, and they already had almost two years of manège practice behind them, while we had none when we entered the detachment.

After the review Palitsyn was abashed and looked gloomily at us. But we volunteers were simply crushed. For us it was a blow, since it turned out that we could not be admitted to the officer's examinations that year at all.

For me personally and for my fiancée this was simply tragic, since all my dreams of getting set up in life and getting married were connected to being promoted to officer's rank, and now it had been put off for a whole year! (Volunteers, like soldiers, were forbidden by law to get married.) We seemed to have no alternative: we knew very well that Colonel von Schweder was implacable and stubborn as a bull . . .

But all the same an alternative was found! And we were rescued from this nasty situation by, of course, *a lady* . . .

Our savior turned out to be Varvara Mikhailovna Zhilinskaia, the wife of the chief of the General Staff and the aunt of Mishanchik Osorgin. On the first Sunday Mishanchik went to see her cap in hand, and told her about our misfortune, and as a result the very nice general's lady, always a little overenthusiastic and deeply concerned about other people's misfortunes, wrote a short but eloquent note to General Bernov. This was enough. The kind general could refuse anyone you please, but not Varvara Mikhailovna!

A day later it was announced in the orders of the day that we had satisfactorily passed the review and were being sent to prepare for and take the officer's examinations at the Nicholas Cavalry School.

The end of our manège martyrdom had come. Palitsyn ceased to be our bogeyman. In our book of life a page had been turned—and all thanks to Varvara Mikhailovna! "It is good to live keeping God in mind," said the great Leo Tolstoy. "It's not bad to live keeping the ladies in mind," I modestly add.

Chapter Four

Studying for the Officer's Examinations

WE HAD TO HURRY as fast as we could to prepare for the officer's examinations, since there were only about two months left until they would start. In that length of time we had to master a two-year course in fourteen subjects, in which the textbook for military history alone was about a thousand pages long! And all the subjects taken together made up thousands and thousands of pages. Involuntarily there arose the terrible question, when would we be able to complete a survey of all this, let alone master it? My comrades and I frankly doubted that it was possible, since it seemed obvious that it was simply physically impracticable; furthermore, we were interested in passing the examinations not only satisfactorily, but with a guardsman's mark, that is, *well*.

All our hope rested on the famous Captain Basevich, whom I mentioned earlier and to whom the four of us set off immediately after the regimental order releasing us was read out. We had already made arrangements with this captain at the beginning of the winter, and he had already agreed to prepare us with great reluctance, since Guards volunteers were thrusting themselves upon him from all sides and he had already taken on fifteen students. So after accepting us cuirassiers, he had nineteen students. Basevich was a captain and commander of a company of the Life Guards of the Pavlovskii Infantry Regiment. When and why he was inspired to take up such a strange private business as prepping volunteers for exams, I don't know. But in my time his name was well-known in the most fashionable cavalry regiments of the Guards, where thanks to Basevich many noble, rich young men, originally volunteers, were fortunate enough to shine as cornets. For two or three months' work, Basevich would earn about 10,000 rubles (if not more) from his volunteers every year, and because of these activities the officers in the Pavlovskii Regiment where he served looked at him askance, considering that he was involved in a dirty and completely inappropriate business. My acquaintances in the Pavlovskii Regiment said they were ashamed of Basevich, that he was close to being the disgrace of the regiment because he had turned himself into a kind of tutor (which is suitable maybe for a poor student, but not for an officer of the Guards). The senior officers of the regiment had more than once pointed out to Basevich that his private coaching practice was incompatible with the high calling of a Guards company commander. They even raised the question of removing him from the regiment, but Basevich didn't care a damn for anyone or anything, and continued his profitable business. They tolerated Basevich in the regiment only because he was one of the best company commanders and his company was one of the most outstanding in reviews. (Basevich was killed while leading his company on the German front, in one of the first battles in 1914, having shown himself to be an excellent leader in battle conditions.) In general the Pavlovskii Regiment enjoyed a well-earned reputation among the Guards infantry as the regiment most suited for combat and the front, and it was famous for its quite special discipline and drill, which had become a regimental tradition.

Although he was an infantryman, for some strange reason Basevich specialized exclusively in the Nicholas Cavalry School, having thoroughly studied the tastes and requirements of its pedagogues, among whom he had a relative and a close friend. It is interesting that he refused to undertake preparation for any other schools, although they had almost identical programs.

Basevich lived on Millionnaia Street, in a regimental apartment. When the four of us came there for the first time, we found classes already in full swing, since we were several days late due to the delay caused by our unsuccessful review.

The first day of our studies has been especially engraved in my memory. When we rang at Basevich's front door, his orderly, a typical Pavlovsk man, snub-nosed, red-haired, and freckled (because according to an old tradition and supposedly in imitation of the appearance of the Emperor Paul I, the Pavlovskii Regiment recruited men of this type), went to announce us to his master. Then we heard the following dialogue behind the door:

"Your Ex'c'lency, four more lads have come to see you. What is your pleasure, should I let 'em in, or not?"

"Go to he-e-e-ll!" someone's hoarse, whining voice resounded in reply. "Don't bother me! . . . So, gentlemen, Sanroberto, a 'Talian antilleryman, established the law of ver-ti-cal low-er-ing of shells . . . Remember that! Yes, gentlemen, there are such generals on earth who never get tired of philosophizing!" (the laughter of several voices is heard behind the door).

"So, therefore this very law—"

But now the voice of the orderly again resounds:

"Your Ex'c'lency, so what should I say to the lads? After all, should I let 'em in, or, what is your pleasure?"

"Oh, Lord! Oh hell, drag them in here too! These must be the cuirassiers. That's right, Vasilii, finish your captain off! Drag a whole regiment in here!"

Having left our greatcoats, helmets, and broadswords in the little entryway, where the coat rack was already groaning under the weight of volunteers' greatcoats of all possible regiments, we followed the red-haired orderly, who opened to us the door into Basevich's study.

This little room offered a strange picture. In thick clouds of papirosa smoke, on the divan, on chairs, and on the windowsills sat about fifteen young men in unbuttoned uniforms, casually sprawling with papirosas in their teeth; their uniforms were bright and multicolored, from various cavalry regiments. There were guards hussars in short white jackets embroidered with yellow cord and boots with gold cockades; cossacks from the Hetman's Regiment in dark blue uniforms; life dragoons with elegant aiguillettes on their shoulders; chevalier guards; an uhlan; and, finally, a Chernigov hussar from the army with the drunken face of a debauchee, in red "crepe" riding breeches and a green dolman. In the corner of the room at a big blackboard covered with formulas stood a short, thickset, chalk-spattered infantry officer with pitch-black, curly, tangled hair and a small, similarly black mustache. He looked harassed. His face was red and sweaty. His military tunic was unbuttoned. Both from the expression on his face and from the positioning of the comfortably sprawling volunteers, finally from the piles of cigarette butts that could no longer fit into the ashtrays, it was clear that this whole motley company had been here for many hours on end.

When we appeared in the doorway the sweaty Basevich only threatened us with his fist, giving us an eloquent sign that we should stand stock-still and not hinder him from finishing his explanation. Basevich spoke deliberately, in a slightly singsong way, stretching out some phrases and distinctly rapping out certain words. He spoke tersely, but so clearly, expressively, significantly, and—most important—simply, that each of his words seemed to gnaw its way into the listener's brain. Looking at his animated and flushed face and listening to his hoarse but precise voice, I immediately had faith in this man and understood that with such a coach we would not fail our examinations. I felt that this man would prepare us and prepare us well. The volunteers listened to him with unusual attentiveness, with their eyes glued to him.

From that day began our new drudgery, which took up all our mornings, all day, all evening, and even part of the night, in a word, all our strength. I have never in my life, neither before nor after that, crammed so hard and worked so hard at various disciplines as we did then at Basevich's, and I could never have imagined that it was possible.

Basevich was an ideal teacher, the most talented pedagogue I had ever encountered. He simply performed miracles with his students and was able to keep them at strained attention for hours on end. He knew how to capture students' interest, and not, interestingly enough, with the subjects themselves but with the bold idea of accomplishing the impossible—of covering in two or three days an entire course on a particular subject. He turned it into a kind of new, interesting sport—the sport of cramming.

Basevich's pedagogical techniques were varied and extremely original. He devoted the first days to artillery, a subject replete with boring, dry theory. Basevich would always expound the points that were most difficult to master in a concise and clear way, and every once in a while he would interject such an unexpected and apt obscenity that the whole room would shake from the explosion of the students' rolling laughter. Such an apt and surprising little word, inserted at the right moment, would always be engraved on one's memory, causing you to remember and understand by association the whole particularly important phrase. The most boring and dry verities would be presented by Basevich in such an amusing and witty way that we assimilated them quite easily. The most difficult and seemingly incomprehensible things became clear, thanks to a felicitous comparison, and would of course be retained in our memory.

The huge sums of money that Basevich accepted from his students were not accepted for nothing, because in exchange for that money he gave all of himself; he would be absent from service and toward the end of the course he had lost a lot of weight, his cheeks were sunken as if after a serious illness, and he completely lost his voice, which had turned into a hoarse whisper. After all, he had to wag his tongue and strain his vocal cords from morning until late at night, since sometimes we would stay at his place long past midnight, until about three in the morning.

Basevich established an amazing relationship with us volunteers from the very first days. I could not imagine that people like us from the lower ranks could behave so familiarly with an officer. We called him not "Your Honor," but simply "Viktor Ivanovich," and in his presence no one was embarrassed to unfasten his uniform, sprawl on the divan, and light up a cigarette. Most of the students regarded Basevich first of all as a clever fellow. Basevich's students, although they loved him for his wit, didn't really respect him, because in the first place, they had bought Basevich for money, and a lot of money at that, which seemed to give them the right to a slighting attitude toward a "hired man." On the other hand, Basevich himself would sometimes permit himself pranks that could not inspire a feeling of deference toward him.

I remember, for example, that during class he would suddenly turn the blackboard away from us and write something on it in chalk that we couldn't see, and then he would suddenly put the blackboard facing us and we would read, "I beg you to pay me tomorrow. This concerns those who haven't paid me a damned thing yet!"

At this point Basevich, pretending to be an embarrassed girl, would cover his face with his sleeve in a theatrical gesture and hide behind the blackboard to the general laughter of the students. For a Guards captain to play the clown like this in front of a group of volunteers was simply unworthy.

For the sake of his business the clever and observant Basevich had studied the examiners of the Nicholas School until he knew them like the back of his hand. He already knew exactly what questions they would ask and what kind of answers they liked to hear. He prepared us with this in mind. I remember that when some confusing verities were not quite clear to us, and one of us would ask for clarification, Basevich would reply quite cynically: "What are you saying, young man, that you want to learn this in earnest? No, my dear, I'm not teaching you in earnest. I'm teaching you to throw dust in their eyes! Remember that. You don't need learning, you only need to pass the examination. If you want to learn these subjects, enroll in the school and study there for two years. I can't teach you any serious subjects in two months. But how to throw dust in the examiners' eyes—that's my specialty. So, young man, what you are asking me now is idle curiosity on your part, since there was never yet a case in which the examiner would ask such a question. Content yourself with the fact that these are the rules of the game. So, can I erase it?" Basevich would ask with an interrogative glance at all of us.

"Erase it!" we would answer in unison according to our custom, and Basevich would wipe the formula or drawing off the blackboard with a sponge and go on to the next question. So we started to use the catchphrase, "It's the rules of the game, go ahead and erase it," whenever someone failed to understand something.

Once Basevich announced to us that he had calculated the time necessary for each subject to the minute, and that he couldn't devote even one day to preparing us for the examination in cavalry field-engineering, and therefore he would not prepare us for that subject at all. "Viktor Ivanovich!" we implored. "How can that be? It's more than 200 pages in the textbook! It involves setting up a telephone, a telegraph, something called 'Dreyer's fuses,' underwater explosions, demolition of iron bridges, millions of formulas! When will we have time to learn this? What can we do?"

"What can you do?" Basevich said with a significant wink. "Here's what: those of you who want to do well in this subject should pay me just another thirty rubles on Saturday evening, and it's in the bag! On Sunday morning we'll go for just two hours to the Engineers' Palace—that's all the time we have. In the palace I'll introduce you to a certain Captain Svirskii (a wonderful fellow), and he'll prepare you in two hours. Oh, have no fear: Svirskii is a very talented captain. By the way, he'll be one of your examiners at the school." And Basevich became completely deadpan.

"Aha! I think I understand . . . ," one of the volunteers drawled out. "So if you're so clever that you understand," Basevich interrupted, "I advise you to be even more clever and not let on that you understand."

It was clear: we had to give the examiner a bribe through Basevich . . . thirty rubles—a paltry sum. But if you multiplied it by nineteen (because there were nineteen of us students), it came out to about 600 rubles, not bad for the budget of an officer of modest means!

I remember that some of us were indignant and out of principle did not want to give a bribe to a Russian officer, preferring to somehow steal the time to prepare this subject on their own. But Basevich was not lying when he said that he had calculated our time to the minute, and we really had no time available for preparing the subject of cavalry field-engineering. The question was put point-blank: either give a bribe, or withdraw from the tests. Although many of us were shaken by this, on Sunday our company assembled, apparently in full, in the Engineers' Palace. Here Basevich introduced us to a short, pale, seemingly sickly field-engineer captain. For an hour and a half in one of the rooms of the palace, Svirskii demonstrated how to set up a field telephone and a Morse telegraph, and also how to regulate the apparatus. Then he wrote down our names on a piece of paper, making some kind of memoranda next to them. A bit embarrassed, he told each one of us what to concentrate on. "Strukov, you do a good study of the paragraph about sabotaging railroad rolling stock, railroad cars, and locomotives . . . Kochubei, pay attention to telephones. Trubetskoi, study the sabotage of station structures: how to explode pump-houses, switches . . . Ilovaiskii, make a thorough study of how to produce underwater explosions," etc. etc.

Do I need to tell you that when it came time for the examination in cavalry field-engineering, our examiner Svirskii gave no indication that he knew us? Do I need to tell you that he asked each of us precisely about what he had assigned us in the Engineers' Palace? Do I need to tell you that each of us received an excellent grade on this examination?

Yes, it was a dirty business—I admit it!

Basevich's students were a motley crew in many respects. There were some young men who had been given a refined and well-rounded education and had finished the university, like the Life Hussar Taneev, the brother of the well-known Vyrubova and son of the court master of ceremonies and head of "His Majesty's Own Cabinet."[1] This young man had completed his university degrees in two different departments. There were princes here: Viazemskii, Obolenskii, Kochubei—all of whom had brilliantly completed their higher education in the lycée or the law school. These were people who were "very respectable" in all senses of the word. There also were people who were not respectable, like the army uhlan P——skii and the dragoon P——ov—principled profligates of the worst tone, meritorious and honorable venereal-disease sufferers, proud of their indecent malady, thrown out of cadet school with a crash for bad behavior, debauchery, and poor scholarly performance—cynical and deeply depraved types, the kind of whom it is usually said that "they are in-

dispensable in male gatherings." There was also the army hussar Andrievskii—dear son of the governor of Oriol—a lisping young dimwit and
carouser who was unable to finish even high school because of stupidity. For
this category of students Basevich was the last bet, the last chance to "enter
the world" and become good army officers. (The path to the Guards was
closed to them forever.) Only Basevich could still save these lost souls, and Basevich went all out—but he saved them! He fleeced them, but he saved them
too. I remember once, before we met with Svirskii, we had a day when we had
all "reached the end of our rope," as they say, from cramming, and we felt so
overworked that we ceased to understand our teacher, and he meanwhile had
completely lost his voice. Our heads were splitting from our studies. The students' eyes, fixed dully on Basevich, were glittering unnaturally; he suddenly
fell silent and looked us over attentively.

"Here's the thing, lads," he uttered hoarsely after a prolonged pause, "I
see that we can't go on like this . . . and I foresaw that such a moment of universal stupefaction would come. That's enough for today. You are free until tomorrow. But today . . . today go have a fling, lads. And make it a good fling—
that's my advice!"

And oh, did we have a fling that day! The whole gay company (with the
exception of the most indecent ones) descended that evening on the mounted
artillery volunteers in Pavlovsk, Prince Gagarin and Baron Meindorf, where
we found the Guards riflemen Prince Sviatopolk-Mirskii and Pokrovskii. The
mounted artillerymen arranged a hot-punch party, and we drank ourselves
under the table.

As if it were today, I can see in my memory the dark room, and in the
middle of it a large wooden jug full of wine standing on the floor. On top of
the jug, resting on crossed sabers, loomed a loaf of sugar, soaked with
warmed rum and ignited. This flaming, intoxicating object was the only illu-
mination in the whole room, where the electric light had been extinguished.
The rum burned with a wavering blue flame that cast a fantastic light on the
multicolored uniforms and flushed faces of the whole company, who were
sitting right on the floor, on rugs that had been spread around the jug. The
ignited sugar, melting in the fire, dripped into the burning wine in large
white-hot drops with an ominous hissing. When the flame began to flare too
brightly, Taneev, who was directing the feast, would pour champagne onto it
from above. The "yorsh" that resulted was cruelly strong. All this was completely out of the ordinary and therefore twice as much fun. Our glasses were
filled out of a scoop with the fiery and highly intoxicating beverage that
burned our throats and seemed to ignite our very brains. After our fever of
studying, it was wonderful to just get drunk. We enjoyed ourselves with all
our hearts.

Many of us were unable to leave the hospitable gunners that night. The hussar Taneev, the chevalier guard Dubasov, the rifleman Sviatopolk-Mirskii, and I, for my sins, spent the night sleeping like the dead in Pavlovsk.

The next day Basevich's lessons didn't go well; our heads were splitting, not from study but from our stupendous hot-punch party of the night before. But a day later we were all healthy, and we took up our cramming with refreshed minds and a redoubled passion. Basevich knew his amazing audience well, and the fling he had prescribed truly turned out to be beneficial for us all. We repeated this fiery fling one more time at the end of our examinations, this time on our own initiative, without the advice of Basevich. This time we had our fling in St. Petersburg in Taneev's apartment—where the devout Vyrubova often sat. This fling was also a lot of fun, but it ended rather unpleasantly for me. At that time I was living on Sergievskaia Street with my aunt A. V. Trubetskaia. My aunt found out somehow about our feast and when I returned from Taneev's she met me, three sheets to the wind, in the entrance hall at two in the morning. With a stone face, my aunt inspected me through her lorgnette with a squinting eye that chilled my soul. It was shameful and disgusting to appear before her drunk, and in the presence of the footman she gave me such a dressing-down that I remember it to this day!

"Now I have to study," I decided, when I had sobered up the next day, "how to cleverly get drunk in such a way that no lady or decent maiden will ever see me 'three sheets to the wind' again!"

From that day I held faithfully to this principle right up to the Revolution. After the Revolution, this principle fell away all by itself. There appeared a new type of Soviet lady, a more politically conscious type that had discarded the old prejudices. This updated type of young lady would not only drink wine, but began to guzzle moonshine, and not in shot glasses but in mugs, almost on an equal footing with men. I'm not knocking these updated and reborn ladies, and I couldn't possibly knock them, because I myself got drunk with them many a time and with pleasure. Before the Revolution one couldn't even dream of such a thing, and to appear drunk before a decent young girl or even a lady was an extremely boorish thing for a "man from society." We could appear drunk only in the presence of a prostitute or cocotte.

Our examinations began very ceremoniously at the end of April. On the appointed day we cuirassiers screwed the golden eagles onto our helmets, laced ourselves into our white parade jackets, and appeared at the Nicholas Cavalry School, excited and "beautiful as gods."

In a large bright hall, over seventy volunteers formed up in one row along three sides of the room. On the right flank were the chevalier guards with the giant Obolenskii at their head, the horse guards, and we cuirassiers; on the other side of us—the cossack guards and the volunteers of the regiments of the Second Guards Division, and finally the army men, of which there were quite a few. Blue, yellow, white, red uhlan lapels, hussar dolmans, crimson, raspberry, and dark-blue riding breeches, helmets sparkling with gold and silver, varnished shakoes, hussar caps with white plumes—in a word, almost the entire amazing Russian cavalry in full parade—a picture worthy of an artist's brush.

The year 1912 was exceptional for the number of volunteers who appeared for the examinations. It was said that in previous years only half as many had gathered.

The festively attired young men whispered excitedly to each other, as if in church. At 9:00 the doors were flung open. There resounded the command: "Right dress—attention!"—and into the hall came the head of the school, General Miller, accompanied by the class inspector, Major General Osipov.[2] Miller was a rather short, young-looking general, built for the cavalry, smartly dressed, pink-cheeked, with a beautiful big mustache, calm and correct in appearance. I had met him earlier at the Zhilinskiis', where he had impressed me as being a true gentleman. Next to him, General Osipov presented a complete contrast—short, fat, quick-moving, with gray hair and the angry and mean yellow face of a superior who is accustomed to blowing up at his subordinates. (We already knew that Osipov was the terror of the school, the evil genius of the cadets.) Miller greeted us with a note of well-bred correctness, letting us know both through the expression on his face and the intonation of his voice that he was treating us not as simple soldiers but as "gentlemen." After greeting us, he began to walk from one volunteer to the other beginning on the right flank, standing to attention with a youthful bearing before each of us in turn. In the deathlike, attentive silence, each of us in turn reported our name and the name of our regiment distinctly and at top speed. He looked each of us straight in the eye with the amazingly calm and cold gaze of an imperturbable and dignified man. Osipov, on the other hand, stared at us with such dissatisfied eyes, as if angered in advance, that it made us feel somehow uncomfortable and even terrified. Osipov had the kind of mug that made it seem as if at any moment he would burst out into furious shouting (which in fact happened often).

After the ceremony of introduction we were divided into two equal groups, because there were too many of us, and they let half of us go home. Our cuirassier division ended up in the second group, and therefore we were to appear for the examination the next day. But the first group had to begin to be "grilled" that very day. The first examination was one of the most difficult—on artillery. That very evening we learned the results. They were murderous: a good half had already flunked . . . on the very first subject! If that was how it was, who would be left standing at the end? The hussar Andrievskii, a student of Basevich, who had ended up in the first group, flunked with a resounding crash. It's true, he was a real dolt, but after all—he was a student of Basevich! This was unheard of. Basevich, who was hardly less agitated than we were, couldn't stand it and rushed to the school to sniff out what was happening. We awaited his return in his apartment on Millionnaia Street, listening with gaping mouths to the unfortunate Andrievskii's tales of how they had slaughtered the volunteers that day. After about two hours Basevich brought news that was hardly consoling: this year the school had received an instruction from above: to test the volunteers as strictly as possible so as to promote only those who had thoroughly mastered all the military sciences. An unusual number of the volunteers who were preparing that year had displeased someone for some reason. In a word, there was an order from above to "slaughter" us, and this order was now being put into effect zealously by the directors of the school, who had decided that with the very first two examinations (on artillery and tactics) they would make the most merciless selection and cut off the weakest candidates all at once. This would make the further process of the examinations significantly easier for the examiners.

That night I slept badly and prayed to God as I had never prayed before. I recalled all my sins. It turned out that there were a lot of them, and I was terribly afraid that because of this God would not hear my passionate prayers and would allow me to fail. But then what would happen with my marriage? How would I be able to look at my fiancée? My soul became troubled and pained.

There are all kinds of excitement—joyful and disgusting. The most repulsively disgusting kind, that really gets you in the pit of the stomach, is the excitement connected with examinations. With a dry mouth and nausea in my soul and in my stomach, I sat the next day in the spacious classroom at the school, where thirty agonizing volunteers sat petrified at their desks, not daring to move a spur, with glittering eyes fixed on the terrible examination table, at which the committee headed by the angry and jaundiced Osipov sat. His enraged physiognomy terrorized us.

A second officer conducting the examination, hirsute and red-haired, callous and inaccessible, was tormenting the poor volunteers, speaking venomously and carpingly, apparently with the clear intention of flunking them.

"What a ba-a-a-stard! What a lout!" I could hear someone's hate-filled and barely audible whisper behind me whenever the red-haired officer flunked one of us.

Many failed . . . Our Sashenka Iskander, with eyebrows raised high in perplexity, was perishing hopelessly and agonizingly, having stumbled on the diverged and converged battery sheaf, in which he lost his way in broad daylight—and he was a student of Basevich, who in his day had graduated from the Imperial Lycée! Now the chevalier guard Strukov had started to scrawl out something hardly decipherable at the blackboard and with a trembling hand was drawing such an improbable and strange trajectory that he was immediately driven away from the board. Now the cossack Beskudin flunked beautifully and crashingly, with lightning speed, without having answered a single question. Although he flunked, he did it with dignity and imperturbability.

"Prince Trubetskoi!" Unexpectedly they called me to the table, loudly and in a voice like nails on a blackboard, and immediately my knees began to shake unpleasantly. I went up to the board, convinced that I would fail. I walked with a gallant and artificially cheerful "dashing" gait, trying with all my might to hide my agitation from my comrades. I walked as if to the scaffold, repeating to myself: "company in distress makes the trouble less!" (I had already worked out the night before the handsome and dignified demeanor with which I was going to perish that day.) I went up to the terrible table, whose green baize covering suddenly appeared distinctly before me with its two inkwells, pens, pencils, slips of paper, and other horrible details. "I'm done for!" I thought with painful melancholy, and clicking my spurs, I cheerfully pulled out the first ticket on the edge, No. 13, I seem to recall—the most foul and mystical number possible! With self-possession I made the most precise turn to the right—hep, two! —gallantly walked up to the board, again turned like a peg—hep, two!—to face the committee, drew air deep into my lungs, and, narrowing my eyes, looked at the ticket . . . In the first moment I did not yet realize that I was saved. Suddenly I realized it. I had gotten a question about shrapnel shells, time fuses, and the trajectory of shells—I knew all this. I answered the red-haired officer cheerfully and gallantly. I correctly solved the problems on saturation bombardment. I only stumbled a bit when the red-haired officer, departing from the examination ticket, began to drill me on the whole course and asked me trick questions. Finally the red-haired officer coldly muttered: "Dismissed!"

Whe-e-e-w!!! What a sigh of relief, and with what happy feet I tumbled out of the classroom! Ten points—that was my grade, more than was needed for a "guardsman's grade."

I was seized by a feeling of great pride. I wasn't worse than the rest. What is more—it turned out I was better than many of them. How beautiful was God's world at that moment! The men who had failed looked at me with envy, and I felt that I had begun to "get on in the world."

On the next two days both groups were grilled on tactics. On this examination almost all the same volunteers who had failed artillery, plus a few more, failed decisively. This was not an examination but a real rout. On maps with a scale of two versts to the inch [one verst = 3,500 feet] we had to solve tactical problems applicable to the movements of a cavalry division and a mounted battery, we had to write dispositions and then answer questions relating to the whole course. The examination lasted several hours, and we were examined by officers from the General Staff. In tactics I received only eight points, but even that grade was lucky—not many people did better, and a whole slew of people failed.

After these two most difficult examinations, no more than thirty people remained in our two groups. The students of Basevich had done better than anyone. Basevich himself, who had thoroughly sniffed out what was going on in the school, kept cheering us up and consoling us with assurances that now, after tactics, they wouldn't be slaughtering us any more. He turned out to be right, and in fact all the rest of the examinations went comparatively smoothly for everyone.

Encouraged by my first success, I gained confidence in myself and gave myself up to the examinations with passion. I thought of nothing but the examinations and fought for my future happiness at the price of a huge strain on my nerves, brain, and all my moral forces. I was inspired by the thought of my fiancée. Having always been a terrible student and a lazybones all through secondary school, now unexpectedly for myself I suddenly acquired the reputation among my comrades of being the cleverest of men. People with a university education had done worse than I had, and many of them envied me. My self-satisfaction and pride knew no end.

I had correctly understood the spirit of the school and had devoted a great deal of attention to my purely external manner, how to behave before the examiners, trying to please them with the precision of my answers, with my gallant, cheerful bearing, and with a kind of tactical deception that succeeded very well for me. It's true, deception alone without knowledge of the subject wouldn't have gotten me far, but all the same my ability to deceive or as they say now to "bluff" contributed to my success. There were volunteers who knew the subjects better than I did, but who got lower grades on the examination simply because they did not know how to pull the wool over the examiners' eyes, or if they tried to, did it tactlessly and without skill.

I remember that my pious cousin Mishanchik Osorgin, a serious and important specialist in church matters, who had an enthusiastic interest in the history of the church, got only ten points on the examination in theology and scripture, because he was not polished and eloquent. But I, who of course knew the subject ten times worse than Osorgin, contrived to get a score of twelve points, gaining the affection of the kind priest by making respectfully pious faces at him as I answered and giving my voice the most touching intonation as I recited the hagiographies of some remarkable martyrs. I was just as brilliantly successful in the examinations on fortification, military administration, jurisprudence, military geography, equestrian matters, and military hygiene. I studied each examiner as he was questioning my comrades, and then I tried to adapt to his tone. Sometimes I would get a difficult ticket on a subject I had a mediocre knowledge of, but I was always rescued by the confident manner with which I answered, my ability to evade and cover up my weak spots, and finally by my expressive eloquence. In a word, I had a good knowledge of the subjects, but I bluffed so virtuosically that often as I was answering, the other volunteers exchanged significant glances. Out of thirty men only the highly intelligent Taneev and maybe at most two others got better grades than I did.

The very difficult examination in military history was conducted in a very curious fashion. For this examination we had to cram the organization of our army in virtually all historical epochs, and also all the battles in which the Russian army took part, beginning with the time of Peter the Great and ending with the last campaign of the Russo-Japanese War. The endless wars between Russia and the Swedes, the Prussians, and Napoleon were full of the names of Russian and foreign generals and of bloody battles that we had to be able to narrate without mixing anything up and with a critical overview . . . Suvorov alone caused us such trouble . . . God almighty! It's no wonder that many of us became real cowards right before this examination. Basevich recommended that all the cowards have recourse to a certain Kudriavtsev—a modest and inconspicuous employee of the school who occupied the post of porter. It was said that this fellow had rescued the volunteers on the history examination for several years running. You had to grease his palm, and per each "mug" he took only twenty-five rubles. You could often encounter this small, unprepossessing man in a black civilian jacket in the corridors of the school, where he hung around with a businesslike air. He was rather colorless, gloomy, and silent, but in his small, lackluster eyes seemed to be written: "I am no fool." We waylaid him in the bathroom and won him over in a trice, handing over on the day of the examination several hundred rubles that we had collected from almost all the volunteers.

The examination in military history was especially solemn. General Miller himself was present and personally administered the questions to the volunteers. Opposite the examination table stood a blackboard on which the porter Kudriavtsev hung large maps of one battle or another, depending on the ticket that had been drawn. The volunteer who had been called up to the examination table would pull out a ticket and, after calling out the number, would take a printed program in his hands and approach the board. Then Kudriavtsev would get the appropriate huge map out from a corner, and using it as a cover, would slowly pass by the volunteer under examination, hiding him from the eyes of the committee for a moment. With the dexterous movement of a professional magician, Kudriavtsev would shove into his program a slip of paper with a beautifully composed synopsis in fine print that corresponded to the ticket that had been drawn. Having performed this number, he would gloomily hang the map on the board, then slowly go off to the side, looking bored and indifferent. We were given several minutes to prepare, and the volunteer, turning to the map, would pretend to be looking at his program but in fact would hastily memorize the synopsis in front of the whole committee. All this was carried off so adroitly that no one was ever caught at the scene of the crime. Of course, it was a big risk, and if any of us had been caught with one of Kudriavtsev's synopses, he would of course not be allowed to take the rest of the examinations but would be kicked out with a resounding crash. I remember that when I was standing in front of Miller with the synopsis in my hands, I suddenly became afraid that I would be caught, so having hardly looked at the synopsis, I tried to hide it as soon as possible. Despite this, I still answered rather smoothly and got a grade of nine for history. These synopses helped many of my comrades a great deal. For example, the chevalier guard Prince Shirinskii-Shakhmatov, whose father had died the day before the examination, had wanted to withdraw from the examination since because of family circumstances he couldn't prepare for it, but at the last minute he decided to take a chance, and he was successful only because of Kudriavtsev's synopsis.

Kudriavtsev's services were used not only by the volunteers but also by the cadets, so it's safe to say that Kudriavtsev earned a goodly sum on the history examination. Of course he was risking the loss of his job if his bosses caught him.

One can only be amazed that these tricks, which were repeated year after year, never came to the attention of the school administration. But the cadets in the Nicholas School formed an amazingly tight-knit caste, and they had their own special mores. A hellish discipline and an extraordinary *Zug* were a firm part of the tradition.[3] In general I must admit that I never encountered an institution where the force of tradition was as great as in the Nicholas School.

In the Nicholas School, which the stern Emperor Nicholas I loved to visit in olden times, the cadets were divided into the Squadron and the Company. Those in the Squadron became officers and the regular cavalry. Those in the Company became the Cossack Horse. There was a well-known antagonism between the Company and the Squadron. The fiercest *Zug* reigned in the Squadron, where the senior cadets according to tradition were supposed to haze the junior cadets. Each senior cadet had his own so-called "beast," that is, a first-year cadet whom he got to bully and mock to his heart's desire. The younger cadet not only had to stand to attention before the elder, showing respect for his rank, but he also had to carry out the most absurd whims and orders the elder gave him. The cadets slept together in dormitories, both senior and junior. Sometimes if the senior cadet wanted to go to the toilet at night, he would wake up his "beast" and ride him as if on horseback to take care of his needs. This did not amaze anyone and was considered completely normal. If the senior cadet couldn't sleep, often he would wake up the junior cadet and amuse himself by forcing the latter to tell a dirty joke, or would say to him, "Junior Cadet, tell me the name of my beloved *right now!*" or "Junior Cadet, tell me the name of the regiment I'm going to join as a cornet *right now!*" The awakened "beast" usually answered these questions correctly, since he was obligated to know by heart the names of all the women beloved by his elders as well as the regiments they intended to join. In the case of a wrong answer the senior cadet would punish the "beast" on the spot, forcing him to do thirty or forty squats, saying, "Hep, two! Hep, two! Hep, two!" They especially liked to make the junior cadets do their squats next to the heater in the toilet. "Junior Cadet, tell me about the immortality of the soul of a grouse *right now,*" the senior cadet would command. And the junior cadet, standing at attention, would report: "The soul of a grouse becomes immortal when it lands in the stomach of a noble cornet." The seniors, even though they were only cadets, would demand that the juniors call them Mr. Cornet. Sometimes a senior cadet would get the following fantasy into his head: "Junior Cadet!" he would order, "follow me and bellow like a whale." And the junior cadet would "bellow like a whale," following the senior cadet persistently wherever he went, until the senior cadet commanded: "As you were!" Sometimes the senior cadets would make the juniors write essays on the most unbelievable topics, like for example "The influence of the moon on a sheep's tail." And the juniors would carry out all this nonsense unquestioningly, since tradition did not permit them to disobey the orders of a senior cadet.

The best cadet in the unit was appointed sergeant major. The cadets called him "the earthly god," and rendered him particular homage, almost holding him in higher respect than the head of the school himself. Officially, this cadet had a particular disciplinary power, but unofficially, his power over the cadets was almost limitless.

Particular respect was also paid to those cadets who had been held back in the school for two or three years because of their poor academic progress. For their length of service these lads were awarded the title of "generals of the school" by the other cadets. They walked around the school like big shots, felt themselves to be heroes, and would haze anyone they pleased any time they pleased. In general it was considered bad form in the school to show an interest in academics. But to go on a spree with a good-looking girl, to go drinking with a wild crowd, or when the opportunity arose to punch some civilian intellectual in the mug or pick up the kind of illness that cannot be talked about in good society—these were worthwhile pursuits, much more interesting than any academic subjects.

With their merciless *Zug* the senior cadets steeled the juniors and subjected them to terrible discipline, producing a very particular gallant bearing by which one could recognize a Nicholas cadet from a mile away. The school administration and the officers of the school in general rather approved of the *Zug* tradition, and if they didn't directly encourage it, at most they shut their eyes to it, because most of them were themselves alumni of this remarkable school, from which in his day, strange to say, the famous poet Lermontov emerged as a cornet. A monument to Lermontov modestly adorned the school courtyard.[4] By the way, it is characteristic that the Nicholas cadets never said "the poet Lermontov." In the school it was customary to say "the cornet Lermontov," for to the cadet's ear "cornet" of course sounded much better and more significant than "poet." In fact, people did not go to this school to learn how to write poetry. They went in order to become dashing cavalry swordsmen.

When you tell stories about the unbelievable school *Zug* and the mockery of the junior cadets by the seniors, you can't help but expect to be asked why the junior cadets always put up with these offensive tricks, why they never lodged complaints against the seniors, and why in general they so unquestioningly submitted to this completely illegitimate school tradition. I must explain that when a young man entered the school he was asked first thing by the senior cadets how he wished to live—"according to the glorious school tradition, or according to the regulations?" If the young man answered that he wanted to live according to the regulations, he would, it's true, be exempted from the *Zug*, but no one would treat him as a comrade. Such a cadet was called a "red." A "red" cadet was boycotted and deeply despised. No one would talk to him. They maintained a strictly official, service relationship to him. The "earthly god," the sergeant major, and the platoon cadets would not forgive a "red" cadet the smallest mistake in service, they would annoy him with extra duties or deny him leave, because according to the regulations they had the right to do so. But the most significant thing was that after finishing school, not a single Guards regiment would accept such a "red" cadet into its officers' ranks, because every regiment included alumni of the Nicholas School, who always kept in touch with their alma mater, and thus would always have information about which of the newly graduated cadets were "red." But I should note that the "red" cadet was a very rare phenomenon. The Nicholas School was extremely famous, and every young man who wanted to enter the school knew in advance what he was getting into, and therefore usually agreed voluntarily to live "not according to the regulations but according to the glorious tradition." No matter how strange it may seem, the Nicholas cadets really loved, even adored their school, and every officer it turned out would for many years afterward lovingly recount to his comrades his school recollections, which were always softened by the fact that every first-year cadet who was hazed turned into a hazer in the second year.

Yes, the school had its own society—unflaggingly cheerful, dashing, and most important—firmly united. We volunteers were tested separately from the cadets, and therefore we had little interaction with them, only meeting them by chance in the corridors and the lavatories, where we often were witness to very curious scenes of cadet hazing.

A great contrast to the Nicholas school was "His Majesty's Corps of Pages."[5] This school made officers for the Guards regiments out of the most well-educated young people, whose noble parents often registered them as "pages" in early childhood. The Corps of Pages had junior classes with the general education program of a secondary school (which also existed in other cadet schools) and two senior classes which provided junior officers for Guards regiments of all branches, that is, infantry, artillery, and cavalry. It took years to complete the program of the Corps of Pages, and therefore this caste-based military school stamped its alumni with a particularly refined bearing and good form. In the Corps of Pages firm discipline also reigned, and the principle of *Zug* was not unknown to the pages, but it didn't exceed the bounds of human dignity and strict propriety. In the Corps of Pages academic subjects were given their rightful place, and it must be admitted that this institution probably produced the most cultured officers in the Russian army.

The young men who entered the Corps of Pages had come in contact with the court atmosphere from their earliest years (and of course the very word "page" bears a purely court connotation). Among the students of the Corps were youths who had been personal pages to the empresses and the grand duchesses. At court ceremonies and solemn palace appearances these pages were dressed in beautiful gold-trimmed uniforms, chamois breeches, and jackboots, and clad in this brilliant attire they would hold the trains of their "lofty and regal ladies," carrying out their petty personal errands. The pages were very proud of this and looked down on the other military schools. It goes without saying that the privileged position of the pages and their contact with the great ones of this world made it impossible for them to ever display "bad form," profligacy, or conspicuous soldier's crudity. What was required here was refined manners above all. If the Nicholas cadets while still in school were not yet even contemplating a career, the young pages, on the contrary, while still in elementary school often had started dreaming of a brilliant military-court career and the aiguillettes of an aide-de-camp, and were forming brilliant plans for the future, having imbibed since childhood careerist ideas, influenced of course by their relations with the court.

The pages were firmly united among themselves. Before being promoted to officer's rank a whole class would order identical modest gold rings with a wide steel outer rim.[6] The steel symbolized the firm (steel) cohesion and friendship not only of the whole class but of all the people who had ever graduated from the Corps of Pages and who wore a similar ring. The pages usually remained true to this principle, and an alumnus of the Corps of Pages who made his career and attained the heights would as a rule drag his former Corps comrades along with him, pulling strings for them in all kinds of ways, and thus it was former pages who more often than not occupied the high military and even administrative posts in the empire.

There was a rather strong antagonism between the pages and the Nicholas cadets, despite the fact that both institutions sent their alumni into the Guards. This antagonism was so great that long after having been promoted to officer's rank, former pages and former Nicholas cadets serving in the same regiment would treat each other with a certain suspicion. These two institutions were very different in spirit: one could immediately recognize a Nicholas officer by his bearing and his soldierlike bluster. One could recognize a page by his emphatically proper air of a "boy from a good home."

Of all the cavalry officers from a given class, seniority in the service was given first to graduates of the Corps of Pages, then to the Nicholas cadets who had received Guards-level grades on the final examinations, then to volunteers who had received Guards-level grades, and finally to alumni of the Tver and Elizavetgrad cadet cavalry schools. Despite the fact that volunteers were lower in seniority than graduates of the Corps of Pages and the Nicholas School, many young men from the nobility chose the volunteer route to a military career, because it was the fastest route: volunteers were spared a whole year of study, because the pages and cadets were required to study two years in their institutions.

Chapter Five

Topographical Tests in the Countryside

BEFORE I HAD finished my examinations a joyful event finally took place in the Trubetskoi family. My cousin S. P. Trubetskaia married the very nice young Count N. Lamsdorf. This wedding, at which I performed the role of best man, was celebrated festively and gaily, after which the atmosphere of gloom that had prevailed in the house of Trubetskoi since the absurd and tragic death of my uncle Piotr Nikolaevich was significantly relieved.

In the middle of May our examinations in St. Petersburg on all academic subjects were finished. All we had left to pass were the practical tests on topographical surveying and tactical problems in the field. The school moved to its Dudergof camp near Krasnoe Selo, and we volunteers made our way there too, having said a warm farewell to Basevich.

The life hussar Taneev, Osorgin, and I rented a three-room dacha in Krasnoe Selo and every morning we would appear at the picturesque Dudergof camp near a lake for topographical work. They appointed a certain Captain Nevezhin to us volunteers—a very correct and humane person, who was in charge of us during all the tests.

The tests began with plane table surveying, and each of us was assigned a separate parcel of land in the vicinity of Dudergof, which we had to plot very precisely on a map with a scale of 200 sazhens [426 meters] to the inch. We were given little village children as assistants, who would drag the base chain and help us to place the landmarks. I was assigned a rather difficult parcel, which included one of the steep and oddly shaped slopes of the Dudergof mountains, dotted with dachas (this was the very mountain that is mentioned in the cadet song that begins: "It's as dark as a Moor's a[sshole], / And the advance-guard camp is sleeping, / And on the top of Dudergof / An eagle-owl is plaintively crying . . .").

Besides this slope of the famous mountain, my parcel also included the old Pavlovskii redoubt, a plowed field, vegetable gardens, shrubbery, and part of the Baltic railroad line, which intersected with a broad country road. The slopes and the whole relief had to be carefully plotted on the map with contour lines. I had to perform the work in the space of a week. From early morning until night I would be on my parcel with a tripod and plane table, sighting individual landmarks, telegraph poles and spires on dachas, and composing an intricate and confusing triangulation on paper. Nevezhin would make a circuit of all the parcels on horseback twice a day, checking up on us. From time to time General Miller himself, on a beautiful bay horse, would appear on our parcels.

The weather was unusually beautiful. It was a lovely, joyful, early and luxuriant spring. The apple and cherry trees were blossoming in a riot of intricate lace, and the little birds, as is their custom, were singing hymns to the spring, inspiring naughty erotic daydreams and moods in young people. Toward noon the heat would become unbearable, as in the South, and all the volunteers who had come to camp exhausted and pale from their nocturnal study sessions in St. Petersburg became as swarthy as Moors during the very first days, their noses and the backs of their necks peeling from the sun. After the Petersburg fever of examinations and maniacal cramming in Basevich's quarters which had become so hateful to us, our topographical tests in the bosom of spring nature were a kind of joyful vacation for us all. We had a feeling that no one was going to fail at this point, and that we could consider our success to be in the bag. Since I had picked up an average grade of more than 10.5, I personally considered that no matter how mediocre my grades in topography, I would still get an average Guards-level grade. So I did not put in too much effort at this point, giving in to the general reaction that had overcome all of us. No one wanted to work seriously any more and we all took it easy.

The most original approach to the surveying was that of a certain Pr——v, the scion of a well-known Moscow millionaire factory owner, who had become a volunteer in the Life Guards Cavalry Regiment under the aegis of Grand Duchess Elizaveta Fiodorovna. This bumpkin, who before entering the service married the lovely daughter of a well-known, rich Duma statesman, did not have the slightest desire to work now. He sent for an experienced surveyor from St. Petersburg, for whom he rented a separate dacha near Dudergof. The mail-order surveyor did all the work for Pr——v, and Pr——v limited himself to sitting on his assigned parcel in the bushes, where he and his young wife enjoyed the charms of a country idyll. Pr——v also hired special "signalers" in Dudergof, whose job was to watch out to see whether any officers were coming. When the latter would appear on the horizon, the signalers would immediately alert both Pr——v and his surveyor. On such occasions Pr——v would jump nimbly out of the bushes and stand by his tripod with the air of a person absorbed in his work, and the surveyor would run as fast as his legs would carry him to hide in a ditch or in the very same bushes where Pr——v's lovely wife was secreted. When the officers had signed Pr——v's plane table and gone away, the surveyor would again crawl out of the bushes and take up his interrupted work, and Pr——v would return to his interrupted pleasures. Is there any point in adding that Pr——v got a better grade in topography than any of us? Pr——v, although he was serving in one of the most "expensive" regiments of the Guards, and despite his high patronage, was not accepted as an officer in that regiment and entered one of the Hussar army regiments instead. In fact, one must say that Pr——v conducted himself rather tactlessly, always advertising his millions and boasting of his wealth, throwing money around ostentatiously, which wasn't very clever in his position, since it was seen as the typical sign of a rich upstart of rather poor form. In the Guards this was never forgiven. One was supposed to throw money around in a different, more seemly manner and style.

For us volunteers, who were spending every day from morning to night on our parcels, the question of entertainment was solved with the help of the so-called jackals. "Jackals" were special tradesmen who roamed with large baskets on their heads around the Krasnoe Selo military field during cavalry exercises and who darted about the environs of Krasnoe and Dudergof, supplying all kinds of snacks to the pages, cadets, and volunteers who were carrying out their surveying. In the jackal's capacious basket one could find any sort of delicacy—cheeses and sausages of all kinds, tasty meat pies, smoked eel, pressed and unpressed caviar, canned lobster, duck pâté, chocolate, mineral water, lemonade, vodka, cognac, and even foreign champagne. The jackals understood perfectly that they were dealing with healthy young men whose stomachs were empty and finances tight, and thus they made us pay through the nose, readily offering us unlimited credit.

The profession of jackal was apparently very profitable, because after several years of activity the jackal usually acquired a dacha in the neighborhood of the Krasnoe Selo camp, which he would rent out in the summer.

My jackal was a respectable and shrewd little peasant with a broad and thick light-brown beard. He was called Gavrilych. He would bring me greetings from my comrades on the neighboring parcels and loved to look at my plane table with the critical air of an expert, making respectful comments on my work and even giving me advice: over the many years of his jackal activity he had learned a thing or two about the science of topography.

The jackals made out especially well with the officers during exercises on the Krasnoe Selo military field. But we will speak of that later.

After the plane table surveying, we carried out surveying by eye and route surveying. This work was done not one by one but with our whole cheerful company, in which to everyone's delight Taneev was designated the head. We worked very harmoniously, everyone's mood was carefree, and as a result we had amusing adventures.

For example, I remember once as our whole group was going out to work in the morning, we met the jackal Gavrilych and arranged a rendezvous with him at noon, instructing him to prepare for us a substantial and tasty snack opportunity with the corresponding drink opportunity. Wishing to please us, Gavrilych had arranged a real picnic for us in a grove near the road. We all drank quite a bit, but especially the Aleksandrinskii hussar Geine, who suddenly got into such a state that he could no longer stand on his feet without external help. Supported by his comrades, Geine, who had lost his cap God knows where, unexpectedly on the road began to vomit from mouth and nose everything he had eaten and drunk at the picnic. Trying to sober our comrade up as quickly as possible, we began to drench him with water from a little swamp, and Taneev, who was experienced in such matters, armed himself with a twig and brushed away two amazing strings of snot that were hanging mournfully over the hussar's chin . . . All this would be well and good, but to our misfortune, at that very moment from around a bend in the road quickly came a coach and pair, and in the coach a general with a very solemn air.

Taneev commanded, "Attention!" and we froze over the corpse of the fallen hussar. Seeing this outrage, the general ordered his coachman to stop and beckoned us with his finger. We started telling His Excellency in a rather confused way that our comrade was suffering from sunstroke because he had been working without his cap. It was hard to believe this, however, because as ill-luck would have it, the day was rather overcast and the sun kept hiding behind the clouds, and besides Geine at that moment suddenly came to life in a most inopportune fashion and began to howl something loud and outrageous.

"I'll give you sunstroke!" His Excellency uttered ominously, and having noted Geine's name and regiment in a little book, the general set off on his way, threatening us with his finger in a manner that boded no good.

Meanwhile Geine was absolutely unpresentable, and it was quite obvious that he would not be himself for quite a while. At every moment we could expect another terrifying encounter with some terrifying officer. We had to hurry back to camp to hand in our work, and we just couldn't figure out where to hide our tipsy young hero.

The jackal Gavrilych came to our rescue. He ran to Dudergof to get a coachman and told us that he knew some kind dacha inhabitants who would give Geine refuge until he sobered up. When the coachman arrived, Taneev and I carefully lay Geine in the cab and delivered him by a roundabout route to the address that the jackal had given us. It was a large dacha with a front and back garden at the foot of the Dudergof mountain. Our knock at the garden gate was answered by a lovely maid in a cap, and then by the mistress herself, a middle-aged lady of very respectable appearance. Taneev and I did not expect this at all and were very embarrassed. To ask this unfamiliar lady to give refuge to our drunken comrade was somehow ridiculous and even awkward, so we were ready to withdraw, but the lady had already noticed Geine, who was hanging out of the cab like a corpse. "Who sent you to me?" she asked in a rather severe manner. In embarrassment we named the jackal. "O-o-h-h, Gavrilych . . . ," the lady drawled with a smile, "well, in that case, come in. I'm happy I can be of help. Your ailing comrade is welcome to have a rest at my house. He seems to be having some sort of fit?" We dragged the unconscious Geine into the house and laid him out on a fine bed in a cozy little room, whose walls, I seem to recall, were hung with Chinese fans, lanterns, and pictures. With a knowing smile the lovely maid prudently placed a chamber pot near the head of the bed. Convinced that our comrade was now out of danger, we politely took our leave from the mistress of the dacha, thanking her sincerely for her assistance.

"I'm always happy to be of use to noble and well-brought-up people. Please don't forget the way to my home," she said with such a genteel air that we gallantly kissed her hand in farewell.

The next day we met the revived Geine at the school camp. He was gloomy and came down on me and Taneev: "Why did you drag me to N——? Who asked you to do that?"

"But where were we supposed to put you, you wretched hussar! You should thank us for setting you up in the home of a respectable woman."

"Stop making fun of me! You took me to a brothel!"

"Wha-a-a-t?"

"Please stop pretending. I woke up yesterday in a brothel, the madam of which, by the way, I know to be the craftiest scoundrel in creation!"

And to our general amazement and pleasure the unfortunate Geine related in detail how yesterday he suddenly and unexpectedly woke up in the evening in the very gay company of several "dear but fallen" creatures, out-and-out prostitutes, and what resulted from all of this.

We laughed until we cried. We laughed at Geine and at ourselves, remembering how we had gallantly kissed the hand of a 100-percent gangster's moll, taking her for a respectable lady.

I never encountered that attractive personage again, but several of my comrades noted down her Dudergof address just in case, and later when under the influence they visited her cozy dacha.

As for the general who met us on the road with the drunken Geine and promised to give us sunstroke, fortunately he forgot about it and did not make a complaint about us.

Strange things happened near Krasnoe and Dudergof, teeming with lively military men!

After the surveying we solved "tactical problems in the field," for which we left camp either as a group on horseback or one by one on foot. From these tactical exercises I have preserved one rather vivid memory, which did not, however, have any relation to tactics.

Once I was wandering along the bank of the dammed-up river Ligovka, with the assignment of finding a convenient ford for artillery. The place was secluded, overgrown with willows and alder trees that bent poetically over the water, and in the air one could scent the happy month of May—that month when young people become particularly foolish.

Suddenly around a sharp bend I heard the splash of water and someone's young feminine voices. At that moment I caught sight at my feet of someone's little shoes, stockings, and two little virginal white dresses. Another moment, and beyond a willow bush from out of the water emerged before me two charming little heads—one blonde and one dark. As I already said, it was the month of May, and therefore I stood as if rooted to the spot. For a minute the girls were not aware of my presence, and I had the opportunity to ascertain that they were swimming without swimming suits.

"Enough, Lika! I can't any more . . . I'm completely frozen!" resounded the ringing chest-voice of one of the girls.

At this point I coughed loudly and significantly.

Another moment—and the two nymphs plunged into the water up to their necks, turning their frightened little eyes on me. After a pause the bolder one, the swarthy one, shouted at me in indignation:

"Go away from here at once!"

"Forgive me, young lady," I answered, "but I cannot go away. My officers gave me the assignment of finding a ford on the river, and this place seems to me to be the appropriate one."

"You are an insolent fellow, and we will complain to your officers if you do not leave here immediately!"

"So what . . . I will be only grateful to you if you inform my officers about me, they will of course thank me for the zeal with which I am carrying out their orders . . . Tell me, is it deep here?"

"Get out of here, I told you!"

"I repeat my question: is it deep here? After all, I don't know whether you're standing up straight or perhaps you're squatting?"

"Get out of here this minute! You're an impudent fellow!"

"Forgive me, young ladies, but I have no time to waste, and since you refuse to inform me whether it's deep here, according to my military duty I am obliged to check the depth of the river personally."

With these words I sat on the grass and slowly began to pull off my boots. At this point my naiads raised such a squealing and shouting that you could hear them a mile away. Panic horror was expressed in the eyes of the blonde. "He-e-e-lp!" the swarthy one howled frantically.

"Ladies, why these horrible cries? I have no intention of murdering you. I only ask that you inform me what the channel is in these waters. The sooner you answer me, the sooner I will leave you, despite all the pleasure your society affords me! So, is it deep here?"

"On your honor, will you really leave if we tell you?" the swarthy girl suddenly asked with touching naiveté, after thinking it over for a moment.

"On my honor."

"It's not deep here . . . Well, why aren't you leaving?"

"And what's the bottom like here? Silty? Rocky?"

"No . . . it's just sand . . ."

"Merci, and now tell me: over there, farther to the right, beyond the bush, is it deep?"

"There? We didn't swim over there."

"Well, go over there and tell me!"

The swarthy one submissively went over to the bush and shouted: "It's very deep here! Now, go away finally! I'm frozen stiff!"

"Well, and by the other bank?" I continued imperturbably to torment my nymph. "Please go over there. I like to be thorough."

The swarthy girl carried out this demand as well, while her blonde friend, hiding behind a bush, kept stealing alarmed glances at me.

"By the bank it's quite shallow!" the swarthy girl shouted to me.

"Please stand up straight, otherwise I don't have a good idea of the true depth."

"But this is outrageous! You're making fun of us! If you don't leave this minute, you're a base and dishonorable man!"

"First show me your little leg, then I'll go!"

"That's disgusting!"

"I repeat: until you stick your leg out of the water, I'm not going anywhere!"

Complete helplessness was reflected in the eyes of the girl, who was turning blue and shivering from the cold. In a weak voice she said, "This is dishonorable of you . . . ," and weeping bitterly, she turned her back on me.

At this point I realized that I had gone too far and without saying another word I hastened to leave. When I told my comrades about my joke, they laughed, and one of them remarked that it would have been even wittier to hide the swimmers' dresses and underwear.

In the evening, when going to bed, I again remembered the swimmers and I was suddenly ashamed of my "tactical exercises" that day. The girls I had forced to tremble from cold and fright would not go out of my mind. I remembered my mother, who had often told my brother and me that the boor and the true gentleman can be recognized above all by their behavior toward women. "Noblesse oblige" was one of my mother's principles, and if in her view a member of an old noble family could marry only a noblewoman of good birth, this did not at all give him the right not to be a gentleman in relation to any woman, no matter what her social status, because in woman one must above all respect feminine honor, dignity, and chastity.

How would I have reacted if I had learned that some boor had allowed himself to joke in this way with my sister or my fiancée? Indeed, according to the customs of the day I would have been obliged to either beat in the face of such a lout or demand satisfaction from him. "Stick your leg out of the water . . ."—that's how I harassed an unknown young lady, whose honor could not be defended at that moment by any man. With my loutish tricks I brought to tears girls who might be sisters of Russian officers, that is, people who have cultivated very particular and punctilious ideas about honor in general. I felt sick at heart from the realization that I had played the boor and that I had a long way to go to be a true gentleman. In those days in Russia the external aspect of behavior was completely different. Now everything has become much simpler. These days half-naked women, fat and thin, middle-aged and young, go swimming and lie around on common beaches, not at all embarrassed by the presence of men, and no one sees anything immoral in this. But in those days—there were different ideas, and feminine chastity was valued in a completely different way.

The story of the "nymphs" did not end there.

About three days after the incident I have described, on my way to spend Sunday in St. Petersburg, I was strolling on the platform of the Krasnoe Selo railroad station and waiting for the train. Suddenly I heard a suppressed female voice behind me: "Look, Marusia, it's him!" I looked around and saw my charming naiads, who were staring fixedly at me. Meeting my gaze, the young ladies quickly and shamefacedly turned away, lowering their little heads in consternation. I thought at first that it would be most prudent to ignore them and pretend that I hadn't recognized them. But a twenty-year-old young man is by no means always prudent and logical. After about three minutes I had bought two boxes of candy in the station kiosk, and a minute after that, having lain in wait for the young strangers in a secluded corner of the platform, I went up to them, touching my fingers to the peak of my service cap.

"Please forgive my boldness," I addressed them both at once, "but do not refuse to accept this candy from a man who is sincerely repentant for the indiscreet and unsuccessful joke that he had the audacity . . ."

"You're out of your mind!" the swarthy girl interrupted me, blushing.

"No! Today I'm in my right mind, but three days ago, when I first met you, I was out of my mind."

Apparently there was a lot of sincerity in my voice. In any event, the young ladies very soon stopped pouting and finally deigned to accept the candy from me.

I made their acquaintance without giving my real name. The swarthy one was called Marusia, and the blonde Lika. They turned out to be seniors in the Gatchina high school and they knew a few of our cuirassier officers.

Later I sometimes encountered the two friends either in the Gatchina train or on the street, and I always joked with them. It turned out that after our second or third meeting Marusia, against all expectations, was smitten with the kind of love for me that only an inexperienced high-school girl is capable of. She found out my real name, and later, when I was already a married officer, she openly declared her passionate love for me, wrote me notes, found out somehow when I was on duty in the regiment and would often call me on the telephone right in the officers' club, demanding that I agree to a rendezvous with her. She was pretty, rather large-breasted, always with burning cheeks, and with a charmingly arched nose. But . . . in those days I was a happy newlywed and I wasn't terribly interested in any Marusias. Her harassment reached the point that I, like Evgenii Onegin, once even had to read a lesson in morals to the passionate high-school girl. But my Marusia turned out to be much more insistent and pushy than Pushkin's Tatiana . . . May Allah forgive her!

I was living then, as I have already mentioned, in a dacha in Krasnoe that I shared with Osorgin and Taneev. I got along very well with the latter, in spite of the difference in our ages. Apparently this intimacy was fostered by the cheerful personality we both shared. I liked everything about Taneev, whom we called "Siza" or "Tania." I liked in him the dashing elegance with which at a bachelor gathering he would pop a champagne cork to the ceiling; I liked the tactful and at the same time independent manner of a true nobleman with which he would conduct himself in the presence of our officers; I also liked his inborn affectation of speech, his inability to pronounce the letter "r" properly; finally, I liked his attractive face with its kind and expressive light-blue eyes and somewhat melancholy nose, sharply pointed downward. There was a silly period when I tried to imitate him in everything.

Taneev was rather strange. Undoubtedly intelligent, broadly educated, extremely capable, sensitive, I would even say talented, far from devoid of feeling for the beautiful, at the same time he was very frivolous, loved drinking bouts and the gay company of inane comrades who were far from worthy of him, and he was a great one for thinking up funny practical jokes. He drank a lot, not because he was an alcoholic but because it was fun. Only at times did it seem to me that he was drinking in order to drown some kind of bitter secret thoughts—perhaps thoughts of an unhappy love. Despite his ostentatious frivolity, one sensed that Siza Taneev had his own closed and fine little world where he contemplated serious and secret ideals, and he did not let anyone into that little world. When it was necessary, he could be very restrained. Thus he spoke about his sister Anna Vyrubova in a very guarded way, never mentioning her exceptional position in the tsar's palace or her friendship with Rasputin, but meanwhile at that time in high society, gossip and ru-

mors that were very compromising to both Vyrubova and the Empress Aleksandra Fiodorovna herself were being spread.[1] It was obvious that Taneev,
who loved his sister as an intimate relative, suffered a great deal from these
rumors and gossip. Taneev had no dealings with Rasputin and never mentioned him, because as I was aware, he was not one of his admirers. But despite my close friendship with Taneev, I almost never touched on this delicate
question with him, because at that time I personally was rather aggrieved
when I heard someone in society say bad and unseemly things about the empress, whose honor, according to my ideas at that time, every loyal subject, especially a member of the nobility, was obligated to protect, just as if it were a
matter of the honor of one's own mother or sister. In high society, however,
this was by no means a unanimous opinion. On the contrary, they often rel-
ished gossip about the tsar's family—gossip that more often than not that year
originated with the garrulous lady-in-waiting S. I. T., who had once been a
governess to the tsar's children. With the characteristic tendency of old maids
to "make a mountain out of a molehill," T. would wash the court's dirty laun-
dry in public, as they say, conveying to her good friends her sensational news
items, to which her old maid's imagination and old maid's chastity undoubtedly lent a certain tendentious coloration. The not-too-bright T. apparently
had no idea what a fatal hole she was digging for the throne and the dynasty
by this activity. Then the little people, who always love to discuss and gossip
about what great people are doing, picked up the stories of the lady-in-waiting
T., embellished them in their own way, added their own commentary and suppositions, and in this way, the gossip spread by the tsar's governess snowballed,
quietly passed by word of mouth and rolled all through immense Russia, en-
gendering in people's minds an evil and negative attitude toward the empress.
It is interesting that the empress knew that this lady-in-waiting had a tendency
to blab and was spreading nasty stories about her. Nevertheless, although T.
was relieved of her duty as governess at her own request, she was not deprived
of her honorary title as lady-in-waiting.[2] It is a strange fact, and I believe it can
be explained by the special character of the empress, who was by no means
devoid of magnanimity.

So I became friends with Taneev, and from this friendship my pious
cousin often had to suffer, as he suddenly became the roommate of two inveterate debauchee-martyrs, who were constantly thinking up something outrageous. We were a strange trio. But I hasten to correct myself—it wasn't a
trio but rather a quartet, since Mishanchik had brought along to the dacha in
Krasnoe his loyal tutor Evmenchik, who now served all three masters at once
with great zeal . . . And poor Evmenchik really took a lot from us! One day Taneev and I would arrange a hot-punch party, and Evmenchik and Mishanchik
would tremble at the thought that we would burn down our wooden dacha.
The next day we would arrange a party and invite the volunteer chevalier

guards. The day after that we'd play cards until dawn. The day after that, in pursuit of honey, we would let loose a cloud of bees in Mishanchik's room out of the special glass hive that Mishanchik, as a lover of nature and agriculture, had brought with him to Krasnoe and set up in his room near the window. The day after that—again an intimate hot-punch party and panic. "Have the fear of God!" was all we would hear from cousin Mishanchik. After a week of such torture both he and the servant Evmenchik began to beg, categorically protesting against the practice of hot-punch parties in view of the clear danger of fire. "You'll burn down the house, gentlemen!" Evmenchik said. "Accidents will happen . . . We'll have a fire and won't be able to get out!" These protests gave rise to a new amusement of ours, namely the conducting of fire drills. Taneev and I worked out a special fire task sheet, according to which each of us (except Mishanchik) had his duties. We all four lived on the second floor, which was reached by a narrow wooden staircase. The fire drill was based on the idea that this staircase would burn and therefore it was impossible as a means of escape.

"Fire! Fire!" one of us would suddenly start to howl in a voice not his own, and then an unbelievable outrage would begin. Taneev and I would grab a bucket of water or a jug or a tub, and with this rescue equipment we would of course set off first to Mishanchik's room.

"Mishan, you're engulfed in flames!" we would howl in panicked voices and instantly drench both Mishanchik and his bed. He would become furious, but we had already started "saving" his belongings, throwing them quickly out the window.

"The staircase is on fire!" Taneev would howl, "save Evmenchik!!" And having finished with the master, we would tumble head over heels onto his servant, tying him up and trying to lower him from the balcony onto the street on a rope made of sheets tied together, upon which the respectable man would flounder helplessly and squeal like a piglet. To top off the fire drill Taneev and I would ourselves descend like lightning on the sheet-rope from the balcony, nobly saving ourselves only at the last.

I remember one evening, at the height of one of these drills, precisely at the terrible moment when Taneev and I were forcibly rolling the tied-up Evmenchik over the railing of the balcony, and on this occasion our servant was squealing like a wild boar out of terror, that suddenly right beneath the balcony there resounded a terrible cry: "What is this outrage???" We looked down and were horribly confounded to see right in front of our dacha the lanky figure of the Grand Duke Ioann Konstantinovich, who then was a lieutenant of the Horse Life Guards Regiment. Attracted by Evmenchik's squealing, the grand duke, who was by chance passing along the street, stopped and looked into the front yard of our dacha, where he saw a very strange and completely incomprehensible picture. "What's going on here? Immediately stop this outrage!" the grand duke shouted, looking us over in perplexity, while Taneev and I had frozen on the balcony, respectfully standing at attention. Drenched with water and tied up in a sheet, our loyal servant, involuntarily imitating his masters, had also assumed a respectful pose, standing at attention along with us. Wet as a mouse and with whiskers disheveled, at that moment Evmenchik looked so funny that the grand duke obviously was having trouble restraining a smile. "I'll show you volunteers how to commit outrages!" he shouted at us threateningly, quickly turned away, and strode away without looking back. "Oh, gentlemen, gentlemen, what will happen to you now if the grand duke makes a complaint against you?" grieved Evmenchik, who was always touchingly concerned about our welfare. "So, you caught it? You caught it?" Mishanchik maliciously rejoiced.

After such "fire drills," Mishanchik and Evmenchik of course grumbled at us, but not for long, because it's impossible to be angry at cheerful people for long, and our cheerfulness sometimes infected them too. Besides, Taneev and I asked their forgiveness and promised to reform, but as soon as we reformed we immediately thought up new crimes, since the constantly emphasized good behavior of Mishanchik and Evmenchik couldn't fail to inspire a feeling of protest in us and sometimes provoked us to play dirty tricks.

Once when Mishanchik and Evmenchik were out, we staged a scene of burglary and the bloody murder of Mishanchik, for which purpose we dressed a pillow and a couch bolster in Mishanchik's dressing gown, placed his boots on boot-trees at the "corpse's" feet, and stuffed it under the bed. Next to it we formed a pool of blood made of red wine, and stained an axe with wine, giving it a most criminal appearance. For greater verisimilitude, we turned everything in the room upside down, as if a desperate struggle had gone on there. Having set up our joke, we left, leaving the dacha unlocked. (Mishanchik and Evmenchik, both very careful about the household, were always terrified that someone would burglarize the dacha, and watched keenly to see that it was always locked.)

We had wanted to play a charming joke on Evmenchik, and in our frivolity we did not expect that this little joke would nearly cause him a heart attack and evoke indescribable indignation in Mishanchik.

Another time, I remember, on some holiday, after Taneev and I had gone on a spree in Pieter [nickname for St. Petersburg], we returned to Krasnoe accompanied by the brass band of the Ligovskii fire brigade, which we had intercepted by chance at the Baltic Station. The trumpet players, paid and gotten drunk by us, had been delighting our ears in the train-car all the way to Krasnoe, to the great pleasure of the young female dacha inhabitants, whose favorite pieces we had ordered the orchestra to perform, and to the great indignation of the older, staid dacha-dwellers, who tried to file a complaint against us, for which they even brought in a policeman. Luckily for us,

216

no officers rode in third class and this whole racket passed without any consequences for us, even though we appeared at our dacha to the thundering and solemn sounds of a fanfare that gloriously announced to all Krasnoe Selo the arrival of two drunken Guards NCOs. To this day I don't understand how we got away with it! But one can't count all the pranks Taneev and I got up to during this mischievous period of topographical surveying and tactical assignments in Krasnoe Selo.

This was one of the most amusing months of my life. I realized that I was going to get married soon, and although I was awaiting my wedding day with great impatience, I also was fully aware that my marriage would drastically change my behavior. I knew that simple respect for my wife would never allow me to so stupidly and amusingly act the fool and go crazy as I hastened to do now, taking full advantage of my last few days of bachelor life, far from my strict family.

Chapter Six

Regimental Exercises in Gatchina

THE LAST EXAMINATION passed almost without my noticing it. Finally the long-awaited day had come, and I breathed a deep sigh of relief. The object of my dreams—the grade that qualified me for the Guards—was in my pocket. Of us four cuirassier volunteers, only I had had the good fortune to receive such a grade. My cousin Mishanchik received only an army-level grade. Speshnev and Iskander had completely flunked.

Yet another little page in the book of my life had quietly been turned over: Basevich, cramming, the Nicholas School, the terrors of the examinations, topographical surveying, and my jolly volunteer comrades—all this suddenly was behind me, sunk all at once into oblivion. A new stage in my life was beginning.

We were all immediately posted back to our regiments, where we were to await our promotion to the rank of officer in a little over two months. It was a tradition for Guards cadets to be promoted to officer by the tsar himself only on the Feast of the Transfiguration, August 6.

Our regiment was still in Gatchina, since it was one of the last to depart for the Krasnoe Selo camp, just for the brigade and divisional exercises and maneuvers. In Gatchina there was a large, high-quality military field and a well-appointed target range, and so all the regimental exercises of our regiment were carried out in Gatchina, while the other regiments, which did not have suitable space at their winter quarters, went to the Krasnoe Selo camp for this purpose.

The regimental officers were kind enough to give Mishanchik and me a week's leave after the examinations. Mishanchik went to see his parents near Kaluga, and I, after picking up my childhood friend Valerian Ershov and my cousin N. Trubetskoi in St. Petersburg, took off for Vitebsk Province to visit my sister at her husband's wonderful estate called Beshenkovichi. We were joined there by my mother, my brother Kolia, and . . . my fiancée.

Situated picturesquely on the banks of the Western Dvina River, the exemplary estate of Beshenkovichi was surrounded by marvelous forests, where we took delightful walks. The very old manor house, of a strange and unusual architectural style, was extremely interesting. This house was remarkable for the fact that during the war with Sweden, Tsar Peter I stayed there, and later, during the 1812 campaign, Tsar Alexander I lived there for a time and Napoleon stayed there during the Russian retreat. In one of the rooms was preserved the bed on which Napoleon himself had slept, and in the library was a French book on which there was some kind of inscription made by the hand of Napoleon and his autograph. The house had the particular scent of the deep past, and was filled with an air of romantic poetry.[1] I was received by my relatives in triumph, as a person who now was indubitably ready to go out into the world. Announcements of my betrothal to Princess Golitsyna were sent in all directions to our numerous relatives and good friends. Finally, after almost three years of secret betrothal, I was officially recognized and announced for all to hear as the fiancé of Princess Golitsyna, and my pride at this good fortune was boundless. My fiancée was received warmly and affectionately at Beshenkovichi, like one of the family, and during this short visit my mother, who had always liked Princess Golitsyna, came to love her as her own daughter, finding the woman of my choice to be a kindred spirit and just as noble and aristocratic in her spiritual qualities as she was a *true princess* in her appearance. My mother highly prized such spiritual aristocratism in people, and ascribed a particular significance to it.

During those days at Beshenkovichi, my fiancée and I were a remarkably happy couple, and we were very well aware that now no power on earth could stand in the way of that to which we had so long aspired. We often went off by ourselves, either to the park, by the little round lake strewn with blossoms, where swans floated, or to one of the rooms in the old house, where we amorously gave ourselves up to our romantic dreams and talked about our future.

My mother, who considered that I was too young, first insisted that our wedding take place only when I had become 21 years old, that is, in 1913, but my fiancée's mother felt that the year '13 was an entirely unsuitable year for a happy marriage, since the number 13 is an unlucky number. According to my future *belle mère*, the number 12 was very lucky, and so she insisted that the wedding be no later than 1912. The older generation was not at all free from superstition and attributed significance to all sorts of omens. My dear mother was not devoid of this weakness either, despite all her education and enlightenment. All this talk of lucky and unlucky dates, of course, simply played into the hands of my fiancée and me. In any event, it was finally decided during this visit to Beshenkovichi that we would get married in the autumn of the year, as soon as the elder Princess Golitsyna could take care of her daughter's trousseau and my mother could arrange the furnishing of our future independent family house in Gatchina, where we were to have a lovely and cozy little nest. The few days we spent at Beshenkovichi flew quickly by like a good dream from which you don't want to wake up. Now I said goodbye to my fiancée in order to meet her next as a Guards officer; that is, a real, legitimate person, worthy of being her spouse in the eyes of society and our relatives.

After we returned to Gatchina, Mishanchik and I both found ourselves in the Third "Standard" Squadron, as it was called. When we arrived at regimental headquarters, the period of shooting practice and squadron exercises on the military field had already ended. We arrived at the best time, for the regimental cavalry exercises, when every day the whole regiment would be occupied no more than an hour and a half or two hours in the morning.

Thanks to my tall stature and my imposing appearance, I was named guard to the regimental standard, and from that day I indefatigably followed behind that object sacred to the regiment, at exercises and on maneuvers, right up to my promotion to cornet.

The regimental standard was a rectangular light-blue silk panel on which the face of Christ was depicted. This panel was hung by two gilded chains to a tall, heavy carved pole, crowned by a golden two-headed eagle—the same kind of eagle that crowned the cuirassier helmet, but a bit larger. Our standard was kept in the imperial palace in Gatchina, and a cuirassier guarded it around the clock. The standard was considered a sacred object for the regiment—in a way, the soul of the regiment—and it was rendered particular honors. Young soldiers and officers swore allegiance to the standard, and even generals saluted the standard, standing at attention. In the vicinity of the standard no one would dare to use curse-words or even an angry word. Civilians and local people were obliged to remove their hats upon meeting the standard. When we were in regimental formation, the standard was met with special music and the men were ordered to "present arms!" drawing their swords and saluting with them. The regiment could not exist without the standard, and if the standard were lost in battle, the regiment would be subject to disbandment. The standard was the symbol of regimental honor, regimental valor; I felt very flattered and even proud that I was the guard to this remarkable regimental holy relic. The standard was assigned a particularly reliable and strong horse. In our regiment this horse was named Vorotilo and was the pride of the Third Squadron.[2] It was the tallest horse in the whole regiment, a real knight's horse of gigantic proportions, mighty and stately as a monument, with a remarkably beautiful neck and noble head, and its brown coloration with bronze spots seemed to intensify its resemblance to a monument. Vorotilo had a kind and calm nature.

The standard-bearer, a noncommissioned officer, was well matched with the standard-bearing horse. He was a handsome, hefty Ukrainian lad, with an athletic build and a sensible mustachioed face. I can see him as if at this moment, astride on Vorotilo with the standard in his hand—a sculpture, a monument of a hero, and that's that!

The regimental exercises were carried out in the following order. At the appointed time, the sergeant majors would separately form up their squadrons in mounted formation near the stables in two columns, after which the platoon officers, starting with the most junior, would ride up to each squadron, prancing on their own beautiful horses, stupendously well-groomed, and would greet the men in turn. For the arrival of each senior officer, a junior would command: "Attention! Right dress! (or left dress!) Gentlemen officers!" At this command the soldiers would jerk their heads all at once in the direction indicated, and the junior officers would salute either in the usual way or with their swords, depending on the position of the person they were greeting. The squadron commander was the last to arrive, and after taking report from the sergeant major, he would greet the men. Then, after looking over his squadron with a proprietary eye, he would lead it onto the street, in front of the barracks, where all the squadrons were forming up into a single regimental line in an extended front with squadrons in numerical order, with the choir of trumpeters on the right flank. Here, after the general line had been painstakingly drawn up, first the junior and then the senior aides to the regimental commander would ride out to the regiment and also greet the men. Meanwhile a platoon of the Third Squadron, along with the regimental adjutant, was detailed to the imperial palace to receive the standard. Near the palace the adjutant and the NCO standard-bearer, after calling out the chief of the patrol, would go into the palace to get the standard, while I held both my own and the standard horse Vorotilo by their reins. As the standard was carried out of the palace, the platoon would present arms, the adjutant would approach us with ceremonial step, his hand at his cap in salute, and after him the NCO standard-bearer with a regular gait would carry out the standard itself and would give it to me while he mounted his horse. Every time I took the standard into my hands, I always felt an involuntary shiver at the thought that I was holding a very sacred object, and I was terrified that I would somehow suddenly drop that sacred thing. After handing the standard back to the standard-bearer, I would mount my own horse, and the whole platoon with the standard would return at a trot. As we approached, the command would resound: "To the standards! Present broadswords, lances to hand! Gentlemen officers!" At this command the regiment would clank their weapons with a warlike sound, and in an instant hundreds of long steel blades, drawn out of their sheaths, would gleam identically over the men's heads, and the orchestra would play in unison a particular piece of music, very old and ceremonial.

After the receiving of the standard, the senior colonel would turn the regiment to the right, and having stretched out in a long column, loudly clattering hundreds of hooves, to the sounds of the gay and bravura march, the regiment would pass by the palace and cross the Baltic road into the military field, spacious, even, and green as a billiard table. Here the regiment would again form up in two columns to greet the regimental commander. The commander at that time, who had been appointed in place of the ludicrous Bernov, was a new, gallant general from the emperor's suite, Piotr Ivanovich Arapov, a good officer who knew his business well, a great landowner, an excellent cavalryman, and a passionate lover of and subtle expert on horses.[3] On his fabulous fiery mare he would ride at a gallop up to the regiment, which would greet its commander with the rattling of its naked steel weapons and the sounds of the regimental march that was supposed to be played for the welcoming of important officers. In a lordly voice Arapov would greet each squadron in turn, tossing off brief remarks appropriate to a superior officer, like: "Cornet Such-and-such, get your horse under control!" or "Captain Such-and-such, is that any way to draw up the fourth platoon?" Arapov greeted each squadron in a different way. For each squadron he had a special vocal intonation: "Hello, lads of Her Majesty's Squadron!" he would toss off in a coarse baritone. "Hello, Second!" he would cry out in a particularly abrupt and careless way. "Hello, lads of the Standard Squadron!" he would enunciate precisely in a completely different manner, a sort of thin tenor; and finally: "He-e-e-e-l-l-l-o-o-o, Fo-o-o-u-r-r-r-th!" he would bellow like rolling thunder, apparently finding in this variegated style of greeting a particular sort of military chic and also pleasure, no doubt. The general was a thickset, round-faced man with a small broken nose, the result of a fall from his horse a long time before. He had a closely cropped little gray mustache and liked to stand with his arms dashingly akimbo. The general was magnificent and apparently was aware of it himself.

Regimental exercises began with the regiment, deployed into two extremely long ranks, crossing the military field back and forth several times at different gaits, from a walking pace to a fast gallop, while maintaining the strictest alignment, as if connected by a thread, and not allowing the line to break in the slightest, which was particularly difficult since the line was so long. This whole mass of excellently trained horsemen had such perfect control of their horses that toward the end of regimental exercises the commanders had achieved such an ideal monolithic order that not a single horse's muzzle, not a single tip of a horse's tail stuck out an iota from the general unified line. This was achieved through persistent drilling, the expertise and patience of the commanders, love of effects appropriate to military reviews, and firm discipline.

Next in the exercises came various re-formations and maneuvers, sometimes rather complicated, which required great precision and automatization, achieved by virtue of the fact that each individual platoon and each squadron had already been exceptionally well trained during the previous period of platoon and squadron exercises.

All these re-formations were performed at trumpet signals which sounded very bellicose. Then came the so-called mute exercise, during which the whole regiment had to silently carry out one maneuver or another, following only a single mute gesture by the general—a gesture that all the squadron commanders repeated at the same time. The precise performance of the mute exercise was very hard to accomplish at first, and therefore, although the exercise was "mute," there was more shouting and cursing associated with it than anything else. Nevertheless, thanks to the experience and patience of the commander, finally it all worked very smoothly, harmoniously, and well, while observing a true "silence of the grave," which was very striking.

About twice in the course of our exercises, in order to let the men and horses catch their breath, the command would be given: "Ha-a-lt! . . . Dismo-o-o-unt! . . . Put your dress in order . . . Have a smoke!" At this point the soldiers would joke with each other, hastily smoking little cigars, holding their horses by the reins, and the gentlemen officers, having given their horses to the orderlies, would walk forward and surround the regimental commander, who liked at such moments to wag his tongue, retailing the latest news and anecdotes from court life, because, having been an aide-de-camp since his youth, he was close to the court. He also liked at these moments to gossip about other Guards regiments, good-naturedly poking fun at his colleague generals and even at his own superiors. The general would sweeten his discourse here and there with a magnificent and apropos French phrase. Sometimes, adopting a stern air and nervously puffing a papirosa in a little amber cigarette-holder trimmed with gold, the general would address the officers: "Gentlemen, come closer . . . even closer . . . get up really close . . ." In such cases everyone already knew that the gentlemen officers were going to hear some *dirt,* which should under no circumstances ever reach the ears of the lower ranks. The general liked to preface such deliveries of dirt with subtle hints, and would talk for a long time in an allegorical way and in long parables, without naming any names. After a long, obscure foreword, he would suddenly blurt out, slightly raising his voice: "Yes, sir! And Cornet Such-and-such and Lieutenant Such-and-such should be ashamed of themselves! . . . Yes, sir!" At this point the general would give a short bow, which was the sign that the "dirt" was finished. Then all the officers would salute and click their spurs as a sign that they had well understood the general's parable, and the latter, as if nothing had happened, would already be giving the shrill command: "To your horses . . . Mount!" And the exercises would continue.

During regimental exercises we often had run-ins with pilots. The recently established Gatchina aviation school for military pilots was located right next to our military field, which served simultaneously as an airfield. At that time it was, if I'm not mistaken, the only aviation school in all Russia—a school that in the World War produced many brave and self-sacrificing pilots who acquired great fame and glory for their military feats.[4]

It would happen that at the height of our cavalry maneuvers, there would suddenly appear on the field with a deafening crash a slow, clumsy, and awkward "Farman," which resembled a kind of big, ridiculous bookcase.[5] Moreover, this crashing bookcase would slowly and ponderously fly over our heads at a height of only a few yards, almost touching the sharp tips of our lances with its wheels. This monstrous object would frighten the horses terribly, drowning out the commands of the officers and the signals of the trumpeters, introducing an awful muddle into our exercises. Despite the fact that the military field was large, the Gatchina pilots for some reason aimed to fly precisely into that spot where our regiment happened to be at any given moment, clearly intending to act like hooligans. Military aviation was then still in an embryonic stage. People were interested in it more as a new and curious form of sport than as a military factor, the power of which was doubted by many old generals, who had an ironic attitude toward planes. The Gatchina pilots of that time—these pioneers of aviation in Russia—were young officers of an adventurous bent, who were sick of the drudgery in their own regiments. These pilots, who were carried away by their new occupation, had dashing but also boorish ways. In the new school discipline was weak at first, and the young pilots apparently derived pleasure from spoiling our exercises and simultaneously the mood of such earthly creatures as us cavalrymen.

At the appearance of the "Farman," our general would as a rule fly into a rage, threatening the pilot with his fist, and the regimental adjutant, digging his spurs into his horse, would fly at full gallop to the director of the flight school and demand that he halt the disgraceful behavior, which the director of the school could not always accomplish, since he did not know a way to make a primitive airplane flown by a joker-pilot turn back. Our general—a fanatic for cavalry exercises—would demand that the pilot be punished for hooliganism, but the director of the flight school—no less a fanatic for his own occupation—would always find an excuse for his officers, stressing the fact that we did not understand the technology. Not bold enough to enter into an altercation with such an influential general as Arapov, the flight school directorship proposed in the future to coordinate the schedule of exercises on the military field, but the coordination didn't help, and the reckless pilots continued as before to annoy our gallant general and the zealous squadron commanders. This was an expression of the antagonism between an old, obsolescent arm of the service (such as our heavy cavalry) and a new, nascent military technology that was loudly asserting its rights.

The regimental exercises ended with two "mad" cavalry attacks in close-order and extended-order drill, to the booming "Hurrah" of the entire regiment, when at the command "Forward!" we would fly like a hurricane, with our lances in a horizontal position and with sabers drawn, toward the "designated enemy," which consisted of several mounted cuirassiers, holding in their hands various multicolored signal flags. These flags served by convention as signifiers of one or another military formation of the supposed enemy. After the attack the general would usually thank the regiment in a loud voice for its "dashing exercises." The regiment would again form up in marching order and return home with a majestic step. The command "Singers, forward!" would ring out, and the dashing singers with their loud-voiced choir leaders would ride to the head of each squadron. They would delight us with gay or mournful soldiers' songs, in which either some beauty named Dunia would be extolled, or the valor of Russian arms, or, finally, "bottle-bottle-bottle—my dear little bottle!" There was an endless supply of such songs, and some of them were very old. It was mostly Ukrainians, great lovers of all kinds of music, who volunteered to be singers. Although these men sang on command, they always obeyed the command with great eagerness.

The period of these exercises ended with the *review of the exercise*. This review served as an index of the whole year of training and drill for each individual horseman as well as each separate platoon and squadron—in a word, of the whole regiment, which became at the moment of inspection a well-proportioned and monolithic body. At this review it was as if all the work done by the junior and senior commanders both on the human and equine staff of the regiment, the difficult and painstaking work of many months, was being summed up. According to regulations, the review was to be carried out by the commander of the First Guards Cavalry Division, Lieutenant General Kaznakov. This general had a reputation as a strict, demanding, and fault-finding commander, who was not easy to please. But our regimental commander found a beautiful means of obtaining the very best commendations for the review. The means was the following: Arapov, as a general attached to the court, would invite to the inspection of the regimental exercise none other than the most august patroness of the regiment—the old Empress Mariia Fiodorovna, who liked to spend the beginning of the summer at the Gatchina Palace. Empress Mariia Fiodorovna was very favorably disposed toward General Arapov, who since his youth had served all his life in regiments that were under her patronage. (In his youth Arapov was a chevalier guard, then he commanded the Second Pskov Dragoon Regiment of Her Majesty, and finally the Blue Cuirassiers.) Thanks to Arapov's cunning and resourcefulness, it almost always turned out that the regimental review was received by the empress, and thus the captious chief of the division, Kaznakov, was present at the review only as a secondary personage. Obviously the empress knew very little about the regiment's drill exercises, and therefore she could do little but go into raptures about her handsome young cuirassiers, who carried out such staggering and dashing attacks on her tent that the earth trembled all around. When attending our reviews, the old empress, always gracious, after every maneuver or re-formation of the regiment, would order the staff trumpeter standing beside her to play us a trumpet-call in thanks, expressing in this way her delight and praise. Obviously, the chief of the division (a man rather experienced in the subtleties of court life) could find nothing better than to echo our most august patroness, assuring her that in all his years of service he had never seen such a dashing review. After all, he couldn't very well criticize what the empress herself had praised! But I do have to say that we did in fact perform conscientiously at our reviews, without a hitch. There would of course be a rehearsal the day before the review. We would be formed up on the field, after which the empty carriage of the empress, harnessed with a pair of her favorite black stallions, driven by an impressive old coachman with a broad, thick, graying beard, would drive past us. This empty carriage would be greeted by the regimental march, and the commander, galloping next to it, would greet us. This was done in order to make sure one last time that the imperial horses would not shy from the music and the cuirassiers' greetings, conscientiously shouted from hundreds of throats simultaneously.

On the day of the review, a beautiful white canvas tent, its floor covered with carpets, was set up on the martial field for the empress. Soft armchairs were placed in it. The empress would ride out to the field in her carriage, accompanied by some elderly court lady or other. The commander of the regiment would meet her with a report, and then the noble, amazingly beautiful black stallions would convey the empress along the front line of the regiment at a gentle trot.

Small, slender, with a slim, cinched-in waist, all in black and in an old-fashioned little black hat, the old empress would sit in her carriage as erect as a girl. Smiling with a particular affability, she would look at the men, motionlessly sitting on their enormous steeds, and as she passed by each squadron commander, she would nod gracefully, with a light, inimitable gesture that had evidently been perfected through years of having to constantly represent the imperial family. (The thought comes to mind that even the best actress would be unable to invest in that tiny gesture so much majestic grace and cordiality.) At this nod of the head, the squadron, fixing hundreds of eyes on this little smiling old lady, would shout in harmonious unison: "To your health, Your Imperial Majesty!" Having ridden along the whole front line, the empress would ride off to her tent, where the footmen would help her out of her carriage. Then at a signal, an orderly officer and staff trumpeter would ride at full gallop from the regiment to her tent, after which the review of the regimental drill would begin, constantly interrupted by the empress's praise, con-

226

veyed to us by a trumpet-call. At each such call, the regiment would roar in answer: "Very good, Your Imperial Majesty!" At the review we were all very excited and jumping out of our skins so as not to disgrace ourselves. We tried to pass the review in a brilliant fashion. Every platoon officer, and even every simple soldier, felt that if he made a mess of things he would bring shame on the entire regiment and call down a great storm of indignation on his own head. The mere presence of important officers always has an inspiring influence on subordinates, and thus the men, who were at such moments extremely tense, in fact usually passed the review so well that even the fault-finding commander of the division had to be satisfied, even if the empress had not been present.

The apotheosis of the review was a fierce attack in close order, carried right up to the empress's tent to the sound of a thunderous "Hurrah!" This was a spectacle that would grip one with its precipitous surge. At ten paces from the tent, the center of the attacking line would abruptly stop after attaining full speed, calling forth the most enraptured praise of the empress, who, after thanking everyone one more time, would dismiss the regiment.

As we were passing over the St. Petersburg-Warsaw railroad line, the regiment would be overtaken by the pleased and radiant regimental commander, who would shout to his cuirassiers: "Thanks, my good men, for an excellent review! A bottle of beer for everyone from me!" (The commander was a rich man!) "We thank Your Excellency most humbly!" the regiment would roar in answer. At this point all the officers would start to display their generosity. The squadron commanders would treat their squadrons, and the platoon officers their platoons, to a bottle of beer, and after they returned home, the whole regiment would celebrate with a merry feast. The officers would celebrate in the officers' club, and the soldiers in their barracks, where the merrymaking would continue into the evening. The commander of the regiment, his aides, and the squadron commanders would usually be invited immediately after the review to breakfast with the empress in the palace. This breakfast would not last long, so that these officers still had time to return to the officers' club and catch the merry feast at its height, where champagne was flowing in rivers and innumerable toasts were proposed to the commander and the regiment and the regimental standard. As a rule, the divisional commander was gotten dead drunk, despite his entreaties and protests. In such cases the cuirassiers knew how to be "hospitable" hosts.

Chapter Seven

The Third Squadron

WHEN I RETURNED to the regiment, the gentle and kind Staff Captain Iskander, who had commanded the Third Squadron, had retired. In his place the squadron was taken by Staff Captain Edvin Iogannovich Lindgren, a Finn. Although no one could say anything bad or at all blameworthy about Lindgren, this tall, red-haired man with a gleaming pincenez did not inspire love in either the officers or the soldiers. Always polite and demonstratively correct, he was also petty. He was a martinet in the fullest sense of the word, a pedant to the marrow of his bones and also a stick who couldn't understand either a good joke, a witticism, or strong Russian humor. He was easily offended and spoke Russian poorly, with a strong foreign accent. He stuck his pince-nez into all the petty details of the squadron's life and made his subordinates heartily sick of him. He knew how to wear them out with his monotonous, nagging complaints, never raising his voice and never swearing. Practical, a good manager, always conscientious and sober, he was in essence a quite good squadron commander and always a useful regimental toiler. He was a great patriot of Finland and subscribed to a Finnish newspaper that he always carried around. He loved to talk about Finland's past and to hold up his compatriots and their customs to everyone as an example. Lindgren's comrades could sense that, although he never expressed it, he did not like and even despised Russians. It was astonishing that this strange fellow had chosen to serve precisely in a Russian Guards regiment, to which one might presume he would have a hostile attitude. Besides, serving in the Guards did not afford him any material benefits. But he served not only honorably, but with the highest degree of conscientiousness, and he perished somehow unnoticed and humble at the head of his squadron, at the very beginning of the World War, from a well-aimed German bullet.

In the Third Squadron the senior platoon officer was the Lieutenant Prince Urusov Senior, who in complete opposition to Lindgren was a typical Russian nobleman and the kind of Russian patriot who adored "Daddy Tsar." He was a good comrade, a very jolly fellow and a joker, who loved good company and good liquor. A lively and vivid regimental personality, Urusov Senior, besides the service and carousing with and without women, had the most varied interests, up to and including theosophy, for he read Blavatsky and Leadbeater and all kinds of spiritistic books.[1]

A graduate of the Pages, Urusov dreamed of a military career at court and the rank of aide-de-camp, but all the same he never disdained to have a joke and a chat with the soldiers. As an officer he was rather lazy and not terribly assiduous, and maybe it was for this reason that the soldiers liked him, always greeting him with a restrained affable smile. The soldiers saw him as a lively, gay officer who didn't press them to work too hard—they saw him as a man above all.

Urusov Senior was especially popular with the cabbies of Gatchina, whom he loved to tip and with whom he would engage in long conversations as they drove. Sometimes you would be walking along the street and would see in the distance a cabby riding along, having dropped the reins and turned his torso toward his fare, gesticulating eloquently, sitting on the box almost backwards. You would know that it was Lieutenant Prince Urusov Senior, arguing with his cabby on some impossible topic.

When I was promoted to officer, I very quickly became friends with this always jolly and boastful lieutenant. He had a rather imposing appearance. He was a bit stout, young but already balding, with a long nose and black mustache, always smelling of champagne. Urusov had a slight stutter, and this speech defect suited him very well, because it seemed to emphasize the wit he often displayed in his arguments with his companions.

I remember the following incident, which was very typical of Urusov.

In Gatchina a well-respected retired general died. He was buried, as was proper, with a parade to which military detachments from all units of the Gatchina garrison were assigned. From our regiment was assigned a representative squadron under the command of Urusov Senior. The squadron went out in mounted formation in parade dress, that is, with jackets, helmets, and cuirasses, but without rifles, which were never carried when cuirasses were worn. The whole parade was to be commanded by a colonel from an artillery brigade quartered in Gatchina.

When our squadron had already formed up near the cemetery, the artillery colonel rode up to Urusov and demanded that our men fire a rifle salute over the general's grave, completely overlooking the fact that according to regulations, cuirassiers do not carry rifles on parade. In answer to the colonel's request, Urusov, glittering with gold, putting his hand, sheathed in a blindingly white gauntlet, to his helmet, said in the most courteous tone, stuttering a bit, but in such a way that the whole squadron could hear him: "It's a great pity, Colonel, that you didn't let us know ahead of time: I would have ordered that my men be fed peas." "What do peas have to do with it?" asked the bewildered commander of the parade. "But, Colonel, you see, if you feed the men well with peas, they can fire a salute even without rifles." "What is your name?" the colonel asked sharply, with a frown. "Lieutenant Prince Uru-urusov Se-ee-eenior, Colonel, sir!" answered our hero, saluting with the most obliging air. There was a pause, during which the whole squadron held their breath so as not to burst out laughing, and meanwhile the colonel, who finally understood his mistake, shrugged his shoulders in embarrassment and rode quickly away. The next day the unlucky colonel sent an official memorandum to the commander of our regiment, in which he demanded that Lieutenant Prince Urusov be subjected to a disciplinary punishment for giving an impertinent answer while in formation. Our general called Urusov in to explain himself, but after learning all the details of his transgression, he had a hearty laugh, and not only didn't he punish him, on the contrary, in the order of the day he thanked Lieutenant Prince Urusov for his quick-wittedness.

Good regimental commanders always shielded their officers from officers of other regiments. Moreover, there was a distinct antagonism between the artillery and the cavalry.

The cousin of Lieutenant Prince Urusov Senior, the cornet Prince Piotr Urusov Junior, a junior platoon commander in the Third Squadron, was of about the same type. He was empty-headed and frivolous, but a jolly fellow—always up to the eyes in debt and finally expelled from the regiment for his escapades. Both Urusovs could do wicked imitations of all Lindgren's mannerisms and ways, which provided great enjoyment for the whole squadron. Urusov Junior was killed in 1914 on the German front.

The cornets Batorskii, Rozenberg, and von Baumgarten the Second, the last killed in 1916 by shrapnel, round out the list of platoon officers of the Third Squadron, who all stuck together, as if united by common antipathy to the squadron commander.

An important role in the life of any squadron was played by the sergeant major. The post of sergeant major was the highest position and highest rank that the lower ranks could attain. In the squadron, the sergeant major was the senior noncommissioned officer, and was specially selected by the commanding officers from among the men who had served more than their required term. The sergeant major was the direct superior of all the lower ranks of the squadron and the closest subordinate to the squadron commander in squadron management (in the infantry and artillery the rank of sergeant major corresponded to the *Feldwebel*).

In our Third Squadron the sergeant major was a certain Bazdyrev—a remarkable personality in many respects, and most of all for the fact that he was the most senior sergeant major in the whole regiment, who had served more than twenty years beyond his initial term. He was an inveterate "hide-skinner" [nagging, fault-finding commanding officer]. He knew the ins and outs of the service so well that even the regimental commander had to reckon with him, and he carried out his duties with such zeal and diligence that he earned many silver and gold medals from his superiors, and along with them the hatred of his subordinate soldiers.

He had a giant's physique, high cheekbones, squinty, swollen eyes, and spoke in an insinuating, slightly nasal voice, which he didn't like to raise even when he was chewing out the soldiers.

The barracks, the stables, the squadron armory—he kept it all in perfect order, and to do him justice, he not only knew his business, he was a fanatic about it, and also a zealous patriot of his Third Squadron. (Bazdyrev always spoke of the other squadrons in the regiment with a certain irritation and semi-contempt in his voice.) With a sergeant major like Bazdyrev, the squadron commander could always have peace of mind, because Bazdyrev was not a whit less, and perhaps even more concerned about the reputation and well-being of the squadron than the commander himself; moreover, he was capable of foreseeing every eventuality and knew every soldier like the back of his hand, as if he could see right through him.

Bazdyrev was particularly irreplaceable during reviews and parades, which he adored. To prepare the men and the horses for parade and bring them out to review like clean little toys—that was Bazdyrev's favorite hobby! You had to see the voluptuous pleasure with which he inspected the men in parade dress formed up in the barracks before he let them go out on parade. Squinting his eyes, he would inspect each soldier individually, from the front, from the back, from the side, from head to toe, checking each button, each little hook, and changing countenance at the sight of some barely noticeable little spot on a uniform or greatcoat, or an ammunition belt adjusted with insufficient care. Bazdyrev never engaged in "mug-bashing," for in the regiment in my time it was strictly forbidden. But in place of mug-bashing, Bazdyrev had other methods of influencing soldiers who were not too neat: "Nesterenko! . . . Your helmet's been put on not too well for some reason," he would say in a soft, affectionate voice. "Here, let me put it on a little better." With these words Bazdyrev, without removing the helmet from the soldier's head, would begin knocking on it with his weighty fist, from the top, sides, and back. The soldier's eyes would pop out of his head from pain—but in a moment the heavy, five-pound brass helmet would be sitting irreproachably on the soldier's head. "Why are you blinking, Nesterenko? Well, why are you blinking, you idiot? You don't seem to be a young soldier. It's time for you to know how to put on your helmet. When you get back from parade, you'll stand here in front of me for two hours in full battle dress! And you, Sikachov, why are you so badly shaven? Come on, you idiot, tell me, can you really go on parade with a mug like that? What is this? Just look!" Bazdyrev would say in a nagging, nasal voice, pulling little hairs out of the soldier's chin with his own fingernails. "What a disgrace! Look alive, Sikachov, and get yourself over to the barber: a soldier on parade has to be like an eagle! Tsyganov, the hook on your collar is sticking out for some reason. That doesn't look good on parade. Haven't you gotten that into your head yet, idiot? Well, after the parade you'll stand in full battle dress for a couple of hours, then maybe you'll develop the proper outlook on the essence of things! You're serving in a standard-bearing squadron, not just any old place!"

Before particularly important parades, Bazdyrev and his friend and myrmidon, the platoon officer Kuriatenko, would personally put rouge on the soldiers' cheeks, using the juice of red beets. A few of the soldiers had their mustaches dyed, so that all the men would look equally handsome. This was all done without joking, seriously and even reverently.

Before leading the men on parade, Bazdyrev would weary them with rehearsals, greeting the squadron thirty times and making them answer him as if he were a general or the grand duke or even sometimes the tsar. Here in the barracks, with windows and doors closed, he got such a precise and harmonious answer out of the squadron that it seemed to be some kind of operatic recitative.

"You're answering pretty crudely, idiots! The commander of the corps likes refined voices. Answer in a refined voice. Now—greetings, lads!—No, it's still crude. Come on, more refined. Greetings, eagles! You idiots, before you answer take a breath, take a deeper breath into your chests. You can't growl at the corps commander. Only a divisional officer or brigade commander likes growling. You have to understand whom you're answering. Can't you narrow your throats for the corps commander! Come on, one more time: Greetings, lads!" And so on, until he obtained precisely the kind of answer that this or that important Guards commander liked. And Bazdyrev had made a thorough study of the tastes of all these important officers in the course of his long service.

Bazdyrev behaved with marked politeness toward young officers, but without ever losing his sense of dignity, and always with a certain shade of superiority, as if letting them know that, although young cornets had beautiful gold shoulder straps, still they could not possibly have the same subtle knowledge of the service as he, Sergeant Major Bazdyrev, who had given half his life to the service of the Third Squadron. How many young officers of all kinds had been replaced right before his eyes over the years, squadron commanders and high officers of the Guards! And how many of these brilliant young cornets manage to attain even the rank of staff captain? Just look, some fashionable little cornet serves a couple or three years in the regiment, and then he gets sick of regimental life, or he gambles away his money and gets into debt, applies to the reserves, and he's gone from the regiment! Sergeant Major Bazdyrev outlived everyone in the cuirassier regiment and never once received an official reprimand, and for this the high-ranking officers honored and respected him.

Over the course of his service Bazdyrev had accumulated some means. According to regulations he lived in the barracks permanently, in a separate room, although everyone knew that he had his own little house in Gatchina which he would rent out. Bazdyrev had apparently attained his material well-being in an honest fashion, for no one could say he was an embezzler like some sergeant majors in the Guards, who had the opportunity for significant machinations and manipulations with the fodder if their commanders were not on their toes. Bazdyrev would never have permitted himself such a thing, if only because he would not have been able to bear the disgrace if at the regimental exercises the horses of his squadron were the slightest bit thinner than the horses of the other squadrons.

In general one must say that the sergeant majors in the Guards were rather well provided for. Just as in the best foreign armies, in the old Russian army the high command tried to retain in the service after their appointed term the excellent noncommissioned officers, the soldiers who were most skilled, capable, and trained. In order to induce such men to reenlist voluntarily, they were offered all kinds of privileges, like for example permission to get married and have their families nearby. Their living conditions were improved. They were given a significant salary raise, and this increase in the salary scale continued to grow at regular intervals. The reenlisted men also got improved food and clothing, the latter adorned with special signs of distinction, like broad and narrow gold and silver chevrons sewn on the sleeves of their uniforms. They also got a certain provision for the future in the form of the so-called recommendation certificates for entry into government service (most often the police), as well as pensions and one-time allowances that could be as much as a thousand rubles for long military service. Besides all this, squadron commanders in the Guards were in the habit of giving their sergeant majors monetary and other gifts for New Year's, Easter, and their name days. The junior officers often did this too, not to mention the volunteers, who also gave the sergeant majors tips and little presents in order to get a gentle horse or release from duty. Thanks to these customs, sergeant majors in the Guards had a pretty good life.

Sergeant Major Bazdyrev liked to show concern for the morals of the lower ranks in the Third Squadron. I can well remember the speech he would give year after year in the barracks the night before the regiment would move from Gatchina to the camp in Krasnoe Selo. This speech would be given in front of the soldiers lined up after evening roll call. He would speak very solemnly, and his speech would be supplemented by the commentary and notes of platoon officer Kuriatenko, a great friend of the sergeant major, also a long-serving "hide-skinner," who would stand next to Bazdyrev during the speech. "Lads," the sergeant major would say in his insinuating nasal voice, squinting his eyes, "tomorrow we are moving to Krasnoe Selo. There are a ton of temptations in Krasnoe—but there are also a ton of high-ranking officers in Krasnoe. In Gatchina it's one thing. In Krasnoe it's something else entirely. Let's take for example the female sex. If in Gatchina you embrace or kiss some woman in the evening—you get away with it. In Krasnoe it's different. In Krasnoe they're not women but bitches: if you embrace or kiss a woman in Krasnoe, she'll inform on you as if you committed a sin against her. A woman in Krasnoe won't have any words with you. Where will she go? Straight to the commander of the regiment, the bitch! And you, you idiot, where will you go then? [Pause.] To the penal battalion—that's where you'll go because of your caresses. Now, about vodka. In Krasnoe there are tons of taverns, lads, and again I say: in Gatchina it's one thing, in Krasnoe it's something else entirely. If in Gatchina you have occasion to drink a half-bottle of wine at a little cele-bration, and you breathe accidentally on your officer—he won't kill you for it, he might just give you extra duty or stick you in the regimental guardhouse for twenty-four hours. In Krasnoe it's different. Just try breathing wine on an officer from another squadron there—he won't have any words with you. Where will he go? Straight to the commander of the regiment! And you, you idiot, where will you go then? [Pause.] To the penal battalion—that's where you'll go for a little glass of wine."

At this point in the sergeant major's speech, platoon officer Kuriatenko's bass would interpose: "Vasilii Grigorievich, don't forget to tell them about the raspberries."

"There are tons of gardens and orchards in Krasnoe," Bazdyrev contin-ued in his nasal voice. "If you have occasion to pass a garden by day or night, it would be better to give it a wide berth: if you pick a single raspberry, the lady of the house will inform on you as if you cleaned out the whole garden, be-cause in Krasnoe they're not women but bitches. She won't have any words with you. Where will she go? Straight to the commander of the regiment. And you, you idiot, where will you go then? [Pause.] To the penal battalion—that's where you'll go because of a single raspberry! Yes, lads, don't let me hear about those raspberries or about wine in Krasnoe. But more than anything, lads—womenfolk, keep away from womenfolk in the camps! Understood?" "Yes sir, Sergeant Major, understood," several voices would answer quietly and not in unison. "Dismissed!" the sergeant major would command in a tenor. "Dismissed!" the bass of platoon officer Kuriatenko would repeat like an echo, and the cuirassiers, made wiser by the sergeant major, would dis-perse, jingling their spurs loudly.

As a matter of fact, in Krasnoe Selo, where the regiment was quartered in private houses, the soldiers lived a much freer and gayer life than in Gatchina. Thanks to this, discipline grew slack in Krasnoe. Foreseeing this, the cunning sergeant major purposely frightened the young soldiers in advance, depicting all kinds of horrors in Krasnoe Selo that in fact didn't exist. It was Bazdyrev himself who more often than not had to hear complaints about the soldiers from housewives and smooth over the soldiers' little scandals involving raspberries and the harassment of women and girls. Such trivia of course never reached the regimental commander except in very rare instances. Bazdyrev was a great diplomat and was well able to settle such conflicts all by himself. A good sergeant major could get by even without the help of the squadron commander, whom he would never consider it necessary to disturb for petty matters.

Although the soldiers hated Bazdyrev, he was an undoubted authority in their eyes, and they were so afraid of him that when soldiers were asked for their complaints, no one ever complained about the fact that the sergeant major would pluck hairs out of badly shaven soldiers' chins with his fingernails, or that he would fit the helmet on a soldier's head with his fist. And by the way, the sergeant major could have really caught hell for such deeds from a good superior officer! That the sergeant major had to be a hide-skinner and a bastard—this in general was accepted as a kind of axiom by the soldiers, and as a result all the acts of Bazdyrev, whom the commanding officers so trusted, were regarded by the soldiers as a necessary evil: what else can you expect from a hide-skinner, they'd say. Being a volunteeer at that time and willy-nilly hanging around in the barracks and stables, I, although I was a little nobleman's son, stood in a much closer position to the mass of soldiers than any officer did. Not once did I hear from the soldiers an angry or indignant grumble against the sergeant major. The soldiers were amazingly good-natured and forgiving: when Bazdyrev was riding some soldier hard, the others usually would cheerfully tease the victim, sending merry jokes and witticisms his way.

At the beginning of the World War, Sergeant Major Bazdyrev was killed in the same action where his squadron commander Lindgren perished.[2] How the sergeant major fell, cut down by a bullet—no one saw, and this gave rise to a few rumors in the regiment that he had died not from an enemy bullet but at the hands of his own soldiers. The only basis for such an assumption was the well-known hatred of Bazdyrev by the lower ranks of the Third Squadron.

Fairness compels me to note that not all sergeant majors resembled Bazdyrev. Our other regimental sergeant majors, although they were on excellent terms with the commanding officers, did not commit atrocities and did not pluck hairs from the chins of unshaven soldiers. The most mature non-commissioned officers were assigned as sergeant majors. Over their long years of service and their daily interactions and conversations with the squadron commanders, sergeant majors usually acquired a certain air of polish and culture. For instance, the sergeant major of the Second Squadron, Golantsev, was educating himself under the direction of the commander of the squadron, Captain von Briummer, who gave him good books to read. The sergeant major of the Life Guards Squadron, Ivan Klementievich Kvasnyi, was even promoted to officer's rank during the World War and transferred to the so-called Wild Division, which was then commanded by Grand Duke Mikhail Aleksandrovich, who had at one time been commander of the Life Guards Squadron of our regiment and who had personally promoted Kvasnyi to the post of sergeant major.[3] By the way, although he was a mere sergeant major, Kvasnyi maintained a constant correspondence with the grand duke, who stood godfather to his children. A very handsome man, in my time Kvasnyi carried himself with great style around the regiment and expressed himself in a highly literate way.

Every detachment, every squadron, had its own icon. This icon would be located in the barracks, in a special icon case, and would be adorned with a silver *riza* [frame that reveals only the face and hands of the image]. A lamp would burn before the icon day and night. The Mother of God or saint depicted on such an icon was considered to be the patron of its squadron. The saint's day was a day of squadron-wide celebration. On that day the squadron activities would be suspended and no one would be put on guard duty. For the squadron celebration, a feast would be given for the soldiers at the expense of the officers of the squadron. The festivities would begin with a prayer service in the barracks with the regimental commander and all the officers of the regiment who were at liberty present. After praying and hearing the *mnogoletie*, the drinking bout began, for which everyone moved to the squadron mess hall.[4] Here the tables had already been set up for the soldiers in a horseshoe shape, spread with clean tablecloths and groaning from the weight of the snacks. In the corner on a special table stood a bucket of vodka. In the same room nearby a special table was set for the officers. When the soldiers had taken their places, the general himself began the drinking bout. He went up to the table holding the vodka, where the sergeant major poured him a shot of vodka, scooping it out of the bucket with a ladle. "Well, lads, I congratulate you on your holiday from the bottom of my heart and I drain this glass to your health!" the general would proclaim in a gallant baritone and, after making the sign of the cross over himself with a broad gesture in peasant fashion, he would dashingly toss back the vodka. "We thank you most humbly, your Excellency!" the soldiers would answer staidly. After the general, all the officers present went through the same procedure in turn, beginning with the most senior and ending with the most junior. This ended the official part of the ceremony, and at this point everyone could sit down and set about eating and drinking to their hearts' content, without any constraint. The officers drank champagne, the soldiers—vodka and beer. Toward the end of the festivities, the singers performed, a concertina appeared, and dancing began. Despite the abundance of hard liquor, the whole celebration usually passed in a rather orderly way and there was no loud carousing, because these well-disciplined men did not forget their military bearing and respect for rank.

Thus were the "humble" squadron celebrations conducted. But in addition to these, there was also the grandiose regimental celebration. In our regiment it was celebrated on St. Nicholas's Day, May 9, because our regimental church was the Church of Nikola the Wonder-Worker, who consequently was the patron of the Blue Cuirassiers in heaven. This was an exceptional feast and cost the officers a pretty penny.

To the regimental celebration came nearly all the former regimental officers who had served the regiment with honor in their day. They would appear on that day in tails and top hats, and some in chamberlains' uniforms. Even some former lower-ranking soldiers who had long been transferred to the reserves came for this celebration. Honored guests were invited, like grand dukes, important generals, and the high command of the Guards.

In the morning, on the square in front of the imperial palace, the whole regiment formed up on foot, wearing summer uniforms, with the trumpeters on the right flank and on the left the noncombatant detachment and the regimental school of cantonists, consisting of little kids, also dressed in our cuirassier uniform.[5]

For the honored guests and ladies of the regiment, a special carpeted area was set aside on the square, and all the ladies were given large bouquets of roses, intertwined with white and dark blue ribbons (the regimental colors). After the greeting of the commanding officers and a tedious prayer service including an acathistus and *mnogoletie,* the lectern was quickly removed and in its place immediately appeared a little table covered with a tablecloth, and on the table a lovely silver carafe of vodka and a little silver cup on a gold saucer. The most senior of the important officers present, after pouring vodka into the cup, proclaimed several toasts to the tsar, the empress, the heir to the throne, and the regiment, and each such toast was drowned out by shouts of "Hurrah!" and the thunder of the orchestra. After the toasts the command rang out: "To the ceremonial march! From the right, platoon by platoon, at platoon interval! Trumpeters straight ahead, regiment to the right! [Pause.] First platoon!!!" At this point the commander of the first platoon of the Life Squadron would turn around to the left like a peg and command: "First platoon, right dress! Quick march!" At this command, the whole regiment as one man caught hold of the hilts of their sabers and jerked their heads sharply to the right. "March!" the platoon officer would shout abruptly. The trumpets and drums would deafeningly take up the fervent, rhythmic music, and throwing their left feet forward simultaneously, hundreds of men would pass by the guests in perfect formation, eyes fixed on their senior officer. The squadrons would disperse to their barracks to await the feast.

This feast was astounding and would last all day with breaks, so that toward evening there was not a single sober cuirassier to be found in the whole regiment. The soldiers were given an excellent entertainment. Besides abundant liquor, they were also given presents.

In the large, elegant hall of the officers' club (where ladies were never admitted, by regimental tradition), a long table sparkled with the ceremonial silver, in the form of all kinds of wine bowls, carafes, and *surtouts de tables* [decorative vases]. Our civilian club cook, a great master of his trade, outdid himself on this day with the magnificent victuals that were offered in abundance. Fine, expensive foreign wines, French champagne, liqueurs . . . but it goes without saying: "Her Majesty's Cuirassiers/Of lots of liquor have no fear!" was the favorite saying of our young men. "This is how the cuirassiers do it: drink—but don't drink your mind away!" was the favorite song of our oldsters. The rest is easy to imagine! At dinner congratulatory telegrams from the tsar and the dowager empress were read. After dinner, which lasted about three hours, usually the most senior and important officers, whose high position did not permit them to get properly drunk, would leave. Then the whole regiment would gather in the manège, where a stage and benches had been set up. In the first rows sat the officers with their guests. In the back sat the soldiers. Actors who had been sent for from St. Petersburg offered an amusing performance and a lengthy variety show with magicians, ballerinas, acrobats, and singers of satirical couplets. After the show, on the parade ground in front of the stables, various games and humorous competitions for prizes were organized for the lower ranks. These included a sack race, which was won year after year by the blacksmith of the noncombatant detachment; there was also climbing of a soaped pole, on the top of which was attached a prize in the form of a concertina, a pocket watch, or a pair of boots. This prize was won by the agile fellow who could remove it without sliding off the soaped pole. There were many such diversions.

In the evening a supper was rolled out in the club, which far from everyone was capable of attending. The next morning everyone in the regiment had a splitting headache and a terrible stomachache, and in the officers' club a few people were groaning and scratching the back of their necks, calculating what Nikola the Wonder-Worker had cost the gentlemen officers. Every year he cost thousands. But he gave all the cuirassiers a miraculous party!

I remember, in either 1913 or 1914, on the eve of the regimental celebration, quite unexpectedly, there suddenly appeared an ancient man in his seventies, wearing a military jacket in terrible shape, discolored, patched, and coming apart at the seams. He was wearing some kind of strange striped cavalry trousers worn outside his boots. In my time not a single regiment had such a strange uniform. But it was our old uniform, and the old man himself turned out to be a former cuirassier soldier who had served in our regiment in the 1850s! With touching naiveté and simplicity the old codger explained that in his native village (somewhere near Voronezh) the young people laughed at him and pestered him unmercifully on Easter because he would dress in such a worn-out uniform, in which it was shameful to enter the house of God on a great holiday. Stung to the quick by this mockery, the proud old coot undertook a long journey and came to our regimental celebration to honor Nikola the Wonder-Worker and at the same time to see if we would give him a new uniform.

The old codger's visit was a real sensation. He was photographed in all guises: in his old shabby uniform, and in a brand-new one which was, of course, given to him before the parade. On parade the old man brought up the rear in the ceremonial march, conscientiously stepping out right after the cantonists' school, that is, the very youngest cuirassiers.

The old man told the officers many interesting stories about his former service, the old customs of the regiment, and past cuirassiers. He stayed in the regiment as a guest for a whole week after the celebration, and he was pampered in every way. He returned home with a gleaming new uniform, riding breeches and boots, and generous presents from the officers. I can just imagine what a furor he caused when he returned to his native village!

I spoke earlier of the abyss that existed between men dressed in officer's uniform and men dressed in soldier's uniform. This was a matter not only of class. The extreme degree of respect for rank that had been cultivated in the army over the course of two centuries, as well as the very position of an ordinary soldier, who irrespective of class was virtually without rights in the army, could not help but deepen the abyss that separated the officers from the soldiers. In such a situation could people who had been forcibly enlisted in the military really love their unit or their commanding officers? Based only on what took place in the cuirassier regiment, I would answer this way: Yes, the majority of our soldiers, after getting accustomed to the service, were devoted to the regiment and loved their squadrons, often giving themselves up to a narrow, purely squadron-based loyalty. As for their attitude toward their commanding officers, they didn't like some of them and were indifferent to others, but still others they loved and respected—moreover, there were quite a few in our regiment whom they truly loved. As for the soldiers' life in the regiment, I must note that although a Guards soldier was almost without rights, still many people were concerned for his welfare. The living conditions in the Guards were incomparably better than in the regular army, and for this reason the Guards were justifiably considered the most reliable and loyal bulwark of the throne.

Despite the well-known caste-based character of the Guards officership, it was more cultured than that in the army, and this meant a great deal for the interrelationships of commanders and subordinates. As for the material existence of the soldier, in the Guards it was of course quite decent. First of all, the Guards soldier was fed heartily and well. The official soldiers' ration in the Guards was better and larger than in the army. In peacetime in our regiment, strict care was taken that the soldiers' food be of high quality and tasty. This was conscientiously verified by the squadron commanders themselves, who were usually men of means and not only did not steal from the soldiers' rations but, on the contrary, tried to make the soldiers' mess better in every way, and officers often bragged to each other about this. The soldiers usually didn't eat their whole ration because they were full. Every day the squadron received the uneaten leftovers, which were given to the pigs who were kept in the squadron. These pigs were slaughtered for a squadron holiday, for Christmas or Easter, so as to offer the soldiers a good meal to break their fast. For important holidays the officers often treated the soldiers to beer and special dishes at their own expense, and for Shrovetide they even had *bliny* made for the soldiers.

The Guards soldier was very well dressed and shod (I am speaking of peacetime). He kept himself clean and in essence led an entirely healthy life under the observation of senior and junior regimental doctors, who concerned themselves with the soldier's bodily hygiene and periodically examined all the soldiers.

Now, in regard to the officers' relationship with the lower ranks, we can say that these relationships differed and depended on purely individual human qualities, interests, and on the character of the officer.

When on our Soviet screen I now see a Guards officer, who, according to a well-established cliché, is always depicted as a cruel monster who foully mocks the nice, sweet soldier, and this soldier is beaten in the face for no reason at all; when I read in contemporary novels by some of our writers about loathsome Guards officer tyrants and their unfortunate victims—soldiers who, as a rule, secrete a venomous malice against their officers in their hearts, a malice that at any minute is ready to pour out into open mutiny or revolt— I cannot suppress a smile.

I am writing this not only because I would naturally wish to shield myself as a former Guards officer from all the monstrous behavior that is attributed to people like me. I would like to relate simply and straightforwardly how people who were so divided from each other both by uniform and by class and certain abnormal conditions of their former lives managed to interact and get along together.

I never served in the regular army. It had its own ways and customs, which have been beautifully described by Kuprin in the novel *The Duel*.[6] I served in a model regiment of the Guards, and first of all I must say that in our regiment any sort of "mug-bashing" was out of the question. As far as I know, it also didn't exist in the other Guards cavalry regiments. In three years of peacetime service that I spent in the regiment, I learned of only two cases in which an officer hit a soldier. In both cases the officer was Lieutenant Sokolov—not a bad man, I assure you, and as often happens with good people, very passionate, temperamental, and irascible. Once he "bashed in the mug" of a young Polish soldier, a malingerer who was caught stealing, and moreover I happen to know that Sokolov's act evoked sympathy and approval among the soldiers, because each of them would himself have smacked the thief in the face with pleasure. Another time Sokolov (a passionate connoisseur of horses) gave a good-sized black eye to a clumsy soldier because by his error and stupidity he injured in the stable one of the best horses in the squadron.

Sokolov did not, however, get off scot-free from this incident. The next day the regimental doctor, when examining the soldiers, noticed the injured man and immediately fired off a report about Lieutenant Sokolov to the regimental commander. The commander was so angered that he almost decided to put Sokolov on trial, but the senior officers prevailed upon the commander not to do this so as not to disgrace the regiment. The question was raised whether Sokolov should be thrown out of the regiment, but finally they had mercy on him because he was an excellent officer, and they limited themselves to imposing a disciplinary punishment on him. Whether Sokolov was involved in any other cases of corporal punishment, I don't know. In any case the soldiers valued him highly and displayed an unmistakable sympathy for him, seeing in him a responsive, simple, passionate, but just person. I remember that when Sokolov was the commander of the regimental training detachment, the soldiers on their own initiative took up a collection and presented him with an officer's saber with a good blade and an appropriate inscription. Far from every officer was shown such consideration by his soldiers. This was precisely the kind of officer of whom the soldiers say that he is "like their own father." In the war Sokolov showed great bravery and self-sacrifice and was the first in the regiment to receive the highest battle decoration, the officers' St. George's Cross.

The only "physical coercion" that individual officers (like Palitsyn) infrequently permitted themselves, and then only during horseback acrobatics training, was to occasionally and as if accidentally flick the tip of a whip on a soldier's backside. As I said earlier, even volunteers were subjected to this. It was done in such a way that it was hard to determine if it was done accidentally or on purpose. Soldiers did not take offense at such a well-aimed flick on the backside, because everything relating to the human backside was most often regarded as something humorous, and they usually laughed good-naturedly at the men who got a flick of the whip during acrobatics.

Nowadays you often hear that regular officers in general did not regard soldiers as humans and treated them like cattle. I can only say that among my regimental comrades I did not know any such officers. It's true that one encountered both senior and junior officers who behaved indifferently, so to speak officially, towards the soldiers and had absolutely no interest in the soldiers' lives and needs, but one cannot conclude from this that they must have regarded the soldiers like cattle. In our regiment, even to call a soldier a vulgar or obscene name was considered bad form for an officer.

I remember once during platoon drills on the military field, Cornet D., who was zealously pressing his platoon, started abusing the men with some choice obscenities, which by chance reached the ears of the senior captain, Danilov, who was on the field at the time. This Danilov was one of the bosses of the regiment. An intelligent and sober-minded man, he enjoyed great authority. In my presence Danilov summoned the cornet who had gotten all hot and bothered, and told him off good and proper: "Listen, my friend," the captain said in a fatherly way, "when you use indecent words to insult men who are dressed in the same uniform as you, you are insulting your own uniform and consequently also the regiment which we all love and are obliged to honor. Don't forget that you are dealing not with lackeys and boors, but with soldier-cuirassiers of Her Majesty, who are called to the honorable service of the sovereign himself. We must develop in our soldiers a feeling of pride, not humiliate them. You may and are even obligated to take your subordinates in hand and punish them for infractions, demanding of them the highest level of discipline, but to insult them with obscenities—that's loutishness, my friend. Leave your loutishness to some army second lieutenant in a godforsaken provincial army regiment. You and I, it seems, are serving in the Life Guards, and so we are not allowed to be louts. All right, now, off to your platoon, and don't let me hear the word 'mother' out of you again!"

If by force of convention and established traditions and prejudices officers addressed soldiers with the familiar form "thou" and never shook hands with them, this does not mean that officers despised their soldiers. One can after all address a person with the polite form "you" and even shake his hand, and yet despise him in one's heart. In our regiment, not only did they not flout and belittle the human dignity of the soldier, on the contrary, they tried to instill a feeling of valor, heroism, and a particular pride and even haughtiness about being in the Guards. This was manifested even in trivial things. Thus for example, when a soldier was allowed to go home for Christmas on leave, he was always readily given a parade helmet with eagle, a jacket, and sometimes even a cuirass, so that he could show off and brag a bit about his regiment in his native village.

To the young soldiers in the regiment, those official words of the old military regulations, which said that "soldier is a celebrated name," were always emphasized. It was instilled in the soldier that his was an honorable service because in the regulations it was stated that the soldier serves the tsar himself and is "the defender of the motherland from external and internal enemies." In regard to internal enemies, it was explained to the soldiers that these were bad people who went against the tsar. And could you really have created an Imperial Life Guards in the true sense of the word without all this?[7] Could you create a reliable Guards soldier, if he was treated like cattle? Of course not! That is why in a guardsman they strove to cultivate a bold martial spirit of valor, of love for the regiment and for the tsar. Discussions of this were usually conducted by the officers in charge of new recruits and young soldiers in the squadrons. The commander of the training detachment also spoke to the soldiers about this, as well as the regimental priest, who was charged by General Arapov with the responsibility of conducting in the squadrons and detachments regular "religio-moral discussions with the lower ranks." It was a simple policy that was instilled in the soldiers: "for the faith, for the Tsar, for the fatherland"—those were the three whales that embodied the entire Guards ideology of that time.[8]

The regimental patroness—the old Empress Mariia Fiodorovna—used to visit the regiment often, especially when her favorite son Mikhail was serving in our Life Squadron. The empress would appear in the barracks, would look in at the regimental infirmary; she had a gift of sociability and of appearing gracious and attentive.[9] The significance of her visits was inflated by the regimental command, which turned them into a kind of tool of political agitation, pointing out to the men their interaction with the "great ones of this world," and therefore the honored purpose that had fallen to their lot.

Our soldiers often saw the tsar, both on maneuvers in Krasnoe and at reviews. They saw him only in exciting, ceremonious circumstances and in a halo of glory, when each of his appearances in the midst of his huge, glittering retinue was greeted by the majestic trumpet sounds of the very beautiful anthem, and the lowering of the regiment's proud standards, which we respect above all else. The soldiers saw how, at the appearance of the tsar, the countenances of the most important and proud Guards commanding officers changed, as they suddenly were transformed from haughty masters into anxiously respectful servants of the sovereign. The might of the tsar, the unlimited power of this absolute ruler of the immense Russian land, and finally the faith instilled by the regimental priest in the divine origin of the tsar's power (for the tsar was considered the "anointed by God"), all this could of course not fail to have an emotional influence on the ignorant mass of soldiers, torn from the countryside, and as a result there appeared a naive but sincere devotion of the old Guards cadres to their supreme leader. And it's strange to think today that it was precisely those cadres—devoted and politically reliable—who were the very first to be thrown into the fire of the World War.

When in February 1917 the Reserve Battalion of the Life Guards of the

Preobrazhenskii Regiment, stationed in Petrograd, was the first to join the rebellion, there was nothing "Preobrazhenskii" left in it besides the epaulets and collar-tabs: the true old Preobrazhenskii soldiers had completely disappeared from the face of the earth by that time.[10] During two and a half years of the World War, the regiment had a complete changeover of its personnel nearly three times over, losing all the old reliable cadres, so that in 1917 the rebellious Reserve Battalion consisted of men gathered haphazardly from everywhere—men who were never polished the way the soldiers were in the peacetime Guards. Let us take the following incident as an example: when in 1905 in Moscow the bright flame of an armed uprising of workers flared up, the tsarist government sent the Life Guards Semionovskii Regiment to Moscow, because the government could not rely on the army units of the Moscow garrison at this acute and critical moment. The guardsmen who had been sent to Moscow, without flinching, carried out everything the regime expected of them and put down the popular revolt, despite the fact that the Semionovskii Regiment consisted mainly of simple Russian peasants.

In speaking of the devotion of our cuirassier soldiers to their regiment, I should point out one factor that played an important role in the soldiers' education. I am speaking of that purely sporting spirit that strongly infected the whole regiment. The remarkable world-class athletes Staff Captain von Exe and Lieutenant Pleshkov had managed to group the young officers around them and get them hooked on sports. Many pages and cadets wanted to become officers in our regiment precisely because of the reputation for athletics that our regiment had established in recent years. Carried away by sports, the young officers involuntarily infected the soldiers with their enthusiasm. Rather than a rote, formal attitude towards such activities as relay riding, horseback acrobatics, saber drill, shooting, and gymnastics, the young officers invested a sportsman's passion in them, arousing interest and a spirit of competition in the soldiers. Although the word "competition" was never spoken, the principle of competition existed in all the detachments, for it is inseparably bound up with the idea of sports . . . Ivanov is a great marksman, so let me try to shoot even better than Ivanov!

Purely individual competitiveness inevitably became collective: whose platoon is best at jumping hurdles, whose squadron shoots best. On this basis a kind of squadron patriotism arose among the soldiers. It was expressed especially vividly at the regimental marksmanship review, and also at the soldiers' competitions for prizes that were often organized in the regiment. There were competitions in saber drill, and fencing, and hurdle-jumping races. Our soldiers got very excited about these competitions, displaying passion, pride in their team, and a feeling of squadron honor. This cultivation of sport did much to bring officers and soldiers closer together and caused each to respect and admire the other, often smoothing over and softening the differences that had to exist between junior officers and their subordinates, making their relationship more human. In general, when they ended their service in the regiment and were transferred to the reserves, soldiers left the regiment without hard feelings, and the regiment always gave the departing men a warm send-off. I can well remember the scene of saying farewell to soldiers who had served their term and were going home. They were formed up in the manège. The regimental commander for a final time solicited any complaints, then he gave a short speech to the departing men, thanked them for their service to the motherland, and ended with the words: "Well, lads, now God be with you as you go to your homes. With all my heart I wish you everything good, and don't forget me and your cuirassier regiment and remember us kindly! To your health—Hurrah!"

"Hurra-a-ah, hurra-a-h!" the soldiers would roar at the top of their voices, many of them wiping away tears. "Well, now disperse! Now you can break ranks!" the commander ordered, and the soldiers, leaving their ranks, would surround him in a crowd, lift him into their arms, swing him with shouts of "hurrah," and with joyful laughter carry him out of the manège. Although they were all happy to be going home to their towns and villages, still they were obviously sorry to say goodbye to their own regiment, for over the years of service they had gotten so used to it that they considered the regiment also to be something like their own home.

Chapter Eight

The Camp at Krasnoe Selo

AFTER PASSING THE regimental drill review, the regiment left Gatchina for a few days of so-called patrol duty, so that the squadrons could practice performing field patrol duty according to the regulations for field service. While on patrol we were quartered in villages, and this short period of exercises was organized by the officers as a pleasant and at the same time useful period of rest for the whole regiment. On patrol everyone was in an equable mood; no one put pressure on anyone. After designating the front line of the imaginary enemy, we dispersed into sectors and pickets on which guard and listening posts were set up, and reconnaissance parties were sent out, but in fact no one did anything, because everyone was overcome by a kind of blissful laziness after the intense period of spring exercises and the platoon, squadron, and regimental reviews.

On patrol we were often quartered near the estates of landowners, with whom the gentlemen officers were always eager to become acquainted, in those cases where young ladies were on hand in the landowner's household. The unexpected arrival of an entire cavalry regiment was always a great event for the landowners, an event that introduced a lot of gaiety into their monotonous country seclusion, jolting family-oriented people and homebodies out of their everyday life. When the landowners were nice and there were young people in the house (and most of the time this was the case), an evening party, with the regimental singers and a delicious supper, would be arranged for the landowners in the capacious tent housing the officers' club, since the club's cook always followed the regiment with two huge vans loaded with all necessary supplies for providing a feast. The local landowners, if they were well-off, would in turn have a party for the officers in their homes, trying to boast of their Russian hospitality.

During patrol duty we lived like gypsies, never staying in one place more than two or three days, always moving from place to place. One day we would meet and become friendly with one set of "decent people," the next day we would forget them, because a new meeting was on the horizon, promising love, merry adventures, and new alluring prospects. The young officers loved

246

these chance and fleeting encounters, especially with young ladies—encounters that at times smacked of a strange romanticism and were sometimes accompanied by violent fallings-in-love and unexpected affairs arising like a flash of lightning. In regard to the latter, the young Staff Captain Baron Taube particularly distinguished himself.

Short, slim, quick-moving, with pale eyes and rosy complexion, in a rumpled service cap worn dashingly on the back of his head, he was not handsome or even elegant, but he was a true ladies' man with an undoubted gift for making himself liked, and in amorous dealings he was extremely enterprising and resourceful, turning love into a kind of sport. Baron Taube's rivals in the pursuit of the ladies were the always merry and cheerful Lieutenant Grossman and the youthful-looking Cornet Elvengren, who had the face of a typical "military lover-boy." All three of them were in the Life Squadron. And how many pairs of magnificent branching horns these three regimental Lovelaces placed on the heads of respectable landowner husbands during patrol duty—only Allah knows![1] It used to be that the trumpets of the regimental orchestra would not have time to finish thundering next to the club tent, where a slightly tipsy landowner husband was finishing his goblet of wine, clinking glasses with a gaily winking colonel, while on the grass in front of the tent the landowner's sisters and female cousins were dancing with the amiable cornets, when before you know it, the landowner's dear little wife, agitated, happy, and flushed, was already looking around warily, trying to catch a convenient moment for going off unnoticed with our "dear baron" to some secret avenue of lindens in the park, where the thick foliage made the transparent twilight of the white night less immodest . . .

The baron was irresistible. The trumpeters and regimental singers had already fallen silent, the guests and hosts had gone off to rest, but for a long time yet in the most secluded corners of the old linden park the old night watchman could hear someone's muffled talk, languid sighs and kisses, interrupted now by the tender jingling of spurs, now by the sweet trilling of the nightingale.

Early in the morning the cuirassiers saddle their horses, joking with each other (soldiers are no slouches either; you can rest assured that in every squadron there was an enterprising lance corporal who had managed the night before, behind the back of his platoon commander, to fool around with a bold peasant lass!). The regiment forms up on the street and makes its way at a walking pace out of the village onto the high road, hooves making a soft sound on the country road. One or two of the young officers cast a last glance at the cozy landowner's house fronted by columns, hoping that perhaps one of the lowered curtains will suddenly be raised, revealing the sweetest little face in the window, all the enchanting freshness of which can still be felt so distinctly on the lips. But the landowner's ladies are either resting in bed, smiling happily in their sleep, or are tormenting themselves with belated repentance, not at all suspecting that someone's searching eyes are fixed at that moment on the curtained windows of their bedrooms. Baron Taube, short on sleep and sporting suspicious wrinkles and dark circles under his eyes, yawns and tiredly stretches in the saddle. "Well, how are you doing, Fedia?" the regimental adjutant hails him jokingly, overtaking the Life Squadron at a gallop. "Lousy!" the baron answers curtly, nervously shrugging his shoulders and for some unknown reason punishing his completely innocent horse with a sharp spur.

The landowner's house suddenly disappears behind a grove of birches. Everything is over. Forever? Well, of course, forever!

The command rings out: "Singers forward!" and the green grove suddenly resounds with the fervent, dancing sounds of a sprightly cuirassier song:

> I'll marry an uhlan, but I'll live with a cuirassier,
> Tra-la-la-la, tra-la-la-la,
> I'll live with a cuirassier. . . .

Everything is over.

After patrol duty, the regiment immediately went to camp for the whole summer in Krasnoe Selo—a huge, gray, dusty town, filled to overflowing with military men of all ranks and branches of the service, since by this time the whole Guards were concentrated here. The officers were quartered by twos and threes in unprepossessing gray and yellow wooden dachas. Our soldiers and horses were quartered in private village courtyards, except for the Fourth Squadron, which for some reason had wooden stables in Krasnoe of the semi-barracks type. The infantry was quartered outside the town, in tents. Some units were quartered in neighboring villages.

Every morning we rode out to the enormous Krasnoe Selo military field, which occupied several square miles—a gray, unattractive field trampled flat by thousands and thousands of horses' hooves from eleven cavalry Guards regiments and horse batteries, which exercised here every day for several hours at a time. There was not a single blade of grass on the entire huge field. Everywhere dust, endless dust.

At first we participated in brigade drills on the field together with the Yellow Cuirassiers, who were part of our brigade, then there were brigade maneuvers of short duration in the Krasnoe region. Then there followed a period of divisional drills and maneuvers. Then (all on the same field) grandiose drills of the entire Guards cavalry at once were conducted—drills that were always led personally by Grand Duke Nikolai Nikolaevich, and which the tsar himself sometimes came to admire. At the end of the summer the Krasnoe Selo camp assembly culminated in large-scale maneuvers by the entire

Guards corps with the combined participation of all the branches of the service, including even the air corps, represented by a single miniature, slow dirigible and a few airplanes, which at that time were entrusted only with narrow reconnaissance tasks.

The troops received most of their tactical training in Krasnoe Selo. In this regard I consider it pertinent to quote an excerpt from the book by A. M. Zaionchkovskii, *Russia's Preparations for the World War.*[2] A distinguished military specialist and also an active participant in the yearly Krasnoe Selo camps as a former brigade and divisional commander, Zaionchkovskii offers the following interesting evaluation of Krasnoe Selo:

The tone of the entire training of the Russian army was set, strange as it may seem at first glance, by the St. Petersburg military district and in particular the Krasnoe Selo camp. The Commander-in-Chief of this district was Grand Duke Nikolai Nikolaevich. . . . At the camp exercises of this district both the minister of war and the commander of the General Staff often were present. Army units from other districts were also brought here every summer; finally, Guards staff officers received the majority of army regiments, and the high-level schools that trained staff officers were very closely connected to the Krasnoe Selo camp. Its influence on the training of the Russian army is indisputable. So what did the Krasnoe Selo camp give the army? With complete impartiality I must say that it gave it a great deal. The experience of the Russo-Japanese War was taken into account; infantry, machine-gun, and artillery fire were accorded the greatest significance, sometimes to an inordinate degree (a regimental commander whose regiment did not earn an "Excellent" rating at a marksmanship review had to resign), and this led involuntarily to certain undesirable contrivances in peacetime. An infantry attack was allowed only after active training in rifle, machine-gun, and artillery fire. Particular attention was paid to the connection between the infantry and the artillery, but there was a failure to insist on the fact that in the heat of battle the artillery should choose a position close to the infantry.

Battle formations were greatly broadened; attacks in file were replaced by massing and the rudiments of group battle and an excellent adaptation to the landscape. Particular attention was paid to individual training in marksmanship and to the development of independence on the part of junior officers.

All the drills and maneuvers were exclusively oriented toward encounter battle and toward training the troops in the spirit of decisive active operations. But the training at Krasnoe Selo also had its negative aspects.

The conditions of service in Krasnoe Selo forced the troops to pay a large tribute to the demands of review, which inevitably was reflected in field training. The exercises had the character of actions by small detachments, with no clear idea of the interrelationships of larger groups. The cavalry was trained primarily for mounted actions (although it too paid great attention to marksmanship training) and for close-order attacks, and no attention was given to training the cavalry for strategic work or combined battle. While training the troops for active battle, little attention was paid to engineering training and technology in general.

Little attention was paid to training the commanding officers, and there was no maneuver practice for the officers in directing divisions and corps. . . .

From this short outline it is evident that most attention was paid to training small formations, which indeed gave positive results during the first period of the war of movement, when regimental troops were still active. But there was absolutely no attention given to the workings of large groups and to training senior officers to lead them. . . .

From Zaionchkovskii's assessment one may conclude that the tactical training of our cavalry was somewhat worse than the training of the infantry, because our cavalry was often given less training than it should have been. Indeed, when I remember our exercises then on the Krasnoe Selo military field, I can't help but be dismayed at how much time and effort we expended on learning the technique of mounted frontal attacks, always performed in close-order extended line formation, when whole cavalry brigades and even divisions, lances held in horizontal position, would fall upon each other like a whirlwind and engage in hand-to-hand combat. Only the infantry attacked at tactical interval. Such picturesque cavalry battles were appropriate perhaps a century earlier, but with modern technology and arms we could hardly expect to actually apply such tactics under the conditions of a major war. Meanwhile, not one of our drills on the military field, not one maneuver took place without such attacks, which were usually the culmination of all maneuvers, whether on the brigade, divisional, or even corps level.

The main reason for this curious state of affairs, it seems to me, was Grand Duke Nikolai Nikolaevich—a cavalryman of the old school and a great adherent of the cavalry in general, and moreover a man who was quite temperamental and what is called "dashing," and who therefore demanded dashingness from us at all costs! And one must do him justice: the Russian cavalry could attack in close order or extended order with large formations just as remarkably as with a single platoon. It is not for nothing that during the World War, neither the German nor the Austrian cavalry, even in the smallest formations, would as a rule engage our mounted attacks, but would always evade them, preferring to hurry behind the lines and send rifle fire at us from there.

On August 6, 1914, near the small town of Kraupischken in eastern Prussia, there was even a case where one squadron of the Horse Life Guards Regiment, which was part of our division, frontally attacked (true, in extended order) a German battery in its position![3] Having lost a good half of his men and horses to German grapeshot, nevertheless the squadron commander galloped with his surviving men right up to the guns, a pair of which they immediately captured. The Germans managed to save the other pair by hastening to flee, and the exhausted cavalry squadron no longer had the strength to pursue them and take these guns that had been hurriedly carried away. In this amazing attack (which the writer of these lines witnessed and which, I believe, was the only one of its kind in the entire war), the influence and training of Krasnoe Selo could undoubtedly be detected. By the way, the commander of the Horse Guards squadron was Captain Baron Vrangel, who thanks to this attack on the battery acquired great fame and popularity in the Guards and rose quickly to prominence, but ended his amazing career ingloriously as the defeated leader of the Whites.

I will now attempt to describe how our maneuvers were carried out.

It all began with two huge vans on springs leaving at dawn from the officers' club with the club staff, headed by our civilian cook—a portly man who looked more like an arrogant marshal of the nobility than a cook. Fat and round-faced, he had an imposing, neatly trimmed round beard, a beautifully tailored gray jacket, and a beaver bowler hat. When he went out to the maneuvers, he would take a seat on the box of the first van with the air of an important lord, holding on his lap a military map with a scale of 1.3 miles to the inch, showing where the bivouac site was, where he had to arrive before everyone else in order to set up the officers' club tent and prepare a delicious meal for the gentlemen officers. What didn't the cook take with him in his black vans!—expensive club silver, starched tablecloths and napkins, batteries of champagne and liqueurs, and an endless assortment of hors d'oeuvres. The cook was a clever man but also a first-class rogue. But to hell with him!

After this preliminary action (which had an undoubted influence on the success of the coming operation), the regiment began to saddle their horses, form up, and endlessly salute their officers. When in the morning the regiment finally left the limits of Krasnoe and dismounted near the town, the regimental commander would summon all the officers to him and read out loud to them the general assignment he had received from the divisional command and the so-called tactical situation. Often it consisted of the fact that according to data provided by aerial reconnaissance, an enemy landing force that had disembarked in the Gulf of Finland was advancing in the direction of Krasnoe. We were supposed to either pretend to be this advancing force or, on the contrary, repel its attack.

In the first case, after joining the other regiments in the division, we would undertake a prolonged march, sometimes more than forty miles, after sending quartermasters ahead of us. After arriving at our bivouac, one of the regiments would be assigned to outposts. After quartering the squadrons, the hungry and tired officers of the remaining regiments would immediately begin having a party. While the soldiers received their dinner from field kitchens, the officers would have a large open-air picnic, with remarkably abundant and varied hors d'oeuvres and drinks, because on maneuvers everyone worked up a devilish appetite. These picnics were an integral part of all maneuvers.

Meanwhile the regimental commanders, brigade generals, adjutants, and staff officers, after a quick snack, would gather at the divisional commander's for a discussion of the plan of attack, and after working it out in detail, would also join one or another regimental picnic, which sometimes lasted long past midnight, frequently to the music of the trumpeters. In bivouac one could hear from afar the Yellow Cuirassiers, Chevalier Guards, and Horse Guards "having a spree." The officers always partied in the tight company of their own regiment, very seldom inviting their neighbors. An exception was made for the mounted artillery, whom everyone was glad to invite, because the mounted artillery of the Guards completely lacked that regimental arrogance and snobbism that were so typical of many Guards units.

The officers, always smartly dressed in brand-new uniforms, permitted themselves while on maneuvers to wear old, worn-out clothes, acquiring the look of battle-hardened warriors. Everyone was in a merry mood, and never were so many jokes and witticisms cracked or so many anecdotes told as on these bivouacs.

During the day our young officers, who were crazy about sports, would often gather the local urchins and arrange prize competitions for them in running, swimming, jumping, and wrestling. Many sports fanatics who had long ago lost their minds over horse racing, organized pari-mutuel betting according to all the regulations, placing bets on one or other of the boys; they set up all sorts of "heats" for "three-year-olds" and "five-year-olds" and drew handicaps, sometimes pulling even respectable generals into this foolish business. They went to bed very late, either on a haystack or somewhere under an overhang, preferring to set up their camp-beds in the fresh air rather than in the stuffy, dirty, and bad-smelling huts teeming with cockroaches, bedbugs, and fleas. (Guards officers, despite their battle-hardened appearance, were very squeamish!)

At night the young cornets would get up to mischief like children. Out of the open door of a barn one hears the impressive snore of the senior Colonel von Schweder; the terror of the officers, the terror of the entire cuirassier regiment is resting peacefully on his camp-bed. At the head of the stern colonel's bed stands an overturned bucket. On the bucket sits a large cup full of water, and in the cup—the colonel's teeth, which though false are numerous. The cornets Prince Urusov Junior and von Baumgarten the Second are great practical jokers; one of them quietly steals up to the sleeping colonel and carefully pours into his huge, toothless, open mouth some bedbugs and reddish cockroaches that they have caught in the hut. The other, frozen on the neighboring camp-bed, watches with a happy smile as those lips, the fiercest in the entire regiment, which seem to have been created by Mother Nature in order to shower unpleasant reprimands, lectures, and reproofs, now twitch helplessly. But now one can see the little wiggling whiskers of a cockroach in the corner of the colonel's mouth; a fat, wet bedbug runs in panic out onto the colonel's puffed-out lip. Another has apparently lodged in the colonel's throat and caused a tickle there. "Kha-kha!" he coughs like thunder and jumps up onto the bed like a crazy man, eyes bulging threateningly. The cornets turn away quickly, pretending that they are preparing for bed. "Ugh, hell, how disgusting!" the colonel angrily grumbles, spitting in disgust, and without understanding a thing, turns furiously onto his side. The "green" cornets laugh and exult quietly, heads stuck in their pillows.

At dawn we would finally get down to serious business. After a detailed briefing, mounted patrols and reconnaissance squadrons were sent out toward Krasnoe (if they had not already been sent the day before). Finally the whole division along with its artillery set out in reverse, with the advance guard ahead and march pickets on the flanks. The war game would begin—a game that often was truly engaging both for many officers and for some soldiers, who would get very excited, especially on reconnaissance, trying to capture "enemy" scouts, who were sometimes in the heat of the moment given a beating. But there were also many officers who had an indifferent or one might say purely formal attitude to the maneuvers, limiting themselves to carrying out their assigned tasks in a more or less conscientious way and nothing more.

We often had to practice night marches, which were very tedious but caused great difficulty for enemy reconnaissance. Under cover of night it was easiest to deceive the enemy, carrying out a "deep" circuitous maneuver and suddenly turning up in a place where one was least expected. The commanding and staff officers really liked such turning movements.

Now, after a tedious night march, our division is stealing up to Dudergof at dawn. At this point the reconnaissance party has unexpectedly fallen upon the "enemy's" major forces in the person of a Cossack Guards battery or the Second Cavalry Division. In the advance guard there is confusion: it turns out that someone confused someone else, someone went round someone else, someone missed someone else. Both sides overreached. The "enemy" is burning with the desire to engage us, and having suddenly discovered our main forces, they are pressing upon us at full speed and, moreover, not from the direction we expected.

The decision to attack is made at lightning speed by both sides. The command rings out, the crashing martial signals of the staff trumpeters thunder forth, and the whole division deploys in an instant, at full career, from the long, extended marching column into a close-order front, bristling with lances. This maneuver is performed to perfection. The orderlies gallop off at breakneck speed. Our batteries gallop to the side, and taking up some kind of unbelievable positions behind us, they open fire. In the first rays of the dawn the sabers pulled out of their sheaths flash with fiery sparks. Ahead of us the enemy's batteries are already banging.

"March—march!!!"—we fly forward like a hurricane, raising clouds of hellish dust behind us, the reserve after us in echelon formation. The earth hums under thousands of hooves, the wind whistles in our ears, we shout "Hurrah!" and the entire Second Division is already falling upon us in an irrepressible solid wave of horsemen, screaming exactly the same victorious "Hurrah!" at the top of their voices. Six, or even all eight cavalry regiments collide at full career . . . Well, in fact, no one "collides," because the regimental and squadron commanders galloping ahead stop the two sides ten paces from each other at the last possible moment. The staff trumpeters sound retreat. The maneuver is over. Its critique begins. "Ha-a-lt! Dismo-o-ount!"

The horses, snorting and dark with sweat, are panting quickly and heavily. The rushing "enemies" are immediately transformed into good old acquaintances, and in clouds of all-enveloping dust they exchange friendly greetings.

"Hey, Geowges," a lisping Horse Guards cornet cries to his opposite number, an officer of the Life Hussars, "are you going to Petersburg today?"

"Yes!"

"And where are you going to pawty tonight?"

"I'll start at the Kiuba [a fashionable Petersburg restaurant], does that suit you?"

"*C'est entendu!*"

As if sprung by magic out of the earth, the ubiquitous "jackals" appear between the lines with their baskets. The officers have a quick snack, usually without managing to get their change from the cunning tradesmen; meanwhile to the side, the senior officers and umpires, sputtering and getting offended with each other, argue until they're hoarse about who was the true victor in the "battle." Usually the victor was acknowledged to be the side that managed to turn the enemy's flank even a little bit, or to open fire earlier.

These encounter attacks, carried out by several regiments at once, were a very striking, I would even say thrilling spectacle, and we more than once pondered what would happen to our squadrons if we were to attack each other seriously. In such a case the officers galloping at the head would have a particularly hot time of it, because they would inevitably be the first to fall, as if in a pincers, onto the points of the lances, both of the enemy and possibly of their own men, attacking from behind in the kind of irrepressible rush that only heavy and zealous cuirassier horses are capable of.

After such a maneuver a "day's rest" was usually announced. The officers would dress up in new uniforms and some would leave for St. Petersburg, others would stay in Krasnoe, where in the evening they would appear, dressed to the nines, in the cozy Krasnoe Selo theater to watch an operetta performed by excellent actors.

On days when there were no maneuvers, as I have already mentioned, we would go out onto the grim military field for cavalry drills. All these drills, both brigade and divisional, were very monotonous, and they essentially resembled the Gatchina regimental drills described above: the same re-formations, the same maneuvers and attacks, just on a larger scale.

At the risk of boring the reader, I will nonetheless permit myself to say a few more words about the drills of the entire Guards cavalry, in order to give as full a picture as possible of the Krasnoe Selo camp.

At 5:00 A.M. or even earlier, after reveille, all of Krasnoe Selo would resound with the melodic sounds of the very old "general march," which the bands in all the cavalry regiments would begin to play simultaneously. From the very first sounds the men would begin to saddle their horses. Then the regiments would form up on the main street to meet their standards and commanders. By 6:00 A.M. the regiments and their bands would come out onto the space of the military field in long columns from all directions, greeting each other according to an old tradition, by playing regimental marches. Thus, for example, if our regiment encountered the Life Cossacks, our band would play the Life Cossack march, and the Life Cossacks would answer us by playing our cuirassier march. In all, eleven Guards regiments would ride out onto the field at once (the Chevalier Guards, the Horse Life Guards, His Majesty's Cuirassiers, Her Majesty's Cuirassiers, the Cossack Life Guards, the Ataman Life Guards, the Combined Cossack Life Guards, the Mounted Grenadier Life Guards, the Dragoon Life Guards, the Uhlan Life Guards, and the Hussar Life Guards), along with four mounted batteries plus sometimes two army cavalry regiments as well, since every year several army regiments whose patrons were "imperial personages" would be brought to Krasnoe Selo from other districts. An incredible cacophony would arise on the military field, thanks to the simultaneous playing of eleven or even thirteen different marches at once.

Finally, all the regiments and mounted batteries, in the order of their brigades and divisions, would form up in a single enormous common line and after carefully dressing, would dismount to await their commanding officers. At different times, five brigadier generals would ride onto the field. We would again mount, form up, and play our regimental marches to greet the generals, then we would again dismount to await the divisional commanders, and when they appeared the whole rigmarole would be repeated. After greeting with pomp and circumstance the last divisional commander, we would finally dismount to await the Grand Duke Nikolai Nikolaevich himself. More than an hour was taken up by all these ceremonies.

The grand duke would come out onto the field in a large gray open car, and would stop at a little distance from the regiments in a prearranged spot, where he was awaited by orderlies, who held by the bridle a saddled noble racehorse of exceptional beauty, and by a Cossack with a big bright flag. As soon as they caught sight of the grand duke's car in the distance, the appearance of which was announced by specially placed signalers, the commanders would begin to get nervous, fuss about, and dress their units with exceptional zeal and attentiveness. Some generals would seem to suddenly change countenance, losing all their importance. One could sense that from the moment Nikolai Nikolaevich appeared on the field, all the commanders, and especially the major ones, became deeply agitated, because Nikolai Nikolaevich was considered the terror of the Guards with full justification. "How's it going to go, today's drill?" was in everyone's mind. Meanwhile the grand duke, with the help of the orderlies, would mount his steed and, putting it into a gallop, ride out to the perfectly formed-up units, which at that moment seemed to have been frozen. He would ride along the front line, beginning with the right flank of our division, that is, the Chevalier Guards, greeting each regiment separately.

The grand duke looked very striking on horseback. Despite the fact that he was enormously tall and had extremely long legs, he had that ideal, almost coquettish "Nicholas" seat of an old-school cavalryman, a seat that so became the horseman, causing him to merge with his horse into a single indivisible and harmonious whole. Nikolai Nikolaevich was dressed in a khaki jacket with an adjutant general's gold aiguillettes and a simple field ammunition belt. He wore a rumpled khaki service cap on the back of his head, cavalryman-style, and on his long legs he wore riding breeches with bright red stripes down the sides. At that time he was already advanced in years, but he still had a youthful look. His face, which ended at the bottom in a small beard, was tanned and irregular. It was not a handsome face, but it was a memorable one, because it wasn't the ordinary military face of a vulgar general. It was the very particular face of a great leader—an imperious, stern, open, decisive, and at the same time proud face. The look in his eyes was intent, predatory, seeming to see all and forgive nothing. His movements were assured and unconstrained, his voice was incisive, loud, a bit guttural, accustomed to giving commands, and shouting out words with a sort of half-contemptuous carelessness. Nikolai Nikolaevich was a guardsman from head to toe, a guardsman to the marrow of his bones. And there was no one else like him in the whole Guards. Despite the fact that many officers tried to copy his mannerisms, he was inimitable. His prestige at that time was enormous. Everyone trembled before him, and it was not easy to please him at drills.

After riding along the front line of the cavalry, the grand duke would ride at a brisk gallop to a small hill a little distance away, accompanied by a Cossack with a bright flag in his hands. Suddenly stopping his racer, the grand duke would order the trumpeter who accompanied him to sound the assembly of the commanders. It was funny to see how at this signal, pompous middle-aged generals would fly at breakneck speed to the grand duke along with the green cornet orderlies sent from each brigade. Surrounding the grand duke, the commanders would salute and the orderlies would "present themselves." After explaining the program for the drill, Nikolai Nikolaevich would send the generals back to their units, and the grandiose drill would begin.

These were the same long-familiar formations and re-formations, but because of the mass of regiments participating in the drills all at the same time, the drill became very difficult, especially since the grand duke did not wish to make any allowances, and demanded the precision and accuracy of automatons from everyone. And this was no laughing matter: on the military field at that time, not counting the four mounted batteries, as many as sixty-four squadrons(!) were galloping, which at a mere wave of the grand duke's hand had to simultaneously perform the same movement and the exact same formation, hitting their marks precisely! Sixty-four squadrons—just imagine the scene!

Only thanks to the prolonged drilling of these same squadrons well in advance was it possible for the grand duke to achieve the ideal coordination and order at the grandiose Guards cavalry drills.

And what a tiny, insignificant blade of grass the simple soldier participating in this avalanche must have felt himself to be.

If from the contemporary tactical point of view such mass drills seemed pointless, on the other hand they undoubtedly developed a keen eye in the commanding officers, and sharpened their attentiveness and the general discipline.

The tiniest blunder on the part of one of the commanders often entailed a general muddle, and then the grand duke would give free rein to his cavalryman's temper: summoning all the commanders, he would not spare his expressions, so as to further smarten up the already smart and obsequiously trembling generals, who on such an occasion took on the appearance of guilty schoolboys.

I can remember as if it were yesterday the following scene:

Shading his squinting predator's eyes from the sun with his hand, the grand duke fixedly inspects his cavalry, which is completing its final re-formations before an attack.

"Orderly!" Nikolai Nikolaevich tosses out curtly, not even looking around at the officers following him, and with a careless movement of his finger he summons the closest orderly, whose face instantly turns bright red from excitement.

"What are your orders, Your Imperial Highness?" the young cornet asks in a strained voice, riding up to the grand duke and saluting.

Not looking at anyone, the grand duke stretches out his arm in the direction of the cavalry's flank and quickly raps out:

"Gallop to General N. and tell him that he should . . ."

The grand duke speaks so quickly, and the cornet orderly is so excited, that he cannot make out the order he's been given, and meanwhile the grand duke is already saying impatiently, "Get going! Get going!"

In other circumstances the cornet orderly would perhaps have asked his commander to repeat the order, as was proper to do in such cases, but the expression on Nikolai Nikolaevich's face was so stern that looking at it the cornet is stunned, and after shouting furiously, "Yes, sir, Your Imperial Highness!" he spurs his heated horse and rushes at top speed to the general in question, without looking back.

During this short trip the cornet is seized by torments of desperation: What is he going to tell the general? With his pitiful cornet's mind, the young man tries to guess the grand thought of the grand duke and suffers terribly, thinking up some kind of fantastic dispositions all on his own to convey to the general. Now he gallops up to him, and having failed to think up anything sensible, salutes with a dismayed air and mumbles indecisively: "Your Excellency . . . His Imperial Highness orders you . . . orders you . . ."

"Well, what does he order me to do! Tell me quickly!"

The cornet's position is horrible. After all, he can't just tell the general nothing. "You are ordered . . . to move to the right!" the unfortunate orderly finally blurts out the first thing that comes into his head and, horrified at the crime he has committed, composes in his head a prayer to the Almighty. "To the right?" the general asks, shrugging his shoulders in bewilderment.

"Yes sir, Your Excellency!" the cornet answers in a weak voice.

"Regiment! Right wheel!" the general commands shrilly. "At a gallop . . . Ma-a-arch!"

"My God, what have I done? What will happen now?" the orderly whispers to himself, and with the decisiveness of a suicide returns at full gallop to the grand duke.

"Cornet, did you convey my order accurately?" the grand duke asks in a strangely quiet voice, in which one senses the brief calm before a storm.

"Yes, sir, Your Imperial Highness!" the orderly answers with a trembling jaw.

"Return to your post! Trumpeter . . . assemble the commanders," the grand duke orders even more quietly, and with a nervous movement he lightly taps the top of his boot with a bamboo riding crop.

The crashing trumpet of the grand duke's signaler pours out in its familiar passionate call. From all directions middle-aged, decorated generals come rushing on their expensive horses, saluting.

The grand duke waits patiently until they have all assembled and pauses. It smells of a thunderstorm. The commanders are tense and silent.

"Your Excellency!" the grand duke finally raps out, turning to General N. "You should not be commanding a regiment . . . You should be herding swine!" he suddenly shouts out, baring his teeth angrily. "Did I send an orderly to you? Did I?"

The general has frozen like a statue, his hand in salute.

"What did I order you to do? What did I or-der you to do-oo? to form up in a reserve column! And if you don't know how to do that, then what kind of commander are you, devil take you? Where did the devil drag you off with your regiment? For shame!"

General N. is terrorized. It would seem the simplest thing to immediately explain that he received no order concerning forming a reserve column, but that he merely carried out conscientiously what the orderly conveyed to him. But General N. is destroyed. "I'm sorry, Your Imperial Highness," is the only answer he can find, which causes the grand duke to soften a bit, while the true culprit in the mess—the little cornet—heaves a sigh of relief and, reborn in spirit, offers a heartfelt prayer of thanksgiving to the Almighty.

After shouting for a few more minutes and finally cooling off, the grand duke dismisses the commanders, and the drill continues.

I describe this little scene, which I once had occasion to witness, in such detail because I was very intimately acquainted with its participant, the young orderly.

In every fold of the military field, under every stunted little bush, a jackal was hidden who never for an instant lost sight of our cavalry. The jackals, from their many years of Krasnoe Selo experience, knew when and where this whole mass of galloping horsemen would turn. They knew as well as Nikolai Nikolaevich himself when and where he would order his regiments to dismount, put their dress in order, and rest for a few minutes. This was the moment they were waiting for; they surrounded us, constantly moving behind us, and when we actually dismounted to rest—the jackals would be right there with their baskets. There was already a cluster of officers around each jackal. Each one was hurrying to drink a bottle of fruit-flavored mineral water and to gulp down a ham or cheese sandwich. A jackal seemed to have ten hands, and managed to serve each man with amazing adroitness. There was not a moment to lose, because at any minute the command would resound: "Mo-o-ount!" and the officers would run to their orderlies who were holding their horses by the bridle, chewing the last of their sandwiches on the run.

"Hey, grandpa, what do I owe you?" a mustachioed lieutenant with a sanguine countenance impatiently asks, holding out a pink ten-ruble note to the jackal. At this point the jackal is transformed from a sprightly lad into an imbecilic mumbler.

"Just a minute, Y'r Radyunce . . . so, let's see, five meat pies at five five-kopeck pieces each . . . one ruble twenty-five kopecks. Didn't you deign to have some chocolate? A ruble seventy kopecks . . . now, then, mineral water . . ."

"But I didn't have any mineral water!"

"Excuse me, Y'r Radyunce: I had a little gap in my memory. Now let me count it up right away . . ."

And the jackal squints his eyes pensively, as though calculating a complicated mathematical formula in his head.

"Mo-o-ount!" the squadron commanders call out the order from behind.

"Oh, to hell with you, you crook!" the sanguine lieutenant shouts angrily, quickly joining his squadron, leaving his ten-ruble note in the hands of the jackal.

A good half of the officers fail to receive their change from the jackals. Of course, it was usually only small sums that they overpaid, but in total the jackals would do fantastic business in only a few minutes at these drills.

The grand duke would make us go onto the military field for several hours every day, thoroughly wearing out our horses. Every drill of the Guards cavalry ended with a quick field gallop for a long distance, for which all the participating regiments, following each other in squadron formation, had to describe on the field a figure eight with a huge radius. The challenge in this figure eight was two artificial obstacles—an earthen rampart and a wide ditch, across which all sixty-four squadrons flew one after another.

The military field was so trampled up that in dry weather each horse left a cloud of dust behind it. You can just imagine what was raised on the field after thirteen regiments had passed over it at a quick gallop, one following the other! Usually in each squadron the second rank could barely make out the tails of the first rank's horses because of the dust. We galloped in a thick, solid yellowish shroud that made it hard to breathe and that blinded us, but meanwhile—we had to keep our eyes peeled! For those galloping in the second ranks, the obstacle would loom up suddenly and would only be noticeable right in front of the horse's muzzle, but the experienced line horses, carried away by the herd instinct of universal unrestrained rushing of the whole gigantic avalanche, never shied, and with a sudden powerful bound into the air, would overcome the obstacles.

Of course there were isolated falls, sometimes resulting in injuries, and for this reason, field hospital wagonettes with doctors and medics stood next to every obstacle.

We would return home from drills after noon, so dirty and dusty that one could not make out the color of the men's shoulder straps and caps. I remember once as our regiment was returning from drill and we entered the main street of Krasnoe Selo, suddenly the order came from behind along the column: "Attention! Left dress!"

Grand Duke Nikolai Nikolaevich in an open car is overtaking the regiment. He comes even with the regimental commander, riding at the head, and ordering the driver to slow down, he summons the commander with one finger.

"In your Fourth Squadron, in the first platoon the flank man's hardware hasn't been cleaned . . . Take care of it!" the grand duke says in a quick patter.

And as his car gathers speed, General Arapov is already flying to the rear of the column to the Fourth Squadron.

A scandal . . . an earth-shattering drama. And indeed, in the first platoon, on the curb-bit of the flank horse, rusty spots clearly appear! The commander of the squadron is given a reprimand. The commander of the platoon and the sergeant major are given a stern reprimand. The platoon NCO and the flank man are sent to the guardhouse. And for a long time in the Fourth Squadron the men talk and gossip, shaking their heads: "What an eye Nikolai Nikolaevich has! What an eye—it's pie-e-ercing! It doesn't miss a thing, doesn't miss a thing!"

Chapter Nine

The Imperial Circuit at Krasnoe Selo

AUGUST 1912 WAS approaching. One could count the few little days until my promotion to officer, and for this reason I was up to my neck in errands: getting fitted out was no laughing matter.

Every day after drill I would go to St. Petersburg, where first I would visit the esteemed Nordenström—the famous Petersburg military tailor who dressed the flower of the Guards dandies and also the young "imperial personages." There I endlessly tried on my officer's jacket, frock coats, regular uniforms, high-collared jackets, overcoat, Nicholas greatcoat [cavalry greatcoat introduced under Nicholas I], and short and long riding breeches and narrow cavalry trousers with side straps for parade, drawing rooms, and everyday.

In Nordenström's spacious, bright, and respectably furnished atelier on Nevskii Avenue the work of several most experienced craftsmen was in full swing under the keen and tireless observation of the owner himself—a stern, pompous, lame, and obese old man, who was rightly considered the king of Russian military tailors.

Old Nordenström charged a pretty penny for his work, but he was a true artist in his field. Certain unprepossessing and clumsy figures, when they donned uniforms and frock coats made by him, suddenly, as if by magic, acquired shapeliness, elegance, and a noble bearing. Uniforms and coats cut by Nordenström bore precisely that stamp of stern elegance and good form that so advantageously distinguished the appearance of Petersburg fops from their provincial colleagues.

When I looked in the huge triple pier-glass in Nordenström's atelier, I was filled with amazing joy and at the same time I felt strange at the very thought that this shapely and most elegant Guards officer in the austere black frock coat with white silk lining who was looking at me from the depths of the mirror was none other than I myself, in my very own persona!

From Nordenström's I rushed to Fokin—the Guards' favorite store for "officers' accessories." Here I would order field and dress ammunition outfits in the form of all sorts of dress sword belts and regular sword belts, gold cuirassier cross-belts, silver cartridge pouches, tricolored scarves, holsters, shoulder straps, epaulettes, gauntlets, gloves, and sword-knots for broadsword and saber. At Fokin's, too, the most beautiful gilded officer's helmet with light-blue silk lining was crafted specially for my head, and a golden cuirass was fitted to my skinny figure. It was also there that after a careful process of selection I acquired a broadsword, saber, and sword, with the aim of someday showing off the remarkable ornamented steel of their blades to my connoisseur comrades. But most remarkable of all were the famous Fokin service caps, which were made only to order and were acknowledged in the Guards cavalry to be the quintessence of good form. With a small, fairly soft crown, they were a little bit rumpled in a very particular style, which gave the guardsmen a certain refined foppishness. A huge dark-blue saddlecloth embroidered in gold and with gleaming stars in the corners, placed in a massive oak case, crowned my orders at the famous shop of Fokin. Having finished there, I immediately rushed to the no less famous bootmaker and ordered magnificent dress boots, ordinary line boots, and all kinds of shoes—dress, ballroom, patent leather, and "ordinary," which were also extraordinary, because they were the creation not so much of a bootmaker as of a true artist.

I of course bought my spurs from Saveliev. It's true, both in the Guards shop in St. Petersburg and at Fokin's one could find an enormous selection of spurs of all types—large, small, nickel, real silver, nail-on, hussar-style, cuirassier-style, bent upward, straight, with bows, without bows, bulldog spurs [toothed spurs], spurs on straps, on hooks, etc. But no spurs in the world could compare to real Saveliev spurs in the "nobility" of their ring; and the sound of spurs at that long-ago time was extremely eloquent. If you heard behind you on the street a loud, bellicose, and challenging clang, without turning around you could confidently state that behind you was either a policeman or some headquarters pen pusher from the commandant's office. If you heard a thin, passionate, coquettish, or clamorous ringing—you would know that somewhere nearby was proceeding a "dashing" provincial army man or hussar in red pants. But if a soft and nobly jingling melody reached your ears, you could rest assured that the creator of that divine music was a refined, well-educated Guards officer, skilled in the rules of propriety and good form—an officer wearing the famous Saveliev spurs, made from some magical and of course very expensive alloy.

I would end my busy day of errands in St. Petersburg at a well-known saddler's, where I looked at a creaking officer's line saddle with all the accoutrements, and ordered a light sport saddle with flat wings extending forward in the Italian style. I also ordered elegant checked horse hoods and horse cloths with coronet and monogram for my own horses.

The horse question was in general the most critical one. I was supposed to acquire two horses, and the regimental command warned me that any horse I bought, before entering the regiment, would be given a preliminary inspection by the regimental commander and senior officers, who would never admit into the cuirassier regiment a horse who might by his points spoil the general regimental harmony. The horses of the gentlemen officers had to be irreproachable. In this difficult matter General Arapov himself met me halfway, and offered to sell me, for a thousand rubles, a huge, very elegant golden-chestnut horse of a heavy—typically cuirassier—build, with a croup as fleshy as a ripe Antonovka apple and a well-muscled neck. This horse was called Jodhpur, and it was far from embarrassing to cut a dashing figure with him on parade or to caracole on him in the presence of ladies. I was sold a second horse, of a purely sportive type, a real competitor in the steeplechase, by our regimental adjutant, Lieutenant Pleshkov—a well-known Russian athlete who kept outstanding horses on which he was always winning prizes. This Zum-Zum he let me have was in appearance the complete opposite of Jodhpur. A very tall dark chestnut horse, very sinewy and lithe, with a "dry" [refined], thin, long neck and long ears, with "dry" legs and sharply outlined tendons, he possessed a powerful shoulder and girth. He was trained with clockwork precision and was impossible to tire. Pleshkov sold Zum-Zum only because he had only won second and third prizes with him, and this did not suit such a capricious and spoiled athlete as he was.

All this bother with getting fitted out took up lots of time and money, but it afforded me an inexpressible, purely childish joy, the joy of a youth who is just getting ready to throw open the doors and go out into "the world."

From the time I had finished my exams and returned to the regiment to await promotion, only a few weeks had passed. But over that short period the attitude of the men in the regiment towards me had noticeably changed. My own relationship to the cuirassier regiment had also changed.

The sergeant major and platoon NCOs, to whom I was still subordinate, suddenly became very gracious to me and displayed great tact when addressing me on service matters. They knew that in a few weeks, when I would put on the gold cornet's shoulder straps, an impassable abyss would appear between me and them, suddenly and all by itself.

Now even our junior officers, when I would stand to attention on meeting them, would answer my greetings more graciously than before, not disdaining to talk to me and even offer advice on my outfit. The terrible Palitsyn, and the regimental commander himself, already singled me out from the other volunteers, greeting me with a gracious, encouraging nod and a few warm words. This was a natural change: the officers had already consented to receive me into their midst, and I had gotten an excellent grade, high enough for the Guards. Only old Colonel von Schweder as before either paid absolutely no attention to me or glowered at me.

264

On the other hand, if during last winter's training period, which took place to the eternal accompaniment of Palitsyn's *Zug*, I was essentially indifferent to the cuirassier regiment, now, after tasting the charms of the camp, I began to feel more and more sympathy and attachment for the regiment.

Regimental life, which required neither intellectual exertion nor philosophical meditation, began to be positively congenial to me in its clarity, liveliness, mobility, and primitively romantic character. I began to love the cuirassier regiment, its vivid characters, its beautiful chestnut horses, its simple but strict customs. I liked it when our regiment did something better than the other regiments on maneuvers or at drills. Conversely, I was sincerely dismayed when another regiment displayed its superiority to us in some area or other. In short: I was gradually becoming a true and confirmed cuirassier, a process which perhaps was assisted by my constant contact with the regimental standard—that inanimate object which nevertheless represented the soul of the regiment. By training myself to respect the standard, I learned to respect the regiment itself.

Every young man who became an officer in the regiment was obligated to acquire a copy of the history of the regiment. It had been published in two volumes, very lavishly produced, with beautiful illustrations by the artist Samokish, photographs, maps, and the plans of the battles in which the regiment had participated. This history was written in a tasteless and somewhat bombastic style, but I set about reading it with great interest.[1]

It turned out that our regiment was one of the oldest of the existing Russian regiments. It had been formed by Peter the Great in 1704. Originally it was called the "Dragoon Regiment of General Portes." Under Peter, the regiment fought the Swedes at Poltava and at Lesnaia, and it was in these battles that the regiment particularly distinguished itself, in honor of which there hung in the officers' club a large oil painting depicting our attack on the Swedish cavalry at Lesnaia.[2]

When in 1731 at the suggestion of Field Marshal Münnich, heavy cavalry was first introduced in Russia, our regiment was renamed the "Life Cuirassiers." During the reign of Empress Elizabeth the regiment, now the cuirassiers, participated in the Seven Years' War and after the taking of Berlin received a remarkable reward in the form of several silver trumpets decorated with precious stones, which trumpets in my time were mouldering somewhere in the bowels of the enormous regimental armory. The regiment also fought in wars under Catherine. For the Fatherland War of 1812 and the Battle of Borodino, the regiment received a reward of twenty-two silver St. George's trumpets, and from that time the instruments in our band were always entwined with St. George's ribbons.[3] The regiment received the rights of the Guards relatively late—only in the 1850s—but it received them exclusively for its many past services in battle.

All this was remarkable and delighted me. But most remarkable of all was the recognition that the life of the regiment, which began under Peter I, had flourished for over two centuries without a moment's interruption—that since the time of Peter up to my day, some men were gradually replaced by others, and at any era there were always old-timers who remembered the previous men, previous commanders, previous customs. One generation of cuirassiers replaced another not all at once but gradually, inculcating in the newcomers its views and regimental traditions and transmitting orally to the young the old songs and sayings. Thanks to this continuity the face of the regiment remained unchanged.

Just as in the body of a living person over the years some organic cells and corpuscles are replaced by others, but the person himself continues to live his life, almost not changing in character, so the old fighting regiment, gradually replacing only the men who played the role of the cells of an organism, never changed its essential identity but only adapted and accommodated itself to new eras and demands. It was pleasant for a young nobleman of a patriotic and somewhat dreamy bent to serve in such a regiment, and at that time I was still a great dreamer in many respects.

At the time when my fate was still being determined and it was decided that I would enter the cavalry, I assumed that I would devote my entire life to the military. I imagined that in time I would undoubtedly enter the Academy of the General Staff in order to become a serious, highly qualified military man before whom, thanks to the academy, the broadest future prospects and possibilities for advancement to high commanding posts in the army would open up. I planned to end my career as none other than the commander in chief of a military district or maybe even a minister of war.

But in 1912, a few days before my promotion to cornet, I suddenly realized clearly that one could reach the top by completely different means—less difficult and more pleasing to one's vanity. This turnabout in my thinking came about, strange as it may seem, after the so-called imperial circuit of the Krasnoe Selo camp and the accompanying ceremonial parade in the presence of the tsar.

Two years before, namely in the summer of 1910, when I was sailing on the destroyer *Horseman*, I would see the tsar every day, since the *Horseman* had for more than a month been stationed to guard the imperial yacht. We rode at anchor next to the yacht in the skerries and in the Baltic port near Revel. I used to conceal myself somewhere in the deckhouse or at the mine apparatus and stealthily direct an 18-power telescope at the deck of the elegant imperial ship and spend hours watching the activities of the tsar's family, who of course had no suspicion that anyone's indiscreet eyes were watching them.

In the telescope the tsar was as distinctly visible as if he were standing or sitting next to me. I could see him get a papirosa from his cigarette case and light a match; I could see his lips move soundlessly as he conversed with his wife or children. I could see every little feature, every little wrinkle on his face. During these hours of leisure his tsar-ness was not at all in evidence. He looked like an ordinary forty-year-old man of a pleasing but by no means outstanding appearance. One could see that the people surrounding the tsar—his children, his wife, and Anna Aleksandrovna Vyrubova—treated him with complete ease and human simplicity.

When the tsar reviewed our destroyer that summer, he again failed to make a great impression on me, perhaps because he came wearing a modest navy jacket, without regalia, without an opulent entourage, but accompanied only by the elderly Admiral Nilov and some young aide-de-camp, thus lending the whole review the intimate character of a mere visit, which was further emphasized by the simplicity and spontaneity with which the tsar treated our commander.

But the tsar appeared to me in a completely different light now, in 1912, during the circuit of the camp and the parade of the Guards.

It was a quiet, sunny morning. On the enormous field near Krasnoe, in a gigantic symmetrical horseshoe, the entire Imperial Guards was stretched out at full strength, with its historical banners and standards, from which the black leather cases had finally been removed for the occasion of the parade.

Thousands and thousands of men were so strangely and tensely silent that, merging into the solid masses of regiments, they were transformed into wooden, inanimate parallelograms.

From a distance I could see a soldier with a light-blue ribbon over his shoulder, riding a dark horse, approach the Preobrazhenskii Regiment at a walk. Behind this man followed a huge cavalcade of horsemen not in formation, who were also wearing ribbons, scarlet and dark blue ones. In the morning air the Preobrazhenskii band precisely and solemnly struck up the deep chords of "God Save the Tsar," and with the marvelous precision of a monstrous machine, through the entire Guards cavalry, in two sharp beats, the gleaming rifle bayonets moved and again fell still as the men presented arms: "One-two!" With the impassiveness of a machine, the first regiment quickly banged out: "Greet—Y'r—Imper—Maj'sty," and suddenly a "Hurrah!," no longer a mechanical but a real, powerful, human "Hurrah"—a living one, produced by thousands of chests that had deeply breathed in the cool morning air. Suddenly into this human roar, new trumpet sounds of the anthem, now from the Semionovskii Regiment, seemed to fix themselves. Then the Izmailovskii, then the Chasseurs began to trumpet . . . The Grenadiers . . . and so on, and so on . . .

The ever-growing and all-flooding river of sounds was irrepressible.

Again and again swelled new shouts of thousands of men and singing of hundreds of trumpets, merging together, shading and complementing each other. These sounds, rolling in waves, filled the air with strange dissonant peals, calling forth a feeling of unreasoning excitement and a strange feeling in the spine, like little ants running along the skin.

The circuit of the front line of the Guards lasted an agonizingly long time, and from tense expectation one's nerves finally began to be on edge. You could not drop a single word or make a movement. But the wave of human roaring and music was rolling ever nearer.

The tsar, riding at a walk the whole time, had already passed the line of infantry and artillery, and turning in the direction of the cavalry, was already coming even with the Chevalier Guards, which shrilly took up the general howl of the troops. Now he had passed the Horse Guards. The peals of "Hurrah" were resounding right next to us, turning into an unbearable fortissimo, and suddenly I saw our old gray-mustached kettledrummer, seated on a stately white-legged horse in front of our band, raise his suede-trimmed drumstick over his head. A second—and the old drummer lowered his hand with a sudden energetic movement, touching the skin of the old cuirassier drums, embroidered with gold on a blue background and fastened to the saddle on both sides. In the ever-strengthening human howl there suddenly arose with new force and solemnity the martial sounds of our regimental trumpets, singing an anthem full of majesty.

One felt a disturbing lump in the throat, and the feeling of ants running along the spine was intensified.

Yes, what can one say: the old Russian anthem was well composed. What inspired Mr. Lvov, a little-known and not terribly gifted composer, I do not know, but in the stern and serene harmonies of that short chorale he managed to instill an enormous sense of strength and majesty.[4]

If there had not been this furious human howl of thousands, directed at a single man, if there had not been this marvelous solemn music that sang also of him, this person would not have produced such a tremendous impression on me. But I was a dreamer, and what is more, I had been extremely impressionable since childhood, and this whole situation in which a single man was being glorified and celebrated could not help but captivate me. My place was next to the standard. The tsar came even with me. And suddenly the standard, our proud cuirassier standard, before which civilians bowed obsequiously and old generals stood at strict attention, our standard with the image of the Heavenly Father on it, smoothly bent to the very hooves of the tsar's horse, almost touching the image of Christ's face to the muddy earth. Tears suddenly clouded my eyes. I looked at the tsar and for a brief fraction of a second his eyes met mine. I could barely recognize the tsar. This was not that cozy, rather short family man whom I had so often watched two years ago through the telescope lens. I could now only with difficulty recognize the tsar thanks to the completely new expression on his face—an expression that I could not guess the meaning of.

His grayish face was strange and calm, and it was impossible to tell whether it expressed concentration or a separation from everything earthly. At that moment it was a far from simple face . . . I was a terrible dreamer, and I seriously imagined that the gaze of those silent eyes wished to say: "Yes, you're right, I am more than a man. I am the most powerful person on earth. That is how it must be, and you know it."

In the regiment, heart-rending voices shouted "Hurrah!" The tsar rode slowly by, looking closely into the faces of the soldiers. Behind the tsar followed his enormous entourage, consisting of men covered with stars, decorations, and broad ribbons, scarlet and dark blue, thrown over their shoulders. They all rode by without looking at us—guarded, silent, serious, and stern. The giant Nikolai Nikolaevich rode by silently, wearing the Order of St. Andrew, along with adjutant generals, major generals of the suite, aides-de-camp, and foreign military attachés in strange uniforms.

The "hurrahs" and the music rolled over to the Cossack Brigade and further into the Second Division. The regiments as before seemed in their deadly immobility to be brightly colored wooden parallelograms, and from this tense immobility of thousands of men it was hard to believe that it was they who had produced the chaos of howls and trumpet sounds. One imagined that the whole hubbub had been torn out of the bowels of the very earth, as if all of suffering and ancient Rus had suddenly begun to howl, militant and autocratic.[5] I looked around and (I remember this clearly) saw the old gray-mustached drummer, glove removed, wiping his eyes wet with tears.

Almost all the parades in the imperial presence began just like this. They would end with a general ceremonial march, and the infantry always marched first to the sounds of the tsar's favorite old marches—"The Taking of Paris" and the old chasseurs' march—and the cavalry rode at various gaits past the tsar.

I had occasion to participate in several parades in the tsar's presence; I saw him many times: on maneuvers, at drills, and at great ceremonies. But it was that first big parade I attended in the summer of 1912 that evoked in me theretofore unknown sensations and a sharp turnabout in my thinking. I suddenly felt that I passionately loved the tsar. Why? I could not explain it to myself at all. It occurred to me that it would be a great happiness for me to someday become a member of his glittering entourage. To be always near the tsar, to accompany him, to serve him personally, to do his personal errands, even to serve his tsar's caprices—this would be both honorable and marvelous. That's it! A brilliant military-court career—that was my future, which without any "academies" would someday win me the respect of others, influence, power, and glory. To hell with the great academies and general staffs!

At that time I was only twenty years old and, as I said, a dreamer.

I realize that the description I have just given of the feelings of a young participant in an imperial parade may seem either incomprehensible or exaggerated to a present-day reader. I realize that such a description of events and attitudes may even grate upon the feelings of the contemporary reader, who may see the author himself in an unfavorable light—but what is to be done? In order to be completely honest, I can describe these long-past attitudes and events only in the way they were perceived by me at that distant time. As for the parade I have described, I can offer the proviso that it was of course not perceived identically by all participants, and if the soldiers all shouted "Hurrah" and trumpeted "God Save the Tsar," they did it not from the fullness of their hearts but because that was the long-established custom and the order of the commanders. But if some participants received from the imperial parade only an impression of long-established official procedure, others were shaken and agitated, thanks to the artificially created situation of universal tension and great solemnity. In any case I can say that at that time in my thoughts and dreams I was not a sole exception, and there were many young Guards officers who were dreaming similar dreams. As far as love for the tsar is concerned, among the young this was more a kind of infatuation than love. Just open Tolstoy's *War and Peace* and read the passage with the description of the imperial review in which young Nikolai Rostov participates.[6] Apparently young people in all eras were inclined to fall in love with their sovereigns.

Chapter Ten

Becoming an Officer

NOW THE LONG-AWAITED day of August 6, 1912, had finally come. This little day was awaited with impatient longing by hundreds of young Russians, counting the hours and minutes until that massive and firmly closed door—the door out "into the world"—would finally fly open before them.

It was morning. On a little green meadow not far from the Preobrazhenskii camp, which on that day was solemnly celebrating its regimental holiday, the graduating cadets formed up in a horseshoe without rifles, in the order of their schools. On the right flank were the pages, girded with broad white patent-leather belts; then the *pavlony,* the pupils of the Paul Infantry School, famous for its regimentation; then the cadets of the Michael Artillery School; and finally the lads of the Nicholas Cavalry School. We too gathered, old acquaintances, the cavalry volunteers, formed up on the left flank under the command of Captain Nevezhin. Everyone—the pages, the cadets, and the volunteers—had come wearing simple khaki soldier's blouses, soldier's caps, and peakless caps with modest soldier's cockades. All were wearing riding breeches made of durable government-issue soldier's cloth. But if at that moment you were to rummage in the pockets of those very riding breeches—in each one you would find a pair of gold or silver shoulder straps—brand-new, glittering, real officer's straps with little stars. In each pocket you would also find a brand-new officer's cockade. All the faces were festively glowing and a little agitated—after all, only about an hour remained . . . a half-hour . . .

When Mass was over in the camp, the tsar came to us on horseback, accompanied by a small entourage. He was riding a large dark-bay horse and was dressed in a Preobrazhenskii uniform.

For the last time in our lives as simple soldiers we were given the order "Attention!" At an unhurried pace the tsar rode along the line of cadets, looking seriously into their eyes, as was his custom, and saying in a calm and even voice, "Hello, pages! . . . Hello, Michael students . . . Hello, volunteers!" And to these greetings we answered as soldiers for the last time in our lives.

After finishing the greetings, the tsar rode out to the middle of the green grass plot and in the same calm voice addressed us all with a fairly long speech. He spoke unhurriedly, smoothly, very distinctly, in a slightly pompous style, but without particular expressiveness. The tsar spoke of the significance of commanders in the army, of the honorable calling and mission of a Russian officer—a defender of the fatherland. He indicated that an officer's relationship to his soldiers requires justice towards the latter. The tsar mentioned that all Russian military men without distinction should become not only good comrades to each other but brothers, and it seemed to me that he wanted to allude to the antagonism among the individual arms of the service and the units of the army. The tsar particularly emphasized the role of an officer during war in time of battle, which requires mutual assistance and support and seems to bring to the fore the principle "One for all—all for one!"

Holding my breath, I listened carefully to the sound of the tsar's voice, catching each intonation. The very fact that he was speaking for us, including for me, seemed a remarkable thing. It was a little strange that he spoke like everyone else, in the most ordinary human voice, since now, after the recent experience of the tsar's parade, I expected from the tsar the manifestation in all respects of something unusual and exceeding the bounds of the "human."

The tsar ended with the words: "I congratulate you on your promotion . . . Good-bye, gentlemen officers!" The last words he particularly emphasized, raising his voice. He had hardly finished when we all began to shout, "Hurrah!" How we shouted! How we strained our throats!

Our reincarnation had been realized. Just five minutes ago I was a soldier, but now! Was I really an officer? Was I really a person, a real person?!!

The tsar left us, to the accompaniment of a frenzied and this time most sincere "Hurrah."

Many of us were in a state of ecstasy, which Captain Nevezhin brought us out of. "Well, congratulations," he said, firmly shaking our hands, "now you may disperse." We all had silly, happy faces and silly, embarrassed smiles. The cadets broke ranks and right there, without any constraint, began to rip off one another's cadet shoulder straps and affix the officer's straps. I also followed their example.

The handsome Nicholas cadet Cherep-Spiridovich and the pages Polivanov and Goncharenko approached me. They were also entering our regiment. We congratulated each other.

"Let's go quickly and change clothes, and go all together to the officers' club to introduce ourselves."

Overtaking each other nearly at a trot, we rushed uphill to Krasnoe Selo.

My cousin Mishanchik, a little embarrassed, lagged behind. He hadn't gotten a grade good enough for the Guards. He didn't want to go into the

army and hadn't ordered a uniform for himself. On this very day he was to report to enlist as a reserve officer.

At home I was awaited by my officer's summer dress uniform, made
ready for me by Evmenchik.

It was strange to feel the light shoes on my feet instead of my accustomed line boots. The stiff starched collar, which long resisted my attempts to
fasten it, propped up my neck in an unaccustomed way. The cartridge pouch
that was hung on the cross-belt and passed through the broad Guards waist-
band hampered the movement of my arms, and I felt awkward. But I had to
hurry, they were waiting for us in the officers' club. On the occasion of today's
ceremony a gala dinner was being prepared for us there.

How would I be received there and how should I conduct myself before
all these completely unfamiliar people, in the presence of whom just yesterday I dared neither sit nor even stand at ease?

For the last time I looked at myself in the mirror, smiled foolishly, and
with a certain alarm in my heart set off for the regimental office, where we,
four newly fledged cornets, had agreed to meet.

We were led into the club by the regimental adjutant. The door into the
long, bright dining room flew open. Our eyes were struck by the long, long
table, set for a gala meal. Through the open door we could see a chorus of
trumpeters forming up on the balcony. The hall was packed with officers.

"And here are some newly fledged ones for you," the adjutant joked
loudly, pointing to us.

"A-a-h! O-o-oh! He-e-ey!" we could hear various voices from all sides.
Everyone there looked us over, smiling kindly.

"Hello, hello! Come in, come in!"

We looked for the regimental commander in order to officially "present
ourselves" to him. But the general was absent and had informed everyone that
he would be late and asked us to begin without him.

The eldest of the new officers, Cornet Polivanov, short and seemingly
on springs, stood gallantly to attention before the senior colonel and dashingly
reported in a ringing tenor:

"Mr. Colonel, I have the honor to report on the occasion of my promotion to officer and enlistment in the Life Guards of Her Majesty's Cuirassier
Regiment . . . Cornet Polivanov."

During this speech and the similar performances by each of us that followed, it suddenly became quiet as the grave in the dining room. Everyone
present instantly got rid of their smiles and, standing at attention, took on
stony expressions.

"Well, ceremonies for later, but let's eat now!" the colonel finally said
gaily.

At these words the hubbub in the room began again. We were grabbed by the arm and dragged to the balcony, to a special hors d'oeuvres table, covered with hot and cold snacks, shot glasses, and carafes holding vodkas and herb and fruit liqueurs.

"Well, young men, stand firm!" the tall, lanky Palitsyn boomed in his bass voice. "Let me see what good you are! Pour them a drink, pour them a drink! That's it . . . Wha-a-a-t? You refuse?!!! What a lack of discipline! Who trained you?"

"Young men, remember once and for all: Her Majesty's Cuirassiers / Of lots of liquor have no fear!" said Lieutenant Sokolov, twisting his cockroach whiskers and supervising the glasses.

None of the older men drank more than one or two glasses: to get drunk on vodka, as we already knew, was considered in the regiment to be very bad form. One drank vodka only in moderation, before dinner, to stimulate the appetite. But they set about getting us, the newly fledged officers, totally smashed—that was the custom on this day, and we obediently tossed back shot after shot.

"My God, what is this going to be like?" I thought with a certain horror. "This is only the preliminary snack . . . Dinner lies ahead! If only I can maintain decency!"

One of the officers mentioned my cousin Mishanchik. One way or another, he too had been promoted to officer today. True, an army officer, but still! They immediately dispatched someone to get Mishanchik. He arrived, embarrassed, wearing a soldier's blouse to which someone had managed to attach officer's shoulder straps.

The whole company finally took their places noisily at the table. The trumpeters on the balcony thundered a deafening march. We were served soup and along with it madeira, which was poured into crystal wineglasses of imposing size. We new officers were seated apart from each other and were not permitted to stick together. Next to each new officer sat an old experienced cornet who ordered the orderlies to pour the wine. My neighbor turned out to be Cornet Rozenberg, who from his place drank *Brüderschaft* with me and kept repeating:

"Trubetskoi, hold on to your style! Drink, but don't lose your style, that's the first rule in life. Remember that if you need to go to the john to barf—even that, from now on, you have to be able to do with style. Style above all, understand?"

My head was spinning. I had spots before my eyes. The white tablecloth merged with the white plates, the fanfares of the trumpeters merged with the loud talk and laughter of the dining men.

"My God, my God!" I prayed. "I beg you, let me not lose my style today!"

A roast was served, and orderlies in white blouses surrounded the diners, holding large trays with goblets of champagne and large bottles wrapped in blindingly white napkins.

Now it began!

"Trubetskoi, let's drink *Brüderschaft!*" cried someone across from me.

"Hey, Prince, let's drink 'na ty' [using the familiar 'thou' pronoun]," they shouted from left and right, from all sides.[1]

From everywhere, goblets full of foaming wine were held out to me. With each one I had to kiss and drink—drink up the full goblet "from the heart to the bottom." Behind my chair, as behind each of the new officers, an orderly stood rooted to the spot, holding a bottle, and no matter how often I emptied my goblet, it was always full.

Suddenly everyone noisily jumped up from their chairs and instantly fell silent.

"Trubetskoi, the commander of the regiment has come," Rozenberg whispered to me, "present yourself, take your cap in your hand, and watch that you don't lose your style!"

I looked around; as if in a fog, dozens of faces jumped before me. I felt an unbearable spasm in my throat. My legs seemed to be filled with lead. With difficulty my gaze finally found the round physiognomy of the general with a little broken nose.

Making a great exertion of self-control and gathering all my willpower into a bundle, I walked right toward him, trying to march smartly in a front-line style. I managed after all to stop in time and give my report to the general as prescribed. The general extended his hand to me with a good-natured smile and congratulated me. Someone's voice nearby said quietly:

"Well, at least this one knows how to drink."

"I'm very glad to hear it!" the smiling general responded. "I appreciate it when people know how to drink!"

What happened after that I don't know. In my memory remained only some large silver platters with toasted salted almonds, and the striking concentration on the face of cousin Mishanchik, who was beating a large drum with swinging blows.

What happened in our officers' club was happening that day in all the other regiments of the Guards cavalry without exception. Tradition required that on that day the new officers be gotten blind drunk, and that the old cornets, lieutenants, and staff captains drink *Brüderschaft* with them, because in a Guards regiment all officers had to address each other with the familiar form "thou," no matter what the difference in their ranks and ages. This too was required by ancient tradition.

How I got home—to this day I have no idea.

I woke up in my bed the next morning, ill and worn-out.

In the next room cousin Mishanchik was quietly moaning and groaning, calling on the name of God.

A great abstainer, yesterday he had gotten drunk for the first time in his life, and blind drunk at that.

"Mishanchik, have the fear of God!" I teased him, despite my own sufferings.

"Well, how did you like 'going out into the world' yesterday?" he teased me back.

In the entryway resounded the jingling of spurs, and quite unexpectedly the loud Lieutenant Urusov Senior came into the room, immediately plopping down on the sofa. "What do I see?" he cried, "a cornet still in bed? Wha-a-at? You're sick, you say? What nonsense! How you feel is of no concern or interest to anyone. Her Majesty's Cuirassiers / Of lots of liquor have no fear! Have you really not mastered that yet? And besides, my dear, you're talking nonsense, your head can't possibly hurt: in the officers' club they drink only Mumm *sec cordon vert* (a brand of dry French champagne with a green border on the neck of the bottle). A wonderful brand! Yes, yes . . . and one never ever gets a hangover from it. If in your life you only drink Mumm, and only *sec,* and only *cordon vert*—you'll always be fine. I beg of you only one thing: never drink *demi-sec* (semi-dry wine)! Believe me, Prince: any *demi-sec* is, in the first place, barf-inducing, and in the second place, it's the same kind of boorishness as detachable cuffs or traveling in second class. So: Mumm *sec cordon vert,* got it? Well, get up, we're going to the club. Over there I'll fix you up in an instant. By the way, there's news: I saw the commander today. You've been assigned to the Life Squadron, and it will be in the order of the day. Are you glad? What?—you say you'll miss the Third Squadron? But my dear, you can't stay in the same squadron where you served as a simple volunteer-pup! Just think of the soldiers' attitude toward you! Well, get up quickly. Hey, help the cornet get dressed!"

How I drank "na ty" with the lieutenant the day before and what we conversed about—I could not remember at all, but today he came to see me like an old friend, with an air as if he had known me all his life, and while I occupied myself with my toilette, he managed to give me a heap of most useful advice and recount tons of news.

At the club the lieutenant in fact cured me quickly, personally preparing something like slops out of several drinks and offering the appropriate hors d'oeuvre to go with it. Meanwhile yesterday's newly fledged officers arrived at the club—rumpled, flaccid, and visibly suffering. While Urusov Senior set about curing them, the senior Colonel von Schweder came in, prim and official as always. We jumped up, and the colonel quite unexpectedly invited all of us "young men" to follow him into the next room for a "little talk."

Eduard Nikolaevich von Schweder was a dry, well-built man of about forty years old, of medium height, with a well-bred "nobleman's" face. His black hair was always sleeked down in an irreproachable pomaded English part. The black bristles of his mustache were trimmed to a length of precisely 0.1 millimeter.[2] His energetic jutting chin was always freshly shaved, and his lower lip protruded a bit peevishly. His nose was large and aquiline, and from below his black eyebrows his shining dark-brown eyes leaped out—angry, stern, official. The colonel spoke in a quiet, low baritone, a bit nasally. At the mere sight of this always smart colonel one involuntarily wished to smarten oneself up, and every officer upon meeting him involuntarily looked himself over.

"Close the door," Eduard Nikolaevich said sternly, as soon as we had followed him into the adjoining room; the colonel did not invite us to sit down and he himself did not sit. He looked at us so coldly and impressively that we four newly fledged officers involuntarily formed up in a row, at attention.

"Gentlemen," he said quietly, "the cuirassier regiment did you a great honor by accepting you as officers in their midst. Yesterday you put on the officer's shoulder straps of the cuirassier regiment. I—your senior colonel—demand of you that—no matter where you are—you never forget that on your shoulders are the officer's insignia of our regiment. These shoulder straps commit you . . . Yes, these shoulder straps commit everyone who has the honor of wearing them to worthy acts, decency, and decorum. Remember that in the eyes of society and the world, each unbecoming act or even gesture you perform will be ascribed not so much to you personally as to the whole regiment, because a regiment, in accepting an officer into its midst, thereby guarantees his decency and good breeding. An officer who does not know how to protect his dignity and the dignity of the regiment, an officer who does not know how to conduct himself, will not be tolerated in the regiment. Now—as for monetary matters (I am speaking to you about this for the first and *I hope* the last time). In this regard I demand of you the utmost scrupulousness. The regiment demands of its officers that they live in a decent fashion, but . . . if you do not have the means for this, do your best to leave the regiment as soon as possible. Living beyond your means, unpaid bills, debts, and promissory notes—all this finally leads an officer to committing unbecoming, even dishonorable acts. Remember this and draw the appropriate conclusions. This is clear . . . But I personally warn you: at the very first unbecoming or indecent act—I give you my word of honor—you will have to leave the regiment within twenty-four hours . . . Yes, gentlemen, the regiment will not tol-er-ate this and will not forgive anyone, no matter who he is and no matter what his connections.

"I demand that you observe the strictest discipline while on duty, and in the club I demand that you pay respect to every senior comrade, even if he is only one year senior to you or even in the same year as you."

The colonel gave a brief, official bow as a sign that the talk was ended. We clinked our spurs and hastily bowled out of the room. The colonel knew how to make an impression and how to be most unpleasant.

Very soon after this talk, namely at the very first General Assembly of the regimental officers, we ascertained that Eduard Nikolaevich was not exaggerating and that he never wagged his tongue for nothing. But I will speak of that meeting later.

So, after hearing out the edifying speech of our senior colonel, I devoted the whole morning to official visits to my senior comrades; for this purpose I again donned parade dress. The soldiers of our regiment saluted me when they met me, standing dashingly to attention, and "devoured me with their eyes." I will not hide the fact that on that day this made me somehow ashamed and a bit embarrassed, especially when I met soldiers from the Third Squadron. Each soldier in the regiment knew me well—the former volunteer and guard to the standard, and this was somewhat unpleasant for me.

Towards evening I wished to tear myself out of the regiment in order to be free and to feel like a real person. I now wanted to show myself to unknown people and see what impression I would make on them in my new role as a complete person. I decided to take a ride to St. Petersburg. For this I no longer had to ask either permission or the humiliating leave-pass.

Now the cabby is driving me up to the Krasnoe Selo railroad station. But how much should I pay him? I know: a decent Guards officer never bargains when he hires a cabby. He doesn't ask "how much," but silently gets out his wallet and sticks money in the cabby's hand without looking. But how much? Should I give him a fifty-kopeck piece? No, I should probably give him a ruble. But what if the cabby suddenly says, "You're stiffing me, master." How ashamed I would be! I would be degrading myself, my dignity as an officer, my regiment . . . So after getting out my wallet, I carelessly thrust a whole three-ruble note into the driver's hand. I don't look back and hurriedly run up the steps of the portico, as a respectful "Very, very grateful, Y'r Radyunce," resounds behind me.

I resolutely throw open the door leading to a place that was forbidden to me only yesterday morning—the waiting room for first and second class. A slow-moving, portly lieutenant general in a gray greatcoat with a red lining and riding breeches with broad stripes down the legs comes toward me. At such a sight, the usual reflex is instantly engendered in my brain, imperiously ordering me to stop, clink my spurs, and stand smartly to attention like a soldier, fixing my eyes right on the general's eyes. I have only to take one more step and . . .

"Oh, hell, what am I doing?!!!" I suddenly catch myself at the last moment. And so, instead of standing to attention, I just walk past the general and touch my hand to the peak of my Fokin service cap, trying to lend the gesture an elegant air of indifference . . . but in my breast there is a joyful bubbling.

There are a lot of people on the platform. I walk slowly back and forth. Ding—I hear the sound of distinctly clinking spurs. I look around—some artillery volunteer, at attention, is saluting me. The poor man doesn't even suspect that just yesterday morning I was the same sort of nonentity as he is. But today . . . Today I have no conscience and I carelessly wave him away, barely raising two fingers to my cap and behaving as if I long ago grew tired of these marks of respect.

Now a completely unfamiliar lieutenant, a horse grenadier, coming even with me, to my amazement walks right up to me and silently extends his hand. Mechanically I reciprocate. We greet each other—and only now do I remember that according to tradition all officers of the Guards greet each other upon meeting with a handshake, regardless of whether they know each other or not. A beautiful tradition that signifies comradeship and the mutual respect of the regiments.

At every step a new sensation awaits me. Just yesterday morning I did not dare to smoke in public, but now I reach in my pocket and light up a papirosa with an independent air, not constrained by anyone's presence.

The train approaches. I climb unhurriedly into the dark-blue first-class car and sprawl on the velvet settee. Gods, how unused I have gotten to a soft-seated train-car! In front of me is an elderly civilian gentleman, and I look him over a bit contemptuously, with the superior air of a Guards officer. In fact, I feel that I deeply despise my neighbor's soft felt hat, his civilian manners, and his entire civilian worldview, although he remains silent. The first stop is the "Racetrack" platform. Into our compartment comes a beautiful and elegant young lady. From the very first glance I determine that she is from high society; it is evident both in her special self-assurance and in the elegant, exquisite taste with which she is dressed. In her face and her whole figure there is something familiar . . . But I know her very well! It's Ella Pushchina, née Countess Kleinmikhel, formerly one of our Moscow young ladies, with whom I used to dance at children's balls in Moscow.[3] Three years ago she married the rich Petersburger Pushchin, a captain of the Horse Guards, and I remember her brilliant wedding, which I attended along with many other guests. How she had changed since then. What a self-assured, somewhat standoffish air she had taken on, and what a new expression of calm and a certain fatigue there was on her beautiful face.

"Don't you recognize me?" I ask.

Pushchina looks at me with amazement for a minute.

"Oh, yes, now I recognize you. Just imagine, I didn't even know you'd become a cuirassier. How strange that we didn't meet in St. Petersburg all this time! Don't you go out anywhere?"

I want to tell her of my happiness and the fact that I became an officer just yesterday, but for some reason I restrain myself. It's more pleasant for me if people think that I came out into the world long ago. With an ingenuity that amazes me I explain to Pushchina that I have not gone out into society for a whole year because of the mourning period for my uncle Piotr Trubetskoi. We recall our mutual acquaintances in old lady Moscow, of whom we speak with a barely perceptible tinge of contempt. Pushchina has heard rumors of my betrothal to Princess Golitsyna. She congratulates me. With enormous satisfaction I ascertain that this young lady of high society is conversing with me in a new way. She is taking me seriously. In her eyes I now have a position and a certain specific gravity. Pushchina pays absolutely no attention to our neighbor in the compartment, the elderly gentleman. For her he is an empty spot, a nothing, while I am a real person! God, how good it is and how new!

I am terribly glad to see Pushchina. She is the first of my former acquaintances on whom I have tried out the efficacy of the wondrous metamorphosis I have undergone.

And now I am in the capital. I'm a twenty-year-old child. Like a happy little boy, I want to laugh and jump for joy, but today I am playing at being an adult, and the game is fascinating and affords me untold pleasure. But instead of smiling, I affect an air of tired indifference. In all my movements I restrain myself. I try to copy precisely the most mannered and refined Guards fops I know. I copy their walk, the slightly contemptuous expression of their faces, in a word, all their ways—and I feel that I am extremely successful at it. In any case, the inhabitants of the capital take me seriously. None of them smiles, looking at me. No one guesses that in essence I have only existed in the world for a single little day. My perfectly cut Nordenström clothes and Fokin cap are my faithful allies. They help me achieve new effects, and I never tire of trying out my new possibilities.

Now on the broad sidewalk of Nevskii Avenue, some young civilians in student caps come toward me. They walk with the free-and-easy civilian step of carefree young students. As I come even with them I assume the haughty air of a person who is used to his own superiority; I walk so erectly, proudly, and confidently, that the civilian youths instinctively make way for me and move aside so as not to brush up against me.

Smart capital-city policemen in white gloves take on a respectful expression at the sight of me and salute as firmly as if they saw before them an important dignitary.

In the eyes of the women I meet I also read something new for me today. By their glances I feel that they are attracted to me and that I'm making an impression. Some young ladies cast glances at me that last two or three seconds longer than is customary for noting the ordinary passerby, and in the glances of some ladies today I read a certain invitation and desire. I am enraptured by myself and so self-satisfied that at times I'm even ashamed of myself.

I of course end the day in a place that for a year I would not even have dared to think of entering. I end this day at "The Bear," the famous, fashionable St. Petersburg restaurant. Over dinner I wearily order Mumm *sec cordon vert* and display the true style of a decent Guards officer, drinking barely one glass of the entire bottle of expensive wine I've been served.

To sum up this marvelous day, I ascertain that everyone I met today without exception behaved in a new way towards me. This new thing accompanied me today at every step, and I read it in the eyes of the train conductor as well as in the eyes of the taxi driver, the cabby, the policeman, the restaurant waiter, the modest young lady, and the elegant lady of the capital.

On this day I suddenly felt a certain firm foundation beneath me.

On this day I saw myself with unusual clarity as a brilliant aide-de-camp, setting the tone for the Guards. I saw myself as a young major general, caracoling on my horse in the sumptuous entourage of the tsar, I saw myself already as an adjutant general respected by all, carrying out the crucial personal commissions of the tsar himself. I imagined that I was a court commandant, a minister of the tsar's court . . . the devil knows what I imagined on that remarkable day!

There was only one thing I didn't see. I didn't see at all the specter of the coming revolution—that most grandiose power that in one day destroyed all my ambitious plans and transformed me into a déclassé nothing.

Chapter Eleven

The Mores of the Regiment

AFTER PROMOTION, ALL junior cornets were usually given a twenty-eight-day leave by the regiment. But I decided not to use my leave now but to postpone it until my wedding, which was set for November.

The question of my wedding was not entirely simple. Officers did not have the right to enter into marriage before a certain age, and since I had not yet attained that age, I had to immediately submit a petition "addressed to the Emperor" asking for permission to get married. In a meticulous Guards regiment the matter was, however, not confined to this, and in each separate case the question of a comrade's marriage was decided at a General Assembly of the officers. A Guards officer could not get married to either a peasant woman or a woman of the lower middle class or even a rich merchant's daughter, no matter her upbringing, without being obliged to leave the regiment. A Guards officer could marry only a woman of noble birth, and before allowing a comrade to enter into legal matrimony, the society of officers of the regiment made inquiries about the fiancée herself as well as her conduct, reputation, and family.

I will not conceal that it was strange and even somewhat insulting to my self-respect to ask my new comrades for their consent to my marriage with a girl whom I considered to be the height of propriety and every perfection, but there was no way I could avoid it. Every officer had to reckon strictly with the established tradition and with the customs of the Guards; otherwise he would immediately be noisily "chucked out" of the regiment. But the senior officers hastened to assure me that in the present case no one could possibly have any doubts, and that the matter would amount merely to the observance of an established formality. So, having hardly managed to don my cornet's shoulder straps, I was plunged into a new activity as commander of the third platoon of the Life Squadron, that is, the first squadron, still termed in the official language of regimental orders "Her Majesty's Squadron."

This squadron was commanded by the senior captain of the regiment, Mikhail Fiodorovich Danilov, whom I had occasion to mention earlier. He was a sober, composed, and tactful officer. A typical careerist and subtle intriguer, he was far from stupid and knew how to obtain the respect of the high command and acquire authority in their eyes. He was an officer of the Life Squadron throughout his entire career. He loved the squadron, and despite his careerism, he was a true cuirassier patriot who had the regiment's interests at heart.

The senior officer in the Life Squadron at that time was Staff Captain Baron F. N. Taube, already familiar to the reader. Both these officers from the very first days behaved quite well towards me, like real senior comrades. But Danilov, who was many years older than me, was so respectable that I could not become close with him, nor with Baron Taube, with whom I turned out to have little in common, because it seemed that in essence the baron was interested only in women. But with Cornets Arshinevskii and Kliupfel (especially the latter) I very soon became close friends, and thanks to this I did not feel lonely in the Life Squadron.

The question of my relationship with the soldiers disturbed me a little in my first days. There were several men in the Life Squadron who had taken the training course with me in the regimental training detachment. They were witnesses to all Palitsyn's scoffing at the volunteers. While in the training detachment, both soldiers and volunteers were in the same position as simple line soldiers, and we confided our service misfortunes to each other. Now I had become a commander to these men, whom they were obliged to glorify with the epithet "Your Radiance." I was afraid I would not have the necessary authority in their eyes. And what if at the very first, circumstances forced me to urge them on, cuss them out like hell, or subject them to punishment?

All this embarrassed me greatly, and I cannot conceal that my first appearance before my third platoon was very agitating for me. I had to overcome a feeling of great embarrassment in order to greet my men like a commanding officer. Fortunately, everything came off much more simply and naturally than I had imagined, and if I was able to display a certain tact towards my subordinates, they met me in a no less tactful way, and thanks to this, in three or four days I was completely at home in my role as a commander.

At the time of my promotion the maneuvers near Krasnoe were in full swing. I was lucky from the very first days. Commanding an officers' mounted patrol, I had an opportunity to distinguish myself and attract the attention of the high command. Pure accident helped me to supply our detachment with valuable information about the strength and movements of the main forces of "the enemy." I repeat: this happened by accident, but it already seemed to me as if it was my innate passion for hunting, that is, for tracking beasts, that helped me in this affair.

Thanks to my early successes, our regimental commander General Arapov paid particular attention to me and from the very first days began to treat me with great favor. I began to notice that the general was more favorably disposed towards me than towards other young cornets. Frankly speaking, I do not think the reason for this was only the capabilities I had displayed, because many of my comrades proved themselves to be excellent workers on maneuvers. The reason for General Arapov's favorable disposition toward me, it seems to me, was something else. The fact is that at the very first maneuver, I had occasion to find favor with the famous Guards General Petrovo-Solovovo. This general was distantly related to our family and had once been friendly with my mother and my late father.[1] I had known him since childhood, when he was still an officer of the Life Hussars. On holidays he would come to Moscow and always came to our family's Christmas party. He loved to spoil us children, running around with us and having snowball fights. He was a lively and cheerful man. We children called him "Black Uncle Boria." In his day Petrovo-Solovovo commanded the fashionable Life Hussars regiment, was very popular in the Guards cavalry, and also enjoyed the personal favor of Grand Duke Nikolai Nikolaevich himself. He was a rich, independent, and good-natured man.

When I reported to Petrovo-Solovovo on maneuvers, he was surrounded by generals who were subordinate to him that day, including our regimental commander. Petrovo-Solovovo immediately recognized me, as soon as I identified myself, and was glad to see me in a very unaffected way. Abandoning his serious conversations with the generals, he began to ask me about the health of my mother and aunts, asking me to send his regards to my home. The general recalled our merry childhood Christmas parties with a happy smile. I also was very happy to see my "black uncle," who vividly reminded me of my childhood. I unaffectedly called him "Uncle Boria," as a relative, and spent about five minutes chatting with him without any constraint, as with an equal.

I am ashamed to say that this insignificant episode, witnessed by our regimental commander, did not fail to influence the latter's attitude towards me. General Arapov was above all a general attached to the tsar's suite, and frequent contact with the court had accustomed him to single out people with good connections. The unaffectedness and spontaneity with which I got into conversation with my good-natured "Uncle Boria," who was then in favor with the all-powerful Nikolai Nikolaevich, of course could attract the attention of General Arapov, who by court habit could draw the appropriate conclusion, and this conclusion was of course to my advantage. All this, added to my famous name and my coming marriage to a titled fiancée, could only add to my luster.

One way or another, my service became easy and pleasant from the very first. But I would like to think that in the final analysis Arapov felt a sincere sympathy for me, because to the end he treated me with a fatherly warmth.

From the very first I accumulated many new impressions. But I was perhaps most impressed by my first General Assembly of the officers, which was called several days after my promotion. This meeting has been well preserved in my memory. It was a matter of regimental honor, and the regimental commander did not attend such meetings. The regimental commander, although he wore our cuirassiers' uniform, since he was a former chevalier guard, that is, someone from another regiment, was not considered a native blue cuirassier. For this reason, tradition officially did not permit him to participate in the discussion of intimate and delicate regimental questions concerning the tight officers' corporation of the regiment. Moreover, the commander was obliged to reckon with the decisions of the General Assemblies, even if they went against his personal desires. Such was the situation in the Guards. The regimental commander himself could appoint and call General Assemblies under his chairmanship, but only to discuss service and organizational matters, and also for "raking over the coals." But officially, it was as if matters of honor did not concern him at all.

The regimental military civil servants, like the bandmaster, armorer, and doctors, also were not allowed to attend these meetings. Although they bore officer's arms, they had civilian ranks and wore civil servant's cockades on their caps and narrow civil servant's shoulder straps. No one considered them to be cuirassiers, and in the officers' club they could only have meals and play billiards. They were considered unworthy to discuss intimate regimental questions, since the body of officers in general had a bit of a patronizing attitude towards them.

The General Assembly I have mentioned took place in an atmosphere of secrecy. The doors of the hall were carefully locked. The club servants were sent away. No outsider was to know what was to be spoken about at the meeting. The presiding senior Colonel von Schweder had a particularly official and somewhat mysterious air. During the whole meeting only he spoke, and he spoke in an undertone. Everyone present sat in deep silence.

As his first duty, von Schweder informed us of the shameful action of our Cornet Z——. This cornet lived beyond his means and got into debt. The frivolous young man, in order to put off having to pay his creditors and to extract yet more money from them, convinced them that he was the nephew and heir of our rich regimental commander, who supposedly had promised to help him out with money. All of this was a pure fiction. The carefree cornet in his naiveté did not suppose that finally one fine day his creditors would appeal to the general himself to pay the debts of his "nephew." This happened before the cornet could get hold of the money he needed to pay his debts.

"Gentlemen," Eduard Nikolaevich quietly addressed us with flashing eyes, "this shameful action by Cornet Z—— not only sullies him, it sullies the entire community of officers of the regiment, who admitted into their midst a man capable of deception for the sake of money . . . The senior officers consider that there is no more place for Cornet Z—— in our regiment, and for this reason we are proposing to him that within three days he report for transfer to the reserve or to an army regiment. I hope no one objects?"

Deathly silence was our answer.

"Thank you." The colonel bowed coldly and moved to the second question, which amazed me by its unusual nature:

"Gentlemen," the colonel began again, lowering his voice even more, "it has come to our attention that a few days ago one of our officers, namely Lieutenant Khan Erivanskii, while in St. Petersburg, permitted himself to appear in a theater loge in a small company, among whom was included a certain lady you know of. A lady who at one time cast a shadow on our regiment through her actions, and who (as you all well know) incurred for the regiment the displeasure of our most august patroness—our adored empress. It would seem that this alone would be enough for our officers to break off all relations once and for all with this personage who has blackened the regiment. To my deep regret, we nonetheless have an officer who has not wished to understand this! The appearance of Khan Erivanskii next to this lady in a public place can be regarded as a disgraceful demonstration, as a kind of protest against the court—an action that is by no means worthy of a cuirassier! Gentlemen, there are things we have no right to forgive, and the senior officers consider that from this day there is no place for Lieutenant Khan Erivanskii in the cuirassier regiment. The lieutenant is asked to report for transfer to the reserves within twenty-four hours."

Everyone sat as if struck by lightning. By the faces of a few of the officers, whose heads were lowered, one could conclude that they were experiencing unpleasant moments. There was a pause.

"I hope no one objects?" Eduard Nikolaevich asked, looking over all present with angry eyes.

Silence.

"Thank you!" the colonel bowed and, after a pause, continued,

"The incident with Lieutenant Khan Erivanskii compels me to warn you again, that if any of you contrary to expectation has not by now broken off acquaintance with this personage—that he do so with-out de-lay. If it comes to my attention that any of our officers continues to bow to this lady upon meeting her, I warn you: this officer will instantly meet the fate of Lieutenant Khan Erivanskii. You do not have the right to associate with her, or greet her, or even utter her name in public. So, gentlemen, I consider the General Assembly ended."

The colonel bowed and solemnly left the hall.[2]

"I don't understand a thing," I said quietly to the officer sitting next to me. "Who is this ill-starred woman whom we are forbidden to know?"

"Countess Brasova," my neighbor quietly whispered in my ear.

The story of Countess Brasova was the following.[3] For several years the former heir to the Russian throne and younger brother of the tsar, Grand Duke Mikhail Aleksandrovich, served in our regiment and commanded our Life Squadron. For the regiment this was of course very flattering, because thanks to this circumstance the regiment acquired a prominent position in the Guards. Grand Duke Mikhail riveted to the regiment the attention of his mother, the old Empress Mariia Fiodorovna, who from the moment of her son's joining the cuirassiers began to show particular goodwill to our regiment. The Blue Cuirassiers came into favor, acquired the reputation of a fashionable Guards regiment, and at the court the cuirassiers began to be jokingly called *"Les petits bleus de Sa Majesté"* ("the little blue boys of Her Majesty").

Everything went well, until one fine day the grand duke conceived a strong love for the wife of one of our officers, namely the wife of a certain Lieutenant V. It so happened that Madame V. in her turn also fell deeply in love with the grand duke. They began an affair.

Despite the fact that the grand duke was a very shy man and behaved very modestly, the rumor of his affair spread and was talked about in court circles and in high society in general.

From my senior comrades I heard that General Bernov, who commanded the regiment at that time, in his thoughtlessness fostered this affair himself and apparently even brought the lovers together in order to please the grand duke. In this respect Bernov acted directly against good Guards tradition, which by no means permitted affairs between ladies of the regiment and their husbands' comrades. The principle of comradeship was cultivated to such an extent in the regiment that it was considered extremely reprehensible for any Guards officer to steal the wife of a regimental comrade. Such affairs, if they did not end in a duel, in any case entailed the inevitable departure from the regiment of the officer who made advances to his comrade's wife.

Meanwhile the rumor about the relationship between Mikhail Aleksandrovich and Madame V. reached the empress herself. True to the family ordinances of the late Tsar Alexander III, who in his personal life adhered to the strictest and most unshakable family foundations, the empress demanded of her son an immediate break with Madame V. But the grand duke was so captivated by the lady of his heart that he went against the will of his mother. In view of the fact that the husband of Madame V. had a rather passive attitude towards the whole business and seemed not to cherish any particular feelings for his wife, the grand duke quickly succeeded in obtaining a divorce for Madame V. and entered into a morganatic marriage with her, legitimized by a church ceremony. As compensation the grand duke offered Lieutenant V. a prominent position in the court administrative office, a position that the lieutenant hastened to accept, immediately leaving the cuirassier regiment.

In view of the fact that grand dukes were supposed to marry exclusively "princesses of the blood" and persons belonging to one or another ruling house, his marriage to Madame V. of course took on the dimensions of a noisy court scandal, which distressed the old empress very much.

The grand duke immediately had to leave our regiment, and at the court, streams of mud flowed onto his unfortunate wife. She was accused of intentionally enticing and seducing a modest, inexperienced, and moral grand duke. To please the old empress, the poor lady was awarded the titles of an intriguer and debauchee, although her only fault consisted of falling in love with the grand duke. All society turned away from her. The tsar himself was very displeased by the misdemeanor of his younger brother, who as a kind of punishment was sent to the provincial town of Oriol, where he had to accept the command of the humble Chernigov Hussar Regiment in the Seventeenth Army.

But the matter was closed: one way or another, Madame V. was the legal spouse of the grand duke. As a morganatic spouse, however, not all the rights of her highly placed husband extended to her and her children. She was born a "mere mortal" and thus did not have the right to take either the title or the name of her husband. In such cases a provision was usually made to grant the morganatic spouses of highly placed personages the title of countess or princess. Some new last name was invented for them, and in this way the former humble Madame V. was transformed one fine day into Countess Brasova, a name taken from the name of a great estate belonging to Grand Duke Mikhail Aleksandrovich.

This whole story took place about three years before my joining the regiment, but in my time my senior comrades still felt it keenly, especially now, in 1912, when the grand duke had returned from Oriol to St. Petersburg, bringing his wife.

The tsar had finally had mercy on his younger brother, and after two years of "exile" the grand duke was offered the command of the Chevalier Guards Regiment at the beginning of 1912.

At that time I occasionally visited in the palace one of my elderly relatives, Ozerova, who was at the court of the old empress. From her I heard that when Mikhail Aleksandrovich was offered the Chevalier Guards, the old empress hoped her son would not drag his wife along with him to the capital. A transparent hint to this effect was even made to the grand duke. But when the grand duke, contrary to the hopes of his mother, all the same turned up in the capital together with his wife, the minister of the court, old Count Frederiks, was authorized to convey to the grand duke that he should content himself with a standard commander's apartment in the Chevalier Guards Regiment and should not move into the palace to live. Mikhail Aleksandrovich reacted to this very simply, and without grumbling occupied a modest official apartment that was at the disposal of the regiment.

He and especially his wife had many bitter experiences in St. Petersburg. As before, all of society turned away from Countess Brasova. To please the court, no one wished either to know or to receive her. Especially painful for Mikhail Aleksandrovich was the attitude of his subordinate Chevalier Guards officers: not one of them paid a visit to his wife and not one of the guardsmen bowed to her—even as the wife of the regimental commander. It was not for nothing that the Chevalier Guards were considered the most court-oriented regiment in the Guards, or that their patroness was also Empress Mariia Fiodorovna.

Of course, our cuirassier regiment had nothing to do with this whole affair that had caused such a fuss. But the somewhat ambiguous conduct of General Bernov, and especially Lieutenant V., who could not or did not wish to protect his wife from the advances of an imperial personage, incurred the displeasure of the empress, a displeasure that extended to our whole regiment.

Now no one at the old court gave us the affectionate nickname "*Les petits bleus de Sa Majesté.*" On the contrary, wrinkled old court ladies now spoke of us, shaking their gray heads: "Look how they turned out to be, those Blue Cuirassiers and their ladies!"

This displeasure with the regiment in high places was intensified thanks to yet another love affair that unfolded almost in parallel with the one I have just described.

This was the affair between the tsar's younger sister, Grand Duchess Olga Aleksandrovna, and again one of our cuirassier officers, Lieutenant Kulikovskii.[4] Both Mikhail Aleksandrovich and Olga Aleksandrovna loved Gatchina because of their childhood memories, since the late Alexander III in the last years of his life was in the habit of living with his family for long periods in the Gatchina Palace. When Mikhail Aleksandrovich joined our regiment, his sister Olga naturally visited him frequently in Gatchina. Mikhail Aleksandrovich behaved very unaffectedly, and our cuirassier officers were constantly present in his intimate company.

The husband of Olga Aleksandrovna, Prince Oldenburgskii, a sickly man, was indifferent to his spouse, and therefore there was nothing unnatural in the fact that one fine day the grand duchess felt a strong attraction to the handsome and well-built Kulikovskii, whom she often saw together with her brother and who seemed to her to be an interesting and worthy man in all respects.

Kulikovskii did not fail to respond in kind to the awakening feelings of the tsar's sister, and since the latter, despite her high rank and position, conducted herself too freely and independently, their love affair was very soon being talked about in society. Olga Aleksandrovna began to appear more and more frequently in Gatchina, where she had the habit of behaving like an "ordinary mortal," avoiding all etiquette and pomp. One could often meet her riding around the streets of Gatchina in a simple cab, accompanied by Kulikovskii. One encountered them in secluded corners of the Gatchina park, strolling arm in arm like an ordinary, vulgar couple in love.

If General Bernov, who commanded the regiment at that time, had possessed sufficient tact and intelligence, he would perhaps in his capacity as a general of the suite have pointed out to Kulikovskii the impermissibility of such casual relations with the sister of the tsar, at least in full view of the broad public, because any advertising of such relations with the grand duchess could only compromise her. But the dim general not only did not do this, he, as they say, was sincerely glad about his officer's success, because in his opinion, this success was only to the regiment's advantage, since it would make it more fashionable. The conduct of Olga Aleksandrovna and Kulikovskii led only to the fact that their affair began to be openly talked about in society. Again a court scandal—a scandal in which again the name of our cuirassier regiment was mentioned! And when all this came to the notice of the old empress, she again became angry and distressed.

The story with Kulikovskii, especially combined with Mikhail Aleksandrovich's affair, decisively embittered Mariia Fiodorovna against our regiment, and after that she ceased her former intimate and "gracious" visits to the regimental infirmary, church, and barracks, to the great chagrin of all the senior officers, who did not feel themselves to be at all at fault and who dreamed of restoring their former kind relations with our patroness. But during my whole time in the regiment, the empress limited herself to visiting our regimental drill review and to sending an official congratulatory telegram on the day of our regimental holiday. She was much more gracious to the Chevalier Guards.

As for the fate of Lieutenant Kulikovskii—so as not to be parted from the grand duchess, with her assistance he easily arranged to become the personal adjutant to her husband, Prince Oldenburgskii. This adroit man with the figure of the god Apollo, although he removed the uniform of the regiment, exchanging it for one of an adjutant general, continued to be listed among the regiment's officers, as was done for all personal adjutants to the imperial family. He did not lose contact with the regiment, and in my time he had a certain influence over our youth, affiliating himself with the party of the athletes von Exe and Pleshkov, and taking part in regimental intrigues. Fate had pity on Grand Duchess Olga Aleksandrovna. She and her sister Kseniia succeeded in emigrating after the Revolution, and Olga Aleksandrovna finally joined in legal marriage with Kulikovskii abroad. They say that Olga managed to inherit part of the small capital that was once transferred on some occasion, by order of her brother, from Russia to a bank in England.

In her day Olga Aleksandrovna was a fairly good artist, and I have heard that her talent for painting was of some material assistance to her in emigration. Among the bourgeois collectors and amateurs of curiosities, there were some who were interested in owning a painting with the autograph of the last Russian emperor's sister.

I well remember my first encounter with this grand duchess. It was in the first year after my promotion.

I remember I was awaiting the arrival from St. Petersburg of a female relative, and for this reason I was strolling under the glass vault of the Gatchina railroad station, waiting for the train. Among the large crowd on the platform, there was one rather short lady who seemed to be about thirty years old. She had a face that was not pretty but lively, and seemed familiar to me. She was wearing a simple dark short jacket and a modest little black cap. But the appearance of this lady was so ordinary that I noticed her only when I saw that the director of the station had made her a low and obsequious bow, and the station policeman respectfully saluted her. Only then did I guess that I saw before me Grand Duchess Olga Aleksandrovna, whom I had had occasion to see earlier. I felt very awkward and ashamed, since I had twice passed by her without saluting, and she had been looking at me. On my part this was a big gaffe—a Guards officer should know well by sight the members of the ruling house and should salute them, standing at attention. To correct my mistake now was awkward, and therefore I retreated to the farthest corner of the platform, so as not to encounter the grand duchess any more and to be as far as possible from her. Suddenly I saw three of my senior comrades come out onto the platform. They were already acquainted with the grand duchess, and I saw her summon them. After about two minutes I noticed that she was pointing me out to my comrades, and to my embarrassment one of them came up to me and said: "Grand Duchess Olga Aleksandrovna has taken an interest in you and would like for you to be introduced to her. Let's go!" My comrade immediately introduced me. Taking off my cap, I took the hand of the grand duchess and, bending respectfully, I raised it to my lips, as was required by custom. Unexpectedly for me, at the moment when I unclasped my fingers in order to release the grand duchess's hand, the latter quietly squeezed my fingers in hers, and without letting go of my hand, began to converse gaily with my comrades, not looking at me. I quietly removed my hand. The grand duchess seized it even more firmly and began to swing it from side to side, continuing to chatter. I was in a most foolish position. Etiquette did not permit me to free myself in some more energetic way from the hand of an imperial personage, and I felt that I was turning bright red, both for myself and a bit for Olga Aleksandrovna, since I realized that a grand duchess was not supposed to behave in so free and easy a manner in view of a crowd that was watching us with curiosity. I felt that in this behavior of Olga Aleksandrovna there was something vaguely improper and provocative, but she continued to squeeze and wring my hand ever more strongly, causing me utter embarrassment. This went on for about three minutes, which seemed to me to be an eternity, and I don't know how much longer it would have continued, if the approaching train had not to my good fortune appeared; its arrival put an end to the whole scene. Letting go of my hand, Olga Aleksandrovna gaily and a bit provocatively smiled and said a few insignificant words to me, to which I replied calmly and respectfully, quickly getting control of myself.

I remember that after this encounter I tried for a long time to find out the significance of the grand duchess's strange behavior, but I never succeeded. Did she wish by this action to punish me for indifferently walking by her without saluting, or did she simply have a whim to amuse herself by embarrassing a young, inexperienced cornet to the point of tears? Was it a simple manifestation of purely feminine coquetry on her part? I don't know. I know only that I was struck and somewhat disappointed, because up to that time I . . .

[*The manuscript breaks off at this point.*]

Notes

INTRODUCTION

1. See B. G. Berg, "Kniaz'ia Trubetskie, Kievskaia vetv'," *Novik* 3 (1941): 22–25; and S. G. Troubetzkoï, *Les Princes Troubetzkoï* (Labelle, Quebec: Troubetzkoï, 1976).

2. The Russian titles "prince" and "princess" are the most widespread titles of the Russian nobility and do not indicate that the bearers are members of the imperial family (Vladimir Trubetskoi was also a prince). Members of the imperial family are given the titles "grand prince" and "grand princess," conventionally translated as "grand duke" and "grand duchess."

3. Cited in P. P. Gaidenko, introduction to Sergei Nikolaevich Trubetskoi, *Sochineniia* (Moscow: Mysl', 1994), 8.

4. Cited in Gaidenko, 8–9. For an account of S. N. Trubetskoi as a philosopher, see V. V. Zenkovsky, *A History of Russian Philosophy*, vol. 2, trans. George L. Kline (New York: Columbia University Press, 1953), 792–811; and Martha Bohachevsky-Chomiak, *Sergei N. Trubetskoi: An Intellectual among the Intelligentsia in Prerevolutionary Russia* (Belmont, Mass.: Nordland, 1976).

5. See the vivid description by Serge Schmemann in his memoir-chronicle *Echoes of a Native Land: Two Centuries of a Russian Village* (New York: Knopf, 1997), 156–58.

6. Emigration did not save Nikolai Sergeevich Trubetskoi from suffering and early death; he died of heart disease at age forty-eight, not long after the Gestapo interrogated him and ransacked his Vienna apartment. For an excellent description in English of N. S. Trubetskoi's life and thought, plus an extensive bibliography, see Anatoly Liberman, "Postscript: N. S. Trubetzkoy and His Works on History and Politics," in Nikolai Sergeevich Trubetzkoy, *The Legacy of Genghis Khan and Other Essays on Russia's Identity*, ed. Anatoly Liberman (Ann Arbor: Michigan Slavic Publications, 1991), 295–389.

7. My outline of Trubetskoi's life is drawn from the sole published source, Vera Pavlovna Polykovskaia's introduction to the "Notes of a Cuirassier": Vladimir Sergeevich Trubetskoi, *Zapiski kirasira* (Moscow: Rossiia, 1991), 3–9.

8. Polykovskaia, *Zapiski,* 5.

9. See the description in A. P. Vergunov and V. A. Gorokhov, *Russkie sady i parki* (Moscow: Nauka, 1988), 362.

10. Polykovskaia, *Zapiski,* 6. The name of the town was changed in the 1930s from the religious Sergiev Posad ("Settlement of St. Sergius") to the neutral Zagorsk ("Beyond the Mountains"). After the collapse of the Soviet Union the name was changed back to Sergiev Posad.

11. Andrei Vladimirovich Trubetskoi, in *Zolotoi vek,* no. 4 (1993): 27.

12. A. V. Trubetskoi, *Zolotoi vek,* 27.

13. Polykovskaia, *Zapiski,* 7.

14. Andrei Vladimirovich Trubetskoi's memoirs recount an odyssey worthy of Homer: *Puti neispovedimy (Vospominaniia 1939–1955 gg.)* (Moscow: Kontur, 1997). See the summary by Schmemann, *Echoes,* 330–31.

15. A. V. Trubetskoi, *Puti neispovedimy,* 192.

16. Polykovskaia, *Zapiski,* 8.

The Extraordinary Adventures of Bochonkin and Khvoshch

HOW WE FISHED FOR GRANDMOTHER

1. These stories are based on Trubetskoi's experiences from 1918 to 1923, when he and his family lived in Bogoroditsk, in the Tula region, south of Moscow (see the introduction).

2. "Pougasse" is the stranger's name for a "fougasse"—a gunpowder charge that is laid under the ground, under water, in ice, or under wire entanglements and exploded, usually by electrical current, at the necessary moment. [*Author's note.*] In the Russian, "pougasse" evokes the word *pugat',* "to frighten." [*Ed.*]

3. The cultivation of fish in ponds was a favorite pastime of [Russian] landowners from earliest times. When they set the fish loose into their ponds, many landowners with nothing better to do would insert golden rings into the fish's gills with an indication of the date on which the fish was introduced. This was done partly for pure amusement and partly to leave a memento of oneself for posterity.

About twenty-five years ago in Tsaritsyn Pond (near Moscow), they caught a huge pike with a golden ring in its gills. On the ring was written: "Inserted by Tsar Boris . . ." The pike was apparently put into the pond by Boris Godunov, and therefore it was about 300 years old. [*Author's note.*]

A TRAP WITH A TRIPLE REHEARSAL

1. By 1919 Russia had been through five years of war: World War I, the Revolution, and the Civil War, which continued on various fronts until 1921.

2. The widow is probably going to start by applying to the People's Court, a

judicial institution created by the Soviet government to have responsibility for low-level civil and criminal matters. A tribunal would be reserved for more serious offenses.

3. General Anton Ivanovich Denikin (1872–1947), leader of the White Volunteer Army which attempted to challenge Bolshevik power in the south of Russia in 1918–20. Denikin managed to occupy virtually all of the Ukraine and to advance on Moscow in 1919 before being defeated by the Red Army in March 1920. He died in the United States. Admiral Aleksandr Vasilievich Kolchak (1873–1920) led a White force that advanced from Siberia and almost reached the Volga in 1918. Kolchak was defeated by the Red Army in 1919 and executed by the Bolsheviks in February 1920.

I GOT THE FOX!

1. The name of Khvoshch's dog, "Dokuka," has the literal meaning of "a tiresome request." Elsewhere in the stories I have provided an English approximation of dogs' names, but I have given up on finding an approximation to "tiresome request" that has the lovely sound of "Dokuka," so I have preserved the original name.

PSYCHO-CURIOSITIES OF SEMION SEMIONOVICH

1. Moscow's major streets are in the form of concentric circles. The "B" tram (now a trolleybus) follows the Garden Ring (Sadovoe koltso) in the center of Moscow. Semion Semionovich fails to exit the tram at his destination in the southwest quadrant of Moscow, and keeps ending up at the Kursk Station on the eastern part of the ring. Each time he completes the circle he is expected to pay another fare.

THE WOLF HUNT

1. Shock-workers [udarniki]—high-achieving workers in factories and collective farms in the 1920s and 1930s. The term originated during the Civil War and reemerged in the 1930s.

BEAUTIFUL MECHA

1. Trubetskoi's stories take place in the Tula region, just north of the Oriol region, where the writer Ivan Sergeevich Turgenev (1818–1883) had his estate and where he set his first important work, A Sportsman's Sketches (1852). This collection of tales used the device of a nobleman-hunter's wanderings as the framework for psychologically detailed, sympathetic descriptions of Russian peasants before the 1861 Emancipation of the serfs. "Kasian from Beautiful Mech" (translated by Richard Freeborn as "Kasyan from the Beautiful Lands") depicts a slightly crazed

but also gentle and attractive peasant who has been resettled from Krasivaia Mech, a tributary of the Don, to a less fertile region. Trubetskoi's story echoes Turgenev's in several ways; for example, the capricious Kasian in Turgenev's story combines the taciturnity of Trubetskoi's cart-driver with the loquacious curiosity of the other townspeople. Perhaps the most significant aspect of Trubetskoi's evocation of Turgenev is the fact that Turgenev's Kasian offers a tough critique of the nobleman's idle pastime of killing game, declaring it a sin to kill free birds and forest animals rather than contenting oneself with domestic animals as food sources: "'A sin it is to be killing such a one, it should be let to live on the earth until its natural end'" (Ivan Turgenev, *Sketches from a Hunter's Album: The Complete Edition*, ed. and trans. Richard Freeborn [London: Penguin, 1990], 132). (This may be why, in Trubetskoi's story, Bochonkin and Khvoshch have no luck killing birds and have to be content with fishing, a pursuit Turgenev's Kasian approves of because "a fish has cold blood" [132].) Ironically, Khvoshch the déclassé nobleman, living in conditions of postwar scarcity, is in fact no longer hunting purely for pleasure but also for survival, as several of the stories make clear.

THE AGGITATOR FROM THE MISSISSIPPI RIVER

1. Papirosa—a Russian cigarette with a cardboard mouthpiece.

THE BLACK-WHITE-AND-TAN SKEWBALD DOG

1. To hunt "gropingly" is an expression designating the chasing of the beast by the hounds when they can't see it but are guided by their scent (tracing the animal from its nocturnal trail to its daytime lair). [*Author's note.*]

2. The Anglo-Russian hunting hound was bred in the second half of the nineteenth century by crossing the Russian hunting hound with the English foxhound and several other breeds. The standard for the breed was established in 1925. The coloration "chernopegaia v rumianakh," which I have translated here as "black-white-and-tan skewbald," is the standard coloration for the breed: white with black and tan spots on the head and haunches (*Russkaia okhota: entsiklopediia*, ed. V. V. Bedel et al. [Moscow: Soglasie, 1998], 244).

3. Trubetskoi never wrote the continuation to this story.

Letters from Exile

1. Vladimir Mikhailovich Golitsyn (1902–43), the son of Trubetskoi's wife's brother. Golitsyn provided the witty illustrations for Trubetskoi's hunting stories published in the 1920s. He was arrested in 1941 and died of hunger and pellagra in February 1943 in the Sviiazhsk prison camp. Dmitrov is near Moscow; Gudauty (now Gudauta) is on the coast of the Black Sea in Abkhazia (Georgia).

2. The Pamirs are a mountainous region of central Asia, mostly in Tadzhik-

istan, south of Andijon, where Trubetskoi is living. Andijon is located in the eastern part of Uzbekistan, about 150 miles from the Chinese border.

3. Lovelace is the gentleman-seducer, hero of Samuel Richardson's epistolary novel *Clarissa; or, The History of a Young Lady* (1747–48). The novel was extremely popular in eighteenth- and nineteenth-century Russia, and the name "Lovelace" became an epithet for a womanizer.

4. In 1927–29, the Soviet state campaigned for the liberation of women in Uzbekistan by mounting an administrative assault on Islamic tradition. As described by Shoshana Keller, the main aims of the campaign were "unveiling women . . . , destroying traditional practices of arranged marriage, bride-price, the marriage of young girls to adult men, the seclusion of women from public life, polygyny, and other customs" ("Trapped between State and Society: Women's Liberation and Islam in Soviet Uzbekistan, 1926–1941," *Journal of Women's History* 10, no. 1 [spring 1998]: 20–44, p. 20). The Soviet Zhenotdel (Communist Party Women's Section) representative organized "large public demonstrations against the veil, where women tore off and burned their veils in public, read political poetry, viewed plays and movies, and listened to lectures" (Keller, "Trapped," 24). By the 1930s, when the Trubetskois came to Uzbekistan, the pressure against Islamic tradition had eased and there was a resurgence of customary practices, including the *parandzha* (Keller, "Trapped," 31). See also Douglas Northrop, *Veiled Empire: Gender and Power in Stalinist Central Asia* (Ithaca: Cornell University Press, 2004).

5. Zags—abbreviation for Department for the Registry of Acts of Civil Status, in which births, deaths, and marriages had to be registered. Registry at the Zags largely replaced religious wedding ceremonies in the Soviet Union.

6. *Basmachi*—native partisans in central Asia who resisted Soviet rule.

7. Mashenka—Vladimir Golitsyn's sister. Her first suitor was a parachutist, and the family jokingly called all her suitors "parachutists."

8. Torgsin—abbreviation for Trade with Foreigners. Torgsin shops sold goods for hard currency, gold, silver, and other valuables, from 1930 to 1936. They were open to anyone with the appropriate currency. The Torgsin stores, which tended to be much better stocked than regular stores, came under heavy criticism for their inequity. See Sheila Fitzpatrick, *Everyday Stalinism. Ordinary Life in Extraordinary Times: Soviet Russia in the 1930s* (Oxford: Oxford University Press, 1999), 57–58, 90, 222.

9. Shock-worker—see note to "The Wolf Hunt," above.

10. Roald Amundsen (1872–1928), the Norwegian explorer who was the first to reach the South Pole, lost his life in 1928 while flying to rescue the Italian aeronautical engineer Umberto Nobile (1885–1978) from a dirigible crash in the Arctic Ocean near Spitsbergen. Nobile and seven others were rescued, but seventeen lives were lost. The *Malygin* and *Krasin* (named for early Russian explorers of the Arctic) were two Soviet icebreakers that helped in the rescue. Trubetskoi's ad-

dressee Vladimir Golitsyn had participated in an expedition in the Barents Sea on the *Malygin* in 1921.

11. Elena Petrovna Golitsyna, née Sheremeteva, the addressee's wife (1904–1992). Their daughter Elena Vladimirovna married Vladimir Trubetskoi's son Andrei in 1948.

12. V. A. Popov, publisher of the adventure-popular science journal *Vsemirnyi sledopyt* (*World Pathfinder*), in which Trubetskoi's hunting stories were published in 1927–28 under the name "V. Vetov."

13. Linochka is Vladimir Mikhailovich's elder sister Aleksandra Mikhailovna.

14. Vovik is Vladimir Mikhailovich Golitsyn, father of Trubetskoi's wife Elia and grandfather of the Vladimir Mikhailovich Golitsyn to whom Trubetskoi is writing; Niks is Nikolai Mikhailovich Golitsyn, brother of Vladimir Mikhailovich Golitsyn the elder.

15. The reference here is unknown.

16. Trubetskoi is quoting a passage from chapter 5 of Pushkin's *Eugene Onegin* (cited here in the translation by Charles Johnston [Penguin, 1977], 132), which he travesties by substituting his own pen name, "Vetov," for that of Pushkin's heroine Tatiana, and by inserting a purely Uzbek detail into the description of a Russian manor—the *duval*, a wattle fence.

17. On January 9 (January 22, New Style), 1905, the St. Petersburg police fired on a demonstration of workers, killing over a hundred people. The incident was one of the factors leading to the revolt of 1905. In view of his own fate, Trubetskoi's references here and at the end of the letter to this harbinger of the Revolution are chillingly ironic.

18. Mikhail Prishvin (1873–1954), a writer known for his nature and hunting stories and sketches.

19. The Sretenka is a street in the northeast quarter of Moscow. The Trubetskois lived there in an apartment in the early 1920s. It was also the location of the Lubianka Prison, and Trubetskoi's son Andrei Vladimirovich believed that Vladimir Sergeevich is referring here to the "cold" of prison versus the heat of central Asian exile.

20. Trubetskoi is alluding to the tenets of socialist realism, enshrined as the official artistic method of Soviet literature in 1932, and officially defined by the Writers' Union in 1934 as "the truthful, historically concrete depiction of reality in its revolutionary development." In addition, "truthfulness and historical concreteness of the artistic depiction of reality must be combined with the task of ideologically remolding and educating the working people in the spirit of socialism" (Herman Ermolaev, "Socialist Realism," in *Handbook of Russian Literature*, ed. Victor Terras [New Haven: Yale University Press, 1985], 430). The idealization called for by the task of "remolding the working people" led to the creation of the "positive hero."

21. S. Istomin—a relative; Ksenia—his wife.

22. As a former sailor, Trubetskoi finds it sad to read about the sea for which he longs.

23. The Soviet campaign in the 1920s against Islamic tradition, in particular the unveiling demonstrations, led to a wave of violence against women. By the end of the 1920s, hundreds of Uzbek women had been murdered for unveiling. Attacks continued even after the temporary relaxation of the campaign in the 1930s (Keller, "Trapped," 25–26, 31–32).

24. This reference is mysterious, because Trubetskoi did not publish any books, only stories.

25. A shrine to a Sufi saint.

26. Makhach-Kala and Derbent—towns on the Caspian Sea in Dagestan. Berdiansk and Genichesk—towns on the Sea of Azov in Ukraine.

27. Alka Bolduin, née Bobrinskaia, a distant relative of Trubetskoi's and a descendant of Catherine II, famed for her many lovers.

28. Cars made by the Gorkii Automobile Factory (GAZ) in a joint venture with Ford.

29. The phrase means "F——k you [referring specifically to sexual intercourse between men]." Translation here and in note 38 by Alexander Lehrman.

30. S. D. Evreinov—a distant relative of Trubetskoi's who fought in World War I. His memoirs have not survived.

31. Marshal Klimentii Efremovich Voroshilov (1881–1969), a leader of Bolshevik forces in the Civil War, famous for his marksmanship and equestrian skill.

32. Vasilii Vitalievich Shul'gin (1878–1976), noted activist in the White movement, who wrote memoirs in the 1920s after emigrating.

33. Commemoration of the Battle of Borodino, in which Russian troops fought to keep the French from reaching Moscow in 1812.

34. The 1913 commemoration of the 300th anniversary of the establishment of the Romanov dynasty.

35. "Vralmann" is a character in a play by Denis Fonvizin, *The Minor* (1782). Vralmann fancies himself a great scientist. (Russ. *vrat'*—to lie or talk nonsense.)

36. A reference to a comic poem by Aleksei Konstantinovich Tolstoi, "Spring Emotions of an Unbridled Ancient" (1859), which describes the universal erotic urges of nature. It includes the lines, "My whole breast is already burning / With a thirst for love, / And every wood splinter is striving / To jump up on another splinter." A. K. Tolstoi, *Sobranie sochinenii*, 4 vols., ed. I. Iampol'skii (Moscow: Pravda, 1969), 1:361 (translation mine).

37. *Tiubeteika*—a small embroidered hat worn by men in central Asia.

38. "F——k you! F——k your dad's soul! [again, intercourse between men]" (trans. Alexander Lehrman).

Notes of a Cuirassier

CHAPTER ONE

1. Count Aleksei Kapnist (1871–1918), the cousin of Trubetskoi's father, later to become a rear admiral and chief of the General Staff of the navy (starting in 1914), in 1911 was in retirement in Poltava. He was executed by the Bolsheviks in Piatigorsk.

2. During the Russo-Japanese War, the Russian Baltic Fleet, sent all the way around Africa to the Far East, was virtually annihilated by the Japanese in the Battle of Tsushima Strait (1905). An armistice followed soon afterwards.

3. According to the 1908 statute on military service, volunteers were men with an education who voluntarily entered active military service in the lower ranks. Those belonging to the first class, men with at least a secondary school education, were required to serve one year of active duty. Only volunteers of the first class could enter the Guards, and then only with the consent of the unit's commander. They were required to pay for their own room and board and were lodged either in the barracks or in private quarters.

4. Trubetskoi's mother was Praskovia Vladimirovna Trubetskaia, née Obolenskaia (1860–1914). His brother, Nikolai Sergeevich (1890–1938, known as Trubetzkoy in emigration), was to become one of the greatest linguists of the twentieth century. As a young secondary school student, N. S. Trubetskoi had already distinguished himself in the field of comparative linguistics and ethnography.

5. Kozma Prutkov was a fictitious writer of humorous and parodistic poetry, drama, and aphorisms, created by Count Aleksei Konstantinovich Tolstoi (1817–1875), Aleksei Zhemchuzhnikov (1821–1908), and the latter's brothers. Part of Prutkov's mystique was the persona that Tolstoi and the Zhemchuzhnikovs created for him, that of a pompous bureaucrat who fancied himself a Romantic poet.

6. The Preobrazhenskii Life Guards Infantry Regiment was one of the oldest regiments in the Russian Guards, formed at the end of the seventeenth century. It especially distinguished itself during the Napoleonic Wars. The Chevalier Guards was formed at the end of the eighteenth century, and was charged with service at court functions and coronations. It also participated in military actions, and, like the Preobrazhenskii Regiment, served with distinction in the Napoleonic campaigns. For this regiment, soldiers were chosen who were tall, blond, and blue-eyed.

7. Mikhail Mikhailovich Osorgin (1861–1939), the husband of Trubetskoi's father's sister Elizaveta Nikolaevna, a former Chevalier Guard. In 1931 he emigrated and was ordained as a Russian Orthodox priest in Clamart, near Paris.

For more on the Osorgin family, see the fine memoir-chronicle by Serge Schmemann, *Echoes of a Native Land*.

Her Majesty's Cuirassier Regiment of Life Guards was formed in 1704 as the Portes Dragoon regiment and changed names several times before becoming the Life Guards in 1733. They were called the Blue Cuirassiers because of the blue trimmings on their uniforms, to distinguish them from the red of the Chevalier Guards and Horse Guards and the yellow of His Majesty's Cuirassier Regiment of Life Guards (the "Yellow Cuirassiers").

8. Mikhail Mikhailovich Osorgin (1887–1950), after entering the reserves in 1912, became the Kaluga marshal of the nobility. He emigrated in 1920, and took part in creating the Theological Institute in Paris, the so-called Daughter Church of St. Sergius, and served as its choir director until his death. (A "daughter church" is an urban church connected to a monastery but located in a different place than the main monastery. In this case, the Paris church claims a connection to the ancient monastery of St. Sergius in Sergiev Posad [Zagorsk in Soviet times], near Moscow. Vladimir Trubetskoi's family lived in Zagorsk from 1923 until his exile in 1934.) Trubetskoi's portrait of Misha is something of an unfair caricature.

9. Mariia Fiodorovna (1847–1928), wife of Tsar Alexander III, became the patroness of the Blue Cuirassiers in 1880. The Gatchina Palace was built for Catherine II in 1766–81 by Antonio Rinaldi; she later presented it to her son Paul (Tsar Paul I).

10. Evgenii Ivanovich Bernov (1855–?) was the commander of the Blue Cuirassiers from 1907 to 1912.

11. Krasnoe Selo was first mentioned as the site of military training and drill camp in 1765, in the reign of Catherine II. Starting in 1823 it became the location of yearly summer assemblies for training and maneuvers of Guards regiments.

12. Grand Duke Nikolai Nikolaevich (1856–1929) was the son of Grand Duke Nikolai Nikolaevich Senior (himself the third son of Emperor Nicholas I). Between 1895 and 1905 he was inspector general of cavalry, and from 1905 to 1914, commander of the Guards and of the St. Petersburg Military District. During World War I he became commander in chief of the Russian armed forces, but was removed in August 1915 at the insistence of Empress Aleksandra Fiodorovna and her adviser Rasputin.

13. Eduard Nikolaevich von Schweder (1870–1919) was a graduate of the Nicholas Cavalry School and had served in the Blue Cuirassiers since 1893. He commanded a hussar regiment in World War I and attained the rank of major general. He was executed by the Bolsheviks in Kislovodsk.

14. Starting in the 1890s, there were yearly horse races in Tsarskoe Selo, Kolomiagi, and Krasnoe Selo (all near St. Petersburg). Cavalrymen were even excused from service in order to participate. Empress Mariia Fiodorovna often attended the races.

15. P. N. Trubetskoi (1858–1911), stepbrother of Trubetskoi's father, was a well-known leader of the Liberal movement. His son Vladimir Petrovich (1885–1954) was a founder of the Assembly of the Russian Nobility in Paris.

The officers' training school in St. Petersburg was established in 1823 by Grand Duke Nikolai Pavlovich (later Tsar Nicholas I), and was named the Nicholas Cavalry School in 1864. The great poet and prose writer Mikhail Lermontov (1814–1841) studied there in 1832–34.

CHAPTER TWO

1. Baron Liov Fiodorovich Girard-de-Sucanton (1855–?), major general of His Majesty's suite, commanded the Blue Cuirassier Regiment from 1905 to 1907. At the time described here, he commanded the First Brigade of the Second Guards Division.

2. Under Tsar Nicholas I, each Guards cuirassier regiment was assigned a particular color of horse. At the beginning of the twentieth century they were the following: Chevalier Guards—bay horses; Horse Life Guards—black; His Majesty's Cuirassiers—dark-bay; and Her Majesty's Cuirassiers—chestnut (First Squadron, golden chestnut; Second Squadron, chestnut with white legs and white blaze; Third Squadron, chestnut with a star; Fourth Squadron, dark-chestnut and brown).

3. In the eighteenth and nineteenth centuries, cavalry regiments were divided into heavy (cuirassiers and dragoons) and light (hussars, uhlans, mounted chasseurs). The heavy cavalry was distinguished by larger horses, soldiers selected for height and strength, and equipment: helmets, broadswords, and cuirasses in the case of the cuirassiers. In battle the heavy cavalry fought in close order.

4. Since all the men could not ride at once inside the manège, they rode in rotation.

5. This seems to be a Russian adaptation of the German word *Zug,* as in the expression *jemand gut im Zug haben*—"to have someone well trained, well in control." Later, in chapter 4, in the discussion of the Nicholas Cavalry School, Trubetskoi uses a purely Russian verb derived from *Zug*—*tsukat'*, which seems to be equivalent to the English "to haze."

6. There are two trotting speeds, leisurely ("manège trot") and fast ("field trot"). "Field trot" is the fastest that the horse can trot without breaking into a gallop.

7. The command "scissors" means that the rider must lift both legs and turn around on the horse's back, using his hands for support.

8. The day-stall is a large stall that can hold several horses during the day.

CHAPTER THREE

1. This incident has been described in the following way by a contemporary of Trubetskoi's, T. A. Aksakova-Sivers (1892–1982):

> In the autumn of 1911 a drama took place in the Trubetskoi family that became known to the whole country. All the relatives of Count Orlov-Denisov

were gathered in Novocherkassk for the transportation of his body: the Trubet-skois, the Kristis, the Glebovs, and the Orlov-Denisovs. The train-carriage of Prince Piotr Nikolaevich [Trubetskoi] was standing on a siding at the station. Kristi, who had burst into the compartment of the carriage and found his wife Maritsa (née Mikhalkova) there with his uncle Piotr Nikolaevich, shot and killed the latter instantly. There was a terrible scandal . . . It was said that Piotr Niko-laevich had invited his niece into his compartment in order to warn her about her obvious infatuation with his other nephew Petia Glebov. However it was, the marshal of the nobility of the Moscow Province had been killed, his mur-derer Kristi was not seriously punished (his punishment was limited to church penance), and Mariia Aleksandrovna Mikhalkova-Kristi divorced her husband and married his cousin. (*Semeinaia khronika* [Paris: Atheneum, 1988], 88–89)

On P. N. Trubetskoi, see note 15 for chapter 1. Vladimir Grigorevich Kristi (1882–1946) was the son of Trubetskoi's father's sister Mariia Nikolaevna. He em-igrated in 1920.

2. Aleksandra Vladimirovna Trubetskaia, née Obolenskaia (1861–1939), the sister of Trubetskoi's mother. She emigrated in 1920.

3. General Iakov Grigorevich Zhilinskii (1853–1918) became chief of the General Staff in 1911. He was chief commander of the Northwestern front in World War I, and was removed from his post after the failure of the campaign in eastern Prussia. In 1915–16 he represented the Russian high command at the Al-lied Council in Paris. He was executed by the Bolsheviks in the Crimea. His wife, Varvara Mikhailovna, née Osorgina (1859–1917), was the sister of Mishanchik's father.

4. Mariia Dmitrievna Apraksina, née Rakhmanova, the stepsister of Trubet-skoi's mother.

5. Baron B. R. von Knorring (1861–?) at the time of narration was equerry at the court of Grand Duchess Mariia Pavlovna. A. S. Ermolov (1846–1917) was sec-retary of state, minister of agriculture and state property, and a member of the State Council.

CHAPTER FOUR

1. Anna Aleksandrovna Vyrubova (1884–after 1929), lady-in-waiting to Em-press Aleksandra Fiodorovna. She emigrated in 1920. See chapter 5, note 1.

2. Evgenii Karlovich Miller (1867–1937?), lieutenant general, head of the Nicholas Cavalry School from 1910 to 1914. During World War I he was chief of the Army General Staff. Active in the White Army, he emigrated in 1920. He was killed in 1937, presumably by agents of the NKVD (Soviet secret police).

3. See chapter 2, note 5.

4. There was also a monument to the composer M. P. Mussorgsky, who grad-uated from the Nicholas Cavalry School in 1856 as a cornet in the Preobrazhen-skii Life Guards Regiment.

5. This privileged military school was established in 1802 on the basis of the Corps of Pages, which had existed since 1759. It prepared young men for military and court service.

6. Such rings, made of steel, cast iron, or iron, had been worn by officers since the nineteenth century. On the inner, gold part of the ring the officer's first and last name would be engraved. The ring served as a token by which an officer killed in battle could be identified. The base metals were used on the external ring so that marauders would not steal the rings off the corpses. Pages could recognize each other by these rings, and no matter when they graduated or what post they held, they would address each other by the familiar "thou."

CHAPTER FIVE

1. Vyrubova was rumored to be facilitating a sexual relationship between the empress and Grigorii Rasputin, a peasant who attained great influence over the empress (and in turn over her husband Tsar Nicholas II) because of her belief that he could heal her son Alexis's hemophilia. Rasputin was murdered by a group of noblemen in 1916.

2. Trubetskoi is speaking of Sofia Ivanovna Tiutcheva. She resigned as governess to the tsar's daughters because of their being drawn into Rasputin's sphere of influence.

CHAPTER SIX

1. This estate, built in the eighteenth century, has survived in drastically altered form. Trubetskoi is not entirely correct about the tsars' visits. Peter the Great traveled to Beshenkovichi three times for a Russo-Polish military council, and Alexander I lived in the palace not in 1812 but in 1821.

Trubetskoi's sister Mariia Sergeevna (1883–1934) was married to the diplomat Count Apollinarii Konstantinovich Butenev-Khreptovich (1879–1946). The family emigrated in 1920.

Trubetskoi's childhood friend Valerian Vladimirovich Ershov (1891–1919) and his cousin Nikolai Petrovich Trubetskoi (1890–1961) were both military men. Ershov fought with the Whites and died of typhus; Nikolai Trubetskoi emigrated in 1920.

2. The word *vorotilo* signifies an enormous lever used to turn windmills toward the wind. As with the dog Dokuka, I have despaired of finding a euphonious English equivalent for this horse's name.

3. Piotr Ivanovich Arapov (1871–1930), major general, graduated from the Corps of Pages. He commanded the Blue Cuirassiers Regiment from 1912 to 1914. During World War I he commanded a brigade in a cavalry division and was awarded the St. George's arms for bravery. He died in Gatchina.

4. In 1911 there were several aviation schools in Russia besides the one in Gatchina—in Odessa, Moscow, and Sevastopol.

5. "Farman"—plane designed by Maurice Farman (1877–1964), French aircraft manufacturer.

CHAPTER SEVEN

1. Trubetskoi probably has in mind *The Secret Doctrine* (1888) by E. P. Blavatskaia and *The Astral Plane: Its Scenery, Inhabitants and Phenomena* (1895) by Charles W. Leadbeater. Blavatskaia and Leadbeater were leading exponents of theosophy, a mystical philosophy that enjoyed great popularity in Russia at the turn of the century.

2. Sergeant Major Bazdyrev was killed on September 18, 1915.

3. The Wild Division was officially the Caucasian (Indigenous) Cavalry Division, formed during World War I with volunteers from the mountain peoples of the Northern Caucasus. It consisted of six regiments: the Kabardian, Dagestan, Tatar, Chechen, Circassian, and Ingushetian.

Grand Duke Mikhail Aleksandrovich (1878–1918), the younger brother of Tsar Nicholas II, was a lieutenant general. In 1904 he commanded a squadron of the Blue Cuirassiers. After Nicholas's abdication in March 1917, Mikhail Aleksandrovich also renounced his rights to the throne and lived in Gatchina as a private citizen. In February 1918 he was arrested and executed by the Bolsheviks in Perm.

4. The *mnogoletie* is a part of the Russian Orthodox liturgy in which long life and health are wished for through repetition of the words *mnogaia leta,* "many years."

5. Cantonists were soldiers' sons who were enlisted from the day of their birth and who studied in special lower military schools.

6. *The Duel* (1905), by Aleksandr Ivanovich Kuprin (1870–1938), paints a bleak picture of army life, with its senseless routines and an officer class of severe spiritual and intellectual limitations.

7. *Leib* in German means "body." *Leib-gard* means "bodyguard." [*Author's note.*]

8. According to Russian folk tradition, the world rests on the backs of three whales. "Three whales" is used figuratively to mean "three basic foundations."

9. Mariia Fiodorovna provided significant financial support for the regiment, including the funds used to build the officers' club of Trubetskoi's time.

10. On February 26 (March 11, New Style), 1917, the Fourth Company of the Reserve Battalion of the Pavlovsk Regiment was the first to go over to the Revolution. The Reserve Battalion of the Preobrazhenskii Life Guards Regiment revolted on February 27 (March 12), 1917.

CHAPTER EIGHT

1. "Horns" are the age-old symbol of the cuckold. For "Lovelace," see note 3 to the "Letters from Exile."

2. A. M. Zaionchkovskii, *Podgotovka Rossii k imperialisticheskoi voine. Ocherki voennoi podgotovki i pervonachal'nykh planov. Po arkhivnym dokumentam* (Moscow: Gosudarstvennoe voennoe izdatel'stvo, 1926), 94–96.

3. According to V. P. Polykovskaia (notes to *Zapiski kirasira,* 202), this attack took place near Kauschen. For his service in this battle, the commander of the Second Squadron of the Horse Guards Regiment, Captain Baron P. N. Vrangel, was awarded the St. George's Cross and received the rank of aide-de-camp.

CHAPTER NINE

1. The publication in question is *The History of the Life Guards Regiment of Cuirassiers of Her Majesty the Sovereign Empress Mariia Fiodorovna,* 2 vols. Volume 1, written by Colonel Markov of the General Staff, covered the period 1704–1879, and was published in St. Petersburg in 1884. Volume 2, written by Staff Captain Mordvinov Senior, covered the period 1879–1904 and was published in St. Petersburg in 1904.

2. In October 1708, during the Great Northern War, Russian forces led by Peter the Great intercepted and destroyed Swedish reinforcements at Lesnaia and captured a supply train that was on its way to King Charles XII in the Ukraine.

3. The Order of St. George (or St. George's Cross), given for bravery in battle, consists of a cross with a depiction of St. George slaying the dragon. It is entwined with a St. George's ribbon of moiré silk, striped black and orange. Besides the medal, one may be awarded St. George's arms, trumpets, or flag, which would be adorned with the same kind of ribbons.

4. Aleksei Fiodorovich Lvov (1798–1870), a violinist, composer, and conductor, was the director of the court chapel choir and also composed church music and operas. He composed the Russian hymn, to words by the poet Vasilii Zhukovskii, at the order of Nicholas I in 1833.

5. *Rus* is the ancient word for Russia (as opposed to the modern *Rossiia*), originally applied to the Kievan state of the ninth to eleventh centuries. Nineteenth- and twentieth-century writers use it when speaking of Russia in high-flown, poetic terms.

6. In book 1, part 3, chapter 8 of Leo Tolstoy's novel *War and Peace* (1865–69), the young soldier Nikolai Rostov participates in a review of the Austrian and Russian troops by Tsar Alexander I and the Austrian emperor in November 1805. Trubetskoi's description of the 1912 review is extremely similar to Tolstoy's: "Every general and soldier felt his own insignificance, was conscious of being a grain of sand in that sea of men, and at the same time felt his own might, being conscious of himself as part of that great whole" (*War and Peace,* trans. Ann Dun-

nigan [New York: Signet, 1968], 301). Rostov is overcome by love for the young, handsome tsar: "Everything about the Tsar—every feature, every gesture, seemed to him entrancing" (303).

Trubetskoi seems to have had a romantic attitude toward the tsar even in childhood. At the age of twelve he sent the tsar a "secret" letter warning him of a conspiracy against the throne, based on conversations critical of the tsar that Trubetskoi had heard in his politically liberal household. The tsar appears to have recalled the letter when meeting Trubetskoi in 1910 on the destroyer *Horseman*, when he said, "I need people like you."

CHAPTER TEN

1. To "drink *Brüderschaft*" is to agree over a drink to use the familiar second-person pronoun. The custom is borrowed from German tradition.

2. It would seem likely that Trubetskoi means 1.0 millimeter.

3. E. K. Pushchina, née Countess Kleinmikhel (1892–after 1930), widowed in 1914, married the author's cousin, N. P. Trubetskoi. She later emigrated to Paris.

CHAPTER ELEVEN

1. B. M. Petrovo-Solovovo (1861–1918?), major general of His Majesty's suite. He was married to S. A. Shcherbatova, sister of the wife of the philosopher Evgenii Nikolaevich Trubetskoi, Vladimir Trubetskoi's uncle.

2. Trubetskoi himself became the center of attention at one of these assemblies in the summer of 1914. One of the Gatchina officers had started a rumor that Trubetskoi was having an affair with the wife of the regimental commander in his absence. The officers' court of honor expelled this guardsman from the regiment and obliged Trubetskoi to challenge him to a duel. Luckily the only victim of the duel was the top hat of one of the combatants.

3. N. S. Brasova, née Sheremetevskaia (1880–after 1930), in her first marriage Mamontova, in her second Vulfert, was the morganatic wife of Grand Duke Mikhail Aleksandrovich from 1910. She died in emigration.

4. Olga Aleksandrovna (1882–1960), grand duchess, wife of Prince A. P. Oldenburgskii, and then of Kulikovskii (1880–1958). Olga Aleksandrovna married Kulikovskii while still in Russia, in 1916. Contrary to what Trubetskoi says later, she was not able to make use of the Romanov capital and lived in straitened circumstances in emigration. She died in Toronto.

Vladimir Sergeevich Trubetskoi (1892–1937) was a member of one of Russia's most ancient and distinguished noble families. His father, Prince Sergei Nikolaevich Trubetskoi, was an important philosopher and historian of ancient philosophy and the first elected rector of Moscow University. Vladimir Trubetskoi served as a cadet in the navy, then in the Blue Cuirassier Life Guards Cavalry Regiment. He fought with distinction in World War I. After the Bolshevik Revolution, Trubetskoi supported his large family by working as a musician and publishing hunting stories in an adventure magazine. In January 1934, he and his eldest daughter Varvara were arrested on trumped-up conspiracy charges and exiled to central Asia, where the rest of the family joined them. On July 29, 1937, they were arrested again and were executed on October 30. The family managed to save part of the memoirs Trubetskoi had written in exile, as well as letters he had sent to his nephew. These writings were published in Russia only in the early 1990s.

Susanne Fusso is a professor of Russian language and literature at Wesleyan University. She is the author of *Designing Dead Souls: An Anatomy of Disorder in Gogol* (1993) and *Discovering Sexuality in Dostoevsky* (forthcoming). She has also coedited collections of essays on Nikolai Gogol and Karolina Pavlova.